ABOVE THE
LINE

OTHER BOOKS BY LAWRENCE GROBEL

Conversations with Capote
The Hustons
Conversations with Brando
Talking with Michener

ABOVE THE LINE

Conversations
About the Movies

LAWRENCE
GROBEL

DA CAPO PRESS

Copyright © 2000 by Lawrence Grobel

Published in 2000 in the United States of America by Da Capo Press.

Library of Congress Cataloging-in-Publication Data
Grobel, Lawrence.
   Above the line : conversations about the movies / Lawrence Grobel.
      p.   cm.
   Includes index.
   ISBN 0-306-80978-8 (pbk.)
   1. Motion pictures.   2. Motion pictures—Interviews.   I. Title.

PN1994.G77   2000
791.43—dc21
                                                                                00-055514

Text Design by Jeff Williams
Set in 10 point Janson Text by the Perseus Books Group

The paper used in this publication meets the requirements of the American National Standard for Permanence of Paper for Printed Library Materials Z39.48-1984.

10   9   8   7   6   5   4   3   2   1

For My Mother—
Stellllllaaa!

CONTENTS

FOREWORD

Joyce Carol Oates

IF THERE IS A MOZART OF INTERVIEWERS, Larry Grobel is that individual. This generous collection of celebrity-film interviews presents him at his most skilled and illuminating. If the Interview as an art form emerges as a predominant prose genre in the twenty-first century, it will be the result of interviewers like Larry who manage to be both invisible and yet subtly dominating. In Larry's case, the Mozartian metaphor has a twofold meaning: the interviewer's apparent ease of execution and the consistently high quality of the work.

I have both read many of Larry's interviews and been a subject of an interview Larry did with me for *Playboy* some years ago. The experience was noteworthy: though I was "guarded" initially, as all interview subjects rightly are, I soon came to feel that Larry Grobel and I were simply conversing, albeit the conversation was more directed and on a generally more elevated plane than most casual conversations. The "art" of the interview is deceptive, because what you read isn't what transpired, but a professional rearrangement, editing and enhancing of what transpired, so that the interview as a prose piece has some of the qualities of a good story. Unlike real life, the interview doesn't ramble and doesn't repeat itself; its dull, guarded segments have been dropped away, and its strongest points brought forward. For the interview subject, as Jodie Foster tells Larry in her excellent interview, the experience is an illuminating one in which you get to "work out" what you think. Of course, it goes without saying that one requires a thoroughly prepared, sympathetic interviewer, one whose intelligence is a match for the subject's.

If Larry Grobel sometimes seems, chameleonlike, to shift his personality from interview to interview, this is surely a sign of his instinctive skill and good taste, but it suggests as well, perhaps more importantly, that the interviewer has a genuine curiosity about and respect for his diverse subjects. Though the general theme here is Hollywood movie- and myth-making, talent, fame, celebrity, and the capricious role of fortune, one can discern in Larry's probing questions a quality of personality that is fundamentally moral, without being moralistic. (For instance, see the interviewer's pursuit of Oliver Stone: "When you hear that two people watched [*Natural Born Killers*] repeatedly and took acid and went on a killing spree, doesn't that get to you somehow?") What makes his interviews with Jodie Foster, Sharon Stone, and Lily Tomlin outstanding is his intelligent sympathy for women, his natural assumption of what might be called the intuitive-feminist perspective. Here, there are provocative questions, but no adversarial edge. The interviewer is able to elicit from these extraordinary women wonderfully frank, even intimate revelations, and from the brilliant writer-director Robert Towne (*Chinatown, Bonnie and Clyde*) the startling observation, "Directing was a lot more feminine than a lot of people thought. Because you're so passive when you're directing. When you're writing, you've got the whole world in your hands . . . but when you're a director . . . you're the only [one] on the set that doesn't have a job." Anthony Hopkins, in perhaps this collection's most iconoclastic interview, reveals a side of himself one would never have anticipated from his exemplary screen roles: "I don't like Shakespeare. I'd rather be in Malibu. . . . What's so special about being an actor? Actors are nothing. Actors are of no consequence."

Here, in this diverse and lively collection, you will find the highest art of the interview.

PREFACE

Lawrence Grobel

THE MOVING IMAGE HAS HAD A powerful influence on the twentieth century. More of us watch the news than read newspapers; more people know about the Mafia from seeing *The Godfather* trilogy than from reading Mario Puzo's novels or Sammy "The Bull" Gravano's memoirs; we understand Hannibal Lecter more than we do Jeffrey Dahmer; we may not get how the phone company works, but we appreciate its power through a character named Ernestine; when we look to myth to teach us about the forces of good and evil, we may quote a few lines from *The Waste Land* or *Ulysses*, but it's Han Solo and Princess Leia, R2-D2 and Chewbacca, Yoda and Darth Vader who have been part of our collective fantasies.

Is it possible to understand the movies by reading what a select few have to say about their involvement with them? To be involved in movies takes enormous drive, an indefatigable ego, a voice screaming inside your head, like Henderson the Rain King, "I want . . . I want." Listen to Robert Evans to grasp the brazen balls it takes to run a studio, to produce mega-hits like *Love Story* and *The Godfather* as well as mega-flops like *The Cotton Club* and *Sliver*. Pay attention to Anthony Hopkins as he explains how he can present monsters like Lecter and Hitler so that we believe their impossible behavior. Hear Oliver Stone describe how he can tackle with such assurance the major historical issues of his generation—Vietnam, the Kennedy assassination, the acid sixties, the greedy eighties, the fall of Nixon—convincing you that he has his magisterial finger on the pulse of his times. Join Robert Towne as he recalls the intimidating meetings he had with Marlon Brando as they worked on scenes involving Don Corleone, and be that fly-on-the-wall as he explains how he got too close to the flame of such friends as Jack Nicholson and Warren Beatty. See how Jodie Foster refines her craft to so convincingly give you rape victims and FBI recruits. Laugh with Lily Tomlin as she takes you through the history of "bad girl" movies behind the brilliance of her solo characterizations. Allow Sharon Stone to tell you how she's helped pave the way for today's younger stars and how unsatisfied she is with all of her own performances. Transpose Harrison Ford's reluctance to reveal himself to how he works as an actor. Imagine the absolute hunger and determination of Jean-Claude Van Damme as he stuck his photo under the windshield wipers of expensive cars hoping to be discovered, and as he kicked his leg up above the head of the one producer who didn't duck but became convinced he could become an action hero. And then let Gene Siskel and Roger Ebert go *mano-a-mano* in their battle to best each other regarding their knowledge of the movies, giving you a report card and index of what to look for, who to root for, and what to rent at the video store.

These eleven people, in ten separate chapters, come to you from the viewpoints of the producer, the director, the writer, the actor, the comedienne, the action adventure hero, the star, and the critic. Individually they portray a part of what makes the movies work from "above the line." These are not the technicians or the investors who work so diligently behind the scenes: these are the people whose names go above the title. They are the ones with the inflated egos who are also riddled with doubts. They are the "talent." Each represents a piece, and as we understand the pieces, the puzzle of the movies begins to take shape.

Movie people often tell you they don't know what they do or how they do it, but if you press them hard enough, they do. You don't win Oscars for acting, directing, writing, or producing, or Pulitzers for writing, or Emmys for performing, if you don't know exactly what you're doing. It takes time and patience to get these people to tell what they know, but the results are worth the effort. What they have to say demonstrates their range of emotion and intelligence. When you get through reading about their lives and hearing their opinions, you may not agree with them, you may not always like them, but you'll have a better understanding of what motivates them, and because they are always in motion you will better comprehend what makes them successful. Each of these people has surmounted obstacles and emerged from the struggle scarred but determined. There is a strength of will in these players forged from childhood hurts, adult failures, and huge acceptance.

As Jean-Claude Van Damme tells us: "I was not born this way. I became."

How he became, how Oliver Stone, Robert Towne, Robert Evans, Anthony Hopkins, Jodie Foster, Harrison Ford, Sharon Stone, Lily Tomlin, Roger Ebert, and the late Gene Siskel became, is the subject of this book. With a little prodding, each brings into focus a picture of the journey to stardom. "I got to be tall and blond and a movie star," Sharon Stone tells us. "That's a lot to get in life."

ACKNOWLEDGMENTS

IN A NEW CENTURY that already seems to be defined by quick cuts, sound bites, cartoons, and entertaining but not very soul-enriching game shows, the need for conversation that is not merely glib or clever but substantive and thoughtful remains important. Indeed, there are fewer places than ever to read what a famous person has to say without some publicist in the room watching the clock, ready to jump in like a protective parent whenever a sensitive subject is broached. Thankfully, there are still editors at magazines like *Playboy* and *Movieline* who expect interviews to be probing and revealing, and publishers who allow enough space for an interview to become a dialogue. I'm grateful to Steve Randall, Arthur Kretchmer, Christie Hefner, and Hugh Hefner at *Playboy*, and to Virginia Campbell, Heidi Parker, Anne Volokh, and the late Ed Margulies at *Movieline* for giving me the opportunity to practice what seems to be a dwindling but necessary art form. My thanks also to John Radziewicz at Da Capo, who liked what he read and wanted more.

No matter how many entertainment shows fill the air, or magazines crowd the newsstands, may there always be a place where questions can be asked and answers given without the feeling that the sand in the hourglass is running low.

THE PRODUCER

ROBERT EVANS

THE FIRST TIME I MET ROBERT EVANS at his office at Paramount Studios, in the summer of 1993, he was sitting behind a round glass table looking at ad copy for *Sliver*, which was about to open. When I entered, he didn't look up, just started talking. I leaned over the table and offered my hand, which he took, but with a puzzled look. "I want you to see this spread," he said, flipping wildly through *Us* until he found the two-page introduction to the summer movie section. He tossed the magazine in front of me. "Look at that," he crowed. "That would make a great ad. It's a hell of a lot better than the ad we've got." I glanced down at the shot of William Baldwin embracing Sharon Stone. Above, the words "Summer Heat" were written in bold red against a bright yellow background. "What do you think?"

"Looks good to me," I said.

"So, can you do it?"

"Do what?"

"Change what we've got to this?"

"You'd probably have to get permission from the magazine," I said.

"Why? It's our still. Why can't you do it?"

I suddenly realized that he didn't know who I was. His secretary had come in before me, but he wasn't listening because he was expecting the head of the ad department. That's why he looked at me queerly when I went to shake his hand.

"I'm not who you think I am," I said.

Now Evans was off balance. If I wasn't the ad person, then who the hell was I? And what was I doing in his office?

"I'm here to interview you."

Evans's face began to wobble. He seemed embarrassed, but just for a moment. Then the woman from the ad department arrived and said she'd look into making the changes he wanted by the end of the day. Later she returned with the ad and he noticed how minuscule the credit type was. "Isn't that too small?" he asked. "The part with all the names, my name included? I mean, contractually shouldn't it be 50 percent?"

"Not really," the woman said. "It's never more than 35 percent."

"What is it now?"

"Twenty."

"I think you're wrong. It's got to be bigger." The woman made a note and said she'd check with the lawyers. Evans turned to me and smiled.

It was a smile that said he was back, with a multi-picture deal, in his old office at Paramount, and he was glad to be there. Just four years earlier people had been saying that Hollywood had passed Evans by, that he was a relic of another generation. Sure, he was head of the studio during its heyday in the late sixties and early seventies when pictures like *Rosemary's Baby, Love Story,* the two *Godfathers, The Odd Couple, True Grit, Paper Moon,* and *Chinatown* were made. But that was all behind him. As were his four marriages to three actresses (Sharon Hugueny, Camilla Sparv, Ali McGraw) and one sportscaster and former Miss America (Phyllis George).

By 1980 he had been busted for cocaine and was on a downward decline. It was a sour decade for Evans, culminating in the suspicion that he was involved in the murder of a man named Roy Radin, who wanted to be his partner in *The Cotton Club.* It was a convoluted story: Evans, in need of financing, wound up dealing with drug dealers, arms dealers, gangsters . . . a lot of bad people. And when one of those bad people didn't like the way Radin was trying to isolate Evans, she supposedly had him offed. Evans had nothing to do with it, but his name was dragged through the story, which brought international attention. And after the disastrous failure of *The Cotton Club,* it was generally assumed that Robert Evans was no longer viable.

But Evans is a man who thrives on challenges and loves to be a player. So he went and found a property that would bring him back and came up with *The Saint.* He went around the world tying up all the rights to the books, the films, the TV shows, then came back and presented it to Paramount. It was a potential industry in itself, he said. Think of Bond, of Indiana Jones. And Paramount bought it. The studio gave him back his office and made a five-picture deal with him. *The Saint,* with Val Kilmer, would eventually flop, as would *Sliver,* starring Sharon Stone.

Evans had worked wonders with Ira Levin's *Rosemary's Baby* in 1968, but he couldn't do it again with the same author and that year's hottest actress. Would the Comeback Kid rise again like a phoenix? Evans had no doubt about it. No doubt at all.

Q: Do you work more at this office or at home?
A: I work mostly here. I have meetings at night at home and work with writers at home. My house is very conducive for working.

How much business got done at your house during the seventies?
There were more deals made in my projection room than there were at Paramount during those days. My home has made Paramount over $1 billion. Charlie Bluhdorn and Marty Davis used to come out here and work out of my house. There were many clandestine deals because of antitrust laws, both legal and illegal, where people weren't supposed to be in the country and they were having private meetings at my house. Bluhdorn used my home as Gulf & Western West.

Who were some of the people that weren't supposed to be in the country? Can you talk about that now?
I can't, because they were private deals that were being made.

Brando told me about harboring Dennis Banks at his home and in Tahiti when he was avoiding the FBI.
Well, for example, the deal for CIC [Cinema International Corporation] when Universal and Paramount bought out Kirk Kirkorian and all the distribution people, they bought out all of Kirkorian's theaters around the world when he owned Metro at the time and business was very bad. Lew Wasserman, Jim Aubrey, Kirk Kirkorian, Charlie Bluhdorn, Martin Davis, myself—met at my house all weekend, back and forth. Kirk Kirkorian walked out six different times, and Charlie Bluhdorn ran down the long driveway to catch him and bring him back, and by the end of the weekend the deal was closed.

Warren Beatty, myself, Jack Nicholson, Sue Mengers, Bob Towne, we always used to sit around casting pictures. I'd like to show you a tape about myself that might help you, if I may put it on.

No, no, let's keep talking. I can see it later.
It tells you very much about the house. I'll give you the tape, okay?

Fine. But why don't you tell me about the people who come to your house.

In my screening room Jack Nicholson comes four or five times a week look-ing at pictures; a lot of directors come to look at their films. *The Godfather* was edited there, *The Two Jakes*. I can go on and on. A couple of years ago I needed new chairs. The old chairs were there for twenty-two years, cotton was coming out of them, it looked like the Salvation Army. I designed a chair and got six of them made and put them in. Nicholson comes over and asks, "Where are the old chairs?" I said I was looking to give them away to the Motion Picture Relief Home so I could get a write-off on them. He said he wanted them. So he sent down a truck and had them picked up. Two weeks later he comes back and says to me, "You gave me the greatest gift I ever got. Those chairs. They're the most valuable chairs in all of Hollywood history. Do you know what happened in those chairs over the last twenty-five years? Mike Nichols wants one, Meryl, Warren, Bernardo . . . everyone wants a chair." I didn't know what I owned. He said, "I may give one to Meryl and to Bernardo. I'm not giving one to Warren." Suddenly I didn't like my new chairs anymore. And Jack won't give me back the old ones (*laughs*).

What has he given you in exchange?
Loyalty. That he's given to me like no one else.

According to the book *The Club Rules*, you are the producer with the most mystique, though no one knows why. Do you?
I'm a loner, that's why. When I was head of Paramount I had a contract that said I didn't have to go out to parties, I didn't have to go to functions. I could always assign someone, from the Academy Awards to the MPAA meet-ings. I just wanted to be involved with film. It's strange. I was invited to a meeting that Lew Wasserman was having at his house, and I didn't show up. He called me, very angry, and he said, "Why aren't you here?" And I said, "I'm editing *The Godfather*, that's why." He said, "That's what editors do. You get over here to the meeting, that's your responsibility." I didn't care. I never showed. He must have been right and I was wrong, because he's counting his millions by the hundreds and I'm looking at the millions I owe in the tens. But I only cared about the film. I was a lousy executive. I designated the po-litical and corporate matters to others, but I did care about the minutiae of film. And product-wise, I turned the product around in the company.

How different is the business today than it was in the seventies?
Totally different. We were four people who ran the company in those days: Marty Davis, Stanley Jaffee, Peter Bart, and myself. I ran it out in California with Peter as my associate, and Marty and Stanley were in New York. We had a hundred actors around. Now there are a hundred executives and four ac-

tors around. That's the best way I can say it. It's a whole different business. It's a committee business, it's a distribution business—you make a picture to make a date, you don't make a picture to make it good. Do I like it? I *hate* it. Am I on my knees glad I'm here? I'm on my knees glad I'm here. Because this is the only game in town.

And all the studios are the same. There is no such word as an "independent" producer. Everyone is a dependent producer. That's the biggest misnomer in the entire film library, that word. The only time that you're an independent producer is when you use your own money. Sam Goldwyn was an independent producer. He spent $6 million of his own money and made *Guys and Dolls*. He owned it, he could do what he wanted, he could tell people to fuck off. When you're being paid—overpaid, as everybody in this business is, including myself—you take the orders. You're not independent.

When I ran the company, it was so different because it went through me, I said yes or no, and there was no one else. We made twenty to twenty-five pictures a year with only two people here. Now there are fifty people here, and they can't get ten pictures made. Why? I don't know. It's become a commodity rather than an art form. And everything is researched, which is nauseating. If a picture goes up three points in a confined period, that's a better picture. It has nothing to do with the quality of the film.

I don't believe in the way they test pictures today at all. It's totally wrong. I believe that a picture has to go out where people spend their two bucks. I'll give you an example. When we took *Marathon Man* out to be previewed, John Schlesinger said, "I will not preview a film." I insisted that he did. We took it to San Francisco. He said, "Well, I shan't change a frame." In the middle of the picture someone stood up and said, "You should be ashamed of yourselves, this is a disgrace!" By the end of the picture they almost threw our car over when we walked out of the theater. We didn't make one change—we made a hundred and ten changes!

Here, if you preview a picture, it's an invited audience. You don't get your highs, you don't get your lows. And you don't know how good or bad the picture is. It's no different from if you came to my house for dinner and my food is lousy but you can't say, "Send it back, I can't eat it." But if you and I went over to Chasen's and the food was as lousy, you can say, "Send it back, it's no good." When you pay for it, you can criticize. When you're invited, you can't.

Are films at all better now than they were twenty-five years ago?
They're not nearly as good. I looked at the pictures when *Chinatown* was up for an Academy Award. There was *Chinatown, Lenny, Godfather II, The Conversation,* and *Woman Under the Influence.* Each one of those pictures was really ex-

traordinary. And you look at the pictures up for an Academy Award today, it's tough to pick five. Today distribution runs the film business. Maybe because it's so expensive, and the numbers are so big today, and the swings are so big. It seems that it's more and more difficult to put pictures together.

And yet you're still doing it. Have you always believed you could pull it off?
I've been a success in whatever I've done. I've never looked at things any other way. The toughest time has been the last five years. It's easy at twenty to be hopeful, but when you're approaching sixty and you're on your ass, you have two places to go: one, the Motion Picture Relief Home, or two, down to live in Palm Springs. When you're successful at my age, it's difficult to stay there, because I'm considered too old. To make a comeback at my age . . . it's like getting out of the grave.

To get back is much more difficult than to get there. This office I'm in now . . . I had a party a year ago Christmas moving back onto the lot. Three years before that I couldn't get into the commissary. I invited everybody from the guards to the Xerox operators to the secretaries to the chairman of the board to Warren Beatty, Jack Nicholson, Raquel Welch—they were all here, over three hundred people. I had a Christmas tree and a present for everybody: a box with a candle, a lighter, and a fake hundred-dollar bill around it, and a saying: "May you open this and may it give you health, love, and a little extra green for the new year." And Jack and I stood outside in front of the awning, and he looked at me and he said, "You know, kid, you're ten thousand to one." That was the miracle in my life. Not getting to where I was. But getting back.

It's tough to get up the ladder, but the higher you climb the further down you fall. And everyone always wants to see you fall.

I was thrown out of this office in 1987. I had been here for fifteen years. I was thrown out because I turned down a million dollars to do an Eddie Murphy film. I didn't want to be Eddie Murphy's nigger. I didn't mean that insultingly, I'm not that kind of producer. I'm not going to be there to say, "Yes, ma'am." Instead, I made something that I'm proudest of in my entire career: *The Planet Is Alive*, America's gift to His Holiness—for the Pope. And everyone thought I was crazy. I put $1.4 million of my own money in it.

Interesting that the man who produced *The Godfather* films says that, since those two films are among the greatest movies ever made.
Filmic-wise, *The Godfather* and *Love Story* are the two for me. The reason I say *Love Story* is, it's a total aphrodisiac. There were more pregnancies from that picture than any other ever made in the history of film. And I was witness to

it. Guys would bring a different girl every night, and for that night they were in love. I'm the only producer still alive who has two pictures—*The Godfather* and *Chinatown*—selected by the Library of Congress to be among the seventy-five films of the twentieth century to be put in a vault for perpetuity.

Why do abnormal people make good actors?
Very good reason: people are not interested in watching normalcy on the screen, it's boring. They see it in life. You have to have a certain craziness, be a little different, otherwise you're not interesting to watch. Interesting to be with possibly. Actors to me aren't interesting people. Most of them are introverted, very dull, scared. But they hold back their real lives and can only act it out in their fantasies. Why, when Jack Nicholson walks on and smiles, does the screen light up? Why can Al Pacino, who's five-foot-six, stand next to a guy six-foot-three on the screen and you don't even see the other guy? Something about him. Nothing to do with size, it's presence. Something off-beat, quirky.

Voices are very important. A voicebox is the most important part of any actor or actress. Humphrey Bogart's lisp, Clark Gable had his voice, Jack Nicholson, Faye Dunaway, Katharine Hepburn . . . you remember their voices. Not the measurements of their height, their breasts, their beautiful looks—that doesn't mean anything. Presence is a strange thing, and it has nothing to do with cosmetic beauty. Nothing.

Marlon Brando never could remember his lines, never studied them well. He's brilliant, though, because he's a presence. He's crazy. Jack Nicholson will be remembered—where actors like Kevin Costner, who's a wonderful actor, won't be after twenty years—because Jack has that crazy look about him. That's why Bogie is and Robert Taylor isn't. Jimmy Cagney's remembered, where Tyrone Power won't be.

Do producers also expect to be remembered the way actors do?
"Producer" is a lousy word today. A producer gets so little respect. He's like Willy Loman. I really feel that way. A producer is on a project longer than anybody else. He usually buys the property, hires the writer, the director, is involved in the production, the post-production, the marketing, and he gets very little credit.

Isn't that because there's such confusion about exactly what a producer does, since there're so many different titles: executive producer, associate producer, assistant producer, line producer, etc.?
No one knows what a producer is. Because a producer means many things: he can be a dealmaker, an agent, the husband or wife of someone. But a real

producer, like David Selznick, Darryl Zanuck, Sam Spiegel, a director needs
him.

Why single out the director?
Because a movie has to be a vision that the two creators see. It has to be that
the director and the producer see the same picture, and they should help
each other. Very few directors have respect for producers, because they're
usually dealmakers. The best thing a director can have is a producer who
protects him. And the best thing they can have for each other is friction
throughout the piece. Because through that friction and grit comes something great. But when the front office is stepping in and everyone has an
opinion and they write thirty pages of notes for every junior executive, it's
counterproductive.

**Since no one knows what a producer does, on a sliding scale of low to
high, which side are you on?**
I'm on the *very* good side of it, and I'm proud to say it. I'm *fucking* good at
what I do. I work too hard and give too much of myself. I ruined my personal life to the detriment of my own health. I ended up in the hospital
twice. They thought I had a heart attack two months ago. They gave me an
angiogram. Fortunately there wasn't anything wrong. My blood pressure
was up to 215. I couldn't catch my breath.

**Critic Richard Schickel said that all of your movies suffer from over-
production: "obsession with detail can ruin a picture."**
I don't think anything I've done has been overly produced. I like things not
overly produced. I think background makes foreground. The difference between *Gatsby* and *Chinatown* was ten minutes into *Gatsby* you knew you were
in the period, and *Chinatown* seeps through. If you call looking for perfection
overproduction, then I overproduce. I'm very irreverent toward what I have
and want to make things better. If that's overproduction, then I overproduce.

What's the biggest chance you've ever taken?
I took a chance becoming the head of the studio when I had never produced
a film. I was there to produce *The Detective*, and circumstance gave me the
chance to become head of Paramount. I was the laughingstock of the whole
city.

***The Detective* was for Fox, wasn't it?**

Which they would have bought from me for half a million. They wanted the property, but I said I wouldn't give it to them unless I got not only offices on the lot but I wanted my picture put in the trade papers attaching me to the project. When you have them, you've got to take the chance to blow a deal, otherwise you'll never make it. I made three other deals while I was there—all controversial projects. One was the life of Maurice Chevalier, another was the F. Lee Bailey story about the Sam Sheppard murders. I had so much going as a kid there without having made one picture that Peter Bart, who was writing for the Sunday *New York Times,* wrote an article in the arts and leisure section about this young producer who in four months had more projects going than anyone in Hollywood. Charlie Bluhdorn had just bought Paramount at the time, and he read this article. And to make a very long story short, I became head of Paramount Studios before I started my first movie.

Before this, didn't you spend some months in London as head of production for Paramount?
They sent me to London first because the action was there. It was the midsixties, and that's when *Georgy Girl, Alfie,* all the hot talent was there. Then they moved me here, and I was a laughingstock. I was called Bluhdorn's Folly. They thought I'd last three days. *Variety* said I'd be fired at the end of the month. I called Bluhdorn once after I had read that I was being let go, and I got him out of a meeting in Spain to ask if I was being fired. "Listen carefully, Evans," he said. "As long as I own Paramount, you're head of the studio unless you call me like this again." And he hung the phone up.

Why was Charlie Bluhdorn so confident in you?
Sense of discovery. It was his pick. And he backed me all the way.

Did you have your own doubts?
Never. I always believed in myself. But I believe I could walk on a court and beat Jimmy Connors in tennis and I won't get a point. You've got to believe in yourself.

Was Bluhdorn a surrogate father figure?
No, not in any way. He was my Knute Rockne. He believed in you and backed you. He was an emotional animal and an entrepreneurial person. He was a unique, brilliant human being.

How much influence did he have on your decisionmaking?

I fought him on everything. When I first came to the company, I got a call from Charlie Feldman, a close friend of mine who was an agent and also produced *Casino Royale* and *What's New, Pussycat?* He told me to come see him on a Sunday morning, and when I got there he said, "I'm gonna make you a winner, kid. *Funny Girl* has just fallen out of Columbia. The bank isn't giving them the money to make it, and I'm ready to give it to you, it'll make you a star." Ray Stark comes in and says he can't do it at Paramount because he doesn't get along with Bluhdorn, and Feldman says, "Ya gotta do it for Bobby. I want him to have *Funny Girl*." So Stark says he'll give me forty-eight hours. I rush home and call Bluhdorn. There were only two hours a week when no one could disturb him, and that was on Sunday afternoon when he would take a hot bath. I took him out of his hot bath and said, "Charlie, listen carefully. I've got *Funny Girl*." He said, "You're crazy, you can't have it." I said I had it, there's a freak thing happening that Columbia doesn't have the money to make it and we can get it but I have to answer in forty-eight hours. Charlie says, "That's my favorite show, I've seen it six times. Stay where you are." He got on the phone and called distribution all over the world, then called me back late that night and said, "We can't go forward with it. No one wants to make it with Barbra Streisand. If Shirley MacLaine would do it that's something else. But no one wants to see that Jewish girl in a picture." I said, "Charlie, don't listen to them. It's your favorite show, it's my favorite show, we've got to do it." He said, "Bob, if you were here a little longer I'd go along with you, but you just came here, it's a very big project, and not one person I talked with wants to do it." "Go on your own instincts, Charlie," I said. "We're never going to have anything better than *Funny Girl*." But he wouldn't do it. Instead we made *Darling Lili*, which almost put us out of business. But from that time on he believed in my instincts.

Does Streisand know this story?
Sure she does. And we made *On a Clear Day* with her, which was a disaster.

Is it true you offered families in for free for *Darling Lili* and still no one came?
That's right. In those days the film business was at its all-time low. Pornography had just come in. The Pussycat Theaters were opening all over the country. In New York *Darling Lili* was playing at Radio City with no one in the theater, and a Pussycat Theater had people around the block trying to get in. It was a real distressing time. We just about sold the studio. By one vote did it miss being sold to become a cemetery. Instead, we ended up buying Desilu for next to nothing. As well as Simon & Schuster, which I bought for the company. And you know what I got out of it? A free trip to Miami.

Did Blake Edwards challenge you to a fight during the production of
Darling Lili?
Yeah. And I'd love to have fought him too. When people challenge you to a
fight, they don't throw the punch.

Have you been in many physical fights?
A lot. I fought in the Golden Gloves. I'm a rough guy. I'm afraid of nothing.
I'm not afraid of being killed.

Doesn't everyone have some fear?
I don't want to have a slow death. That's my fear. I've had a gun put in my
mouth, a gun put at my temple. I won't talk about it, but I can tell you I've
had a gun put on me five different times to talk, and not once have I ever
talked. The last couple of times it hasn't bothered me because I was too well
known for them to have blown me away. Stanley Jaffee said to me, "Why is it
that whenever you get involved with anything there's drama?" It happened
again with *Sliver*. Look what's happened here: Bill MacDonald, my associate,
ends up with Sharon Stone; Joe Ezsterhas is ending up with Bill's wife.
Wherever I am there's an incident. I'm very incident-prone. Some people are
accident-prone, some are health-prone, I'm incident-prone.
    I've always had a theory that has kept me poor but has given me a wealth
of some kind. I like making deals with people where they've got the better of
the deal. Because they'll always come back. Barry Diller said to me once,
about fifteen years ago, "You know, Evans, you're never going to be rich.
You're very bright, you're tenacious, you're as talented as any producer I
know, but you'll never have any money because you totally lack greed." And I
do. I don't care about being the richest guy on the block, it matters the least
to me.

Which of the deadly sins affects you the most?
I like living well. I like seeing things blossom. That's my turn-on.

**When you first came to Paramount, you had to fire a lot of people, you
didn't fill old jobs, and rather than look to the more established talent
you went with new, young talent. How courageous was that?**
We moved off the studio lot. The single most popular man in Hollywood
was at Paramount: Howard Koch. That's why he produced many of the
Academy Award shows, because he could get anyone on them. Everyone
loved Howard. To put me in and take Howard out, from the guards to the
secretaries everyone hated me. They laughed at me. Hal Wallis, Otto Pre-
minger, they all had to report to me. I had to take the prima donnas on like

you can't imagine. There were eight studios, and we were ninth when I came here. The biggest stars we had were [the comedy team] Allen and Rossi. I was greeted with skepticism and disdain. But there's an old saying: When your back's against the wall, the impossible becomes possible. And I wanted to prove that Charlie Bluhdorn was right in backing me.

I wanted to make a picture about an eighteen-year-old boy who falls in love with an eighty-year-old woman, *Harold and Maude.* How do you explain that to anybody? They wanted to throw me out of here. They thought I was crazy.

Didn't you fly to Lucerne to meet with Vladimir Nabokov when his novel *Ada* was still in manuscript?
I always wanted to buy a literary piece of material, and he was my favorite author. *Laughter in the Dark* and *Lolita* were wonderful books. Irving Lazar was his agent, and he said, "Kid, I'm going to give you a break. Nabokov has just finished his new novel, and he lives in Lucerne. Get on the plane and fly over, and you'll be the first to look at it." I fly there. It's eleven in the morning, and there's this long dining room with two old people sitting there, Nabokov and his wife. He said, "You can't be the head of the studio." Because when you're eighty years old . . . I look to him about sixteen. I had to prove to him that I was the head. We ate breakfast, and he gave me this huge manuscript to read. I go up to the room, and we're supposed to meet the next morning for breakfast. And I read and read, and I don't understand anything. I take a Dexamil to stay awake because I think I'm hallucinating. If I had to describe what the book was about, I couldn't talk about it. Now everybody at Paramount—Marty Davis, Bluhdorn—they're desperately waiting. The next morning I come down and I say, "It's extraordinary, I never read anything quite like it." I didn't know what to say.

I fly back to New York and meet with Charlie and Marty, and I say, "Fellas, I don't know how to tell you this. I don't know what I read." Marty says to Charlie, "I told you the kid doesn't know what he's doing." I said, "You know something, Marty, I produced one play when I was an actor, something I read but didn't understand, but I raised the money anyway, and we closed in Philadelphia after one night. I learned when I read something and I don't understand it, let someone else have the success. I can't lie to you, I don't know what it's all about."

Two weeks later Columbia buys it, and they say, "You should have bought it, why didn't you buy it?" Well, Columbia didn't understand it either, they never made it.

And when you do understand material, is it easier to buy?

No one wanted to make *Love Story*. Everybody said, "What kind of piece of shit, pulp junk, is this?" I cried when I read it. I wrote the book with Erich Segal. No one wanted to print the book. They printed 6,000 copies, they were going to give it away as a throwaway. I offered them $25,000 for advertising if they printed 25,000 books. So they did it, and it became the number-one best-seller of the decade.

It was originally a screenplay before it was a book. How did you know to make it a book first?
That's instinct. You can't buy it, you don't learn it, you don't inherit it. You either have it or you don't. *The Godfather* was a thirty-page treatment called "The Mafia." We owned these properties.

In 1970 the studio was going to close and move to New York. I turned in my resignation. I had Mike Nichols shooting *Catch-22* at the time, and I had him do something for me, and I went to New York with this tape. I said to the board, "I'm sorry business is going so terrible. I don't want anything for my severance, I'll sign off now, but I just want you to watch something that I just put together, what I believe Paramount is all about." And I put on this tape for the eighteen board of directors of Gulf & Western, and Marty Davis backed me on this, and it turned things around. (*Shows me the tape: Evans talks into the camera introducing some of the upcoming films Paramount was shooting at the time:* A New Leaf, The Confession, Deadhead Miles (*with Alan Arkin*), Plaza Suite, Love Story.)

Within six years you turned Paramount around . . .
What brought us over the top was *Love Story, Godfather, True Grit*—there were six or seven big hits, and suddenly from being no one we were the biggest studio in the industry.

Yet you rate yourself as a lousy executive.
I'm a terrible executive. I'm terrible at financial things; that's why I have no money.

Is it because you could concentrate on only one or two pictures a year?
I focused on four or five pictures that I took over each year and believed in from their conception. That's my problem, I can't make many pictures. I spend so much time, I get impassioned. To do a *Harold and Maude* you had to have belief in it, it was such a crazy idea. *Romeo and Juliet* was another one.

Is there anybody like you that you know?
No.

How about Streisand?

Barbra is absolutely that way. She's impassioned. But she's a very wealthy woman because she's a talented actress and a singer. I'm not. That's why I have no money. I spend so much time on just one project. And you can spend just as much time on a failure as on a success. That's what Lew Wasserman criticized me for. But I couldn't help it.

Wasn't it on that Streisand picture, *On a Clear Day You Can See Forever*, when you first met Nicholson?

Let me give you a great Jack Nicholson story. I'm making *On a Clear Day*. Barbra Streisand has signed for the picture with Yves Montand. This is a wonderful story. There's the part of Tad, Streisand's half-brother. I looked at fifty actors for the part, and I saw this one guy and asked who it was. The head of casting and talent wanted me to look at someone else, but I kept going back to this guy with a smile. "Find out who the guy with the smile is," I said. Comes back the next day and says, "Some nut named Nicholson, works for Roger Corman." I said I wanted to meet him. But he was in Cannes, he had just finished making two pictures, each one cost $6,000. One was *House of Horrors,* and the other he starred, produced, and directed. But I'm told he's crazy and I should forget about it. I had to fly to New York, and I got a call from an agent who said Jack Nicholson was in town. "Who's that?" I asked. "The guy with the smile," he said. "Oh, that guy. Have him come over to the Sherry, I'll meet him." We hadn't cast the part yet. He walked in with the agent, and this is why I love working at home and not an office. I learned this from Darryl Zanuck. We're sitting and talking for a while, and I said to him, "You know, kid, I loved your smile. I'm going to star you with Barbra Streisand and Yves Montand in *On a Clear Day*, and I'm going to pay you $10,000 for six weeks' work."

He smiled and said, "That's great, but I just finished a picture called *Easy Rider.* . . . " I said, "I don't want to hear about that shit, another motorcycle picture. This is Barbra Streisand. You'll be singing a song with her." His agent said, "Shut up, Jack, let Mr. Evans talk." I said, "No, let him talk." So Nicholson said, "Can I talk to you alone, Mr. Evans?" We walked to the window of the Sherry, it was snowing out, and he looked at me and said, "You know, pal, I just got divorced, I got a kid, I've got no money to pay alimony or child support. Can you make it fifteen?" I said, "How about twelve-five?" "Do you mean it?" he asked. And we hugged and kissed. And that's how we met. And have remained friends ever since.

That could never have happened in an office. Because when you're sitting behind a desk, it's intimidating. Here we were sitting with our feet up on the couch and we could talk. Darryl Zanuck never wanted to meet with writers or artists in an office, because it was adversarial.

Let's go back to your very first deal once you were in that position of power at Paramount: was it *The President's Analyst* with James Coburn?
Yes. And the FBI came to me before the picture started. They came at J. Edgar Hoover's request. They said that the FBI was talked about in the script very unattractively and I had to change it. I said I wouldn't. They said, "We advise you very strongly. Mr. Hoover's asking you to change it." I said, "Tell Hoover to go fuck himself!" I got a call from Charles Bluhdorn. "Bob, please don't cause trouble." So I acquiesced and changed the name to the FBE. And my phone has been tapped ever since.

When you made this first decision, was it harder than any of the others?
No, I always want to do the offbeat. I wanted to do the unexpected. I wanted to be a trend-setter rather than a trend-follower. When I had *Rosemary's Baby,* people thought I was crazy. When I made *Goodbye Columbus,* I used an unknown actress, an unknown director, an unknown producer, Stanley Jaffee . . . and I loved it. I love people stories.

Did you know Ali McGraw then?
No. But I fell in love with her watching the dailies. She didn't want to have anything to do with me. She had been living with a guy for three years, had no interest in me at all, disliked everything I stood for. She was a real bohemian. She was the one who gave me *Love Story* and no one wanted to make it. I flipped for her. I got her to fly out for one night to look at Arthur Hiller's *The Out-of-Towners,* she came here, never saw the movie, never left my house. Until she dumped me three years later.

Let's look at what excited you about the other films you gave the okay to. I'll name the picture, you say what comes into your head.
The Odd Couple.
The Odd Couple was the first confrontation I had with Paramount. Paramount then was looked upon as a B studio. For *The Odd Couple* they wanted to put in Jack Klugman and Tony Randall for the movie. And I wanted Jack Lemmon and Walter Matthau, who wanted a million dollars. Billy Wilder was locked in. William Morris controlled the three of them. And Bluhdorn and Marty Davis flew out from New York. We met at my house for three days, it was like a brothel, with guys coming in and out. I insisted on having Lemmon and Matthau, and they didn't want to spend the money. Well, we

couldn't afford Lemmon, Matthau, and Wilder. So Jack and Walter fucked Billy Wilder over, and he was left out of the package. But that was the start of the turnaround. I got Lemmon and Matthau.

Paint Your Wagon.
That was Charlie Bluhdorn's desire.

The Little Prince, which you thought would be *The Wizard of Oz* of the seventies.
It should have been. I brought Lerner and Lowe back together again, they had broken up. They wrote the most beautiful score for it. Stanley Donen directed it. Frank Sinatra was ready to come out of retirement to play the part, but Stanley wouldn't work with him. Then Richard Burton wanted to play it, he sang beautifully, but Stanley didn't want to work with Burton. It should have been wonderful. I loved it, but it didn't turn out well, it was a big disappointment. No one went to see it. It played to empty theaters. But the picture was good. Bob Fosse had a wonderful piece in it. Gene Wilder. It was a dream that didn't come true.

Blue, which was supposed to star Robert Redford.
Blue was one of the disasters of all time. Redford walked off four days before it was to start and disappeared. Two years later he was going to do *Rosemary's Baby*, and Roman Polanski had a meeting with him, and someone serves Redford with a subpoena because of *Blue*. We lost Redford because of that.

The Molly Maguires, with Sean Connery and Richard Harris.
Disaster! An expensive picture. The only place that did business was in Pittsburgh. It was about the coal business, and it was a big mistake.

Paper Moon.
Wonderful, I loved it. No one would make it. The only way Peter [Bogdanovich] would make it was if he could use Tatum O'Neal, who never did a part. He line-fed her. And Ryan was terrific in it. I'm so proud of that one.

Lady Sings the Blues.
I love to make integrated pictures. I had a very bad back and had a stretcher in my projection room. Berry Gordy and I reedited the entire film. It was a success, but it didn't do as much business as it should have. Diana Ross was nominated for an Academy Award. I'm very proud of that film. And it had all to do with me because no one wanted to make it. They didn't want to make a black picture.

I had a project that I was going to make called *I Love You*. It started and ended on New Year's Eve. I was going to direct it as well. It was about a black girl, a Kelly girl, who meets the guy in Atlanta who's the head of Coca-Cola, a young guy from the wrong side of the tracks, who arrives back from Peking where he closed the deal in China to sell Coca-Cola. It's New Year's Eve, and he belongs to the Riding Club, this top country club which is so restrictive they don't even allow a black senator there. It tells of their romance, and the next New Year's Eve he walks in there, knowing that his career is over, and he says to her, "I don't care, I love you." Those three words. I signed Beverly Johnson to do the part because I wanted to get a black girl who was more beautiful than any white girl in any room, and she was that. And I couldn't get a white actor to play opposite her to get the picture made. That was when Jimmy Carter got in, in 1976. The reason I wanted to make it was that I resented the fact that Jimmy Carter got in because of the black vote and he was the most conservative southerner.

True Grit.
I loved. No one wanted to see John Wayne with a patch over his eye. Hal Wallis and I said, we've got to make this picture. Duke and I were very friendly. He won the Academy Award for it.

Catch-22.
I thought that was brilliant. But it was too sophisticated.

In *Chinatown* Faye Dunaway credits you with changing the music for her love scene with Nicholson, and making all the difference.
It did.

They disagreed on the ending: Towne thought Huston's character should be killed, you and Roman wanted Dunaway killed. Would the picture have been as memorable if Towne got his way?
Never. Never!

Is Towne still angry about it?
Of course.

And what about John Huston? Did you know him before?
I spent some time with John. I liked him. I knew him through Toots as well—Anjelica. John was wonderful on that film.

Did he ever have any ideas that he offered?

He stayed out of it.

Whose idea was it to do *The Godfather* as a period family chronicle rather than another gangster movie?
Francis wanted to show capitalism in America. When I hired Francis, Dick Zanuck and John Cally both called me and told me I was going to be fired from my job. Dick said, "Bob, they're going to throw you off the picture, the guy's nuts." Cally called me and said American Zoetrope owed them $600,000. "We get all his money. You're my friend, you made *Catch-22* with me. Don't use him, Bob, you don't know the problems you're going to get into." He had made only three pictures at that time: *You're a Big Boy Now*, which did no business; *Finian's Rainbow*, which was a disaster; and *Rain People*, which was a slow art film.

So why did you choose Coppola?
For one reason. He was the only Italian director in Hollywood. And I wanted it told from the viewpoint of a second-generation Italian. I made a very careful study. Even after I developed it from a thirty-page treatment into the biggest best-seller of the decade, Paramount did not want to make it. Because there had not been one Mafia film ever made that had made a profit, including *The Brotherhood*, which Paramount had made two years before. They had been written, directed, acted by Jews. And there's a thin line between a Jew and a Sicilian, so that's why I went with Coppola. Because I wanted to smell the spaghetti.

Did you want to replace Coppola with Elia Kazan?
No. At first, because everyone was complaining about Coppola not knowing what he was doing, I called Gadge [Kazan]. He said, "Stick with Francis."

Coppola claims he was fired three times from the picture.
Four. I fired him at the beginning of the film. Two weeks into shooting I got a call from the editors, who said they couldn't edit it. There's a scene where Pacino blows away Sollozzo and Sterling Hayden in the restaurant, which they said they couldn't edit. So I had the film sent to me, and I edited it over the weekend, and it was brilliant. I got on the red-eye, fired the editors, and told Francis he was brilliant. But he was so shaken at the time, no one believed in him. He almost had a nervous breakdown. Charlie Bluhdorn came in and kept him up. When the picture was finished, however, and he edited the film and I saw it, I said it was not releasable. He had taken out all the texture. The picture was supposed to open that Christmas, and I went to the

Paramount hierarchy and said, we cannot open it then. I almost lost my job over it. They pushed it back, and we added fifty minutes to the picture.

What was your initial reaction to Pacino as Michael?
You know how Pacino got the part? I didn't want Pacino. Francis did. He didn't want Jimmy Caan, and I did. So we settled. But you know who talked me into using Pacino? Brando. Pacino didn't test well, and Brando called me. We didn't speak much, but he called me about this. He said, "Listen to me, Bob. He's a brooder. And if he's my son, that's what you need, because I'm a brooder." It was Brando's insight that made me understand why Al would work.

Was Warren Beatty your first choice for Michael?
No, I wanted Alain Delon. He was the type, but he couldn't speak English well. Maybe I did want Warren. I may have thought of Jack too for it. Jack tells me I did, but I don't remember it. Dustin desperately wanted to do it.

Did you eventually warm up to Pacino?
Al did an interview for *The Godfather*. It was the opening night, and a reporter from *Time* was to talk to him. Al was living in a cellar at the time, so he asked to use my suite at the Carlyle. He came up with a little navy pea cap, he looked like a second-story guy, and he said to me, "Can you loan me a fiver? I've got no money for a cab tonight for the opening." And I'm thinking, "This is the lead of *The Godfather*?" So I gave him two hundred-dollar bills. He puts them in his pocket and goes and does the interview.

Ever get the money back?
Of course not. You ever get anything back from an actor? Uh-uh (*laughs*). Marthe Keller told me about Al, that she went with him for six years and she couldn't afford him anymore.

What ever happened to Marthe Keller? She was in *Black Sunday*, which you produced, but then she disappeared.
I can answer that easily: name one European actress who's ever made it in America. You can't. The last one was Ingrid Bergman. Sophia Loren never made it in America. The only actor is Arnold Schwarzenegger. There's a reason for it. Between New York and Los Angeles there's a huge valley called the United States of America. In that valley they want to hear American spoken. Alain Delon came over here, he was the biggest European actor alive, couldn't sell him in America, he was French. Doesn't matter who it is, Anna Brazzi,

Romy Schneider, Brigitte Bardot, Catherine Deneuve, you can go on and on, they never made it in America.

Speaking of foreign actors: did you consider Carlo Ponti or Laurence Olivier for Don Corleone?
No. Marlon was a fraud in this thing. He hadn't even read the book. He needed the part. Francis did a silent test of him. Dino De Laurentiis, when he was told that Marlon was going to play the part, said he wouldn't be able to open the picture in Italy, he'd be laughed off the screen. Marlon had made twenty-two pictures before that, eleven of them were unreleasable. He was as dead as dead could be. Marlon did the part for $50,000. Everyone else got $35,000. And he had one point of the gross after the first $10 million, two points for the second, three, four, and five points up to $60 million. No picture ever did that. Norman Gary, his attorney, called me and said Marlon was desperately in need of $100,000. I told Charlie Bluhdorn, and Charlie said to give it to him but get the points back. We got the points back in twenty-four hours. That $100,000 cost him $11 million.

Did he ever try to renegotiate?
When it happened, he went crazy. And I don't blame him. He fired Norman Gary, he fired his agent. He called me and said, "I'll play the part in *Gatsby*, but I want my deal back." I said one picture had nothing to do with the other. He said, "It's the same company."

Can you compare Brando and Pacino as godfathers?
What's so interesting seeing Brando in *The Godfather* and Al in *Godfather III* is that Marlon was two years younger than Al when he played the part, and yet he had a stature about him that was remarkable. Brando was ageless. Al was forty-seven when he played it, Marlon was forty-four.

What was your bonus after the film's success?
A trip to the Virgin Islands.

And did you buy Francis a Mercedes?
Yes. I had predicted that the picture would do $50 million. He said if it did would I buy him a Mercedes. The day it did $50 million he went and bought the most expensive Mercedes he could, twelve cylinders, and charged it to me.

He made it up to me ten years later. He gave me a second asshole like no one has ever given it to me in my life.

You're jumping ahead, we'll get to *The Cotton Club*, but let's stay with the two *Godfathers*.
Let me make it real clear what happened with those. I did *The Godfather* with Francis, and we had horrendous fights. He only became the *macha* of the industry from that film; he became a genius. If his cut was shown, it would have been on television. When we made *Godfather II*, he wanted total autonomy, and he had it. I had nothing to do with it until we went to preview the picture in San Francisco two months before it was to open. When he walked into the theater, they stood up and applauded him as if he was a king. By the time the picture was over half the theater was empty. What he had done: he left out the entire Havana sequence, the Meyer Lansky–Hyman Roth scene, and had more of Sicily with subtitles. It was a *bore*. And we went back and made over a hundred changes. We put back Havana, which was the best part of the movie. He doesn't know how to structure a movie.

And after he received his second Oscar, he didn't acknowledge you again. Was that hurtful?
On purpose. We stood at the Dorothy Chandler Pavilion in the back. *Chinatown* was a 6–5 favorite against the field. And he said, "You're going to win, Evans." And I said, "No, you're going to, Francis. This is your year." He said, "Isn't it funny. If I win, it's because of you." I said, "I know it." He wins. I'm sitting there. He thanks everybody except me. Then to put the knife in further, he said to me afterwards, "God, I forgot to thank you again." That's how Machiavellian he is.

If you had it to do over again, would you accept releasing the first *Godfather* as a lesser picture if you could still be married to Ali McGraw?
Of course I would have. My priorities were fucked up. When my son was born, I was out here editing, fighting with Francis, instead of being in New York with her.

You were a very hot couple—what went wrong with the marriage?
I fucked up the marriage. She told me before we got married, "I'm a hot lady, Evans, don't leave me for more than two weeks at a time." I left her for four months without visiting her once. Plus she was with one of the most attractive men in the world to boot [Steve McQueen]. Because I was too busy cutting the fucking *Godfather.* All right?

Is it true that you got *Life* to agree to put you and Ali and your son Joshua on the cover—and presented it to Ali as a reason for you to stay together? And she blew up?

No. *Life* wanted us to be on the cover, and Ali refused. I said fine.

Your son is in his late twenties now. What does he do?
He's an actor, director, writer. He's starting his first picture, raised $100,000 to make a movie. He comes to me all the time, not for money but for advice. He's my best friend. I didn't make him go to college, which his mother wanted. I said, go out and make it. He played Tom Cruise's kid brother in *Born on the Fourth of July,* the kid manager of the Doors in *The Doors.* Oliver Stone's crazy about him. He costarred with Denzel Washington and John Lithgow in *Ricochet.* He can't take the shit of being an actor, though. So he's writing and directing now and using my house as a location.

Brando could never take the shit of being an actor and look what he did. He followed *The Godfather* with *Last Tango in Paris.* Did you have a shot at that?
I was going to do *Last Tango In Paris. The Godfather* hadn't come out yet. Everybody turned it down, Alain Delon, Jean-Paul Belmondo, but Brando took it. And I knew how great it was. Yet Paramount wouldn't make the deal because it was an X-rated picture.

Have you ever been involved in an X-rated film?
I made *Tropic of Cancer,* which was X-rated. It was a damn good film. Henry Miller and I were good friends. We used to play Ping-Pong together. He usually won. He said, "You don't have the guts to make *Cancer.*" I got it made, and they pulled it after one theater, it was so rough. Ellen Burstyn was in it, she had a different name: Ellen McGray. She had her pussy showing, lice in her pussy, open legs. When Gulf & Western saw it, they said, "Get rid of this crazo." Then I made another picture they had to pull called *Medium Cool* with Haxell Wexler. It was so controversial that Gulf & Western wanted to get rid of that too. So when it came to *Last Tango,* they turned it down and I was sick about it. I was the one who got Marlon in it. It was a brilliant film. Maria Schneider came on at the last minute. Dominique Sander was supposed to play the part, but she got pregnant and Maria was Brigitte Bardot's stand-in. She was wonderful in that film, as good as Marlon. It was her first movie. I knew her well, used to take her out. She used to dance all alone at Costello's in Paris. What a body she had! Then she got stuck on heroin. When *Black Sunday* came around, she was up for that, she was a total dyke at that time.

After the success of *Silence of the Lambs,* did you think back to *Black Sunday,* which was Thomas Harris's first novel?

Sure. *Black Sunday* was the biggest disappointment of any picture I ever had. It cost me $6 million. I was offered that for my points. And I got a letter from the maven, Bernie Myerson, who said *Black Sunday* was going to be bigger than *Jaws*. It wasn't bigger than *my* jaw. But when it was shown to the exhibitors, they stood up and applauded like no other picture I've ever been involved with. Any film. I thought I had a winner. And I had thirty-seven points of it. Ended up not making enough money to make a phone call.

The reason: the Jews in America they call me a Hitlerite in the *B'nai Brith Messenger*. I had to have guards around my house. The picture didn't play around the world. The Red Army of Japan threatened to blow up every theater in Japan if they played it in theaters around the world. The picture was pulled because it was so real. I showed both sides of the story. The Palestinian side and the Israeli side. And for the one scene where I showed the Palestinian side the sensitivities of the Jewish people were that strong they called me a Hitlerite.

Marathon Man *and* Black Sunday *were made at the same time. Was there bad blood between Dustin Hoffman and John Schlesinger during* Marathon Man?
Terrible. They never talked. There's a gag reel that I made that's locked up in a safe. I have it on video. It was made for one reason: John Schlesinger did not want Dustin Hoffman in the film. He thought he was too old. The reason he really didn't want him was six years earlier Dustin had to screen-test for *Midnight Cowboy* and was paid $60,000, now he was making $2 million.

Dustin is a very difficult actor to work with. Two days before *Tootsie* opened Dustin called Sidney Pollack the bum director of the decade, in front of everybody.

Is it true that you sold *Tootsie* to your brother?
I gave *Tootsie* to him. It wasn't called *Tootsie*, it was called *Would I Lie to You?* My brother was looking to do something in his life. He was bored in New York. He had a terrible tragedy in his life. His wife and two children were burned to death in 1975. He was just a shambles of a person, which was understandable. He was hit with a baseball bat in the balls. He can never recover from it. And I wanted to give him some joy and do something that would turn him on. We used to go away to Palm Springs on weekends, and I wanted to get him involved in something, and I had this script which Dan McGowan had written. It was owned by a theater owner and had been around a long time. I read it after Buddy Hackett sent it to me. I said to Charlie, "This is a very funny piece of material." And he bought it, not from me, from Dan McGowan. At that time George Hamilton was going to do it.

George went into the film business because of me. He became an actor because he said, "If Evans can be an actor, anybody can." He was a pool boy at the Beverly Hills Hotel. We're very good friends. I love George. He's underestimated as a performer. He's a very good comedian. Great personality.

Anyway, Dustin Hoffman was going to do the Renee Richards story. He wanted to do a transvestite story. And Dustin's a tennis player. Someone sent him *Would I Lie to You?* and Dustin liked it. My brother was the executive producer on it. I was happy for him.

Who are your five closest friends?
I don't want to say. But of the top ten, seven are women. Of the top three, it would be one woman and two men. Three women and two men are my five. And fifteen out of twenty are women, and I wish it wasn't that way. Because I do business with men.

During the making of *The Cotton Club* I had to get $2 million to pay the weekly payroll. Money was due to me from Orion the following Thursday, but money had to be paid that Friday. I went to four men to ask them for the loan, guaranteed by Orion the following Thursday, and all four—each of whom I had made $100 million for or more—gave me an excuse why they couldn't give it to me. The first two women I went to gave it to me before I finished the sentence and asked me if I wanted more. Liv Ullmann and Cheryl Tiegs. I rest my case.

What woman have you loved most?
How can I say? Ali, because we're locked at the hip, we've had a kid together. We shared magic together for two years with *Love Story*. She's in my life. She's in my will. Of my three best friends she's one of the three. And I am to her. In her book she said the one 911 number she has in her life is Robert Evans.

None of your four marriages worked out. [Evans married a fifth time after we talked. It also didn't work out.] How difficult are you to live with?
I'm a romantic. All of my marriages put together were less than seven years. I'm easy to live with, that's not the problem. Of my four wives, three of them are my best friends. My son Josh and I were having lunch at the Beverly Hills Hotel in the coffee shop downstairs, and Camilla, my wife before Ali, was sitting at the other end. Joshua had never met Camilla. She came up, and I introduced them, and Joshua said to her, "What kind of husband was my daddy? Because I never grew up having him as a father living with my mother." She said, "That's a very impertinent question, Joshua." He said, "I'd like to know from someone who was married to him, since my mother can't

answer that question to me." She thought and she said, "Your father was the single worst husband any woman could *ever* be married to. However, he spoiled me for the rest of my life for any other man."

All my wives are lovely girls. I was very good to all of them. My priorities were just fucked in life. I don't like a structured life. I'm not a good social planner. I was a flagrant cheat—all the time. That's why my marriages couldn't work out, because I couldn't lie. Camilla found out that I was having many affairs. She didn't want to break up the marriage, but she asked me to at least see a psychiatrist. I didn't want to, but she asked as a favor to her, for her dignity. So she sent me to one, and after the third visit he called Camilla and told her to forget it, to go out and have an affair because I was no good and would never change. For better or worse, I'm not a married type.

Do you still feel that the older you get the less you understand women?
No, I just think that they are more intuitive than we are, brighter than we are. Whether it be a country, an army, a team, a business, a family, a person—it's only as good as its weakest link. And every man has the same weak link: ego. Women don't have that. A good example: you're married to a girl, and she's out cheating every day. When you get in bed at night, you can't think she's fucking around because "she's married to me, how can she do it?" Reverse: you're living with a woman and you fuck around. The first day you fuck she touches you and she can feel it, she knows it. A man doesn't because of his ego. A woman doesn't have that.

How many times I've gone to pick up some of the most beautiful women to take them out, and they won't even go out because they think they look so awful. They don't, they look beautiful. But I always think I look great! If a woman knows how to be fetching as a woman, that's the strongest asset in the world. There's a saying that has nothing to do with sex: the hair on a woman's pussy is stronger than the Atlantic cable. And it's true.

Look at Sherry Lansing. There's not one person who leaves her office who isn't charmed by her. And charmed by *nos,* not just *yeses.* Stanley Jaffee says Sherry is the best closer of any person he's ever known in this industry. Not that she's that brilliant. She knows how to use her femininity, and she's as tough underneath as anyone in the world.

Jack Nicholson has an expression: "Hey, Bob, don't try to figure them out. You can't, they don't play fair." That's a way to look at it.

How would you describe yourself?
I'm a loner. I enjoy being alone. I'd rather be remembered than be rich. And I'm an easy mark: I give to too many people.

. . .

After spending the morning with Evans at his office on the Paramount lot, he asked me to come to his house that evening at 11:30 P.M. to continue our talk. Evans is an insomniac who works while most of us sleep, but I thought that, with a few hours to rest, I could deal with it. However, at 10:00 P.M. he called to say he was still in the editing room at Skywalker Studios and would be there most of the night. Could I come at ten the next morning?

His house is above Sunset, behind the Beverly Hills Hotel. When I arrived, his butler took me through the main house and into the projection room, which is sandwiched between his oval swimming pool and the tennis court. The pool, the projection room, and the court probably contain more Hollywood history than any other house in the Beverly Hills–Brentwood–Bel Air triangle. Evans was late, so I had an opportunity to admire the Picasso and Toulouse-Lautrec prints, the nude drawings by Jean Negulesco, the view of the tennis court. I tried out the leather chairs he had designed, the ones that replaced the chairs taken by Jack Nicholson. I looked at the framed pictures and articles about Evans. And when he arrived, he showed me another: a Polaroid of his caricature from the Palms restaurant, with the words "The Robert Evans" next to it.

"I'm the only one who has that," he said about the "The." "It might work as a title to your piece. It's just a thought."

Evans is a man of boundless energy. He likes to hum when he isn't concentrating, and during the next seven hours he would go between his house and the projection room at least a dozen times, humming as he walked, humming as he approached. It's easy to sense his presence before he actually arrives.

When his assistant came in, he asked her to tell me what she thought of him. "I would describe him as the most generous person, man or woman, that I have ever met in my entire life," she said, speaking like a loyal employee. "He's like nobody I've ever known. I would stop a bullet for him, because he gives and he gives and he gives. And it doesn't really matter who it is. He gives unconditionally. And everybody is still his friend because he is such a wonderful guy, how could you not like him? But he drives me crazy because I worry about him. After the smoke clears, he's given everything away and he's standing there with his finger in his mouth. And it bothers me that people don't recognize what a sweetheart he is, and just back off sometimes."

During our first talk we concentrated on his tenure as vice president in charge of production at Paramount between 1966 and 1974. There was much more ground to cover, including his stint as an "independent" producer—the period that culminated with his bust for cocaine use and the disastrous *Cotton Club* episode that almost destroyed him. His production designer Richard Sylbert said that he had never seen Evans as anxious as he was at that time. "It wasn't just a fear of failure but the big fear of going into the toilet for the last time. He was a man who would do anything. He was in very deep shit."

But in spite of the failure of *The Cotton Club*, Evans managed to come out of that very deep shit. He's a man loaded with ideas, always running on a full tank, hoping to catch the magic once again. And he's not afraid to say what he thinks in an industry that usually prefers to keep the lid on what goes on behind the scenes.

Is film the great art form of the twentieth century?
Oh, by far. More than just a great art form, it's something else. All of us should be proud of this: it is the only product that is manufactured in the U.S. that is number one in every country in the world. The American film flies the American flag higher than any other thing made in this country, and yet we don't even get any respect for it. You can laugh at Hollywood, but that's bullshit. People should praise Hollywood for what it's done. It's done a lot more than Detroit or Pittsburgh or Houston and Dallas have done in cars, steel, oil. The Japanese can't make our product, that's why they have to buy our companies. No one can duplicate the American film. I'm very proud of that. Being in an industry that's number one in America, I don't understand why we don't get more government help, why there aren't schools that are set up for kids to learn, like engineering and doctors.

There are a lot of film schools.
They should be undergraduate schools. There are so many people who have been in this industry a long time who would love to be professors, teachers, who could teach the art of making film. And so many young people want to learn it. I'm a full professor at Brown University. I taught a class there on the anatomy of film four times a year, and I never graduated high school. But no one else could teach my course. And they resented having to make me a professor. But more kids took my course than any other in the entire curriculum. Young people are hungry to learn about film, and there's no one there to teach them. It is definitely an art form, and it is definitely something that no one can knock us off on, because no one can duplicate the American film.

Growing up, did you have any heroes?
Dr. Jonas Salk is my greatest hero. Because he discovered the cure for polio. When I grew up, polio was rampant. I had kids all around me die or become

paralyzed. One summer my mother thought I had it because I had a high temperature, I was throwing up. They closed all the pools, and all the kids couldn't play. Years later, when Salk moved to Palo Alto to work on the immunization of the cell, I wanted to quit Paramount and work for him. I went down to visit him several times, but there was nothing I could contribute except be in awe. He is my hero in life. I was sure he was going to come up with the cure for cancer. He was like my god, Salk.

When you were young, did you have ambitions to get into the movies?
I was a kid actor for many many years. I was under contract to Paramount. When I was eleven years old, I was an actor for radio. I was assigned to a picture when I was seventeen, called *City Across the River,* at Universal, but I got sick, my lung collapsed, and I couldn't do the part.

When your lung collapsed, did you think you might die?
Well, I was leading a wild life as a kid. My parents always backed me, what I wanted to do. Against their friends' advice. My father was a dentist, and all his friends were doctors and lawyers. In those days, when a kid wanted to be an actor, he was looked at as very peculiar. But I was a loner, I didn't play with the other kids. The only reason I wanted to be an actor was so I wouldn't have to face other kids. I always had a good voice, and I did accents very well. I became "the Accent Kid." I played Nazis during World War II on radio. Dicky Van Patten and I used to work together a lot. Dicky's father was a bookie. We used to go up to the Red Rooster in Harlem. There was a whorehouse upstairs and gambling downstairs. We went up with Alfred Lunt's valet. We went for the fascination, because all the girls would pick up their tips with their pussies. And in the eyes of a fifteen-year-old kid, this was something!

I fought on a bet with Dicky. One guy offered me on a dare to fight in the Golden Gloves. I said I was an actor, he bet me $100. So I went into the ring, and after two rounds I couldn't lift my arms. The next thing I knew I was out cold for thirty minutes, they thought I was dead.

But I was very busy as a kid actor. One time I was making more money than my father. And things were tough in those days too.

At fourteen weren't you were earning $1,500 a week as a radio actor?
Some weeks. Some weeks less. Then everything dropped out under me. After my lung collapsed, I couldn't get a job. I became a disc jockey in Palm Beach, then in Miami, then I was invited to Havana, Cuba. By disc jockey . . . it was a show in the lounge of the Copacabana Hotel. I gambled there and probably

would have stayed a professional gambler if it wasn't for not wanting to disappoint my family. I didn't want them to be hurt by my behavioral patterns.

But this business is made up of gamblers: the Louis B. Mayers, the Schencks, Harry Cohn. Darryl Zanuck was busted because of gambling, he had to borrow money from Howard Hughes. David Selznick used to play gin for a buck a point. So did I. I played with Richard Brooks, Willie Wyler, Sam Spiegel. In poker I played with Brooks, Doc Simon, heavy big games. You have to be a gambler to be in this business. To be in a position to put up $20 million on the seat of your pants, because there's no close-out value. It's like Vegas, you drop it. Unlike a car, which you can close-out if it doesn't sell, a film is like a parachute jumper: if it doesn't open, you're dead. You've got to be a gambler.

Your grandfather was a gambler, wasn't he?
He was a degenerate gambler. He'd go out for breakfast and come back three weeks later. He used to win and lose families. It was when there was no money in the family when my father became a dedicated professional. My father wanted to be everything his father was not. I wanted to be everything my father was not, even though I loved him very much. He was so dedicated to a structured family that I wanted to enjoy the celebration of life.

Havana during that time must have been a wild city.
It was the wildest place in the entire world. It was like *Godfather II*. I had to make a very quick exit from Cuba, because I was witness to something I shouldn't have been, which I cannot get into to this day, I don't want to talk about it. I was interviewing Abbe Lane on the radio, and I was brought into a room, blindfolded, taken out and put on a seaplane, landed in Miami on a desolate beach, given $10,000, and told never to come back again.

Was this the government kicking you out or a private party?
I'm not saying who did it. I was seventeen. I had a gun to my head. I shit in my pants, but I didn't talk. That's the truth.

So what did you do when you returned to New York? Is that when you joined your brother Charles in the clothing business?
No, my brother was out of a job at that time. When I came back to New York, I tried to get work in radio, couldn't get much work. I took a job as a male model in a clothing firm. I wanted to get in film. I wound up out in California handling a clothing line and got signed by Paramount Pictures. It was called the Golden Circle then, they had forty actors under contract.

They signed me for $125 a week, and they taught you fencing and riding. I was under contract for six months, and they dumped me.

My brother by then started a little company called Evan Picone, and we decided to go into the pant business instead of making skirts. That was my job: to start women wearing pants in America. I'm very proud of it. Racks of pants weren't allowed in stores in those days, so I had to convince buyers that women would wear pants. I went all over the country doing this. Our whole factory was the size of my office here. I started a fashion that's a lot more important than most of the movies I ever made, and it's something that will remain far after I'm dead. In the fifties women weren't allowed to wear pants. Jackie Kennedy in the sixties wasn't allowed in a certain restaurant because she had pants on. It was taboo, considered insulting to fashion. I got women to wear pants, and I'm as proud of that as anything I've ever done.

Do you feel you have anything in common with Adolph Zukor or Sam Goldwyn, both of whom started in the clothing business?
No. They started as poor immigrants. I was an established person. I was an actor for a decade before I was in the clothing business.

You were "discovered" twice: first by Norma Shearer, who wanted you to play her husband, Irving Thalberg, then by Darryl Zanuck. Most hopefuls wait a lifetime to be discovered once. Were you just born under a lucky star?
If I weren't prepared for my discoveries, I wouldn't have gotten it. If I hadn't paid my dues. Being discovered is bullshit, you've got to be prepared for it. Luck is when opportunity meets preparation. I tested for both parts, they weren't given to me. Certainly I was lucky to have been discovered. But if I couldn't back it up, it would have been hello and good-bye.

How nervous were you acting with James Cagney in your first feature, *Man of a Thousand Faces*?
(*Gets up again to look for an old* Reader's Digest *article that quotes Cagney but can't find it.*) Cagney was my favorite actor. In my autobiography the second chapter deals with going to see *Angels with Dirty Faces* as a kid and then going out and hitting a guy because I was trying to act like Jimmy Cagney. And here was my first experience as a professional actor, having to tell Jimmy Cagney how to act. They picked the wrong scene to start with! What happened was, I walked on to the set, and my father had come out, he was so proud, especially after all the shit he had taken from his friends, and I couldn't open my mouth. They did six takes. Cagney tells the story in *Reader's Digest,* he walked

over to me and said, "Let me tell you something, kid. I'm five-foot-four. The first scene I had was with a guy six-foot-three. When the scene was over, I was six-foot-three and *he* was five-foot-four. Don't be scared, just do it."

Why didn't Hemingway like you for *The Sun Also Rises*?
I didn't blame him. Why should he want me in the picture? He wanted a real bullfighter. I was a laugh. He and Peter Viertel both said: "Pedro Romero? You? No way, not in my story you're not." No one wanted me in the picture, and yet I got all the reviews. (*Takes down a framed* Time *review that says a "handsome" Evans displayed a "fierce intensity."*)

Did you get to meet Hemingway?
I saw him at the World Series after the picture opened. I walked over to him, and he said, "Good work, kid," and turned his head.

Was Hemingway an imposing figure?
Very.

Why did Darryl Zanuck come to your defense?
It's called sense of discovery. There's an ego involved with it. Not that I was the best person for it, but he found me. I was *his.*

When I was on *The Sun Also Rises,* a telegram went out to Darryl Zanuck, who was in London; we were in Mexico. The telegram read: IF ROBERT EVANS PLAYS PEDRO ROMERO THE SUN ALSO RISES WILL BE A DISASTER. SIGNED: ERNEST HEMINGWAY, HENRY KING, AVA GARDNER, TYRONE POWER, MEL FERRER, EDDIE ALBERT, PETER VIERTEL. Errol Flynn refused to sign it. Word comes back that Darryl Zanuck is flying in, and I'm told to report to the *corrida* to do my *quitas* and *veronicas.* I'm sure I'm going to get fired. So I walk into the arena, there's Zanuck on one side, on the other side is Ava Gardner, Tyrone Power, and everyone else, and Zanuck is a little guy with a cigar sticking out of his mouth—he had only met me once, when I was dancing at the El Morocco. I go through my motions with a fake bull, bow to him, and Zanuck takes a megaphone and says: "The kid stays in the picture. And anybody who doesn't like it can quit." Puts the megaphone down and walks out. And that's what a producer is: a boss.

And my whole life has been fighting to stay in the picture, one way or another.

Was that an epiphany for you? You saw all the actors, and you saw the power of the producer . . .

Exactly! I wanted to be him and not me. That's when I made my mind up. My life goes back to the old studio days as an actor. I was under contract for Universal for a while, for Paramount, for Fox. I've been a radio actor, a stage actor, a film actor. I've done everything in this industry. And I love to work with actors. They're very bright. I learn from actors. They're contributors. I'm the only actor who has ever run a studio. And I lasted longer than anyone else in that job, and I had total control.

Before we get back into that, did you date and fuck both Ava Gardner and Lana Turner?
I don't want to talk about that. But I was with both of them, yes. I can show it to you right here. (*Takes another framed set of clippings down from the wall, this one from a 1957* Journal-American, *written by Dorothy Kilgallen, with a headline: "Bob Says Yes to Lana," and from another publication showing him with Ava Gardner sharing a table at a nightclub.*)

Was this when *Photoplay* voted you New Star of 1957?
Yes. Next to Elvis Presley, I was getting more fan mail than anyone at 20th Century Fox. For about five minutes I was very hot.

Did you know Elvis?

Oh sure. We went to a Halloween party together, we played softball together. We were both under contract to Fox. He was a very sweet guy. We didn't hang out a lot, but we knew each other. I liked him a lot.

Were women falling all over him?
He was very modest about it. He wasn't aggressive in any way. A country sort of kid.

You appeared in only two other films: *The Best of Everything* and *The Fiend That Walked the West*. Anything memorable about either of them?
Very memorable. The best thing I ever did was a remake of *The Kiss of Death*, which made Richard Widmark a star. It was called *The Hell-Bent Kid*, which they changed to *The Fiend That Walked the West* three weeks before the picture opened. I was going to be the new big star at Fox as the hell-bent kid. Edward R. Murrow interviewed me on his show because of it, and he only interviewed the biggest stars. They changed the title because they felt that westerns and horror pictures were big. I said, "You can't do this to me." I went to see Charlie Einfeld, the second-highest-paid guy at Fox, head of advertising and PR and distribution. I said, you can't change the title, I wouldn't have

made the film. He said, "You act in them, kid, let me sell 'em." I said, "But you're ruining my career." He said, "Two nights before the picture opens I want you to walk into El Morocco and smack a broad across the face. And I'll say, "The fiend that walked the West is in New York." I said, "Are you crazy? I'm not going to smack a girl." He said, "Bogie used to do it for me in the forties." I said, "Fuck Bogie! I ain't doing nothing." He said, "You're going to have to make a trailer for it." I said, "Put someone else in the trailer, I'm not going to make it." And I walked out of his office. When the picture opened I got terrific reviews, but who looks at reviews of a picture called *The Fiend That Walked the West*? When it's on TV now, Warren Beatty always calls me and imitates me.

Why, after only four films, did you decide to quit acting?
Because I had to make a choice. Our business, Evan Picone, had grown very big. It was over a five-year period, and I was spending nine months of the year in California. I was signed to do two pictures, *The Chapman Report* and *The Longest Day*. I turned down *Murder Incorporated*, the third lead, because I wanted the lead, which was given to Stewart Whitman. Actor's ego. I said, why should he have the lead? I'm a bigger actor than he is. The guy they hired to take my part was later nominated for an Academy Award for it: Peter Falk. It was his first movie. I also turned down *Legs Diamond, The George Raft Story*, a lot of pictures. The parts I wanted I didn't get, the parts I was offered I didn't want. And my brother and his partner, Joe Picone, came to me and said, "Look, you're spending nine months of the year in California, and you're not in the business at all, it's not fair to us. Either sell out your interest in the business or come back and work for the company." They were right. I looked at myself in the mirror—and this was as tough a decision as I've ever had to make, and sometimes it's really tough to look at yourself and call a spade a spade—I said to myself, "You ain't good enough to make it all the way. You ain't gonna be Paul Newman. You're not that good an actor." So I gave up my contract, turned down the two pictures I was supposed to do, and moved back to New York selling ladies' pants. It was the single best decision I ever made in my life.

Even though you were getting so much fan mail?
I was much hotter with fan clubs than I was with producers and directors. One of the reasons was, I was a known commodity before I came to California. If I would have come as a garage man or a plumber or a carpenter . . . but when you're successful in another field and you become an actor, they hold it against you. You're really a hybrid. But I would be working as a waiter at Hamburger Hamlet now if I stayed as an actor.

You mean you have a better shot at becoming a legend as a producer than you would have as an actor?

A legend is someone who dies before his time. Why is it that Irving Thalberg is remembered and Louis B. Mayer isn't? Why is it that Marilyn Monroe is remembered where other actresses with a lot more talent aren't? Why is it that James Dean, who made only three pictures, is the largest-selling poster in the world? Because he died before his time. You outlive your legend many times and fade into either wealth or obscurity. But there's a certain time when you hit heights, and if you disappear at that time, you're remembered.

Why is an actress more than a woman and an actor less than a man?

The man who told me that was Henry Kissinger. The easiest girl to get to, to fuck, is the wife or girlfriend of a movie star or an actor, whether he's the biggest movie star in the world or an extra. Because invariably the woman he's with becomes his mother, he's that involved with himself, and he can't help it. It's no one's fault. But as an actor you need protection, and the woman you're with becomes your old lady. And after a while, when she's depended upon to do everything, including tying his own shoelaces, the woman gets bored with it.

Conversely, a woman needs that same protection as an actress. Really, they're both the same. But in a woman it's attractive, it gives a man a macho feeling to give her that umbrella of protection. Actresses are so unsure of themselves, so insecure, that they come to the man for protection, and it makes him feel good. So on a man, as an actor, it's unattractive, but on a woman it makes her man feel good. Acting is basically a female trait, from makeup to fantasizing, it's not a male trait. That doesn't mean that actors aren't masculine, they are, but it's still narcissism and self-aggrandizement. Very few actors use dope because they're too concerned with their bodies. A lot of actors are alcoholics, though. That's the main thing with actors: they're afraid to face the world, so they become alcoholics.

Why do actors need more protection than people in other professions?

An actor feels, when he finishes a project, it's always his last job. I don't care who it is, unless you're a huge star. Feels like he'll never work again. And it eats him up inside. Invariably they're only happy when they're working. Where you don't have to face the world. It's like going on location is summer camp. It's a different world. And you get more and more into that until you can't face the world.

In the old days actors were under contract to studios who dressed them, made them up, had cars to take them around. Once they were dropped, they didn't know how to face the world, they either committed suicide or became alcoholics. Stars like Robert Taylor: when he was dropped by MGM, he couldn't face the world, as big a star as he was. They didn't know how to function outside the studio system.

Conversely, today there's no such thing as a studio system. But as an actor, the more you become addicted to it, the more you live your own life, and you're always fearing you're never going to work.

As Zanuck had with you, have you also had that sense of discovery with others?
Oh sure I have. It's a big ego trip. I've had it many times. I go to bat for people all the time. And I stick by my convictions. Sometimes I'm right, sometimes I'm wrong. But you have to be wrong in order to be right. You can't bat a thousand. If you do, you're doing something wrong. You've got to take chances.

You took a chance with *Popeye*, which didn't meet the expectations many had for it. Didn't you want Dustin Hoffman, with Hal Ashby directing, until you and Hoffman had a falling out?
I had Dustin, and we had a big falling out because he wanted to fire Jules Feiffer as the writer and I refused. He said, "You're going with Jules Feiffer over me?" And I said, "That's right, because you're not giving him a fair shot." He had an epileptic fit with me, he was furious. Hal was willing to let Feiffer go, I was not. I believe in the writer. The man devoted nine months of his time, and Dustin did not give him enough time, kept him waiting for two and a half days. I lost the picture with Dustin.

You and Dustin didn't speak for six months?
Longer. And our friendship has never been the same. I feel badly about it because he's a very interesting character. We used to play tennis together. He gave me my tennis chair, because of all the bad calls. He still never won after the chair was there. He's a good player too, but he's not a winner. Jack, Dustin, and I have approximately the same game. Jack and I are gutter players. I beat Dustin forty-eight out of fifty times, and Jack beats me forty-eight out of fifty times, and Dustin looks like he could beat us both forty-eight out of fifty times.

Do you think *Popeye* would have made any difference had Hoffman and Ashby done it instead of Robin Williams and Robert Altman?
The real problem was, it shouldn't have been a musical. The reason it was a musical was because I had tried to buy *Annie*. They paid $10 million for *Annie*. *Popeye* was the third most recognizable face in the world. I loved the idea

because it said something very strongly: I am what I am. The celebration of the individual. Robin was wonderful in it. It was his first movie. It's a much better picture than people give it credit for. People watch it and tell us they love it now. Shelly Duvall was great in it.

Was the problem also a lack of special effects? Did the money run out?
That was nothing. By the way, it wasn't a failure, it was a successful film. But not a *big* success. If it were made not as a musical, it could have been very successful. But because of *Annie* . . .

During our talks Evans received calls from Colleen Camp, who is married to John Goldwyn, from Stanley Jaffee, and from his brother Charles. Apparently Goldwyn was blaming Charles for holding up a deal because Goldwyn believed that Evans couldn't make a deal without his brother's permission. Evans admitted that he had had to borrow money from his brother—"so he has a security interest in what I have, nothing wrong with that. I don't want anything for nothing. But it gets back to Paramount that I can't make a deal without his permission. That's how the politics are at the studios. You heard me talk to Stanley Jaffee, the chairman of the board. I just won't take any shit from any-one. Because I have nothing to hide. I learned early in life, when you lead as complicated a life as I do, nothing to do with morality, the easiest thing is to tell the truth. Then you never have to remember what you said. I can walk into any room, whether there's ten people or three hundred, and I don't have to remember what I said to any one of them. I say it as it is. People may like it or not like it, but they can't say I'm a liar. It just makes life easier."

How dark a business is the movie business? Outsiders see the glamour. You're on the inside. What do you see?
There's no glamour in this business. There's accountants, lawyers, agents. For every bit of magic you spend a month of misery in negotiations. It's not glamorous. By the time you start a film, you're tired out. And things get made for the wrong reasons. And you fight on everything. There's more money taken out of the pie for legal in this industry than there is in any other industry. It's not the agents who hurt the business, it's the lawyers. The agents want to close deals, they pay their light bills that way. The lawyers find reasons to build up bills, so they always find things that are wrong. At my table at home Bob Towne, Jack Nicholson, and I put out our hands, we were going to make *The Two Jakes* for nothing. I was going to costar and produce with Jack, and Bob was going to direct and write it. And

no agents and no lawyers were going to fuck it up. We put blood to it. And it got fucked up over lawyers and agents. Even working for nothing. We were all going to take no money up front.

If that would have happened, we would have started a new trend in films, where the above-the-line people would take no money. That's the way films should be made, because then you could make double the amount of films. Because when your above-the-line is so heavy, all the rest goes up too. We were going to make *The Two Jakes* for $11 million, with Jack, myself, Bob Towne, Harvey Keitel, Kelly McGillis, and Cathy Moriarty.

Why should somebody get paid $15 million for a film and the picture dies? That's why, on the other side, the studios cheat you. They have to. You can't give away 50 percent of the profits and incur 100 percent of the losses. That's why you have fancy bookkeeping. When you're overly paid, as we all are, you can't have it both ways. You can't be independent and be overly paid.

When it appeared you weren't going to be acting in it, was Dustin Hoffman ever considered to take your role opposite Nicholson?
No. We couldn't accommodate both of them. The other part wasn't that big, it was like eight scenes. I didn't want to do it. Bob Towne insisted. It was his father, it's a true story. It was boomtown right after World War II, where all the Jewish entrepreneur real-estate guys, the Mark Tapers, came in to build, like his father did. Where the Gentiles had all the oil, the Jews were doing business in real estate. And Jack said in front of Bob Towne, Burt Fields, Ned Tanen, Frank Mancuso: "Listen clearly, gentlemen. I will make *The Two Jakes* for nothing, with Evans. Otherwise, I want $6 million without him. And Towne, I'll buy your screenplay for $2 million and you get out. Because you know what's going to make this picture? The Irishman isn't dumb. Our noses [Evans's and Nicholson's] next to each other, that's what's going to make this picture." That's loyalty. Let me show you the pictures we took. (*Shows me large photos taken by Helmut Newton of Nicholson and himself in profile, their noses close to touching.*)

What did you think of the end result of *The Two Jakes*?
Sad. Bob Towne never turned in a screenplay. He terribly resented Jack directing it. But it was the only way we could do it. He didn't want to direct it. We had a $4 million encumbrance against us because we had our own money up for it. There were lawsuits and everything, and he wanted to clean the slate. He worked his ass off on it, and I was of no help to him, I was a vegetable at the time. He was so kind. I didn't show up on the set because I was embarrassed and ashamed because of the stuff going on in the papers.

To keep me involved in the picture he would bring the cinematographer and other crew members to come up here and watch dailies rather than see them at the studio. He did that throughout the entire picture.

Would Nicholson ever want to direct again?
I don't know. He's such a big movie star. He said to me he so much wanted me in the part. Mike Nichols, who was going to direct it, wanted me. It was such a bad time for me because this was right after *Cotton Club*. The drug thing happened in 1980. *The Cotton Club* was '80 to '84, then *The Two Jakes*, then this Roy Radin case blew up in my face, which had absolutely nothing to do with me. But it did, I made publicity, I made it a celebrated thing, without me it was nothing. I had ten years of Kafka.

Let's talk about those years. Your brother and a friend were caught in New York buying cocaine from an undercover cop. You were in California at the time, yet you admitted to buying into that score. Were you guilty?
I was totally innocent of the charge. I took a dive. But I don't want to get into it. I was guilty of usage, but innocent of the charge. It was the most costly non-blow in the history of the world. If I had to do it again, I wouldn't do it. I never realized the consequences. Robert Redford, Warren Beatty, or Tom Cruise wouldn't have gotten bigger headlines. And the headlines I got around the world, it was above the name of the paper. And I had nothing to do with it! (*Shows me a scrapbook devoted to articles on his drug bust.*) Aljean Harmentz in the *New York Times* wrote what happened, and said that I wasn't there. This made me the Cocaine Kid when I wasn't involved.

Did you save your brother and his friend?
Oh yes, I did. But I never thought it would have the devastating effect it did. To this day, let's say I'm at the Palm restaurant and I have to take a piss. I'll piss in my pants before I'll go to the john. Because if I go people will think I'm taking a snort. And I *have* pissed in my pants rather than go to the john. That will stay with me for the rest of my life. However, during it, I did something which shows that sometimes good comes from bad. I did a show for NBC that turned NBC all around. It was *Get High on Yourself*. It started as a thirty-second commercial, which is what the judge asked me to do. And it became the biggest anti-drug campaign in the history of America. I had every big star in the world go on it.

But how does one stop the drug problem today?

The only way you can stop it is what we did. We did more in six months . . .
let me get the tape and show it to you. Three weeks before it was going to go
on the air I never thought people would show up for it, and everybody
showed up: Paul Newman, Dr. J, Magic Johnson, Henry Winkler, even Bob
Hope, who showed up for a guy who was copping a plea. From a thirty-second commercial it became a year and a half of my life. But it changed programming in television.

The drug agencies tried to disavow what we were doing because we did
more in six months than they did in twenty-five years. They couldn't do anything to me, so they went after Kathy Lee Crosby, who worked on it with me.
They brought out she was a Scientologist and ruined her name, because they
didn't want us to succeed in what we were going to accomplish. And I wasn't
doing this for charity but to pay penance.

Now, I didn't intend to do what I did. All I had to do was have Henry
Winkler go on and say, "Don't take drugs." That's all I had to do. But I don't
do things that way, like an idiot. If the proudest thing I've done is about the
Pope, this is the second thing.

Still, the question remains, how do you keep kids off drugs?
I'll tell you how. My son has never smoked a joint, never used drugs, doesn't
drink. For one reason: he's goal-oriented. Kids have to have a goal. You can
never stop drugs from coming in, it's greed, up to the highest levels of government. But you've got to give the kids alternatives.

Ten years ago it was very fashionable for the kids of the wealthy to take
drugs. It's not that way anymore. Now it's in the poorer neighborhoods,
where they're needing it for survival, where big business is involved pushing
it on kids to sell. Usage has gone down a lot in areas. Cocaine is not the fashionable drug to use anymore, which it was then. Now it's crack, and it's being sold by people right out of Washington, on the highest levels. That's why
they don't stop it. It's called greed.

**How high a level do you suspect it went? All the way to the top, to
Reagan?**
No, under that. Nancy Reagan picked up on our campaign and did her
thing. But it was on high levels and various subcommittees and big lobby-
ists. Too much money is made from the importing of drugs into this country not to involve very important people who don't want to change. And it
will never change by trying to stop it from coming in. They'll always figure
out a way of getting it in.

What was your opinion of Reagan as president?

He was a brilliant communicator and a dreamer. He did through strength bring a cessation to the cold war. I think he's very underestimated.

After that anti-drug campaign you wound up in the headlines again when Roy Radin was killed. It was a sensational case that became known as "The Cotton Club Murder" because Radin was involved with you trying to raise money for your movie. And you were supposedly involved with the woman, Lanie Jacobs Greenberger, a drug dealer who is in prison today for her involvement in his death. Why did you refuse to testify at a preliminary hearing?
No one thought I was guilty of it. The police knew I wasn't guilty. They were pressing me to talk, and I had nothing to say. I would be in court, and there would be 150 photographers there. When I wasn't there, there weren't two photographers. I made careers for people when they had nothing on me. And I would not be intimidated.

Who was guilty in Radin's murder?
I don't know. I knew the person [Lanie Jacobs Greenberger], but I don't know if she's guilty or not. But as horrible a person as she's supposed to be, she could have said something about me to cop a plea and she never did. She had nothing to say, but people can lie. And I had nothing to do with it, and thank God someone was honest about it. When you're a public figure, you're guilty until proven innocent, and I lived with that for eight years. I never opened my mouth, under advice of counsel, and that was the right thing.

Greenberger said she told you that Radin had been killed a week after it happened. Did she tell you?
I found out he was killed. To the best of my memory, I don't remember her telling me, but I don't want to be quoted in this because I want nothing to say about it. A murder case—she's in incarceration now. I don't wish to open up anything. I'm out of it. I've never spoken, I don't wish to speak about it.

What it did seem to show was how one might go to extremes to raise money to make a film.
I didn't need the money, I already had the money. It was all financed. We were in pre-production.

Wasn't Radin involved in helping you finance it?
No, no, not at all. He was trying to form a company of some kind. You know what it was, a media title: "The Cotton Club Murder." It had zero to do with

The Cotton Club. None of them put up any money, and the movie got made, didn't it? It goes to prove it had nothing to do with *The Cotton Club*. But it *sounded* good. It was sexy.

Did you ever live in fear?

Never. I'm not fearful. I only lived in fear for my kid possibly. I didn't do anything. The police were terrible to me, they tried to frighten me, but I had nothing to be frightened about. I was a sexy guy for them to have. I was meat for them. My attorney protected me properly. I refuse to be harassed.

How did all of this affect your life?

I walked into the Palm restaurant with my son, and Michael Eisner was sitting there, and he shouted, "Bob, did you really murder him?" It was a joke to him, but to me it went through me like cobalt. The whole restaurant heard. I walked over to him and said, "No, I didn't. But watch out, Michael, if you don't take my next picture." I made a joke of it, but my son was with me, you understand?

In spite of these troubles, you went on to make *The Cotton Club*. What so excited you about it?

It was the most exciting period in America, the twenties into the thirties. The Jews, the Irish, the Germans, the blacks, the Italians. . . . It was the starting of the Mafia. And Harlem was open territory. The Bronx was controlled by Dutch Schultz, and Luciano controlled Manhattan. Harlem was in between. And the numbers racket was the most lucrative business of them all. For a penny you could fill a dream. But my dream turned into a nightmare. I wanted to do it for my father, who was a dentist in Harlem. And I wanted to dedicate it to him. Instead, I didn't even go to the opening.

Before Richard Gere, wasn't Sylvester Stallone interested in doing it?

Stallone wanted desperately to do the film. During that period he was making *Rocky III*. And I helped him like a brother. The first time *Rocky III* was ever seen was in my projection room—Stallone and his family, my son and myself and my ex-wife. He loved it and thanked me. He used to come over here every day trying on hats, seeing how he'd look in the picture. And I helped him in his life. *Rocky III* opened to a smash, huge. I'm over at the Hotel Ducap in Cannes to meet with three hundred key exhibitors around the world to sell *The Cotton Club*. At 2:00 A.M. I get a call from Sly in Philadelphia. "Bob, they're unveiling a statue of me in Philadelphia. Listen, I didn't like the new script." I said, "What are you talking about? You wrote it." "I don't think I want to be in the picture." "Sly, wait a minute, in seven hours I'm going downstairs to announce you starring in *The Cotton Club,* and you're telling me you don't want to do it? We have a contract. What is it, Sly?" "Well, I got a lousy deal, you know." "You motherfucker," I said, "you no-good guinea cocksucker! Fuck you!" And I hung the phone up.

I went downstairs, and Mario Puzo happened to be over there, and I asked him to join me at the meeting. I had a huge poster that emphasized the action and the music that startled the world. In front of these three hundred men I took up the poster and said, "This is the movie. It's not going to be any better than this poster. If anybody doesn't like the poster, don't buy the movie." There's a guy sitting in the back from Switzerland. He raises his hand and asks who is going to be in the movie. I told him he couldn't have the movie if he paid double his competitor. "Do you know why?" I said. "The man sitting next to me, the writer Mario Puzo, has written five screenplays: *Godfather I, Godfather II, Superman I, Superman II,* and *Earthquake.* They've done over $2 billion. And you're asking me who's in the movie? This is the story of an era. In *Godfather* the highest-paid actor was $35,000, and I worked too hard on this picture to worry about who's in the movie. You can't have the picture. Any other questions?"

I raised $8 million in forty-five minutes, more than has ever been raised in the history of Cannes, with no actor and no script. With a poster.

I came back to the U.S., and I'm thinking about that cocksucker Stallone. I wrote him a letter, which I sent to him, his manager Jerry Weintraub, the *L.A. Times, Variety,* the *Hollywood Reporter,* and *Entertainment Tonight.* They thought he was going to kill me when he got this letter. (*Shows me the letter, which says in part: "Your deportment in our relationship both personally and professionally I find repugnant, cowardly, and ill-mannered and, concerning you, most self-destructive. I hope Mr. Weintraub will find for you the magic property that will elevate you to be a bonafide star without having to wear boxing gloves. . . . I think your wisest move would be to prepare* Rocky IV. *This letter is not written in any way to entice you to come home. At this point in my career I have the luxury of not having to heed to the slippery innuendoes of carpetbag managers who are looking to prove their worth. . . . I do have deep respect for your many talents. Personally, however, you are someone who totally lacks moral, ethical, and professional substance. Evans is wrong again. I should have paid heed to all the doubters. You didn't earn your reputation by mistake."*)

It appears in the papers. Saturday night I'm home alone in bed when the phone rings. "Evans, it's Sly. Hey, what the fuck, are you crazy with this fucking letter? It's appearing in the papers." As we're talking, *Entertainment Tonight* is on, and they start reading the letter. "You must be fucking crazy," Stallone starts shouting. I said, "You deserve worse, you motherfucker. You don't leave someone waiting at the alter when they've been there for you to stop a bullet. You don't do it, you cocksucker!"

"I want to do the picture," he said.

"I wouldn't use you," I said.

"I want to do it."

"You want to do it, then come over on your knees tomorrow morning and apologize."

He came over the next morning and apologized. We sat outside, and I said, "Listen, Sly, no more brother shit anymore. I'm the director and producer, and you're the fucking actor. If you don't like it, don't do it, I really don't care, I've lost all eyes for you. If you're going to ask for one dollar more, then get the fuck out of here now. But if you meet my terms, you're on, because I think you're right for the part, and that's the only reason."

"I'm sorry, I didn't know."

"Hey, Sly, don't give me this humble bullshit." So we shake hands, and then he calls me three days later.

"You gotta come up to my place now," he says. He was living in Pacific Palisades at the time. He had a boxer there training to be a heavyweight fighter. We took a walk down the street, and he said, "Bob, I don't think I can do the picture. But you gotta know why. My cunt wife thinks that if I go to New York with you for a year, we'll be through more broads than there are in all of Manhattan. She told me she'd divorce me. I don't give a fuck if she divorces me or not, but since *Rocky III* came out it's going to cost me fifteen million bucks for the divorce, and I'm only getting paid two million from you, so it's going to cost me thirteen million to make your fucking movie."

He didn't do it because of that reason. Two years later they get divorced and she got thirty million instead of fifteen. True story (*laughs*).

Do you think any actor could have saved that movie?
No, it wasn't the actor, it was Francis Coppola. Richard Gere could have been terrific in it. Film is made in the editing room. In *The Cotton Club* I had *The Godfather* with music, but it was on the cutting room floor. It ended up a slick flick. Francis shot it, it was there. There were seventeen musical numbers taken out. He spent $1.2 million shooting "Stormy Weather," the most important number in the piece, and he didn't put it in the film! I wanted to tell the story of an era, not a slice of life. It was the same thing that happened with *The Godfather.* That was two hours and six minutes and I added fifty minutes to it. We should have done the same with *Cotton Club.* But I didn't have control. He barred me.

We were in New York, and I had given him a birthday party at Elaine's. In front of all the department heads he stood there and said, "Evans, I'm ready to go back to San Francisco. This is not *The Godfather,* Evans, do you under-

stand that? You're not the boss here." He had hostility for ten years he was
waiting to vent, and I had no idea. He said, "You're not allowed on the set.
You can come out and look at the dailies, but I have final cut." I couldn't do
anything about it because we had private financing. If it was at Paramount, I
would have thrown him out the window. I would have said, "Get the fuck
out of here, you fat fuck!" But I couldn't, it wasn't my money, it was other
people's money, and we were too deep into it. It was the single biggest error
in my career, using Francis Coppola for that movie.

I did more research on this project than anything I've ever done. I spent
six years on it, from 1979 to 1985. Didn't make one dollar. Had to put up
my home, mortgage my house—they took away my house actually. Sidney
Pollack begged to direct it, and I said I wanted to direct it myself. Then I
called Francis to ask for help on the rewrite. It was the most expensive call I
ever made.

I said, "Francis, my kid [the script] needs an operation, and I need you to
recommend someone to help me give a rewrite to this screenplay. I want the
best doctor in the world." He said, "It's me. I'll do it for nothing." Ha ha ha.
Call it the beginning of the end. He oozed his way in, and it was brilliant
how he did it. I was like a kid from the Okies next to him. I fell for him like
a groupie. After he did the rewrite, I thought, Jesus, it's Mario Puzo, Francis,
and myself, fuck it, let Francis direct it. He said, "The only way I'll direct it is
if we're Siamese twins, we'll work together and never leave each other's side,
because this is your picture, Bob." He was as genuine in making that statement as Hitler was in saying he wanted the Jews to live. All the time he knew
he wanted to give me a second asshole. And he did.

Did Coppola walk off during the making of the picture?
He walked off in the middle of it because his contract wasn't signed, and he
went to Paris until the deal was signed. It was costing us $40,000 a day. And
I had rough guys putting up the money for me. What he did to us was un-
conscionable. I wrote him a letter that saved my life. It was after I saw the
preview. People named Doumani had put up the money for the film. It was
budgeted at $24 million, and they could have had a completion bond. I said,
please take it. And Francis talked them out of taking it. It cost $47 million,
and Francis put in half the film. After that preview I sat down and wrote him
a letter, and Edward Doumani drove the letter from San Jose to Napa Valley.
After Francis read the letter, he said, "This cocksucker is right, but I'd rather
see the picture do $300,000 than $300 million and see that prick get credit
for it."

What my letter said was exactly what Pauline Kael's review said three
months later. (*Shows me the fifteen-page letter he sent to Coppola, criticizing his cut*

of the film. "What you are about to read bears great[er] consequence to our lives and careers than any decisions we have ever fought over or agreed to in the past," he wrote. Concerned that the previews had all gone badly, Evans wanted to change the movie, putting back scenes Coppola had cut, including seventeen musical numbers. "It is your film, Francis," he wrote, "not mine. . . . [But] not having communication [with you] at this very pivotal moment is so very counterproductive. My God, Francis, if Gromyko and Reagan can meet and have an exchange of dialogue, why can't we? You owe it to yourself if no one else to put personal feelings aside. Use me. Use my objectivity. . . . " The suggestions are numerous and detailed.)

Did you dictate this letter?
I wrote it in a hotel room in San Jose with the Doumanis standing by reading it. It was a painful letter to write. They agreed with me totally.

And were any of your suggestions taken?
None.

Did you speak to Coppola about this as well?
I never spoke with him. The written word is a far more powerful expressor of your thoughts, you're never interrupted, it stays with you, you can review it. I insisted that in my book they had to print this entire letter. People ask what is a producer: this letter gives you an answer.

Why didn't he listen to any of your suggestions?
I think he wanted the Doumanis to go bankrupt, and he'd take over the picture himself. Because what he did to these people is almost legally criminal. These poor guys were putting up money every day. He has ass-kissers around him that if he barks they think it's part of his genius. But the structure, he didn't have people. It's the same thing with *The Godfather*. No different.

What about *Godfather III*? Which you had no hand in and it turned out to be a mess.
That's absolutely Francis, totally. End of story. That says it all. *Godfather III* was a tenth-generation Xerox copy of *The Godfather*.

Had he come to you for help on *Godfather III*, would you have worked with him?
Oh no, I would never talk to him again. Ever. Because he's an evil person. I think Al [Pacino] feels that way about him too. Francis is a direct descendent of Prince Machiavelli. That's the best way I can say it. He's royalty. He is so seductive, so brilliant in his web of bringing people in, he makes Elmer

Gantry look like Don Knotts. He fooled me. He's a brilliant director with actors, but he cannot structure a picture. Not just *The Cotton Club*. It took him three years to edit *Apocalypse Now*. It took him two years to edit *The Conversation*.

Did you ever have to write a letter like the one you wrote to Coppola to anyone else for any other film?
I had to go to this extent with *Sliver,* how about that? Even further. I will show you a letter that I wrote to Stanley Jaffee, chairman of the board at Paramount. He was so angry when he got this letter, the vein in his temple almost burst. Stanley was the one who gave me my break back. He opened the doors and embraced me. We're very close friends for twenty-five years. I'm the dishonorable godfather to his child. And I wouldn't meet with him until he read this letter, which I'll show you but you can't quote from it. Stanley faced me and he said, "Are you threatening me?" I said, "Yes, but I'm saving your ass too." I had to put my job on the line, I had to be willing to quit. He respected that without telling it to me. And whatever I wanted I got.

Can I mention that you wrote the letter?
You can say the passion I had brought me to write a letter on *Sliver*. That's okay. To the point of detriment I have a passion for what I do. I become possessed, more than obsessed. I strive to get something that can touch magic. And for the wrong reasons things happen: for distribution reasons, for lack of communication, for committees. I can't work that way. And unfortunately, I don't have enough money to put up my own money to make a picture and make it the way I want. As long as it's that way, I'm a dependent producer. But no one has the guts to do what I do. I'm not saying that's smart.

So the final cut of *Sliver* is your version, take it or leave it?
Seventy percent, not all. Enough. I went for the money shots. And Philip [Noyce] and I worked together as closely as two brothers.

How important is *Sliver* to you and your new career?
It's the most important picture of my career. Because I haven't really worked in ten years. I had very little to do with *The Two Jakes*. It was a gift to me. I wasn't in condition.

How do you compare it to Levin's other work, *Rosemary's Baby*?
Roman Polanski is the most brilliant director I've worked with in my career. The subject matter isn't nearly as exploitable or as interesting as *Sliver*. Rose-

mary's Baby's subject matter was a cult, which isn't as interesting as voyeurism. But as a film, *Rosemary's Baby* is brilliant because of Roman. On *Sliver* I didn't have that brilliance, but it wasn't Phil's fault, he didn't have time. This picture was rushed. It was like making a sausage. We started in October and had to deliver it in April. It was crazy. Roman could never have done that, he wouldn't have accepted it. An artist needs time on the canvas.

What kind of look did you want for this one?
I wanted it to be like a European film from a woman's point of view. Sharon's character is the one that grows throughout the piece, and it's told through her eyes. I tried to put myself in her body.

Is *Sliver* equally as important to Sharon Stone as it is to you?
It's just as important to her. In this picture it's not Sharon Stone and Michael Douglas, it's Sharon Stone and two young actors. She carries the picture. If it does what I think it's going to do, she'll be on a level all her own. She'll deserve as much as Tom Cruise. She'll raise the price of women in film. She'll get $10 million after this picture, and she deserves it. Thank God there are women who are getting parts now. It's much more difficult writing a woman's part than a man's part. A guy has props: guns, fights, planes, chases. A woman doesn't have that. She has mystery, and that's much more difficult to write than it is to write action. So a writer doesn't spend the time on women's roles. Faye Dunaway in *Chinatown* only has seven scenes, but you never forget them because they're so well written.

You once expressed a desire to go away with Robert Towne for a year and write the definitive erotic film. What would that be?
I think I've done an erotic film now: *Sliver*. And it's not a pornographic film.

Along the lines of *Body Heat*?
More. I'm not saying it's better, I love *Body Heat*. That was an erotic film.

How much do you stand to earn if *Sliver* does well?
I have a good piece of it. I don't have enough money to pay my state taxes now. How about that? I'm in debt. But I have a movie star deal. I deserve it. Of course, because you deserve it doesn't mean you get it (*laughs*).

With all your troubles the last ten years, how have you managed to survive?
I went broke. In 1979 I was a very wealthy man. The only money I earned during the entire decade of the eighties was as a male model for a cosmetic

company from a picture that Scavullo took. I was paid several thousand dollars a month for that picture, selling women's cosmetics. I had to use the money that I saved. I sold my Gulf & Western stock. I made terrible financial decisions. But I didn't change my way of life.

Did you sell the rights to the films you had?
No, I get money from that, but it's nothing compared to my upkeep.

Did anyone offer to help you out?
Jack helped me out. Not monetarily, I'm too proud. My brother helped me, and I paid him back.

By 1989 you were contemplating suicide, and you put yourself into an insane asylum. Why?
I didn't think of committing suicide. I was afraid to. My son could not get a date to his graduation because I was his father. That's how low I got. After this murder stuff came up, I became a media event, just like Roman did. I sold my home, and I was so depressed over it that I was just in a fetal position for months. I had a hundred Nembutal by my bed. If it wasn't for my son, I would have taken them. But rather than have that happen, I checked myself into the looney bin. But I escaped within twenty-four hours, I couldn't believe what I did. I'm not embarrassed to admit it, because if I can come back at my age, anybody can.

On my sixty-second birthday, I was so depressed. Because that day, for some strange reason, *Man of a Thousand Faces* was on television, and I was twenty-six when that was made. My numbers were reversed. And I'm still waiting for the phone to ring. I was all alone, and Jack came around, and the two of us got loaded, just the two of us together until two in the morning. Loyalty's a very important word, and there's a very great shortage of it. You can give it, but don't expect it back. If you get it back one out of three times, you're doing well.

How close is your image to your real life?
People have various images of me. So many people have said they wanted to be me. I'm so many young guys' fantasies: to be Robert Evans one day. Robert Evans has not lived a happy life. I don't believe in happiness and unhappiness, I believe in being turned on and not turned on. Being turned on and doing something with passion is what my happiness is. That's not a normal happiness. I'm not a good parent. I never took my kid to Disneyland, because I wanted him to learn who I was. I read that in Budd Schulberg's

book about his father. His father just let him hang around. If I took my son to Disneyland, to the park, to the ball field, he knew I wouldn't be enjoying it. I let him hang around me, watching me cut films, and he learned to love me that way. I wasn't a good father, but we've been totally open, and now we're best friends.

Do you consider your book, *The Kid Stays in the Picture,* a tell-all memoir?
Not tell-all at all. I don't get into kiss-and-tell. But as an example, at Lew Wasserman's fortieth anniversary there were only forty people invited to his home. I was one of the forty. At his fiftieth anniversary, there were fifteen hundred people invited, I wasn't one of them.

And your book covers the years in between?
Oh sure, before, during, and after. Why my book has the opportunity of being more than an industry book is because when I started it, it didn't have a third act. Now it does. There's no such word as "impossible." In other words, the impossible dream is possible, but life itself has to be respected and protected, and if it's not, then that dream can turn into a nightmare. And to turn the nightmare back into a dream is impossible . . . almost. My story is: if I can come back at my age, I don't want to hear any kid at twenty-five or thirty saying he can't do it.

How much of a struggle was it for you to do the book?
It was *painstaking.* It was heavy therapy. I cried. The book is totally candid, totally. To the point that it hurt a lot. But if you're gonna do it, you want to do it all. It opens with the opening night of *The Godfather* and then goes backward to my life as a kid, and then it goes forward. I spent a year and a half on it.

When you turned fifty, you said you didn't know who you were. You're in your sixties—do you know now?
When I turned fifty, I didn't know where I stood. I went down for ten years at that time. I lived through *Rashomon,* and I got out of it at my age. And I'm proud of myself for doing that, not only for myself, but I can be an example to others. I didn't just get off the floor: I got off the floor as a cripple. And I never gave up.

Where are you going to be ten years from now?
I hope alive. And healthy. And I want to be busy. I have too good a mind not to use it. And I love what I do. I feel I'm a very wealthy man because of that.

You know what I would really love, more than anything? The one thing that's evaded me, and I may never have it, but I sure would love it: peace of mind. I'd love to hear just crickets instead of phones. I'd love to have some silence in my life. I haven't had three weeks off in twenty years. And it's taken its toll.

THE WRITER/DIRECTOR

OLIVER STONE

LOVE HIM OR HATE HIM, OLIVER STONE cannot be ignored. He has become his generation's film historian, taking on huge, disturbing subjects as the focus of his films. The Kennedy assassination, the Vietnam War, the influx of cocaine through Miami, the life and death of a 1960s rock icon, the fall of a despised president, the greed of the 1980s. He won an Oscar for writing *Midnight Express* and two more for directing *Wall Street* and *Born on the Fourth of July*. Those who work for him tell tales that make him sound more like a manic general than a director, but whatever drives Oliver Stone certainly hasn't kept him from being prolific. As a screenwriter he has written or cowritten *Midnight Express, Conan the Barbarian, Scarface, Year of the Dragon, Eight Million Ways to Die,* and *Evita*. He has written and directed *The Hand, Salvador, Platoon, Wall Street, Talk Radio, Born on the Fourth of July, The Doors, JFK, Heaven and Earth, Natural Born Killers, U-Turn,* and *Any Given Sunday*.

Born into a privileged life to a French Catholic mother and an American Jewish father, Stone was put into boarding school in his teens, when his life came to a crashing halt because his parents divorced and left him on his own. His descent into drugs and a search for adventure led him to leave Yale after a brief stay and to head for Vietnam as a teacher. That lasted a year. He joined the Merchant Marine, got drafted, and returned to Vietnam as a soldier. His fifteen months of infantry life changed him forever. He was wounded twice, awarded medals for heroism, and landed in a San Diego prison upon his return for marijuana possession. His first two marriages failed, but his drive to become a filmmaker was so strong that he couldn't be denied.

The first time I met him, in the summer of 1997, the fifty-year-old writer-director was at Todd-A-O West in Santa Monica, where he was screening *U-Turn* for potential exhibitors. The next four times we met were at his offices near the Santa Monica Third Street Promenade. One time he brought in Hiep Thi Le, the young star of *Heaven and Earth,* to talk to me because he was running late. Another time I waited for him while he entertained Sally Kirkland's mentor, Sri Swami Satchidananda, whose white flowing beard and saffron garments made one appreciate that much of the world comes knocking at Stone's door.

As I waited my turn in a room overlooking the ocean, I looked into the glass shelves and read the inscriptions on some of the awards Stone has received. One was the Torch of Liberty Award presented to him in 1987 by the ACLU Foundation of Southern California: "For your outstanding efforts to broaden the public's understanding of civil liberties and human rights and for letting the light of freedom, justice and equality shine through your motion pictures." Another was the Director of the Decade Award from the Twenty-eighth Chicago International Film Festival in 1992: "To America's Greatest Contemporary Director, whose inspired filmwork has chronicled the times of a generation with unique vision and unparalleled artistry."

When Stone finished with the swami, he took me on a tour of his offices, introducing me to his editors and assistants and company executives. In the large conference room he looked at the long table where he holds readings of scripts with his actors and pointed to a chair at the head of the table. "Tony Hopkins was sitting there for *Nixon,* and I was rewriting every night. We had swamps of colored pages. He'd say, 'Oliver, I don't have time to even physically learn what you've given me, much less change anything.' He was so scared. We were starting Monday, and he wasn't ready."

He showed me the large posters on the wall, a red Nixon that looked like "something from the Ruhr Valley." Then the political cartoons: in one he's being shot like Oswald in that Dallas basement, but the shooter is "media critics," not Jack Ruby. "There were dozens of these cartoons. I'm glad I framed a few of them," he said. "Trudeau and *Doonesbury* did a great one, my trail over the years making *JFK* and then getting to the bank at the end—I made it through all the obstacles." He laughed. Showed me the rows of black file cabinets that were filled with paperwork from all his projects. "I've kept everything," he said. "I'm very paper-conscious. Not that I want to one day give it away or show it. I'd have to go through it and censor myself before I did that. There's some very naked stuff in there. The idea is, the older you get the less you have to hide. If you really think about it, at the end it simplifies down to all the basics. The categories get bigger, so that at the end of the day you're shameless. Maybe that's a good thing, because you're ready to move on to another transition or another life. It makes it easy then to keep calm."

He took me to a narrow hallway where framed posters of all his work hung on both walls. "All in order," he pointed out, beginning with *Seizure, Midnight Express, The Hand*. He looked at *Born on the Fourth of July* and said, "That was my first attempt at an epic. The budget turned into $18 million cash. Neither Cruise nor I took anything, we participated. But that was a lot for Universal, and they gave me a hard time. *The Doors* was the same thing. I did that and *JFK*—and this was amazing physically to me—back to back, and they came out the same year in March and December of '91. That was a good year. And they were both reviled. I got nailed, not by everybody, but nothing was uniform about their acceptance at all. It was busy, it was hard. It was all the acceptance and trying to deal with the arguments, and then there was an argument about Ron Kovik's veracities—Pat Buchanan, Bob Dornan were threatened by Kovik because Ron feinted to run for the House and they freaked out, so they started this smear campaign against him, that he'd never been shot like that, that he never killed his own man—it was a really ugly thing. And *The Doors,* the problem there was the picture got maimed. The hardest thing to do was overcoming the history, the curse of this project, the alienations that had already occurred; a lot of obstacles from one of the Doors, Ray Manzarek, for example. He was just unhelpful the whole way."

He walked over to the poster of *Heaven and Earth*. "This disappeared. People who've seen it tell me they like it. A woman who saw it the other day told me she didn't even know it existed. It's the best role that Tommy Lee Jones ever played. He was his most tender, his most mixed. *The Fugitive* was a supporting role, but here he was a full-bodied man."

At *Nixon* he said, "This one was ignored, almost too much so. Because it was dark. I think the music, everything. Nixon was not an attractive man physically, and that doesn't attract people. To go see a film like this is like going to see an Eastern European film, like seeing *Mephisto*.

"It's hard to make that stuff watchable. It's a great challenge. It was three hours and fifteen minutes, mostly interior walls, older white guys talking in those deadly suits, how do you make that work? Very little sexuality in that movie. That was a real challenge. I'm particularly proud because I thought it worked as a movie movie. You could sit there and never get bored. Every scene mattered, every moment was thought about, nurtured, it wasn't sloppy as a movie."

With some sense of satisfaction he glanced at his gallery of posters and said, "I'm different from most filmmakers. Most filmmakers you can say: Marty: *Raging Bull, Taxi Driver;* Steven: *ET, Raiders, Schindler's List.* You *know* who they are. With me, people always disagree. You don't know how many people have told me that *Wall Street* is their favorite movie. *Salvador* is for the buffs, because nobody else has seen it (*laughs*). It's always about knowing more. And *JFK, The Doors, Nixon,* they're all different. *The Doors* I'm proud of because it was wild and it allowed excess to live on the screen. Most of the younger kids, models and chicks, liked it and *Natural Born*—so I have different crowds. Older people who are mature like *Nixon;* older people who are a little wild, *JFK.* Unfortunately, it's not good for your PR, because you don't have a profile. They don't know who I am. John Ford was westerns; Spielberg is entertainment; Marty is nitty-gritty Americana."

Then Oliver Stone looked at me as if I might have been the swami, as a light of realization came to him. "This is our interview right here," he said. "This is what it's all about. This is the ideal situation to talk."

Let's put this conversation in context. You're in between screenings of your latest film, *U-Turn.* **How intense is this time for you?**
I've been working around the clock for two weeks just trying to get it right. I've screened it for the executives, and I'm screening it again for the actors. Sean Penn is there, Billy Bob Thornton, Claire Danes. Plus some of the marketing people. I finished shooting the movie January 14, it's not been enough time to edit, and it's complicated to edit. But it's getting there. The editing process—you go over it on these smaller screens with your editors, and you're sure you've got it right, then you screen it for a room full of people, and you put yourself in the middle of the room, and it twitches your body and you know you fucked it up. The timing isn't right, the shot was in the wrong place, you can sense by osmosis when a scene is not working. I love editing, because not only is it a chance to really rewrite, if you're clever you move lines around, you take a scene and move it up to the beginning—it only shows your vulnerability as a screenwriter—but it's a great intellectual process. Unfortunately, we don't leave ourselves enough time to do it. Like David Lean was famous for taking eight months to a year in the editing room. But now the system is such that *boom,* you're out there. They market you like you'd better have it. I may have made a huge mistake by just having the marketing people from Columbia here today. They have to see it because of Cannes. The music's not done. It's hit and miss. But you hope they have generosity, they see it and understand where you're going.

What's it about?
John Ridley wrote a book called *Stray Dogs*. It's essentially his screenplay, but I would say that Richard Rutowski and myself did a lot of work on it, like maybe up to 40 percent. It's called *U-Turn* now because *Stray Dogs* is not available, it's a Kurosawa title. And U-Turn is what it's about (*laughs*). It's about the day in a life of a man where he reassesses his character. He's a gambler, and he finds himself a Dostoevski figure, but light Dostoevski, going up and down all through the day, his luck changing, and his reaction to that luck. It's a dark tale but with a lot of humor in it. I've never done a picture like it. It's a new genre for me—a sort of neo-noir. It's taking an old genre from the forties and twisting it into the nineties. It's been done before, but each twist takes its own way.

What forties movies might you compare it to?
Nothing. *Duel in the Sun* with Walter Huston, Jennifer Jones, and Gregory Peck is not a noir film, but the fellow from Cannes who saw it thought there was a touch of *Duel in the Sun* and a touch of *A Touch of Evil*. So there's a combination of that noir with the sun. *Film soleil* I call it. Because so much of it takes place in Arizona and it's outdoors.

What's been the most personal reaction you've gotten?
My twelve-year-old son Sean saw it. He gave me some shit. He said, "This is worse than *Natural Born Killers*, Pop."

More violent?
Not violent, sex. I thought this was a tamer film. He said, "No, this is worse." But he's twelve.

I've got a thirteen-year-old daughter. I'd never let her see *Natural Born Killers*. It would be too upsetting.
He sees everything. He saw *Natural Born Killers* in '93 and appreciated it. My ex-wife, his mother, hated it. Hated it. He got it, and he explained it to her.

Did she get angry with you for letting him see it?
No, he lives in Los Angeles, these kids are exposed to so much on television, there's no V-chip in our house that we know of. He's a smart kid. I talked to him before he saw *Natural Born Killers* and told him what it was about, that it was a send-up of what's around us, a mirror, don't view it as a condonation of killing.

Is it more difficult to let your son see something sexual or something violent?

I don't look at sex and violence as entities, which is how a lot of Puritans look at it. I look at it as a process. I'm much more interested that he understand the nature of the movie, the characters, what does that lead to? If it's realistic, it makes sense that he would understand the character and the violence and the sex that resulted. I don't like him to see the pictures that are shallow. The films where the violence is just easily taken for granted, where people knock each other off, kill three hundred Arabs. I pointed out to him, I said, "Look, Arnold is knocking off all these people. It's just fantasy. Think about it." We argued about *Star Wars*. He's a big fan of *Star Wars* too, and I was arguing with him about the nature of the movie.

It's cause and effect. My father took me to pictures, and we always had fun because after the picture he'd say, "Well, kiddo, we could have made it better." And I'd say, "What's wrong with the picture?" And he'd point out the holes in the film. That's the kind of discussions I enjoy having with Sean after he sees a movie. Because he's less demanding. So I'll say, "Well, Sean, did you ever think that if that character had done this instead of that, the picture wouldn't have worked the same way?" That makes him think.

If the sex and the violence grow out of the character in the story, it makes sense. As long as it's rooted.

By the way, Sean stays with me during weekends, and he brings over six kids from his class, and they check through the Internet, and they get into the *Playboy* website, Jenny McCarthy and all that soft-porn, and it's hard to keep an eye on that. But what do you do at that age? They have adolescent urges. You talk about it, you have to deal with it. You can't run away and say, "Put your penis away." There's no such thing as wrong, it's natural. I want to be a good, natural father and discuss things openly with him ahead of time, so then he understands what's happening to him, these feelings, these surges.

Would you show a daughter the same films you show your son?

Probably. I have a daughter, she's a year and a half.

When she's eight, would you let her see *Natural Born Killers*?

Yeah, I would. It depends on how her development comes along. In her mind and where she's understanding nature and society. If she's ready for it, I would show it to her. I'm not actively soliciting my children to like my movies.

Does Sean have a favorite movie of yours?

I think *JFK*. He's a very studious boy, very concentrated.

When you were a boy, were you more into comics?
I had a lifetime subscription to *Uncle Scrooge*. *Classics Illustrated* was my favorite. I had French drawing books. *The Three Musketeers* I read. Then there was a Random House collection—very much distorted my history early, but I loved that whole series. *Tecumseh, Custard, Lincoln*—all American history was written as drama. I subscribed to *Mad*. Unfortunately, I was poked fun at in *Mad* thirty years later. There was a horrendous caricature of me running around in this cartoon—I looked at it and thought, I made it, man. They'll make a movie about [*Mad* publisher William] Gaines. Make him the next pop hero for the next John Waters film!

As a kid, was there anybody you wanted to be like?
There was a lot of hero identification. First as a novelist: Norman Mailer was a hero, J. P. Donleavy, Joseph Conrad. See, I wrote novels when I was a kid. I read a lot of fiction when I was in Vietnam the first and second time, and when I was drifting around. I started to write my own novel, which was called *A Child's Night Dream*. It was based on the language of Joyce and Donleavy. I took that style. And Joyce Cary. The book had different styles to every chapter. It was like a prism, like *Natural Born Killers*. It's a very strange novel. Some people will hate it.

I read that you tossed it off a bridge after Simon & Schuster rejected it.
Half of it was lost. What was left was a bunch of pages all over the place. It was never finished. I threw away some of it. The rest was in a shoebox for most of the seventies. Then finally in the nineties I pulled it out because this editor from St. Martin's, Bob Wyle, saw I mentioned it in an interview, and he asked to read it. I gave it to him without sorting out the pages, he read it and found something there that he felt was special and wanted to preserve. There was a great use of poetic language, which was integral to the piece. I made a deal with them. Last year, after *Nixon* came out, I took six months and reedited and rewrote some sections and tried to put it into one chronological form.

How does it feel to finish a novel you started so long ago?
I'm a little nervous. I'm excited because it fulfills an old ambition of that boy—and I use the third person because I'm no longer him. He wrote and felt a certain way, and he was a very adolescent, strongly emotional boy, twenty years old, the world affected him deeply. And I think of it as giving him his due now. It took thirty years for it to get finished.

Will the critical reception of the novel be as important to you as it is for any of your films?

It's hard to say. I wouldn't judge the book on failure or success. I like it, it achieved what that boy set out to do. He'd be happy with it, that's enough. I don't care if it's ignored. I would be surprised if it was understood and accepted readily. I don't see that happening.

Will you read the reviews?

It all depends. If they're going to destroy me, no. But it's well written, there's some wonderful writing there. The problem is that it will perhaps only be paid attention to because of my film background.

And you'd prefer to be thrown in the ring against Conrad and Jack London?

I was affected the most by Conrad, in terms of moving myself physically to another area. *Lord Jim* put me into Asia for the first time. I joined the Merchant Marine in Asia. It's part of a sequence in my book. Some people will think my book's just about Vietnam. It isn't, it's about three continents: Europe, America, and Asia. I grew up split, my mom was French, I had a European identity. So it's about time and about adolescence, how do you burn off your old life? How do you come around to be an authentic human being? That's basically my quest through the movies too. But it's a very interesting book: part 1, is America; part 2 is the land across the sea in Asia; part 3 is trying to get back home. It moves by free association through time, Proustian really. The novel in its intensity is closest to Louis-Ferdinand Celine's *Journey to the End of Night,* which very much influenced me. The actual prose burns, there's a fire there. The whole concept of the book, as written by a twenty-year-old, is, who am I? What identity and form do I assume in life?

Is it also about the eighteen ways your character tries to kill himself?

There is a strong suicide theme. I don't think I'm so out of touch with what was going on with kids in general. We ignore it, but kids commit suicide a lot, especially now. Back then, same thing. Holden Caulfield comes from the same darkness: boarding school, I was very influenced by that, I left Hill School for two days as a result of *Catcher in the Rye.* Hid out in the Taft Hotel, awful experience.

You were an only child, correct?

I would have been a different person if I had a brother or sister. I was a loner. I didn't get much input.

**You speak of violence when you talk of your childhood. You've said
that there was in you a huge violence when you were born. You were
born in a way that was damaged. You've said, "My life as a kid was
marred by violence. Fights, being beaten up, chased."**
Oh really? That sounds pretty dramatic (*laughs*).

**Harrison Ford told a similar tale, of being chased by kids, beaten up,
thrown down a hill—but he never fought back.**
He's a natural-born Buddhist. I don't remember being beaten up as much as
chased. And definitely scared, because the gangs in New York at that time
were pretty tough. That whole Second and Third Avenue, York Avenue. I
lived on East End, but we couldn't go through the other side of town, you'd
go through that area. And in the parks I was chased. There were Irish gangs,
Puerto Rican kids who stole my bus passes and pushed me around. In
France too there were country gangs who chased me and my cousin in the
summer. We were two against twenty. We would run away on our bicycles.
We were richer, upper-middle-class as opposed to the local toughs. All of this
is revealed in my book, the damages. Among them would be: I was forceps
delivery, a lot of them were done in the forties like that, and that was a very
violent action. It compresses your head, and there's all this stuff in your
body that's the result of that: you get squeezed when you come out, you hit
the light, you're ripped from the light, you've got blood, the doctor spanks
the shit out of you—it's a tearing experience. Babies cry. So when I was defending *Natural Born Killers* I was saying, who are we kidding here? Violence
is a way of life. It's part of us. We've got to stop separating violence as if it's
some kind of thing you can control. Violence is in all of us. That's what
Mickey says in the picture. When we acknowledge the violence within us, we
can begin the journey of having to deal with it, because violence takes many
forms. A father can be very harsh with his child and be sublimating his violence on the child and not be aware of it. Buddhism is very aware of violence
and talks about it because it understands that it's a part of life.

How deeply are you into Buddhism?
Very much so. I practice, I do my meditation every day, I have a guru. It's an
evolution of a form for spiritual exercise. It was always part of my life. That's
what writing is about—writing is an act of devotion, it involves the anti-ma-
terialistic, it involves spiritual and philosophic concepts. I've been doing that
all my life, but I could not find a form in the Christian church that worked
for me. Buddhism was evident in Vietnam. Obviously we went to a lot of
temples, we saw it all over the place, I loved the East, it changed my life, it
was an orphan home for me. My parents had just divorced, and I was alone

in Asia. I was really alone. So Asia became like a mother. And Buddhism was in there. When I did *Heaven and Earth,* Le Ly Hayslip was a Buddhist, and she made me a member of the Vietnamese Buddhist church. The whole picture is based on the concept of not taking revenge, not fighting back. The movie is about accepting and forgiving your enemies. Then I was inducted by Richard Rutowski, who's been a Buddhist for twenty years, into the Tibetan side of it, which is much more accessible to me because of its wild nature and they speak more English. Tibet is a very strange place unto itself. Buddhism is how to deal with the violence. I'm not running away from my violence—it's there. I don't get into fights. I saw enough violence to last me the rest of my life in Vietnam, believe me.

Was going to teach in Vietnam in '65 similar to going into the Peace Corps—a sense of idealism?
Yeah, I think so, though it was based more on Conrad. On Conrad's concept of something being mysterious out there, something that I had to understand that I had never understood. That's what drove me. Maybe I'm flattering myself in hindsight, but it seems to me that I was more interested in knowing more about life, because I was puzzled about life. There were too many pat answers at Yale and in the East Coast of America—to this day (*laughs*).

How long were you at Yale?
I was there twice. A year the first time, half a year the second.

Ever regret leaving Yale?
At times I did. But again, it's part of what I don't know. It was very scary to leave, it was not easy. The second time it was over, I flunked. I didn't go to any of the classes, I got zeroes in everything, and the dean called me in. He warned me to go to work or else I wouldn't make it, because I was already a year behind my class. So I realized it was over, it was sort of an epiphany. And I was scared. I was throwing my fate unto the waters, I didn't know what was going to happen. My dad was really giving me a lot of shit because he paid a heavy tuition to send me there and the money had been forfeited (*laughs*), and also that I'd be a bum and wouldn't do anything with my life. Uncle Joe was always the dark villain in the closet in my family—each family has their Uncle Joe, and he was worried that would be me.

The months before I volunteered for the draft were some of the darkest months. It was winter in New York, and I had little light in my apartment, writing day and night, no social life, no sex, pure pure mind mind mind. It was like a monastery experience for me. Writing a book on which every word, every sentence hung my life.

Were you feeling like Joyce's Stephen Dedalus, that you were out to create the uncreated conscience of your race?
Yes. I was arrogant, I was proud. I didn't boast about myself, but I just felt in my heart that I was on to something big. You've got to laugh.

But have you felt that you've accomplished what was in your heart?
You accomplish the bigness in your own head, but ultimately there is no standard by which you can measure the exterior world.

How much did you heed your father's advice to do something you don't want to do every day?
My father also said, "Don't tell the truth. Because the persecutions are going to come again." That was Jewish persecution. He'd say, "Don't tell anybody you're Jewish." Which I wasn't, I was half-Jewish. He'd say, "They'll get you, they'll come back." And maybe he was right, we don't know the end of the century yet and what's going to happen. He did not want to be a Jew. He didn't practice it, he didn't believe in it, he thought it was a bunch of rabbis with beards and didn't like that ostentation. He was more a man of the fifties, when a man held it all in. You wear short hair, get a haircut every week. He didn't go to church either, but he felt communication with a God. He was very much in communication with *his* God.

Not a liberal God or a Russian God I take it.
No (*laughs*). Not a liberal God. My dad wrote plays, poems. He wanted to be a writer. Perhaps in some ways my own life is a working out of what some of his secret wishes were. As is my mother's life—she wanted to be a movie star. She was a diva. And a very important influence. She loved movies. *Duel in the Sun, Gone with the Wind.* She lived torridly through the Ingrid Bergman-Rossellini affair, she identified with movie stars—Jennifer Jones, Elizabeth Taylor, Carole Lombard, Vivien Leigh. So I picked up on all that as her son. The love of movies. You have to deeply love the illusion in order to put up with so much of the vomit and sickness that you get in this business. It's a hard business, it tires you out, wears you down, beats you up all the time. So in some ways in the movie business I've been able to bring together both parents and fulfill a subconscious desire.

But Dad would say essentially, stay out of trouble. Be anonymous. Do your work well. Put truth in your work. Don't expect reward in this life. None of us are getting out of here alive. A man does good work, and through time it will be its own reward. Unfortunately, he worked very hard at the stock market, he was one of the best, and he didn't make any money from it at the end of the day. He died fairly penurious. So when people say

I'm from a rich family, it's not quite true, because that implies that you're set for life. I was never set.

But during your influential years you came from wealth.
Privilege. Privilege. My life was rock-solid, like some Tolstoy or Nabokov end-of-the-century story. It seemed like it was set until I was fourteen, and it all fell apart. Very treacherous. It was quicksand. And that's an important thing to a fourteen-year-old. My father divorced my mother in a horrible 1960s New York adultery type suit, private detectives were necessary, you had to prove it. He locked her out of the house, then rented the house and moved to a hotel. My mother had no home and went back to France. I had a family one day and then no family, it was as if they'd been shot or taken to a detention unit. They were just not there. They didn't even come and see me at my boarding school. I had a phone call from my godmother telling me that they were getting a divorce. My mother claimed she called me, but I don't remember a call. The headmaster told me.

I wish this would have happened when I was seventeen instead of fourteen, because I would have had three more years of security. Security's important for a child. It really is the foundation for his happiness. Much of the pain I have suffered and put out in my work and also to others is based on insecurity.

Have you ever worked this out with your mother?
To some degree. But you're right, we have to work it out.

Then again, she can say you've accomplished all that you have because of where you've come from.
But you have to be happy as a person. If you don't resolve it with your parents, how can you begin the road? You can't walk away from that. I'm much happier because I've dealt with my mother better now, because I still have a lot of hate for her. It was a treacherous relationship.

Recently, with the birth of this new child, she's become very happy, because she always wanted a daughter to give her jewelry to. And I have gone to therapy, yes, and talked about my mom and all that and am working it out. She's a strong woman, my mother. So was my father. I had two strong parents, and they both rocked my boat.

Did your mother really take you to a nudist colony when you were nine?
Not nine, twelve or fourteen. I was older because I was more excited. It was after their divorce. She took me to Europe on a trip to explain to me what

had happened. Took me to a nudist colony. I couldn't do anything about it, though I felt strong urges. Beautiful women in Europe. I was very embarrassed and shy. I didn't have any pubic hair (*laughs*). That was a real issue with me for a few years: no pubic hair.

Did you become like Donleavy's Balthazar B with his nanny after that? Rubbing yourself against her ass?
I didn't have that kind of nanny. Yeah, maybe I did. She was a big, busty Swiss maid, and my father was fucking her. Great stories: my father and mother, that's another fucking book. But I don't know if that maid ever played around with me at night. I'm still here, and I can't ask her that. She's living somewhere in Europe. I would just bite her and tease her, pinch her ass, make her react.

Is it true that you've had erotic dreams since you were four?
Yeah. Essentially, I seem to have a very strong dream life and very strong erotic impulses. I find it motivating. It's an interesting life force. It can be perverted, it can be lustful, and it can reach excess, definitely. But it's a life force, and I welcome it. I've always had it, even when I was a kid. I would get visuals of women. . . . Of course, I didn't have an active penis at that age, I was three or five. But I'd get excited by visuals.

How old were you when you had your first wet dream?
I don't know. I was a late developer. I didn't even grow to this size until I was about twenty. I was smaller when I went into the Army. I went to boys' schools. I didn't date. I had no girlfriend. First women I really knew were in Asia, hookers—and they were a great introduction because I got to play out a lot of what American teenage boys think about.

I thought your first experience with a hooker was the one your father got you when you were fifteen.
Yeah. Do we have to get into that?

It is an interesting introduction.
It was an effective way. My father was a practical man. See, I didn't grow up in a high school setting. I was very retarded in that sense. In the sixties, when I left Yale, it was still a boys' school. There weren't many women in my life. Because I was different and an outsider I didn't have girlfriends. I was very lonely.

Was your father's gift to you a good experience?

It was great. She was a professional woman. She was nice. I didn't feel the taint of money or anything. It didn't have to be associated with falling in love, thank God, because you don't. Some boys fuck and they have to marry. They haven't learned that lesson yet.

I don't want to condemn my father for doing that, I think he did the right thing because of my needs and insecurity and adolescence. I wish I had a girlfriend, it might have been easier, but that wasn't the time in which women made love very easily.

Were you close enough to your father to talk about the experience afterwards?
That's a good question. I loved my father and respected him, but we never would talk too deeply about any subject, especially when it was personal. He came from another school, those things were kept at a distance. My father wore a tie and a jacket, like Nixon. He had a great sense of humor, but feelings were not part of that man thing.

My French grandfather was a big figure in my life. My cousin, my uncle, they were big men, they were in World War I and II, these guys were really tough, but they also kissed, so I had a whole other example. My father was repressed by the standards of the French man, so I grew up with both sides.

You've said that your father could make enemies with his tongue. Are you like him in that regard?
Yeah. I remember my mother always bawling him out because Dad would be sarcastic and sharp. I would understand that it was done in humor, but it would often hit the person the wrong way, hit their weak spot, and they would dislike him. He was not as popular as my mother. I'd say in my own life I've made numerous mistakes with my tongue by talking without thinking, or saying the sharp thing for the effect of wit rather than for emotion or thinking about the other person's feelings. I've hurt other people that way.

Are you ever apologetic?
Sometimes. But sometimes it's too late. I wish I could go back now and apologize to all the people I've hurt along the way. It was my nature to be a little like my dad. That came also from boarding school, from the East Coast. There's a certain Holden Caulfield cynicism from boarding school. And kids are cruel. Talk about violence—*Lord of the Flies*. I remember in school how they'd pick on somebody, they'd find some nerd or geek and gang up on him. And I'd always be in the role of trying to defend the geek. Then I'd get into trouble and get blacklisted.

Where were you when Kennedy was assassinated?
Hill School Boarding School in Pottstown, Pennsylvania. Most people I
know went with it. That's why the *JFK* movie was structured around the television that first half-hour. It just seemed to me most of us bought everything. There wasn't even a question—Oswald had done it, that was it.

I never bought it.
Good for you. There was a machine out there putting the story out within
hours. They had Oswald's whole bio and everything, he was around-the-
world news as a pro-Communist within like four hours. It was a big preparation to do that.

Did that change the way you thought about things?
No. It was the beginning of the end, in a sense. The divorce was around that
area. I think that was early '63. So '63 is a watershed year. The early sixties is
a really weird time. Marilyn Monroe gets busted in '62. Hemingway buys it,
and he's paranoid about the CIA. The CIA is coming into its full climax—In-
telligences, not just the CIA. They're using mind drugs, they're getting arrogant, they're knocking off leaders, everything comes to a head in the early
sixties. As you know, I believe Kennedy got swept into that mess, into that
detritus.

**We'll be getting back to *JFK*, but of all the corruption you've seen, what
corrupts the most?**
Nothing corrupts as quickly as luxury. All Americans dream for luxury and
materialism, but it's also very corruptive.

**You've said that money was your father's Achilles' heel. What does
money mean to you?**
Most of it I've been separated from (*laughs*). I've lost most of it in a divorce.
I've just never managed it well. They raised the taxes 10 percent so I'm paying 50 percent in taxes. I pay a fixed alimony plus child support. Child support is a California thing which I don't get. You have to continue paying for
the entire household way above what they need. I'm not talking about my
ex-wife, she didn't set out to punish me, it's the system.
   Divorce is a punishing thing for the income earner. It's not about ending
something that no longer works and being sensible, it's really about punishment and cutting off obligation. I'm very stuck in that, thinking, why can't I
just drop out and go to Thailand and just vanish? I'd be a deadbeat dad according to Clinton, who never worked a day in his life as a businessman. The
guy has been a government official all his adult life, and he's talking about

deadbeat dads. Just because he had one he's got to punish all the deadbeat dads in the world. Because of those assholes, which are a small minority, the average good father has to pay a fortune. With no rights. What a stupid fucking system! The legal system . . . on divorce.

It used to be different in the sixties. Now it's supposed to be no-fault. Well, no-fault implies that people are responsible for their fucking lives to some degree. You can't be responsible for somebody for the rest of their lives. That argument doesn't wash. You're not supposed to become a vegetable when you marry, which is what they encourage you to become. There are more women sitting around on their asses not working, with their nannies, living off ex-husbands. It's just unproductive for society and for themselves, they're not using their minds. Any self-respecting woman, or for that matter male partner, should get off his or her ass and work, try something. The irony is that raising a child alone *is* a full-time job, but probably every one of those women needs to have an outside job. There are struggling women, but they don't have anyone to give them money. The system benefits the haves and not the have-nots.

Are you happier married or single?
Both (*laughs*).

So money is a bit of a sore subject for you.
I've never been a materialist, but I was always concerned to have enough to live. I've had to struggle with selfishness, as everybody does, with a sense of what you do with your money. Is it moral? How often I come up wanting, believe me.

Do you ever play the stock market like your dad?
No, I don't like that. I did the opposite of my father. My father rented all his life. He rented apartments, cars, suits if he could, golf clubs. He said, don't buy, don't get stuck. He was always on the move. He died in a rented apartment in New York. He left my mother an insurance policy, and he left me $19,000. After all those years, that was all that was left. But he had given me an education, and he helped me afterwards, and he had been a good father. But tough to understand, to get to. Always a hidden, mysterious section to the man I could never understand. It was as if he was perverted in a way. Perversion is hard to understand, it's like a black hole in somebody's personality. So your father becomes perverse because sometimes he won't wish you well, sometimes he wants to hurt you, sometimes he resents you because you're taking his place or he's getting older and you're younger or you're not good enough. All those thousand reasons are there. Fathers can really hurt sons, deeply, with a word. It's very violent.

How conscious are you with your own son?
Not enough. But working on it. The more sensitive my son is, I see it now, I realize that I've said some insensitive things to him as he was growing up. I was tough on him. I was trying to not overpraise him, because I felt his mother tended to do that.

Did you really once slip acid into your father's drink?
(*Laughs*) Yes. If I tell the story, I hope you put it in a context, because people don't understand that stuff, and that's why I get this reputation as a crazy man. I'm not crazy. I was at war with my father. I came back from Vietnam, and he was treating me like a child. It was a very tough situation. I didn't know where the fuck I was. My life was really crazy. I was living in the East Village here and there, I had an apartment I had painted all red. And he was ragging me about Vietnam—which he called a police action, like in Korea. Well, it may have been to him, by the size of World War II standards, but when you're in combat you're in combat. It was pretty rough for me. I wanted to be treated like a man, which he wouldn't do. He was a Republican until the end of the Vietnam War. In the 1980s he said it had been a mistake, but not before then.

My dad took me to 21, the restaurant, when I came back, and I wore an American flag tie, which was popular at that time, and the owner of the restaurant threw me out. It was that kind of cultural war going on. People take a lot for granted today. It's the same thing with every generation, I suppose. But the sense of sacrifice and the sense of having this materialism was a big achievement in the fifties and sixties. That's why *Playboy* was so popular then—you could buy a stereo that was customized and stuff. People forget that.

So that's the context. Now when did you put acid in your dad's drink?
I was doing acid and a lot of marijuana, and I was talking like a black kid. That drove him nuts: "Man. Groovy. Wow." I'd been really influenced by the black troops, that's where I learned how to smoke dope. I was listening to all that Motown music. I've been smoking grass all my life. If you smoke too much of it, it loses its power. If you smoke a little and you reserve it, then you really get high.

My father just loathed everything about my habits after I returned from the war. I didn't have much money, and I was living for a while at his house. I didn't have any respect for the old forms, and I was struggling to find my way. So somewhere along the way we just clashed one too many times, and I just fucking had it. I put the goddamn acid in his scotch, because he always drank scotch, so he probably only got about a half of it, because it probably settled at the bottom of the glass, but he certainly got off. We were playing chess, and all of a sudden you could see his face change, and everything was being taken really intensely (*laughs*). We were at a strange dinner party in the Hamptons. These unbelievably sexy women were there—not for me, they were more his friends. He always liked women, my dad. He was a bachelor then, divorced. And he was standing out there in the garden holding onto a tree, the whole world was moving. I told him to go to the kitchen and get some milk and cookies, which is what he ate, cookies. And he had this dream about African women, and he could hear the drumbeat. He loved the trip—the next day he was talking about it. He knew that he'd been on something. At the dinner we were thirteen people, I'll never forget that. He stopped in the middle of the dinner, there was a silent pause, you could hear the silverware clank, and he said, "Who's the Judas at the table?" He looked around, and I kept a straight fucking face. I had long hair down to my shoulders. There were Buddhas there too, in the house. I remember the sexy girls dancing to the music. It was a strange night, and he was out of his mind. But he loved it.

Did he know it was you?
I think he did. But I denied it the next day. But he suspected me, and years later he laughed about it. He said, "I'll never forget that night." He liked it, it liberated him. Maybe that changed his life, maybe that's the reason years later he was much more liberal. I felt that you needed a revolution to knock their fucking heads off. These people were so hidebound, they were just not open to reality. The problem to me overall with society is that those establishment people who get the power are always out of touch with reality; they lose it because they work their way up, and all they do is wear blinders to get there. Even I do it. So that they lose touch with that common ground that we have, like being in the Army, being in Vietnam. Those people forgot what war was like. Neil Sheehan called it the "disease of victory from World War II." It's a good line. Because they forgot, and that's why we lost in Vietnam. So Dad—I wanted to knock his block off. I wanted to wake him up. And I was into radical solutions. I wanted to join the Panthers, I wanted to go to Washington, be involved in protests and revolution. Remember Morrison made a movie about shooting people in the streets? It was a very radical thought process going on.

Did any of the bad acid trips you took ever scare you?
I was scared shitless. I took it alone. I took it in the worst circumstances. I took it on the New York fucking subway one time. I was just out of my mind. I would challenge myself in the worst places. They say, get there with friends, be warm. I'd try, but I didn't have that many friends. Sometimes I'd

just take it in the weirdest places. I remember Santa Cruz, California, I got terrified—I was walking alone, the street was going this way and that way. I got busted and went to prison in San Diego, coming back from Mexico with grass. That was a horrible experience.

How long were you in prison?
Almost two weeks. I couldn't get the public defender to come and get me. My dad didn't know I was back from Vietnam at that point. Literally. I had to beg into the tenth day to make a phone call. The prison was so packed with drug people. When I called my dad, he said, "Where are you? Where've you been?" "Dad, I'm back, that's the good news (*laughs*). Guess where I am." The lawyer cost $2,500. It was like the *Midnight Express* scene. The lawyer showed up within three or four hours when he smelled money. He was rubbing his hands together and got me out in two days. I went right from there to the Army prison. I had stolen my Army card, so they thought that I was a deserter. So I spent the night in the brig, and then I got out, but they made me stay in town for a week on parole while the lawyer cleared it up.

Did the experience of surviving in Vietnam unleash confidence and creativity in a way that might not have happened with you had you not had that experience?
It comes from that, absolutely. But it was unleashed anyway before. My mind was in search of adventure and experience. Experience was the only way I could authenticate myself. Because I grew up in a family where I had certain things given to me, like the Buddha. He grew up sheltered, and his father and mother tried to keep him away from anything ugly for many years. And then one day he saw, by accident, an old man, and he thought that was horrible, because old people had been kept away from him. He went out into the world, and his father went crazy, his father wanted him to inherit the kingdom, to be a prince, to have all the riches, and he walked away from it. And a beautiful bride, and children. He walked away from all of it to follow the path that had come to him. It's a very startling story. If Bernardo [Bertolucci] had done just that movie, it would have been very good. No one's ever done it. Did *Siddhartha* ever get made? Do you think we could film *Siddhartha* now? Would you do it modern or period? How would you do it?

It would be interesting to think of it in modern terms.
Yeah, young New York architect (*laughs as he writes on a yellow pad*). I'm getting my story here—not only am I thinking about the movie that's being shown downstairs but I'm writing new story ideas as I'm answering your questions.

The reason I was asking about your Vietnam experience is: you first went to Vietnam to teach, as an idealist, but then you returned as an infantry soldier, armed, to fight against the same people. How does that play with your mind?

You're the first person who knows these facts about me who's asked that question. It's a very good question. There's a turn in character there, and that's dramatic, and part of the mystery of this life. My theory is that it was the opposite of that. I was in hell in New York City, and I was going to go deeper into hell until I got out of hell. I was going to go down. If you believed what you were reading in those days, and I was reading Hemingway and Conrad, a man had to test himself in life. That was the way I accepted it. Like young Indian braves who had to run this course to be in the tribe. I felt obligated to do my part. Of course, I believed that communism was dangerous, my father had convinced me of that. And also, I was driven partly by self-destruction. I was sick of having written a novel, I was disgusted with myself, loathed myself for being so vain and so pretentious, so concerned about only myself—the opposite of my father's philosophy. And out of this need to destroy Oliver Stone I became William Stone again. William Oliver Stone was my born name. So I split my personalities. In all the institutions I was William. Oliver was my secret side, a whole other world. In the book that I wrote I tried to play that out, to get to the bottom of that. You forget that stuff after thirty years, that you had two fucking names when you were in school.

It's been said that you're the only person who went to Vietnam to chill out.

Yeah, right. But I wasn't the only one (*laughs*).

When did the reality of being a soldier in Vietnam set in?

The first day. Like with the *Platoon* character, it was just quick. I had to cut point my first fucking day. They were tough in the 25th, there wasn't a lot of harmony. If you were the new guy, fuck you, you had twelve months to go. They only had four months to go. So you cut point. There was no friendship given that easily. The experience was filled with epiphanies. I woke up. And I could never be the same again. I was fifteen months ongoing in the field, and when you slept out there, you don't sleep. I was more of an animal, I was attuned to being a fox or deer, something in the jungle. To be good at it you have to identify. I became another person. A fascinating experience to me.

You've admitted to smoking dope in combat. Wasn't that a little dicey?

I didn't go into combat on dope. We smoked dope in rear areas. More relaxed areas where we felt safe. Back in base camp, for example. Maybe I said I
was in an area around the beach one day, patrolling, and I got stoned, and
then something happened in the afternoon, so I was stoned by accident and
went into a situation that turned into a major battle. I did all right. In fact,
fuck it, I forgot this! Just now I just remembered—I won the Bronze Medal
that day. So dig that, that's true. For some reason I was bolder and more intense about the experience. I fought more intensely and threw a perfect
grenade that killed a man. I killed a man. That was the first man I killed that
I really saw. I'd been in many combats and never got anything except
wounded and then all of a sudden this happened.

**You've estimated that 20 percent of American casualties in Vietnam
were accidents or people killed by our own side. Fragging was more
common than anyone imagined. And you've shied away from saying
whether you ever shot at an officer. But the sense one gets from reading
about you is that you probably did.**
No. I left it open at that time when *Platoon* came out, in the vein that it was
not something to answer, because you have to leave open the door to the
possibility that I might have. By doing that, I could emblematize the plight
of men who had been in that situation. Now years have gone by, and I don't
feel that same sensitivity anymore. Twenty percent is an understated figure
for fragging—I think it could be as high as forty percent. Modern firepower
is devastating, it's so loud—the noise, the bombs, the airplanes, the confusion—it is impossible to think. There is such an area of chaos that people are
continually making mistakes, calling in wrong coordinates, dropping the
bombs in the wrong spot, artillery is being walked the wrong way, your own
equipment blows up, your own troops dislike you because you're being
gung-ho and they're saying, "Lay back, man, chill, don't get killed, it ain't
worth it," and you're an officer trying to move them along. Those situations
would arise. Any war, American policy in combat is to lay out the maximum
amount of fire with a maximum amount of noise. It's called firepower. It's
supposed to psychologically blow away the enemy. But what it does is blow
away its own troops.

Platoon was about an American civil war in Vietnam. It was about the
struggle for the soul of what we were fighting for, between two forces in
American life. To simplify it, it was the characters Barnes and Elias. It
wasn't much bigger than that. Inside that civil war, the values of the war
and the lies with which it was being conducted led to an unconscious de-
duction of that struggle in the troops and to moral breakdown and disin-
tegration of the collective, which is necessary for war. After I left in '69,

there was a tremendous breakdown with the heroin epidemic that seized a lot of the troops. And racial dissension came heavily into play. All of a sudden you were fighting for your piece of turf. "This is not my war, I'm an angry white man, I'm a black man, I'm a liberal. . . . " It got into all these definitions.

You've said, "I felt I couldn't be an honest human being until I knew what war and killing were." Did killing make an honest man of you?
I was twenty. I felt I had to define myself, to go through fire in order to be a man.

Did you once stop some soldiers from raping a village girl?
Yeah. One of the good things I did. I saved some drowning people once. I think I prevented a couple of killings. I tried to help out where I could. It was a tough situation. It was racist. You were taught to distrust the civilian "gooks." You were supposed to treat them as aliens. And I fell into some of that.

Did you feel like an alien yourself when you left the Army?
When I came back, I was so shocking to my father and friends. I couldn't resume old friendships. I couldn't talk to a boy who'd been in school with me because he continued in school and I'd been over there. As a result, I lost contact, and all my contacts had to be new. That's where acid came into play: you'd meet people under acid trips and you'd become friends with them. Strange girls, strange apartments, strange friends. I joined Scientology for a few weeks because I was chasing some girls. It was a free-floating existence.

Then I had a Henry Miller period later in my life, where I was alone between marriages in New York. I started to believe in Henry Miller. I hadn't succeeded as a writer yet, and he was the emblem of failure and success. There was a moment when I was so intoxicated by him and his great books of Paris with the artists and women and cafés and writing late at night and the endless sex, the freedom of that existence and the beauty with which Henry Miller conveyed it, it really hooked me—I had a great period of Henry Miller liberation.

Was that when you worked as a PA on a soft-porn film and drove a cab in Manhattan?
On the soft-porn movie I remember pushing a dolly in Soho with two others. We decided to band together and do a movie ourselves, and that's how *Seizure* was born. We hooked up and raised the money for it. I worked the

night shift as a cab driver off and on for a year. It was hard because you'd
end up working until 3:00 A.M. Some weird drives, got stiffed a few times,
never robbed. I tried to smoke Js at night but could never get high, driving
would knock off my high. It was hard work. But there would be great runs:
at 1:00 A.M. you could run from 100th Street on Second Avenue all the way
to the bottom of Manhattan in one light, that was just great. Some beautiful
girls tipped me very well at times, but I never had anything else happen.

**Besides feeling liberated by the work of Henry Miller, did you also have
any sense of liberation regarding the movies? And were you influenced
by seeing the work of directors like John Ford, George Stevens, Howard
Hawks, John Huston, Renoir, and Hitchcock?**
Of course they all did, but it would be unfair to the eighty-five others you've
left out. Frankly, you store up a lot of collective memory, and that lays the
foundation for the grammar you use later. I saw a thousand films. Hundreds
of them affected me. I was influenced by *The Robe* as much as by *Lawrence of
Arabia*. They were spectacles, concepts of life greater than 1950 New York
City, America. It was just another world, a dream world. [François] Truffaut
talked about this and loved to run away from school. I felt the same way
about movies—they were something to look forward to. My influences were
very collective, and then when I became more conscious of it—certainly
Kubrick with my dad was really important. I saw *Paths of Glory* all the way
through *Dr. Strangelove, Lolita, Spartacus*. Then David Lean was looked at and
considered. *On the Waterfront* in black and white in '54 affected me. I saw *One-
Eyed Jacks* and thought that was terrific. Fellini knocked me out. *La Dolce
Vita*. So did the French New Wave—*Breathless* was the first one I saw, but I
didn't see it until a year after it premiered, in '61. It just knocked the shit
out of me. I loved it, the speed, the lifestyle. I loved the personal film. The
concept of doing your own life story on film was pretty wild to me—Fellini
was doing it, Antonioni, Truffaut, Goddard, through symbols and
metaphors. It was very direct cinema as opposed to the impersonal American
cinema, which was at that time being derided by the critics, which was unfortunate. Robert Wise, who was a master craftsman and deserved so much
credit for directing films across so many genres, he's one of the most unspo-
ken masters of our era, he edited *Citizen Kane* on top of it—but that kind of
director was being ignored for that European newness. It's always about
something new. But I never thought I'd end up doing it. George Stevens and
all those people didn't mean much. Hitchcock was probably the only one I
knew. Jerry Lewis. Who were the directors? The impression I get with John
Huston, and I love his subject matter, and some of his films are classics, but
I feel that there was a classic waste of talent. So much energy going into bad

scripts or bad movies that were done for money—terribly debilitating to his talent. But I couldn't have told you anything in detail. It was only after I went to film school that I became conscious of the American cinema.

Thank God I went out of synch with my generation in a way, because what happened in '65, when I entered Yale, I would have graduated in '68. But I got out of synch because I wasn't happy, and with these novels, when I returned to college it was when they were starting the idea of a film school, because otherwise I would have never thought of it. Film schools were hot in '68, '69. Marty had come from a previous generation, in '64 or '65, so he was to us a bit of an older fella.

How important was Martin Scorsese as your teacher at NYU?
Oh, very, because he was one of the leading avatars of "buffdom." Marty worshiped the director, the prime focus of his interest. When you talked about films, you talked about Von Sternberg or Eisenstein or Murnau or Sam Fuller, John Cassavetes. He talked about that signature. Marty loved Hollywood filmmaking, and he was a great teacher. He understood style, color, camera, and how to use it. He was very conscious of all that and taught it so brilliantly that you got inspired as a result. We would do these two-minute black-and-white pictures, and he would critique them. It was hilarious—the degree of sarcasm, you had to be there. Everybody would get grilled. You put up your film, and it was like the Chinese Cultural Revolution thing where you sat there and by the time your film was over it was, "It stinks, it stinks!" I traded a little bit of that in that stupid Jim Morrison scene I did in *The Doors*. I played Marty, put a beard on.

Were you thinking about directing in film school or writing?
I was a novelist, then went to Vietnam twice, gave up the idea because the nature of warfare was very uncerebral, it's about sensuality, the six inches in front of your face. That translated to me into movies. So when I went to film school, it was with a desire to make movies as a director.

Was it tough to get into Scorsese's class?
No, he was assigned. He was not a big superstar then. I didn't know much about him. He was a graduate who had been around. His salary was important, it gave him a livelihood, a way to keep going while making short films on the side. He had done that half-picture with Harvey Keitel, *Who's That Knocking? Mean Streets* was very accomplished by the time he made that in '72 or '73.

Scorsese seems to have a strong sense of self. You've said you don't have a very high self-esteem, because you basically whore out your services. Do you really feel that?

I agree with the first part of it, but I don't feel low self-esteem for those reasons. Whore out my services? I don't think I have a record for doing that. I've always written what I wanted to write.

What do you think your impact is?
I don't know. I'm driven by my own inner drives. I've had failure and success, I've had derision and applause in equal measures. If that happens to you enough in your lifetime, you begin to realize the illusion that it is. It's a ploy. Once you accept that as an illusion, it only becomes about your interior consciousness and achieving what your *you* is. That's all it is it seems to me. And I'm on that trip now. I'm in space. I went to the ionosphere. The stratosphere. Without gravity. If that's the ideal state, if you loosen up and go out, you can get without gravity. That's a blessed state, a truly Hindu state, a serenity state. It gives you a feeling of wholeness on this earth. Naturalness.

But you don't seem to put yourself in that serenity state in your work.
I do, I try to. Perhaps I live my life by contrasts, and I need one to excite the other. Serenity inside the chaos is great. I've gotten really good at handling pressure, better than I used to. I was very sensitive to stress. I'd become irritable, or I'd blow out, or I'd lose my control and punish myself or somebody else. It's very interesting to see stress at work. Seeing it when it comes on, feeling it, hearing it, smelling it. You've got to be like an infantry soldier. That's the six inches in front of your face when you're in the jungle. Because that's really what it comes down to: your life is experience, it's authentic feeling. That's all we know. How do we get real feelings in our lifetime? You, me. It's so hard to really know what we think and feel. Because we get all the impostors. We get all the television, the simulations of what to think and feel, it really is an Orwellian media state. And it overwhelms the mind.

You've said that most everything in your life has been failure. That's certainly not how aspiring filmmakers would see you.
If I were to do an honest mathematical assessment of all the efforts I've made in film and in life, most of them would be misses. Many scripts, ideas, developments that went down the tubes. But perhaps I learned from the failures. What is failure and what is success? You should learn from success, but most of us don't because success gives you confidence. I've had some great successes which came at key times, picked up my spirits, like *Platoon*. It was a long time coming. *Salvador* was a failure theatrically. I'd done *Midnight Express*, big hit; but then *Conan* was not really mine; *Scarface* was reviled; *Year of the Dragon* was okay; *Eight Million Ways to Die* was not really mine but was a disaster; *The Hand* and *Seizure* hadn't worked. C'mon, how many failures is that? Maybe I feel like I'm developing as an artist, but it's certainly a slow go.

And you don't develop unless you get some confidence. So I wasn't sure. *Platoon* was really a big shot in the arm. It was worldwide, it wasn't just a critic's thing.

How important is rejection and failure for an artist?
I think you could find maybe a thousand rejections in my files, and there must have been another twelve thousand from phone calls. During that time, believe me, I wanted to give up several times. One of the things that really kept me going—and I don't want to sound immodest, but I don't want to sound overly modest either, because I don't believe in that—the Greeks were right: you should be what you are, don't spend too much energy apologizing for yourself. We live in this fake humble society, it's boring—I was convinced that if I could ever fucking see the daylight, and I was past thirty, that I could become the filmmaker I wanted to be. And what I was learning would come in handy then. And it was true. It's not over, but you get that recognition. But my battles have gotten bigger—not only battles with my own confidence, but there are so many other battles in life that are fought that I hadn't been aware of, people are always coming at you. The will has to be forged in steel and pain and suffering. Now part of the trick is to make joy and creativity work.

I've had so much rejection that I don't get bothered too much when somebody turns me down or somebody disses me. Maybe part of the reason I get so much criticism is that in some karmic way I can handle it.

How sensitive are you to criticism?
Less so over the years. At first, when I became nationally prominent in the mid-eighties and I wasn't used to it, to be criticized nationally was heavy. Then my character was also being slandered beyond the films. I mean, my films were terrible, but my character was also defective. Which was very hard for me to accept. But it happened so much it was like another test which I never thought was going to occur in my life. To be ridiculed. How many ridiculous cartoons were there? I hope it didn't harden me, because that would be its purpose, to destroy your confidence and make you cynical. That's the easy way to go. If you realize that it's your ego that's responding, it's a tough one to deal with. But if you realize it, more and more you can reach a spot where it does wash off you. Because they say so many stupid things, I just have to detach myself. That's the Oliver Stone they see, that's not me.

One idiot I could have sued for libel, because it hurts my career. She said I had a knife on my desk, I was a Vietnam veteran still haunted by war, that if people didn't do what I wanted I'd throw the knife and pin 'em against the wall by a piece of their clothing. What! Where? And she wrote this as if it was serious. Actors read that, people believe that shit, they think, oh, he must be a frightening figure. Well, I don't know what impression you have, but I don't think *frightening* is what people who know me think about me.

I haven't looked for the knife on your desk yet.
There's no knife! I really was pissed off. I called my lawyers, this fucking woman doesn't even fucking call or know anything, just made me out to be a crazy man. And she's allowed to do that by the press. I'm surprised by the limits of the First Amendment, and I'm a big defender of it. But when you destroy somebody's reputation. . . . That portrayal of me as screaming and angry and all that bullshit, believe me, I would not have done eleven movies of this size in ten years if I was making enemies of my crews and friends and actors. Most of them want to work with me again. You have to be fluent, specifically, to get it done in that way. I've had a prolific output. If you behave in a way that's anti-progressive in your thinking, if you're trying to block people, if you're trying to create obstacles, or establish egos—egos get in the way of movies getting made all the time. The director has to be the leader, the visionary. And so he has to see the problem of the ego, and we all have to get the ego together and put it in a place where we all serve the higher ideal of making the film. I really believe in that. I've gotten a collective group of people to believe on a temporary basis that this could be done, and done well. That's the only way. So by having an obtrusive personality or having in any way an egoistic personality, you will not get that done. Maybe make three films in ten years. Jimmy Woods—who's known me a long time, he worked with me on the first one and the last one, on *Salvador* and on *Nixon*—said, and I'm paraphrasing him, that "the thing with Oliver is that he doesn't have an ego, that's what people precisely miss; you can criticize him or say anything you want about him, he wants to get the result and he'll take it from anywhere he can."

People like Sean Penn, Alec Baldwin, have physically attacked the press. Ever happen with you?
Not physically. It's a hard task. It's the malice. I respect the right to opinion. But some critics have become so negative that they don't realize how they destroy people. Kael started it, Sarris, Vincent Canby. They're poisonous people.

Even the early Kael?
Oh yeah. It was more about what she hated than loved. It was always about hatred, negativity, tearing down, destroying reputations. Then building up a

few darlings, okay; but that's not enough. Why are we captive to somebody's collective dream? Why should we believe Pauline Kael's collective mythology of America? It's bullshit. Let her go out and make Pauline Kael movies and make her dream, like I do. She doesn't speak for me, or for Americans. And never did. She was just an elitist bag lady.

I once quoted something by Kael to Al Pacino, and he asked me if that was before or after she removed the shot glass from her mouth.
(*Laughs*) She was good with words, but so what? She destroyed more people than she ever helped. We need good critics who are generous of spirit and who have love in their hearts, who will take any movie and understand that the subject is not criticizable in itself, only the execution is, and allow the filmmaker to speak and not have any preconceptions. That is the true, honest critic. Help the audience understand something in the work that even the artist doesn't see.

Are you saying, if a critic doesn't like something he should pass on writing about it?
No. Charles Champlin in the old *L.A. Times* days had a way of saying something about a movie which he didn't like which you understood, but he didn't have to go and attack with a hatchet the actor, writer, director, producer.
    What I'm saying about critics can only hurt my reputation. I respect them if they're good, but I'm not kissing their asses. It's so depressing, the number of filmmakers and actors who kiss their asses publicly but really hate them behind their backs.
    A lot of the anti-Hollywood sentiment is so boring. The fact that it's made in Hollywood makes it evil—that intellectual nihilism is everywhere. It's insane. Any film made in a grocery store for twelve dollars is valid, whereas any film made for $25 million in Hollywood is a joke. Bullshit! Hollywood has never been monolithic. It still is the most democratic place I know on earth. It's given everyone—as long as they show talent—opportunities to write and direct and produce; it's the land of bullshit and dreams. It's the most egalitarian society I know. And that's why it's so hated by elitists. The work in the eighties and nineties, contrary to critical opinion, has been incredibly varied. There's subject matter on practically everything.

You have also said the opposite about your feelings for this town. "Taste is dictated by a mass consensus of distributors, exhibitors—a floating circle of players." In your *Playboy* interview, you said you were convinced there was a conspiracy to make blander films.
Oh yeah, I remember that. I'm not contradicting myself: it's a subdivision. Inside the Hollywood paradigm, which is a great one, there is, of course, the

worst type of element. But under egalitarianism, it's allowed. Those are people who will make movies to make money. But that is not all Hollywood.

I've been amazed at how resilient you've been, perhaps because you like a good fight.
I don't like to fight. I never fought as a kid, I avoided fights. I just won't step away from one. It's hard for me to run. Sometimes I will run, by the way. I'm trying to be smart about when to pick one. You really think I like to pick fights?

It could be part of what makes you tick. Is it a directorial technique of yours that to get anger from an actor you may enrage him, to get tears you may belittle him?
That's a method of directing. I don't have conflicts with actors, I really don't. Never did.

I've read how during *Wall Street* you had to learn Michael Douglas's MO. Making *The Hand* you spent half your time fighting with Michael Caine. On *Seizure* there supposedly was a crew member who wanted to kill you.
Yes. Two of those three things are true.

So let's start with *Seizure*. Why did a crew member try to kill you?
Which one? (*laughs*). The guy who almost killed me was a special effects man from New Jersey. He had a long pigtail and a machete. He was drunk and chased me. He wanted to kill me because he was fucking my lead actress, Martine Beswick, and he was jealous of me. I had not been with her, but she had eyes for me and I had eyes for her—and we ended up together *after* the film. But during the film he was very jealous. So he ran up the stairs with a machete saying, "I'm going to get that know-nothing asshole director." My crew had to restrain him! Thank God I had a burly, French-Canadian crew that was drunk half the time. They picked him up, and they held him. He was a scrawny little guy, but he was nuts. He was not sane during the whole film. He was out of his mind, he was fucking the lead actress and started to believe that he was a star. He was a special effects man! He wouldn't even come to the set to work when he was supposed to (*laughs*).

And with Michael Douglas during *Wall Street*?
With Michael it was an issue. The whole film depended on credibility, and I had some problems with what he was doing, and I went to him and was straightforward. I said I wasn't convinced that he had gotten the character of Gordon Gekko. We worked it out. I think his ego might have been hurt by

some of the things I said about his previous performance—I didn't say this
to him, but in my mind I was thinking that Michael was resorting to television things he did on *The Streets of San Francisco;* that was my concern, that he
wasn't challenging the role enough. We had a showdown after three or four
days. He got more intense and serious as a result of that. Whatever we did,
he got the fucking Oscar, right? Something happened.

**What happened between you and Douglas that eventually led to that
performance?**
It was himself. It was well written, first of all. Secondly, I felt that Michael
had the drive of his father, I really did. I'd known him socially, he's a very
smart man. Financially acute. Take him for what he is, he wasn't what other
people may have seen him as—that boy from the TV series. Something sweet,
friendly, and affable about Michael that was just easy to get along with. But
that wasn't what I was interested in. I was interested in his slick other side,
which I saw in meeting him, and I used it very well.

Do you see the slick other side in everybody you meet?
Not necessarily. It was in that case because Michael at that time was very financial, very attuned to empire and building, organizing. So what I was trying to do with the script and all the directions and our talks was to push
that side. But only inside the nature of the illusion. In other words, it's over,
we're off the set, and we can joke. He's just Michael Douglas at that point,
and we can have a friendly relationship; he doesn't have to be Gordon Gekko
and carry it around. Tony Hopkins could just drop Nixon in a second. It's
more pleasant to work that way and have full intensity. I find it very irksome
to have to walk around with Jim Morrison for four months. Not that Val
Kilmer did that, but you get a sense of that.

**What about being with Al Pacino when he was Tony Montana in
*Scarface?***
Well, Al is a very interesting character. He influenced me very much. I was
young, working on *Scarface*, saw him rehearse it. Al very much intimidated
me when I started. He was one of the stars that made me feel very nervous
around him. Then he asked me to direct him in a picture, and I got to know
him a bit on *Noriega* also, and may work with him. I'd love to. We're fit for
each other in a way. But he's grown. I find him in another place too, than
where I was. So my answer to Al would be: what do you get out of Al? What
would be the quality that I have not seen him do that I would like to see? In
Scarface it was something very feral, something immigrant and hungry and
decadent. Now I would look for something else in Al, because I've sort of

seen that side. He redid it, not as well, in *Carlito's Way*. *Scarface* is a very special script, we worked on it very hard.

Did you know it's his favorite movie?
No, I didn't. I knew it was good at the time. Talk about getting bad reviews—awful things were said about me, and I was just the writer. I was some kind of weirdo. There were great lines in that movie, and they were not all mine—I took from wherever I could, from Al, from Marty Bregman, Brian De Palma. We worked on it.

Did you have any sense that this would become a cult movie?
Yeah. I thought it was a terrific picture. It was a combination of my dialogue, research, Marty and Al and Brian contributed. It was highly original for its time. Still is. But it was picked up on back then, on the streets of New York in '83, '84, you'd hear it—black kids were getting it, the future rap kids. There were all these white lawyer clubs that used to form—white professional working men who'd get together for a drink and quote the dialogue. There were many instances where I'd go places and hear that.

Was this your personal farewell to cocaine?
I was doing cocaine during the research phase. I went cold turkey during the writing in Paris. That's why I went to Paris. I couldn't break the habit here—Florida, L.A., and New York were the three hot spots. If anything I was surrounded by relationships, and that environment is hard to break.

Do drugs take more of a toll on you as you get older?
Alcohol is harder to recover from as you get older. I view life as a drug. Life is dangerous. We wear down. Life hits our nervous system, it stresses us. The stress factor is the biggest drug of all. People who separate drugs into a category of pharmaceuticals and grass miss the point of the damage of life to our system. I also think we create drugs in our bodies. The hormonal balances we have create our own drug system. We have to move away from thinking of drugs as a separate species. Marijuana, if anything, has a beneficial long-term effect on your life span—it slows you down, calms you, there's less stress, it's enjoyable. You can use any drug, including psychedelics, effectively to improve your life. Which is why God put it here.

If you could rewrite the Constitution, what changes would you make?
I never thought about it. Who would ever give me that power? I would remind people that we're dedicated also to the pursuit of pleasure as human beings. And that we have the right to happiness and pleasure, and that in-

cludes our marijuana—our home-grown, natural, God-given plants. Nobody
said they have the right to get into our abortions, to our private bodies, and
the government keeps encroaching on that.

**Back to *Scarface* and its producer, Marty Bregman. He once said he was
your rabbi. Were you that close?**
Rabbi? That's a good word. It's a Jewish word. Rabbi. No, I think that Marty
thought he was my rabbi. I was in the business without Marty. I had succeeded with *Midnight Express*. My first break came off of Fernando Ghia and
Robert Bolt in '75. Bolt signed me to William Morris, and at least my work
was being looked at. And he taught me something about screenwriting.
Shortly thereafter I wrote *The Coverup* for Robert's company, and Fernando
Ghia was a good producer, he did *The Mission* and developed several other
films. He's Italian, but very austere, very Jesuit, very serious. Then I wrote
Platoon on my own as an original. Marty bought that and shepherded that,
but unfortunately he didn't get it made. So when you say "rabbi," that's
someone who gets it done. But Peter Guber loved the script and hired me to
write this low-budget movie, *Midnight Express,* in England. So I went there in
the cold winter of '77. The picture was a huge hit, it cost $4 million and
made $100 million. So the point I'm trying to make is, my break came a lit-
tle bit from everywhere. It wasn't one person.

**When one saw Brad Davis in *Midnight Express,* one thought, 'here's the
next James Dean.' What happened to him? Was it the lack of direction
which messed up his life and career?**
The lack of sophistication. So many actors I've seen repeat this, even today—a little bout of success goes to their heads, and they believe they're im-
mortal, that they've entered quickly into the realm of the gods. But life is
not made that way. Those who don't seem to get aware die along the way
pretty fast.

Did you ever fear that could happen to you after this picture?
It could have happened. I knew Brad. When the movie was being made, he
was a very sweet kid, very lucky, grateful, a bit like Christopher Reeve. Next
thing you know he was a big superstar, and he couldn't be approached at
parties—he'd be in the corner with his entourage. Doing his coke out in the
limousine. Then I saw him years later, his agent brought him in for something, wanted him to come back into the business, and he was a very bitter
young man. Not towards me, just bitter. His life had hardened him. He
didn't believe in anybody, didn't trust anything. It happens to so many actors, girls and boys. Business is fake, and they all fall for that media line—the

media promotes these people like fucking hotcakes, because they're new, fall fashion, spring fashion, bullshit, and the kids believe it and fall for it. Next thing they know, they haven't done anything significant because they haven't really been honest with themselves. They've been inauthentic people. A lot of them are just out of film school or advertising agencies in commercials. It's a big mistake. It's a fake life. You're creating fake stuff. It's perhaps well done technically, but it runs the risk of being fake to life. That's a hard thing to do: to remain authentic. To realize in this business what your own feelings are, because you're bounced around by peer pressure and psychological pressure. The perception of who you are is sometimes the dominant perception, as opposed to what reality is.

When I was going through some of my most profound personal changes with the divorce, making *Heaven and Earth,* and Buddhism, and Le Ly, it was a period when I was being most ridiculed. The worst motives were always attributed to me, for divorce, for anything. My motives were impugned from *JFK*. Like I did *JFK* out of malice, as opposed to, perhaps, my motives were one of love and great patriotism for this country. But once you accept that my motives were malicious, I can't defend myself. It's like, how often do you beat your wife? That kind of question.

How did the screenwriting Oscar for *Midnight Express* affect you?
It was very helpful to my career. It made me hot for a while, and it led to my directing a picture. I wanted to do *Baby Boy,* a more serious literary work, but I backed off it. It's a love story between two men—about two southern escaped convicts incapable of fending for themselves in the real world and they desperately want to go back to prison. It was a bit comedic, which ends sadly. I actually went through the southern prison system scouting it, but I got cold feet on it as my first major film. I'd done *Seizure* as a horror film. For some reason I loved Mark Brandel's *The Lizard's Tale* and felt more comfortable going back into that genre—psychological thriller. I called it *The Hand.* I did not succeed, and it set me back to being a writer when Marty Bregman hired me for *Scarface. Scarface* didn't do me much good because it was perceived as very violent and brutal. Nor did the other one with Dino De Laurentiis and Michael Cimino, *The Year of the Dragon.* I stalled. I had a very tough period in there. A lot of people were looking for the failure of *The Hand.* There was jealousy of my directing. The reactions were too vivid, too visceral.

When *Born on the Fourth of July* finally happened, Marty Bregman was still hoping to produce, but you didn't want him. Was there still bitterness between you?

There was no way that I would do it with Marty at that point in time. He was paid some money by Universal. A long time had passed. There'd been bitterness on *Scarface.*

You were reported calling Pacino a "schmuck" in an Italian paper, which you later denied. Was it a political denial?
I spoke to Al about that. I was embarrassed by that Italian thing. It was genuinely emotional. I was hurt and upset that he didn't make *Born on the Fourth.* I wanted it to be done so badly back then that I felt that Al buckled early on it. He went to do Jewison's movie, *And Justice for All,* because it was set, there was financing, it was safer. And Al was tired of hanging out waiting for that film. He had his own justification. And whatever Marty told him I wasn't privy to, but certainly Marty had strung him along for a long time on that picture. Marty had kept him in after Billy Friedkin had dropped out. Dan Petrie and him were not seeing eye to eye. Whatever it was, when he pulled out it hurt me. Ron Kovic was the most upset.

One of Al's later concerns about doing Noriega was that he had already played a Latin character in Tony Montana. Did you discuss this with him?
I never felt that. We never discussed that aspect of it. The reason the thing terminated was that we all sat at this table on two separate readings of the script, we read it and it didn't work either time. It wasn't a question of moods, it just didn't work, it lay there, it was lifeless, it was a dead fish. Al and I looked each other in the eye, and we knew we couldn't make it.

Did you write it?
I had done the revisions on Robin Wright's script. The problem was, the tone of the piece was never clear. We didn't know how we felt about Noriega. He was sometimes a buffoon and sometimes this horrific figure. It was varying all over the place. There was no spine. Al and I sensed that both times. I'm glad we didn't make the movie. And Al did not enforce the pay-or-play. He could have. But Al let us off the hook, because it was a big number. We all got off easy.

Many people consider *Salvador* to be your best film. Where do you place it?
A lot of people say that because it's an elitest point of view, it's the littlest seen, and it's the first. It's such bullshit, because I've grown so much since then. I'm not the same filmmaker, I've moved to a different place. If it hap-

pened to catch the *zeitgeist* of that moment, great, but that picture's as flawed as any one I've done.

Did you originally pitch it as a road movie—*Abbott and Costello Go to Salvador?*

That's correct. I was starting from zero. Marty Bregman had hurt my reputation by saying I was difficult to work with on *Scarface*. My career was in the toilet. De Laurentiis's film hadn't gone anywhere. It was a very flat time. I couldn't get going on several things. So I moved aside from the system and wanted to go make the movie by myself with some money I would borrow. Then [Hemdale's] John Daly stepped in, and he was a bit outside the system. He had been a boxing promoter and had done some films. John was a funny guy. A real Gentleman Jim type—white suits, laughs a lot. So when we talked about it, we thought of it being a sort of comedy under dangerous circumstances in Salvador. John Daly helped me the most—he put up the money for both films, and he did it unequivocally. It was also a tax scam. The picture was originally called *Outpost*. They slotted it as a Schwarzenegger film in Mexico because it fit a tax credit that they already had. Schwarzenegger was not going to do the movie, so they had this money because it was a huge ratio from Holland. So the investors would get a huge tax benefit for the investment, but there was no picture, so they put me in as the *Outpost* film.

Do you think it wasn't commercial because it lacked a big star?

Look, you had Brad Pitt and Harrison Ford in *The Devil's Own,* a movie that was very old-fashioned and stodgy, and it just didn't do that much business. That was as purely unsatisfying a movie that has come out, and that was with the two biggest stars. Both with guns, a woman was in it, urban—it had all the ingredients. I guess people didn't feel the story was that enchanting or good.

We've already talked about your time in Vietnam and how it led to *Platoon*. What war films impressed or affected you?

Everything from *All Quiet on the Western Front, Story of GI Joe,* Darryl Zanuck's *D-Day, Men at War* with Robert Ryan, the Aldo Rey one was great but I forgot the title. Numerous authentic, realistic, tough movies. *Sands of Iwo Jima,* that was a tough, bitter picture. A dark film noir approach to war. There have been many good films about war. *Apocalypse Now* and *The Deer Hunter* were both great movies, but mythic in their approach.

During the filming of *Platoon* in the Philippines, did your Filipino crew go on strike because you kicked the head of the crew in the ass?

That's exaggerated, but I booted him in the butt, because I had gotten fed up with the numerous fire engine delays. We had huge special effects, and water towers and fire engines were required. Every time we were waiting for the water truck it was always late, so I had enough and booted him in the ass. Apparently he had a gun and was going to shoot me.

Did the guy get to slap you in the face to save face?
Perhaps so. It was no big deal to me. I apologized to him.

Would you agree with the writer who wrote about *Wall Street*, that you used Wall Street as a backdrop for your vision of Dante's *Inferno*?
I don't remember that analogy. I think Dante's *Inferno* would come up more with *The Doors* because of that look we had in it, Miami, some of the concert scenes.

Val Kilmer so wanted to play Jim Morrison in *The Doors* he camped out on your doorstep and put together an audition video. True?
Partly true. Val's name had been up for a long time. He didn't have to camp on our doorstep, but he did make a tape to show me that he could do it. Val had made a tape for me for Elias in *Platoon*. A lot of actors have done all kinds of crazy things. Val knew that he was the number-one consideration. Jason Patric went through the process of studying singing, and we auditioned him, and he was sore that he didn't get the role. I don't know why he was sore, he got a fair shake.

Kilmer also liked to fuck with your mind too, didn't he?
We fought a few times. He did hurt me, but it wasn't anything dramatic. They hurt me more in the press. I always thought I had a good relationship with Darryl Hannah and Meg Ryan, but I was surprised what they said in the press. I really was hurt. It came out of the blue. The press looks for that, especially with me, they magnetize. How many people have said nice things about me that never get in the press? Anthony Hopkins said marvelous things about me as a director—but I never read one word about it. People are only looking for negative images of me.

Norman Mailer didn't care for *The Doors* but wrote that *Born on the Fourth of July* came near to being a great movie, and he thought *JFK* was the "boldest work yet of a bold and clumsy man. But the first thing to be said about it is that it is a great movie, and the next is that it is one of the worst great movies ever made."

(*Laughs*) That's very funny. What do you say? Mailer writes well, and it was kind of him to do that to help the movie because it was being attacked quite a bit at that point.

He said something else about you: "He is one of our few major directors, but he also can be characterized as a brute who rarely eschews the heavy stroke. All the same, he has the integrity of a brute, he forages where others will not go."
(*Laughs*) Those are funny lines, I forgot that. What he's saying is, with subject matter I'm very frontal, like an infantry soldier. I'm going after big game.

It sounds like Mailer might also be describing himself and his own work.
Isn't it clear?

Would you mind being called the movie equivalent of Norman Mailer?
Not at all. I respect Norman Mailer intensely. He's groundbreaking. Part of what he does is he sacrifices himself, he puts himself out there too. He integrates himself into the piece in his criticism, and in his essays he's very much a presence. Which I'm not in my movies. But to some people I am, and though I don't set out to be, perhaps unconsciously I become so.

It's ridiculous for me to defend myself, but don't you think Van Gogh could get the same attack? In those days they probably were saying, he's a brute. He was sloppy, his edges were bleeding with paint. That intensity that Van Gogh had—he was so lonely and isolated in a strange way. But when painting was flourishing and all painters were starting to be recognized, he was having to go through this horrible period of abnegation and denial and no money and no recognition. That must have been terrifying. And his madness too—I can understand that.

You hoped that *JFK*'s mythology would replace the *Warren Commission Report*, as *Gone with the Wind* replaced *Uncle Tom's Cabin*. Think you succeeded?
Unfortunately, the establishment media went after it big time to try and destroy the film. They saw the danger in it before I saw it. I thought they were overreacting. I had not realized how deep a nerve this was, but I'm glad the film got made. It exposed the nerve. Who knew that it was that deep? I thought you had to be a moron to accept the Warren Commission. I still do. You have to move into primary evidence phase, like what you see, hear, and feel. It's that six-inches theory again. Let's get back to reality here. Go up

there [to the Texas Book Depository], stand in the window, try to do the shots in the time; look at the body of Kennedy. Look at the fucking Zapruder film, which is the most beautiful film made, should have gotten the best short at the Academy Awards in '63. In the film two things that happened are so weird that you have to doubt the official story. If one thing was weird in the film, I could perhaps accept it. But there's two things that happened in the space of a few seconds that are nuts. The first is the one bullet that went through Kennedy and into Connelly that created nine wounds. Just unbelievable. And number two, being shot from the rear and having Kennedy's head flying backwards, which scientists can tell you is the neuromuscular effect, true, but that other thing happening as well, it makes it really bizarre.

Six years after all the hoopla about *JFK*, do you think any minds have changed?
Oh sure, I opened some minds. You ask questions, you make people think for themselves, that was what the film did.

What did you think of Gerald Posner's *Case Closed?*
A disgrace. It was presold. Something smells in the whole thing. Posner's relationships, his past, his past book about the German Nazi guys, his thinking stinks. His desire to close the case, his use of evidence in the case, is done like a prosecuting attorney who has one motive—not the truth, but to get the defendant guilty.

Which is what Vincent Bugliosi is apparently doing now with his Kennedy book.
Yeah, he's another guy whose thinking I really have a strong distaste for. I can't speak for Bugliosi, but there's something rotten about Posner. Posner represents some deep kind of stinky establishment point of view that has to be imposed. He's also dishonest. Just when you read the twelve or fifteen references to me in his book, I'm a straw man, that's all. He just throws me in to chew me down. The president of this computer company that did this analysis pointed out that the computer analysis in defense of Oswald was not used, it was just the prosecutor's computer thesis. And that was used as a big thing at the time, but it doesn't hold up. Check me out on that. Number two, his book was presold. The cover of *U.S. News & World Report,* Harry Evans pushing the shit out of that book, buying ad after ad. Didn't sell, but creating a media stir. And the pickup in the newspapers and magazines. Again, it's the same group. *U.S. News & World* was to me always the rag that led the way for the official story. Always. It attacked Martin Luther King

back in the sixties for a lot of this stuff that was untrue. It's always had this investigative, Mike Wallace–*60 Minutes* intensity of going after something, and always one-sided.

Washington Post reporter George Lardner read an early version of *JFK* and wrote a scathing article accusing you of playing fast and loose with history. You said he had an ax to grind, and he responded by saying: "Is Oliver Stone ever going to shut up? His problem is, it's intrinsically illogical to take a real event, twist it, and describe it as a metaphor for truth. You can't build a metaphor for truth on a pile of falsehoods." Does he have a point?

I would agree that his statement is a correct one: that you cannot build a metaphor upon a pile of falsehoods. I would disagree with Mr. Lardner on what he calls falsehoods, because he didn't really debate at all the statements that the film made. Mr. Lardner has been one of the great obstructionists towards open inquiry since the beginning of the whole affair. He's been on the case since the middle sixties. He attacked Garrison. He has a vested interest, and it's a huge conflict of interest. I called *Washington Post* editor Ben Bradlee from the set and said this was an inherently unbalanced article. Bradlee acted so condescending, so arrogant. These guys are living in another world. The attitude was, "Who is this punk?" At that point we hired Frank Mankiewicz, an old pro in Washington, to help us understand the byways of Washington. Of course, they then criticized us for getting our "flak." Here they opened a broadside: Lardner was prowling around the set trying to find all the dirt he could. He got a copy of the script—which is a violation of copyright. For the press to support that was wrong. It's like stealing plans out of a computer and saying, "This is what they're building." They treated it like the Pentagon Papers. They said, "What does Stone think, the script is private?" Yes, it is private! It is not fucking public. And also, a first draft is quite different from a last draft. I've had stolen drafts on *Wall Street, Nixon, JFK*. This is dangerous territory.

Woody Allen doesn't even let his actors see the entire script.

Why is he concerned? It's not exactly like he's writing *JFK* or something. He's writing movies that probably not that many people are going to want to read (*chuckles*). But getting back to Lardner—who is he to say that he knows the difference of the falsehoods when he's been part of the falsehoods for so long? And he has *not* reported a lot of the important things in the case.

J. Mira Kopell at UC Berkeley felt that the implication of Lyndon Johnson's involvement in Kennedy's assassination caused serious doubt:

"Stone has planted a diseased tree in the center of his historical land-scape of deeply rooted truths. As a result, the whole forest withers and dies."
She's an enemy of the film too probably. What can I say? The way your ene-mies go after a film is, they go after a detail. They find details that are wrong. A Sam Donaldson or a Bob Costas will go after a detail, and then they'll say, "As a result, the whole forest withers." This is typical criticism, what they do to tear down. It's very bad reasoning and bad analogies. It doesn't work. Be-cause a detail might be wrong, it doesn't mean the whole is wrong. Or the spirit of the whole.

If you've seen the film twice, you'd know that all the possibilities, sugges-tions, hypotheses are prefaced by *ifs* and *supposes*. It's very clear in that regard. It never says that Johnson ordered the murder of Kennedy or was complicit in the conspiracy to kill him. It says that he had to know more after the fact, and that he participated in the coverup. That he was a part of a larger con-spiracy to conceal the truth from the investigation—and that I stand by. And he himself said there's a Murder Incorporated down in the Caribbean. John-son knew the score. And I believe that those bullets that went to Kennedy, if you remember, they flew right over Johnson's head. And he was the first guy down. He heard the warning shots: which is, you play ball with what's going on or the same thing can happen to you, LB.

But in your gut, do you think Johnson was involved?
It may not have gone to the top in the Kennedy assassination. It's a tricky thing. Costner as Garrison says *coup d'état* has to work, because you pardon yourself if you get in. It's really clear. It's only treason if it doesn't work (*laughs*).
Why did you dismiss the notion that Jimmy Hoffa and the Mafia were responsible for JFK's death?
Certainly gangster elements were used by the CIA for political murder, no question. They were used in France during and after World War II, to keep the docks running in Marseilles—heavy amount of assassinations. They probably bumped off a few Germans and a few Frenchmen. They learned how from the Germans, the French, and the British. Those were the masters of political murder. Look at history. Then it came over here. Allen Dulles is a very compromised man—both sides: money, connections. De Gaulle fought against Dulles, because he had very few allies as he tried to maintain a free-French position. He was the most sophisticated man politically of our era, and he raised doubt about Vietnam, Cuba, and about Kennedy's assassina-tion. So, using gangster elements is an age-old thing. But for the Mob to or-ganize something of this capacity, where you have to not only knock off the

president but get your men out, get the weapons in and out, and get a patsy to fall for it, and get a history on the patsy—a profile that's going to make the newspapers within two hours—get all that working and not give it away . . . it's a complicated hit. It takes fucking military to do that. Military are the only people in the world who have that sense of hierarchy. I can walk you through any unit, you can get six or seven guys who will kill anything because they are told to, and they will shut up about it and take it to their grave. They wouldn't use fucking Mob guys to take a hit, it's stupid. It was military. There was no security—where was the security that day? Open windows all along the parade route. That's a classic, primer one. People with umbrellas all along the route. It was just bizarre. It was all set.

On the issue of historical responsibility, you've pointed out that directors Bob Zemeckis in *Forrest Gump* and Ron Howard in *Apollo 13* have not exactly met theirs. What disturbs you about those films and how they were directed?
I like Ron Howard and Bob Zemeckis, they're really good guys. I don't want to make any sub-headlines here, because Zemeckis is on the cutting edge of what we're doing technically, I always look forward to his films. *Gump* was brilliantly done. But I do fault the historical message. It was an avoidance message. An avoidance of our past. I was disturbed that anyone who committed to society ended up getting really fucked. Anyone who committed to a behavior, to a role play, beyond being the *idiot savant*, there was no role. Robin Wright dies, Gary Sinese. There was no positive role model beyond the *idiot savant*. It's a Voltairean tale. That's the beauty of it, why it was so successful—it's *Candide* in the 1990s. And brilliantly conceived. Hats off! *Chapeaux bas!* But it bothers me, the moral essence of it. Just does. There was no responsibility for Vietnam, and also, Vietnam was rendered in a very pictorial, romantic way, as a baptism by fire for poor Forrest. It was not really believable.

   Apollo 13 was very well done, but again, at its essence it was a blind celebration of America. There was no critical standard applied by that picture to American consciousness. It was blind patriotism. It works at the box office, but what are the moral consequences of that? These directors make a lot of money, but they are promoting, especially *Apollo 13,* a surefire brand of patriotism that I don't think is correct. We have to move beyond that to a higher consciousness to save this planet. Thinking just America first is not going to do it. It's going to get us into deeper and deeper trouble.

At the Academy Awards gay protesters yelled, "Shame, shame," at you because of how you portrayed gays in *JFK*. Do such protests annoy you?

They said the homosexuality was gratuitous because of the Clay Shaw–David Ferrie connection. But it was not gratuitous. One of the essences of Garrison's case is he had an alias of Clay Bertrand in the New Orleans homosexual underground. Many people, including David Ferrie, knew this name of Bertrand, including the witnesses Garrison tried to bring to trial. I got the requisite amount of postcards from gay members, they're organized that way. And I got the same thing again with *Larry Flynt* from women against pornography. They boycott my movies. By now I would imagine that there are very few people left who can go see my movies (*laughs*). I need a new generation, because I've exhausted the old.

Joe Pesci, who gave a memorable performance as David Ferrie, said he would never work with you again. "He's a terrific director," he said, "but . . . "
". . . he's a piece of shit as a person." I was sad to see that.

He said you beat up your crew and actors. Does it hurt you to hear this?
Yeah, sure. I like Joe, he's a good guy, I enjoyed working with him. I think I got a great performance from him.

Did he call you to deny saying what he said?
No, he wrote me a note of apology for saying it publicly. But the sentiments he felt the same. He's known to have a temper. Joe's a strange guy. In his own way he probably felt threatened, but I didn't pick up on it. How many actors get called a "piece of shit"? You know who else did that to me recently, out of the blue? Gore Vidal was all over the goddamn newspapers saying he hated my work and that he had blown me off when I tried to get him to do *Alexander the Great* for me. Which was bullshit. I was shocked to see that because we were at a private party, so somebody leaked it. It might have been Gore. He said I had no talent at all and that he didn't want to work with me. It was an embarrassing, violent, angry, aggressive quote. I've very rarely seen that degree of hostility. I've known Gore Vidal for years, off and on. In fact, when he offered to write *Alexander the Great* for me in 1990 at his villa in Ravello, Italy, I turned his ultra-homoerotic suggestions down. He's bitten by a temper. It's festered for years. People react to me without my knowing it. Artists are very jealous, angry people. They're the most envious people in the world. I don't like to hang out with them. Artists are very sheeplike, they'll all go in the same direction. When some popular thing happens, a new fad, they all run in that direction like sheep off a cliff. Most of them don't stand for something. Most of them are whores. Brando's right. They're talented whores, but they're whores. If you could convince

them that gratuitous violence is the most important aspect of our society and it is a noble thing, it's sacred, they will make pictures with gratuitous violence, most of them, tomorrow.

I've taken hits from every front: presidents, senators, politicians, artists. It's a lesson in my life. My father used to say, "Don't be too sensitive," because I was an only child and I was sensitive. I would really sulk, I hated to be criticized. My dad always used to piss me off when he'd say, "Don't sulk." And so I entered a profession that's extremely damaging to the ego. It's all about ego. If you can get a healthy relationship with your own ego, then you'll be all right. All these are mirrors: Joe Pesci, Gore Vidal. Their opinion is their opinion. Gore probably wishes he could write a good movie. He's never written a good movie. He's at best a fair novelist. So he's probably jealous. Because of the power of imagination that my films have had on history. And he wants that. His hatred may be based on the fact that he hates himself in some way, or there's an envy that comes because perhaps he views himself as having failed in that historical mission. Personally I don't think he knows me at all. Joe Pesci doesn't really know me. He probably had an image in his mind of: "Fucking director, he's making me do this fucking faggot, I hate fucking faggots. I am not a faggot. And all this fucking guy wants me to do is blow this fucking sleazy faggot. I've got to wear this fucking hairpiece, and I feel like a piece of shit." And then I called him up a year or two later and asked him to play Hoover in *Nixon*. (*As Pesci:*) "All you want me to do is suck somebody's fucking dick!" So I'm tying in, in some fucking way, to his fucking image of some fucking faggot in New Jersey that he hates right from the age of eleven! (*laughing*)

Were Harrison Ford and Mel Gibson your first two choices to play Jim Garrison?

This is a tricky story. There's a short list at Warners, and those three [including Costner] are there. Harrison never said yes, Mel I talked to a long time before it was ready, but I went to Kevin just overlapping Harrison. Harrison is their first choice for a lot of stuff. They were making the movie for $42 million, I'm trying to make them happy, and I had no problem with any of those three actors. But Kevin I chased to England, and he didn't say yes, but his wife made the difference, and Mike Ovitz. Kevin had promised her to take some time off, and she told him to do the movie because it was important.

Before Donald Sutherland, did you go after Marlon Brando to play that mysterious character in *JFK*?

Yeah. First he called me because he liked *Platoon*, so he talked to me about war. He wanted to meet me. I went to his house, but he wouldn't talk there, he felt the government was picking up the airwaves, so he came out, and I had to follow him in his car down into this canyon next to his house. He was barefoot, and he walked over to some bushes, and he sat there, and I had to sit in the bushes with him. We started to talk, and people would walk by in this park, and they must have looked over at the two of us in the bushes and wondered who was this guy, he's crazy? He was big and heavy, but he was very bright. Very sensitive man.

You've been interested in another victim of assassination, Martin Luther King Jr. The King family doubts that James Earl Ray was the sole assassin of Martin Luther King Jr. What're your thoughts?
I'm probably going to cut my own throat, but I know a lot about the case. I met recently with James Earl Ray. We approached the King people three years ago about a movie we wanted to do called *Memphis*.

And you wanted to use Cuba Gooding Jr. long before he won his Oscar.
Yeah, how'd you know that? Wow, that's amazing. We talked to Cuba before he was famous. But we couldn't get financing for it. We didn't have a script either. I turned the project over to my Nixon cowriters, and they just didn't solve it. It's in redevelopment now with Warners. Jerry Weintraub owns a book by Dr. William Pepper called *Orders to Kill,* which is a very good book about his client, James Earl Ray. Pepper's been on the case for twenty years, he's a barrister in England. I respect him greatly. We've combined forces. Not doing an assassination movie *only,* we're doing the life. If you remember *JFK,* there was no character who played JFK. In this case, *Memphis,* we would have a main character playing King. People have really distorted this already. *Time* and *Newsweek* mentioned me negatively. The *New York Times* had a ridiculous column the other day headlining: "James Earl Ray is the only killer of Martin Luther King." They told one-sided stuff. They're really selling us hard on that issue.

But *Primetime* did a piece on the guy who supposedly confessed to being involved with the assassination.
Jowers. Yeah, Jowers has made a confession, but nobody's prosecuted him. Jowers knows something. But Pepper's book shows you what's going on behind the scenes. It's not just about J. Edgar Hoover, it's about the military intelligence that was tracking King for years. Going back to the turn of the century, they were tracking black leaders.

The *Primetime* story showed there might be links to Lyndon Johnson.

I can't say that because Jack Valenti will kill me. Johnson was a bastard, man. The King thing may have come from the top. I think it had to. Because I don't think that military people, who I believe are involved, would do something of that nature unless they had a hierarchical okay.

Do you find it curious, though, that it happened when King seemed to have been losing some support among his people?
He was losing it because he had become more controversial. From the Riverside speech and other speeches where he had said the problem is the system. He got off the black civil rights issue as a single issue, and he made it into a multi-issue about the system. That's when he started to lose his own followers. The young blacks thought he was old hat from the fifties, so he was definitely losing power, but he was also gaining power, because the March on Washington was a big issue. He was going to bring 200,000 black people to Washington, D.C., the following year, and I believe he could have. The Army was much more concerned about a revolution, and a mutiny of their forces in Vietnam, than people give credit to. He may have lost power, yes, but he was still a major threat. And he attacked Vietnam. That was his death warrant. One year before his death in April '67 was when he gave the Riverside speech, I believe—it could have been January—but that was his death warrant.

And what about Robert Kennedy's assassination? Again a conspiracy?
Yeah, but that's not just because of the other two. Though I wouldn't separate RFK from JFK. I feel there were similar patterns between all three murders. The ballistics, the primary evidence, the prima facie evidence, Sirhan's nature, what Kennedy had changed—he was a new Kennedy in '68, he was not the old Robert Kennedy. His avowal to end the war in Vietnam. He would have been president. He would have beaten Nixon, absolutely. He was a serious threat to this country. Three leaders got removed in the sixties. Three. Four, if you include Nixon, who fell on his own sword.

There was also Malcolm X.
Well, I don't include him as an idealist. He's more of a sectarian. He's more in the George Wallace category for me. But those three men were really idealists. You can compare it to the Gracchi brothers in Rome in the 130 B.C. era. The two brothers were reformers, idealists, they remind me of the Kennedys, and they were both assassinated.

You've said that no topic is sacred. Could you imagine taking on Salmon Rushdie's *Satanic Verses*?

Probably at the time I said it, yes. Now, I'm not so sure, because of my perception of a reduced capability, capacity. I'm not sure that's not right of me to say that; perhaps I'm giving up mentally too easily. Perhaps I should be testing myself more.

I don't understand Islam. Islamic scholars say it's not this violence that they talk about. But it seems to me as a religion it promotes the concept of war and violence in pursuit of one god, Allah, Jihad.

I was at dinner the other night with some of the older denizens of Hollywood, like Billy Wilder. Warren too (*laughs*). I had a wonderful moment with Jeanne Martin [Dean Martin's second wife]. I loved Dean Martin. Apparently he had gotten hot, they're selling the rights to his life to Marty. I met Dean once—it took a while to get a meeting because he was a little tired and dazed. She remembered the meeting, and she was telling me her perceptions of his self-destructiveness. She said to me, "Don't do that." She's a tough old dame, not intimidated by anybody; she's hardball. "You've still got a long way to go, you've still got another ten or twenty years. You've got to do like John Ford, you've got to go the distance. You can't feel sorry for yourself now." She read some stuff about me, and she said, "Because they are pissing on you, don't hurt yourself as a result of it. Don't destroy yourself because you've got to make part two of your life."

Do you feel you are self-destructive?
Sure. Haven't you seen that yet? Maybe you don't because you're seeing me in a productive place, working. But I have a very strong self-destructive streak. My whole life. Going to Vietnam was very much that. And it continued in many ways: self-abuse, self-flagellation, whipping myself, destroying my confidence in myself. Having no confidence. Being nervous. In the weirdest way, I've backed into this position (*laughs*). I know I project confidence, perhaps because I didn't have it when I was young. It's the old thing about Demosthenes putting rocks in his mouth. Maybe you overcompensate to try and get some courage because you don't feel that you have it.

[On June 9, 1999, Stone would be arrested in Beverly Hills for driving under the influence. A search of his 1987 Mustang turned up a small amount of hashish. Two months later he pleaded guilty to drug possession and no contest to driving under the influence and was ordered into a rehabilitation program. During his three-year probation sentence he could drive only to and from work and to the drug rehab program.]

Your self-doubt is surprising.
The worst thing that can happen to a filmmaker is to have doubt. Then you doubt everything. You doubt your place in the world. That happens. There's

been a cumulative energy that has hurt me. What's the point? Those people who hurt, what do they get out of it? What, at the end of the day, do they feel good about? Hurting somebody else? What can they take pride in? That maybe their cumulative barbs have stopped some person from making another movie? David Lean lost his appetite and dropped out for a while. I hope I have that freedom and license in my mind, because I've been so criticized for taking license that you shouldn't lose sight of the fact that we need license, we need to feel the wind behind us. You have to be a pirate ship captain. Filmmaking is like hitting different ports. We don't belong to any flag, but we kind of make it. And you need confidence to do that. Sometimes I'm afraid I'm losing it.

One of the sharpest criticisms against you is that you portray women one-dimensionally in your films.
I disagree. *Heaven and Earth* has flaws, like every other film that I've made, but I think it's one of the most beautiful films that I've done. It makes me cry. I don't know why the critics got on that film so badly, it really deserves some notice. Not only was I white doing an Asian experience, but I was also a male doing a female. A lot of angry feminists didn't give it a chance.

Look, I worked with Joan Allen on *Nixon*. I love Juliette Lewis's performance in *Natural Born Killers*. Sissy Spacek as Elizabeth Garrison delivered what I asked, because it was a character who I had met and knew a little bit about. And I like Kathleen Quinlan in *The Doors,* and Meg Ryan got some decent notices. So I have worked with women all through my career.

You've worked with women, but the memorable parts are the men you've directed.
I know where I got the rap—it was based on an unfortunate one-two perception: one was *Platoon.* I took these boys into a training camp. We wouldn't have been able to have made as good a movie without that camp, but that drew a lot of attention. It being a man's movie, I was perceived as a sort of Sessue Hayakawa in *The Bridge on the River Kwai.* A man's guy. There were no women in the movie. And then coming after that was *Wall Street,* and frankly I didn't get along with either of the two actresses in that movie [Darryl Hannah and Sean Young]. But there were interesting roles of women in *The Hand.* There are two women in there, Annie McEnroe and Andrea Markovicci, one's the wife, the other's the girlfriend. There's an interesting psychological portrait that develops between the man and his possessiveness between the two women. So I haven't shied away from women from the beginning.

If I had a highlight clip when I'm ninety, one of the most memorable scenes I would put on it would be Hiep Thi Le with Tommy Lee Jones [in

Heaven and Earth] when they talk about reincarnation. He starts the scene by almost killing her, then he turns the rifle on himself and tries to shoot himself, she talks him out of it, and they unite. It was a bold discovery of a mutual spirit, when she says, "I too was a soldier." It was a great moment, because she talks about her own soul. It's one of the best scenes I've ever done.

What other scenes would you put on that clip?
With a woman? Pat Nixon in the bedroom, or the dining table. I think Mallory [in *Natural Born Killers*] is a great creation—it's Quentin Tarantino's creation, but we fleshed her out quite a bit. Juliette Lewis gave one of her best performances, she became Mallory Knox. I can't tell you how much work is involved in that. So there's three women right there. What do I have to do? What do I have to prove? I'm not going to do anything for politically correct reasons or to correct impressions, it's the wrong way to work.

As a male I'm attracted to women, so it's more delightful to work with somebody who is your opposite. Although I appreciate men and enjoy working with them. If you start disliking people, then you've got to stop being a director, unless you go another way, like a European way where you become sour and cynical and you view the world so sardonically, and all the actors fit into your pattern.

By the way, who was your first choice to play Mallory?
I offered Jodie Foster Mallory Knox. She was afraid of it. That's what her reps told me. Then Winona Ryder came up. But I think Juliette Lewis was born to play that role.

The charge that male artists can't create female characters of depth is not new. Joyce Carol Oates cites Bellow, Faulkner, and Melville who've failed.
That's not true. It's like saying a white man can't do a black man's story. Or a black man doesn't understand a white man. It's all sectarianism, and it's truly ugly and hypocritical. Artists shouldn't do that. And they constantly do that to each other because they're trying to get their own turf. It's the cheapest form of criticism. When *Heaven and Earth* came out, they ignored it and instead were writing about *The Scent of Green Papaya* because it was made by a Vietnamese. It was fine in its own right, but it had nothing to do with my movie. But it was used to say, "That's by a Vietnamese and is a real sensitive story, and here's this American who can't. . . . " They didn't look at my movie.

Both that one and *Nixon* were big movies, I made massive efforts on them, they're some of my best work, and they're unknown movies. *Nixon* is more known than *Heaven and Earth*. Warren Beatty told me he saw *Nixon* on cable. He had problems because we had a bit of a falling out, we had talked about him playing Nixon. But he didn't agree with the script. Still, he had the decency and generosity to pick up a phone after he had seen it and said it was great. He said there was such an outpouring of energy. A lot of people do that with me when my films come out. That's why I wish I could keep my name out of it, just put out the film. People are reacting to my name.

In *Heaven and Earth* you aged Joan Chen to play a peasant mother. How great a stretch was it for her?
She did an interesting job. She gummed herself up, she put black gum all over her. I made them go to Vietnam early, bad guy that I am, and work on a farm (*laughs*). I insisted that they live the farm life. I wanted to get out of the city. Le Ly Hayslip is a peasant, there's a strong earth quality to all Asian peasants. Joan, to me, was the verbal, Shanghai, corrupt, literally out of wanting to be an aristocrat, having no desire to be a peasant. Getting Joan to go back, walk around as a peasant with betel nut, was an interesting journey for me.

Not to say for her!
She ended up complaining that trip that some kind of worm had gotten through the bottoms of her feet and she'd gotten some sickness. She said, "I can act it." But I don't buy that. I said, "You can act it, yes, but show me you have humility too that you can learn that process by which those people came into being. Just reinvigorate yourself." How many times will Joan Chen in her life put a bag of rice on a bamboo pole and carry it with another person? When you do that, you link up with that person, it's an energy between people. I shot a documentary during that movie, staging different phases of planting and harvesting rice, it's a fascinating process. Rice is a key to the movie, because if you understand the relationship to the rice, it goes to the whole earth thing, it gets to the sky, comes back down to the soul, the spirit, and the reincarnation, and the land, the land, the land. And that's the hardest thing to put across: the land. That's why we took such pains to make beautiful shots. We shot great landscapes all over. The colors and textures of that movie are luscious. I love that movie. I just wish I could go back and cut it again, because I cut it too short. I made it for a commercial Western audience, and I was doomed.

How much more time should you have allowed?
Twenty-five minutes. It was two hours and fifteen minutes, which was already pretty outrageous for that kind of movie. I needed 2:40. There were

two solutions: one, I needed to get inside her more early on, so you'd follow
her, because too many people complained that they couldn't follow her, she
was too wooden, and that Tommy Lee was the only guy I pick up on at the
halfway point and he takes me through the rest of the film. We got scared
off some of the village life: we shot a lot more than we used. Then the other
thing I could have done was to edit it the way it was originally written,
which went back and forth in time. I started in Vietnam, then flipped to
America when she first arrived with Tommy Lee Jones and met Debbie
Reynolds at the one-third point, and then out of America she starts to get
another cycle of problems and out of depression her mind wanders back to
Vietnam seeking solace again, so you go through a whole Vietnam episode
where she becomes a hooker and city life almost destroys her. Then that
need for liberation sends her back into an American fantasy. It's like a five-
part sonata: Vietnam-America-Vietnam-America. Great idea. I cut it like that,
but it didn't work. I'd love to have all the elements of that film in my hand
today. I'd go back in that editing room for a month and just sit there.

**Still, you must be proud to have accomplished your trilogy of Vietnam-
related films.**
It wasn't really a trilogy, because a trilogy is the same character, but each one
took me to another area. *Platoon* was into the self-contained world of the
jungle and the men who fought the war. *Born on the Fourth* was about before
going and coming back, it was about America. The third one was really
about Vietnam more, and how Vietnam blended with America and what the
mutual experience was in a large sense. It was through the eyes of a woman
only because the book was so good and moving. If the book had been about
a man, I don't know if I would have done the movie.

**How important is the press for the kind of pictures you make, espe-
cially ones that quickly disappear, like *Nixon* and *Heaven and Earth*?**
We needed a groundswell for those pictures from the press, and we didn't
get it. Making those kinds of movies—I can't do it. Do you understand? If I
know there's going to be the lack of a groundswell, I have to figure out a way
to make pictures that would appeal to stars . . . which is very limiting. I
don't want to sell my name. I have no ego about that. I just want to make
ideas that are provocative and growing with the time. I want to stay in touch
with my time. I don't want to make bad films. I don't want to just be making films because I have the clout to do them. I'd rather stop and retreat. If I
don't have anything to say about what's going on, if all of a sudden I don't
recognize this splurge of attitude that's out there—and I don't. Some of it really puzzles me. All those attitude films like *Pulp Fiction*, which is about

nothing but attitude and behavior, being cool. There's been a slew of that stuff. Where do I fit? I don't know. I don't have that much interest or a role in that, and I don't think I should try to be that. I should stay with what I know, and even if I'm not ultra-popular, if there's a few people who dig it, it's going to last, the message will go on. Maybe I'll be watched again in 2030. Maybe I've got to be after-the-fact to do it.

You're talking as if you were out of the business.
Sometimes I feel like I am.

On the contrary, you've got to be one of the most in-demand directors in the business.
No, I don't feel that.

Well, what do you feel about John Grisham, who said in *Vanity Fair*: "Oliver Stone always takes the high ground in defending his dreadful movies. . . . But there is no humor in *Natural Born Killers*. It is a relentlessly bloody story designed to shock us and to numb us further to the senselessness of reckless murder."
Sarah Edmondson and Ben Darras apparently watched *Natural Born Killers* six times in one night, did drugs, and then went on a killing spree. One of their victims was a friend of Grisham's. Other copycat killings occurred in Texas, Utah, Georgia, Massachusetts—putting *Natural Born Killers* in a class by itself, according to *Vanity Fair*. It's linked to more copycat killings than any film ever made. Grisham wants you in court over this: "It will take only one large verdict against the likes of Oliver Stone . . . then the party will be over."
My God. Grisham's world would be a nightmare for everyone, not just me. It would be a legal paradise for lawsuits. An idea would become a product, and he's arguing for product liability. Beethoven could be sued for inspiring violence or aggression for the Seventh Symphony. Picasso with his fractured people for mutilation from people who didn't understand it or for neurotic reactions. Every single art form would be subject to review. It would be the end of what we call civilization. The concept of civilized debate, that you could have an argument in public without consequences of being libeled. Free speech, First Amendment, I very strongly believe in. Freedom of expression. Where it becomes hate speech, there is an interesting argument. The Fourteenth Amendment.

Natural Born Killers, unless you misunderstand it totally, as Grisham has, is an artistic expression, it's a satire. It was done exactly in that spirit to show back, as in a mirror, partly the state of the mental society as it existed in the

early 1990s America—and still exists. The love of sensationalism; the passing
of sensationalism as news; news for profit; glorification of that world and
making it news—it becomes the lead news. Look at our society in '92, '93,
'94. What had happened? Massive change in the news, from Tonya Harding,
which was front-page headlines in the *New York Times* six or seven times for
two stupid ice skaters fighting over a little riff. It shows the degree of trivialization of the news. Then we had the Menendez brothers, which occupied a
lot of news and TV time. What was it? Two kids' murder of their parents.
The same goes for the woman who cut off her husband's penis. It orgasmed
on the greatest television event of recent times: the O. J. Simpson murder.
Which was a total waste of our American time. They absorbed the airwaves,
the newspapers. It bored me, I never even followed the details of the case. I
don't have time—you can compartmentalize your life, or you can spend it
going through trivia. Americans love to get into these occasional fashion
fads, that will become the hottest thing for half a year, it's a very American
thing. But you have to think of all the money that was made off of the O.J.
story. All the advertising money, the sponsorship. Also think about how
much it replaced things of time and value that one could have been given information about: foreign countries, health, education, welfare, space. There
are so many important things for us to think about as a populace, hopefully
it's the media's responsibility to bring that to our attention, but they're no
longer doing that. It's what works. What gets the news.

You cannot sell the news. And the news is subject to interpretation. But
what we get on the news is the American interest, nightly. You don't get the
Iranian interest, the Afghani interest, the Russian interest, it's a very narrow-
minded news. And it's pacifying news for the most part, or trivialization of
the news. It's terrible. The average kid in Japan or Europe is more knowledgeable about American history than most American kids that I meet. It's
very sad. And Mickey and Mallory is a total send-up of that. Whether you
say it has a sense of humor or not.

**Grisham has replied that it's not a matter of the First Amendment but
one of responsibility: "Should Stone and his ilk be held responsible if,
and only if, a direct causal link can be proven between a movie and the
violence inspired by it?"**
Listen, I cannot be responsible . . .

But does it disturb you? *Vanity Fair* **took your side, but did write that
you "seem oblivious to any sense of responsibility. . . . Worse, shown
the ways in which confused youths interpret his sophisticated message,**

he does not seem inclined to reflection concerning his artistic methods. . . . He doesn't yet see that artists have to be accountable too."
Uch, I read that. That's the kind of talk of the man-in-the-middle Nazi concentration camp guard, that's pablum, it ruins the culture. Because the guy who's saying that is really calling for censorship. When you're saying an artist must accept responsibility, you're assigning the role of responsibility to yourself and to the state, or to a board, or censors, or whatever. Who are you to speak of what's right and wrong? An artist is precisely anarchic because he deals in ideas. And these ideas are explosive. I never said movies are not dangerous, they can be very dangerous to the mind. But they're ideas, we don't act out on them. If someone walks into a movie theater and literally believes that is the real thing, that is a person who has no ability to cross the line and understand that movies are illusions.

***Natural Born Killers* has been compared to *A Clockwork Orange*, which also spawned copycat violence, to the point where Kubrick has not allowed the film to be shown in England. Is Kubrick wrong?**
I don't know the circumstances of the case. In none of these reported cases by the media was it proven. If anything it was talked about briefly, mentioned, and often erroneously. I continue to believe that a pattern of behavior is set, a psychotic pattern of violence is set in that person. The time bomb that that person is, is going to be set off by anything, it could be an argument with his mom, a bad dinner, getting fucked over in a delicatessen . . . it could be anything. It could be a movie. But that doesn't mean it's the root cause.

But when you hear that these two people watched your film six times in a row and took acid and went on a killing spree, doesn't that get to you somehow?
I'm not responsible for the audience and their reaction to my movie. I'm not. I'm responsible to myself and my sense of my own integrity to what I do and put out there. It has to work for me. If there's a psycho, a moron, somebody who says, "That's the way it happened, Mickey and Mallory are my heroes," then that person is really lacking the ingredients in which he can live in society, period. That person is fucked if he'd seen *Pulp Fiction* or *Bugsy* or *Trainspotting*, it doesn't matter. Anything can kick it off. Where does it end? If someone saw my movie ten times on acid and went out and killed somebody and said he did it because of the movie, I would seriously doubt it. I'd go back and examine his root behavior, which, by the way, when Grisham's people [Sarah Edmondson and Ben Darras] were examined, we find

a whole history of errant behavior. I don't know if they made that clear in that article by that moron in *Vanity Fair. Moron!* The guy's a moron. He didn't even talk to me. He made his judgment calls based on my papers. His attitude is fucked. Between the lines he's saying, artists must be responsible. Think about that. That's what Hitler said. That's what the fucking Russians said. The social realism school said artists must be responsible. That was the first call in the revolution, and that was the beginning of the squeeze. If you must be responsible, therefore you cannot be irresponsible. When you start to say that shit, who is declaring what's responsible and what's irresponsible? Then you start to get bored—society, censorship. That is precisely what that guy is saying. If he had any understanding of what we do, he would allow people who make this stuff to determine themselves their limits. If you want to set societal limits with sex and violence by putting ratings boards for the movies . . . we live with it. But then artists can work inside that and maybe make it work better. But this movie [*Natural Born Killers*] was done as a mirror, as a send-up. I adopted the style of television: loud, aggressive, blaring. That was an aesthetic choice. So those who criticize the film often will say I'm exploiting what I'm attacking. It's absolutely not true. It's an aesthetic choice made to show back at society. What the critics are saying is, bring the film down, make it duller, don't make it as exciting, make it quieter, more detached. All right, how do you do that? That's an aesthetic style. Perhaps man-bites-dog is better for some people because it has sort of a documentary flatness to it, but that wasn't the style of this movie. It was an aesthetic choice to go out there and say to people: this is what we are, this is what you're getting, this is the world you're surrounded by, this is our valueless, junk-filled society. Some people say, "Robert Downey's my hero," when they see that fucking movie. I still can't believe that! He's a shallow, craven, monster. And people come up to me and say, "He was cool. I really felt sorry when that guy died." *What!?* I'm not responsible if that's what they think. Those people are really fucked up. They believe all this media shit. He's not my hero in the movie. All five people in the movie were scum. But Mickey and Mallory, because they were young and had the ability to change, were less scum, and they found their way out. They escaped the media society by killing the fucking camera man. And that was their escape. To get away from the madness. The only way to get out of the madness was to turn anti-media and disappear.

But they were a crucial part of the madness.
They were a creation of the madness. They were senseless products of their environment too. Rodney Dangerfield as her father. . . . The idea was that when they got bitten by the poison, the knowledge, the snake, the Indian,

that's when they got past the consciousness. That's why they gave up. After they killed the Indian, the first part was over. The second part was cut to a year later. And Mickey's interview, it's very telling. He says things that are very Nietzschean and very interesting concepts.

Did you get a lot of that from Charlie Manson's TV interviews?
A lot of it was Manson-based, because I was fascinated by that interview, it was brilliant. It was hilarious, because Geraldo Rivera was doing exactly the same thing, he was being superior—"because you're scum, you're in prison, I never did what you did, therefore I'm a better human being." It was an interesting idea, but Manson punctured it and made fun of it. He ran around in circles with it. He laughed. It's a great interview. I saw the unedited version.

I don't condone what Manson did, but he himself said, "I am the devil in this country. I am the evil you want." He grew up the product of displacement. A horrifying existence. Eight years old, he was in a reformatory.

Was it your idea to cast Rodney Dangerfield as the father from hell in *Natural Born Killers?*
I always wanted to work with him. I loved *Back to School.* There are so many of those guys I want to work with that are getting old, but it doesn't come up.

Did you see the anger and negativism in him when you cast him?
Oh yes. Rodney tells a great story, like he came in and wrote all the dialogue. It was that thing Fellini did, *Satyricon,* the clown with the nose, one of the great Roman archetypes. Rodney struck me as a tremendous comedian. I'm surprised we don't use our comedians more. I love him. I'll never forget when he arrived on location we had a dinner for the crew, and he ate like his dish and two other people's dishes, he brought a couple of girls with him, he had a grand old time, he was fun, he just loved life. He's had a hard life, like most comedians. Imagine me working with him, a big star, telling him what's funny. "Rodney, that *is* funny, you're not reading it right." "What's so funny about this?" he'd ask. Then I'd read it for Rodney and he'd say, "Oh, okay, I'll do something with it." But it was hard to convince him that rape, incest, daughters, was funny, I loved that. I'd love to work more with him. I would like to work with Charlton Heston, Bob Mitchum, I wanted to work with Burt Lancaster so badly—I offered him something in *Wall Street,* but it didn't work out.

Last questions concerning Grisham. Have you ever read any of his work?

I've tried, it's not my kind of stuff. He, on the contrary, is a bit of a hyp-
ocrite. I saw *A Time to Kill* as a movie, and I found that to be hypocritical.

Is he suing you now?
Grisham didn't sue us. The lawyer in Louisiana sued Warner Bros. and me
and various people. There is a lawsuit that will work its way out. There's no
way, unless Louisiana goes into some kind of primitivism like Mississippi
did in 1962, but then it would be thrown out on any appeal.

**Because of your financial situation, would it hurt you to make a small
independent film?**
Oh yeah. I could do it, but I would take a beating. What am I talking about?
I didn't take any money to do *U-Turn*. I took a nominal salary and basically
am riding the gross. Which, being a dark film, I don't know if that was too
smart a move.

**You tried to hold up the publication of John Ridley's novel, *Stray Dogs*,
so it wouldn't give away the ending to *U-Turn*. Now, if someone wanted
to make a film of your novel, would you agree to hold up its publication
until after the film? Wouldn't you fear it being then labeled a noveliza-
tion rather than an original work?**
At this point, no, because the book came before the movie. In the case of Ridley, he had no publication. It had been turned down, plus the screenplay
had been turned down. Whatever they say, they were around. He used the
movie deal to force the publication. And it's a thriller with a plot that you
don't give away. It's totally different.

Are you angry with Ridley?
Yeah, I think he's an opportunist. Considering that I also helped produce his
movie? And I asked him to hold it off? What does he get from this? Money?
Is a few hundred thousand dollars the issue? The ethical thing to have done
was to release the book in conjunction with the movie. Instead, he'll bring
out a paperback when the movie comes out. I think he gives opportunism a
bad name.

**Speaking of opportunists, would *The People Versus Larry Flynt* have got-
ten made without your involvement?**
They would have gotten it done without me. But that one I was in at the beginning. I think I helped. Milos Forman had been out of the business several
years. It wasn't that simple or a no-brainer by any means.

What was your involvement?

It's my name. I get involved in how it gets made, who's in it, what kind of script it is. I'm not looking to be the controlling element, but perhaps a helping, guiding one. It's the director's movie, he puts his stamp on it. But I'd like to help create a framework where we'd be proud of the movie. The toughest part was telling Milos how I thought a scene should look, and he's very stubborn in his way. So it was a good mix.

You wrote *Evita*. Did you like the film?

They gave me co-screenplay credit. It missed by a wide mile. I wrote it. Parker—who's got an ego the size of Michael Jordan's presumed dick—says he rewrote it, but it's hard to believe judging by what's on the screen. It doesn't have the soul that it should have had.

Your name has been linked with Hollywood madam Heidi Fleiss, along with Robert Evans, Nicholson, Jon Peters, Dennis Hopper, Charlie Sheen. How damaging is that?

I never met Heidi Fleiss in my life, as far as I know. That surfaced from her boyfriend, the other guy, he threw it out there. I never paid for her services, didn't know her. I knew Charlie, but I never hung around with that crowd. Perhaps because I was a single male at that point my name might have come up. I'm not saying I'm not out there.

Is it true that five of your films—*Salvador, Talk Radio, The Doors, Nixon*, and *Platoon*—are in bankruptcy?

It's a drag. These were independent films, and I can't get access to them. You can't get a *Salvador* video. It's disappeared. Hemdale released it, it was a disaster theatrically, the company went out of business; it did great business for Vestron, which also went out of business. I believe it belongs to Credit Lyonnaise, and they're in trouble because of that asshole from Italy, Giancarlo Paretti, who really screwed it up for all these independents. I don't know the state of the negative, we did it cheaply, we didn't put in any protection, so it's sitting in some vault somewhere in the cheapest possible conditions. It probably looks green and yellow, all the colors might be bled already. *Platoon* is also owned by Hemdale, so there's a confusion on that, although it's a little clearer because Orion distributed it theatrically, but Orion has had so many major problems they haven't issued a new video. *Talk Radio* was with Cineplex Odeon, and I don't know what's going on there, no video is available, it's never on TV. *The Doors* was with Carolco, and they went out of business. So four out of eleven. And now, if Cinergi goes under or is reformed,

Nixon is with them, that will be another one. So those five films are gone in a sense from ability to procreate or recreate.

Well, regardless of who owns your films, you're still making new ones. Assess yourself as a director.
In development. In progress. I've accomplished far more than I ever set out to do. I went further. At NYU film school I had big dreams. Then I had a long period of frustration where I couldn't effect those dreams. Then suddenly I had a period where I could. And that period has become its own self now, and I'm in a new place, a crossroads. I can either go down because some of the feelings of self-destruction can assert themselves again. And partly I can go on and evolve into a new phase. An older phase. Which I hope to do. I can't guarantee it, because it takes tremendous energy to make movies.

ROBERT TOWNE

THOSE OUTSIDE OF THE MOVIE INDUSTRY first came to hear of Robert Towne when Francis Coppola accepted his Oscar for *The Godfather* in 1973. He specifically thanked Towne for writing perhaps the most important scene in that film, the one between Michael Corleone (Al Pacino) and his father (Marlon Brando) when they sat in the Don's backyard and the power between the two men was passed. Towne went on to win an Oscar himself for writing one of cinema's most studied scripts, *Chinatown;* another, *The Last Detail,* garnered him a nomination.

Towne is a man who likes to work for friends, and some of his friends make memorable movies. Besides *The Last Detail* and *Chinatown,* Towne has also worked on three other Jack Nicholson films: *The Missouri Breaks, Drive, He Said,* and *The Two Jakes.* For Warren Beatty he began with a rewrite of *Bonnie and Clyde,* then worked on *The Parallax View, Shampoo, Heaven Can Wait, Reds,* and *Love Affair.* And for his friend Tom Cruise he started with *Days of Thunder,* then *The Firm, Mission Impossible,* and *M:I-2.*

Robert Towne has also had a hand in well over three dozen movies, rewriting scenes or entire scripts and very rarely taking any credit for his work. Though his name may not be attached, Towne's signature is on *The Tomb of Ligeia, Villa Rides, The New Centurions, The Yakuza, Marathon Man, Greystoke, Swing Shift, Eight Million Ways to Die, Tough Guys Don't Dance,* and *Frantic.*

He has also directed three of his screenplays: *Personal Best, Tequila Sunrise,* and *Without Limits,* about the Oregon Olympic runner Steve Prefontaine.

By any standard, Robert Towne, sixty-four, is one of the most influential and sought-after talents in Hollywood. The producer Robert Evans once said of him, "I would rather have the next five scripts of Robert Towne than the next five films of Robert Redford." The critic Pauline Kael once noted that "his characters are so effective on the screen because they have sides you don't expect." Kael also championed *Personal Best,* calling it a "smart and super-subtle movie" that "should be one of the best dating movies of all time, because it pares away all traces of self-consciousness. . . . Only a man who really loves women could have made *Personal Best.*"

Towne grew up in San Pedro, California. He worked summers as a commercial fisherman, dabbled in mortgage banking, and even sold houses one summer in the San Fernando Valley (where he earned a $75 commission for each sale). His father was in the dress business, and Towne has said, "The only thing my father gave me was a love of ladies and an interest in the clothes they wear." He studied acting with Jeff Corey, through whom he first met Jack Nicholson, and they both apprenticed with the B-filmmaker Roger Corman.

No matter where I ran into Bob Towne over the years—at the Playboy Mansion at 3:00 A.M., at one of Goldie Hawn and Kurt Russell's dinner parties, at a movie screening—I always felt I was in the presence of a true Hollywood insider. He was the writer who understood the essence of film writing: without him actors were at a loss for words.

Towne was always very friendly when we talked, and we often wound up sitting opposite each other discussing whatever item was in the news. I left those evenings feeling stimulated and frustrated. Towne was one of those Hollywood figures I wanted to know better. The opportunity to interview him gave me my chance to go further than polite party conversation.

In the summer of 1998 I went to his large, comfortable home in Pacific Palisades, where he showed me some of the rare bird prints on the walls, his swimming pool where he gets his exercise, his upstairs study where he works. We settled down in his living room, lit up cigars, and spoke over two days.

There was a moment when the name Robert Towne emerged from being someone known within the industry to being someone known to the general public, and that was when Francis Coppola accepted his Oscar for *The Godfather* and thanked you for writing a particularly important scene. Did his acknowledgment surprise you?

I knew he was going to do it. Because Francis had asked if I wanted screenplay credit, and I said, "What the fuck for? It was just a scene." I said, "When you win the Academy Award, thank me for the scene." And when he actually got up there to accept the award, knowing Francis, I knew he was going to do it. I was certainly pleased, but I wasn't surprised. I had said it kidding, but I believed there was a good chance he was going to win the Academy Award.

You were brought in late on that film—how did you know it was going to be a classic?
It was obvious. I had seen about seventy-five minutes of the footage, and I was stunned. Francis asked me afterwards what I thought, and I said it was the greatest footage I had ever seen in my life. I could see the look in Francis's eye: he regretted that he had flown me out. Because he thought that I was either a kiss-ass or nuts. He had been so beaten up by other people during the course of that movie that that was not a part of his thinking. You had to come from the outside to see what he had done.

The scene you wrote passing on the mantle from Brando to Pacino wasn't in Mario Puzo's novel, was it?
Puzo never had a scene between them about their lives, and Francis was coming up against it and had no time to think. He was going to lose Marlon, and the scene had to be ready for his last day of shooting. So there was pressure, I had to stay up all night to write it, and I did. A lot was riding on it because Francis felt that their relationship was never going to be resolved without this scene.

How intimidating was that for you, the first time you met Brando?
It was the first and only time I ever met Marlon. It was intimidating. After I wrote the scene, Francis came to pick me up, and I had the two pages on a clipboard and handed it to him. We drove in silence for thirty-five minutes, Francis in the front with the driver. Then he said, "I like it, let's show it to Al." Al read it, and he liked it. "Show it to Marlon," Francis said to me. I didn't know Marlon, and he didn't know me. He was in his makeup chair, and he said, "Read it to me." "Read it to you?" "Yeah." "Both parts?" "Yeah." That immediately pissed me off, because I thought, well, this fucker's got to know that's about as intimidating a thing to do to anybody. I made up my mind about one thing: I ain't gonna read this well (*laughs*). Because I knew if this fucker thinks I'm gonna act for him, that's one mistake I'm not gonna make. He may not like it, but it won't be because I tried to give a performance. So I read it, being thoroughly intimidated, but also I felt the scene

was good. Marlon sat in his chair and said, "Read it again." When he said that, I knew he didn't hate it. Then he did something that only Tom Cruise has ever done since—he took that scene apart, line by line, pause by pause, word by word. There was a moment when he asked me what something meant about Fredo, and I said, "Nothing. He doesn't know what to say." That was okay with him. He just wanted to know absolutely everything in my head that I could tell him about the scene, figuring not unreasonably that since I'd gone to the trouble of writing it that I probably knew at that moment as much about it as anybody else.

Brando has a way of testing people.
In this case he was testing the scene. He liked it and wanted to see if I had put in the kind of thought that he eventually concluded I did. Afterwards Francis asked, "How'd it go?" I said, "He liked the scene." It was a relief. Then the scene had to be printed up and put under the plates and the food and everywhere else for Marlon to be able to see. I wasn't surprised, because he was saying the lines twenty minutes after I showed them to him. The only thing that did surprise me was when he asked me to be on the set that day.

You've been on a lot of sets, rewriting scenes for a lot of well-known movies. Yet you believe it takes a certain arrogance to write a screenplay. Why?
My grandmother was a Gypsy. She was sold to my grandfather, it was his second marriage. She used to read tea leaves and tell the future. Well, screenwriters, in writing a screenplay, have that in common with Gypsies. They're trying to predict the future. What's going to happen at some unnamed time and place when people are going to expend upwards of $50 million, with actors they don't know, with settings and climactic conditions that nobody knows, and what's going to happen when that product is finished and goes into a theater before audiences which may or may not show up. And in that screenplay you're saying that this will be an effective tale, one that will make the investment profitable. That's a level of arrogance that on the face of it is foolish.

If you think that way, how can you even write?
I certainly don't think about that when I'm writing. But if you look at the act from a great distance, that's basically what's involved. But then, like anything, you change that: I'm writing for a certain actor. I know my locations. I'm hoping to get lucky. There are so fucking many variables, the screenplay itself doesn't tie anything or anyone down enough to be able to predict with any certainty whatever the fuck is gonna happen with it! There's just so

much air between the lines—figuratively and literally in a screenplay—how can you tell what's going to happen with it? It's a meaningless document. The screenwriter controls nothing.

He's the Emperor of Ice Cream.
Exactly. But notwithstanding that, there are some of us who try.

You've compared movies to wars: the guy who becomes an expert is the guy who doesn't get killed.
That's right. And it's like a war when it's over with: you can't tell whether you've won or lost. Do you remember the Thurber story "If Grant Had Been Drinking at the Appomattox"? Where Grant thinks he lost to Lee? The truth is, you don't know until somebody tells you that you've won. That's how I feel about it: you don't know who won or who the heroes were. It's like trying to tell who did what to who at an orgy when you were a participant.

You've been through a number of bloody battles, particularly when you directed your first film, *Personal Best*, and wound up sacrificing the one you hoped to next direct, *Greystoke*, about Tarzan.
My life changed forever over *Personal Best*.

Did it make you stronger or more cynical to go through the writers' strike, losing your actors, producer David Geffen making intolerable demands, and your lawsuit against Warner Bros. and SAG [Screen Actors' Guild] for breach of fiduciary duty and fraud?
I don't think it made me more cynical. I survived. If you're dealing with a major studio, or a major star, and also with a billionaire who's hell-bent on opposing you, matching force with force, you're not going to win that battle.

What happened between you and David Geffen?
David and I were at loggerheads. This much I'll say, and it's not generally known: David had taken over the film during the strike, but I hadn't signed documents with David. The fact is, there had been a deal struck even during the strike where David had been financially covered, and that had not been revealed to me. Somebody later did. Assuming at the time that he was at personal risk, I had verbally agreed to the two future commitments he had asked from me. That was the source of our ongoing struggle. He wanted me to fulfill a contractual commitment that was based upon facts that were simply untrue. He had his reasons: he came in and felt he was doing me a favor, and he was. But at the same time I didn't want to feel tied down on the basis of something that wasn't true.

When John Lennon was shot, David's position changed dramatically, because Lennon had recorded for Geffen. It generated a tremendous amount of income for Warner Bros. at a time when they weren't in good shape. So David's request to have Warners take my movie back was at odds with Frank Wells's pledge that it could not come back, but David was able to get the movie back at Warner Bros. And then at Christmas he shut the movie down to see what we had left to shoot. We all had heard rumors that what he was doing was taking away the movie until I signed the documents. Anticipating that, I stole the movie. And the code book. So when they went into the trailer to lock it down, the film wasn't there. I was accused of many things, including being a junkie, but I wasn't accused of the one thing that I was— which was a felon who had stolen $10–15 million of their money. I remember saying to someone, "Why don't they just call me what I am, which is a fucking thief?" Rather than call me a junkie. I stole the negative because, if push came to shove, I felt I'd much rather be sued, because you'd get to court quicker, and if I initiated the suit I'd get [figuratively] killed. They all knew I had the negative, and I did everything but go to the trades to let them know. It was much easier to deal with somebody at that time and place, to cast dispersions on judgments and temperaments because of personal behavior, than the act that was significant, which was, I was a fucking felon!

Let me get this in perspective: you were considered at that time as talented a screenwriter as any in Hollywood. Robert Evans was on record saying he'd rather have your next five commitments than Robert Redford's. Wouldn't you think that guys like Geffen or Wells would avoid giving you such hassles and just let you work?
At Warner Bros. they did that, but those guys were gone by the time this went on. Frank Wells was gone, Ted was gone, all my relations with people I had known intimately were gone. And Geffen felt he made it possible for me to finish that movie and I was an ingrate and owed him, so he lied. So what?

Have you reconciled with Geffen?
We're cordial. You can't afford *not* to be cordial. David Geffen is too rich to be anything but cordial with.

Was the worst result of all of it that you lost *Greystoke*?
Yeah, that's the only really inconsolable event of my professional life. That's as close to death as you can come without it being a living being, for me.

Do you still feel that *Greystoke* was the best thing you ever wrote?

I don't know. I think it would have been the best film I'd ever done if I'd been able to make it.

You never saw the *Greystoke* that Hugh Hudson directed from your script, but did you ever talk to him about it?
I talked to him when he came by to talk to me about the script, which was a disastrous evening. Ovitz arranged that.

Did you ever see what Hudson did with *Revolution*?
Tried to. The only thing I said about him to David was, "In no way am I going to be pissed off with you about *Greystoke,* not after seeing what Hugh Hudson did to the American Revolution."

Your next stab at directing was *Tequila Sunrise* with Kurt Russell, Mel Gibson, and Michelle Pfeiffer. You've said that you hated making it, and hate looking at it. Why?
Tequila is an unfortunate thing for me to discuss. It's a movie whose parts are better than the whole. There's some fine work—Conrad's work, Kurt's work, Mel's. Even Michelle's is good. Michelle has been vocal about disliking the movie and disliking me.

What was it about the chemistry between you that didn't work? And did you ever experience that with anyone before?
Not in that way. She wanted to do it, but she questioned why she had to sleep with the two different characters. I said that's the character. She wanted to change that. At that point I was quite willing to let her go, no harm, no foul. But she said no, she'd do it. The difficulties started there.

Do you feel the end result didn't work?
It could have worked better, but I wouldn't attribute that to her or to her performance. The underlying problem with the movie: if she wasn't going to be killed, he would have to die to prevent it. Then the movie makes sense. Like the moth to the flame, he was attracted to that way of life, and with all the glamour of it, it ends in death—as it can when you fuck around with things like that. That was always the intent—to show the beautiful people, glamorous life, and finally you can't get away with it. The studio would not allow the movie to end that way. So, after *Personal Best,* it would not have been made at all. So I made it figuring I could make it work, but I don't think I quite did.

What were you discovering about directing after these two films?

That directing was a lot more feminine than a lot of people thought it was. Because you're so passive when you're directing. When you're writing, you've got the whole world in your hands—though there's a point where that can get passive too. But when you're a director, from the minute you say, "Action," you're the only fucking asshole on the set that doesn't have a job. Everybody else is doing something. You are doing nothing. But watching. [As Peter Sellers says in *Being There*,] *I like to watch*. And your only job is to be in touch with your feelings. That's very passive. All you're doing is allowing yourself to respond to what's going on in front of your eyes. And do it quickly enough so you're not only able to feel but you're able to articulate how you feel in time to tell the actors before the next take. So first you need to tell yourself what you felt, then figure out how much of that you need to tell the actors. That's a completely passive job. You don't need to know why you're making a movie half the time, or if it's going to be any good, until it's done and then you say, "Oh fuck, that's why I was making it." It's a voyage of discovery, not just of invention.

Is there an advantage to directing your own screenplay?
The advantage of directing a film that you write is that you're seeing the movie as you're writing it, so your preparation is much better. What you lose with having the perspective of another creative force you make up by the force of your own vision. If you are fortunate to have a strong producer, he can provide that perspective that normally would be provided by another writer.

You had a pretty strong producer in Tom Cruise on your latest effort. What sets *Without Limits* apart from your other work?
This is the only time I've ever been involved in the making of a movie about biographical figures, some of whom I got to know. And in a strange way I also got to know Steve Prefontaine, with all the things that I learned and from the people who knew him intimately. As a director or a writer you're not terribly different from an actor in that you are placing yourself in the shoes of the character and trying to identify as he goes through his life. You come to feel the reason for doing the movie is to come to an understanding.

Is Pre's story ultimately about the triumph of losing?
It's a very good way of putting it. Here was a guy who didn't win the biggest race of his life, didn't end up with the woman he loved, and died. And yet his life was a triumph. The voyage of self-discovery may end in victory or in de-

feat, it doesn't matter as long as you squeeze as much living into your life as you can.

Was Donald Sutherland your first choice for Bowerman?
No. I didn't want him. I wanted Tommy Lee Jones. And then a number of other people. I knew I wanted Billy Crudup the minute I laid eyes on him. But in both cases I was very lucky, because I don't think I could have had anybody better than Billy *and* Donald. So it shows you that I was right half the time.

You mean even though Crudup now seems perfect for the role, you never even considered a more recognizable face?
I had seen a couple of people. For silly and not so silly reasons, Tom Cruise was originally going to do it. He loved the story, and I wrote the script right after I finished *Mission Impossible*. But he said, "I don't think I can do this. I realize that I'm in my thirties, I've got a wife and two kids, everybody knows who I am, they're not going to believe I'm sixteen." I said, "But you can look it." He said, "I don't feel it." He was coming off *Mission*, which was his first producing job, and he must have felt a hundred years old. But he said, "I do love it, and I promise you I will make sure we'll get it done. I'll produce it if you'd like." And indeed, without Tom, this movie wouldn't have had a chance.

When did you first get to know Cruise?
On *Days of Thunder*. We became instantly friendly, but where we really became close was on *Mission*. I was there for five weeks rewriting, but not enough was done. My ambitions for the rewrite were really greater. . . . I had warned him, I said, "I don't think it's going to be perfect in five weeks, but it's a start." I was trying to do more than could be done neatly in that time frame. He was a little disappointed. But Tom and I worked on the rewrite by phone and by fax every night while he was shooting. Working in such intimacy and under that tremendous pressure, we really got to know each other. He was just fun. There's nothing like a guy under unbelievable pressure who's also fun to work with. There's something exciting about that. I like working under pressure, and he's just a champ under pressure. We accomplished what we felt we had to and enjoyed the experience, and the movie was a huge success.

What did you think of the film?
I liked it. I had only one wish for the film. We had created more of the story between him and Emmanuelle Béart that had to be cut down. By the time

the movie was over her English was much better, but in the course of it her English didn't work as well for those scenes as it could. I wish we could have held on to a bit more of that. And the other thing is, I wish the mix on the film had been able to make a little more separation between the effects, the music, and the dialogue. It was too finely mixed. Had it been better, the people who said they didn't always understand it would have.

You're a man who has cultivated friendships with some pretty impressive people—do you consider Cruise among them?
The relationship I have with Tom is in some ways the purest I ever had with anybody. I always feel there's nothing extraneous in my relationship with him.

Do you ever talk about his beliefs or interest in Scientology?
If Scientology is what makes Tom what he is today, I feel exactly about it the way Lincoln felt about Grant and booze: let's give it to my other generals.

What do you know about it?
Nothing. I have never asked, nor have I ever engaged in a serious discussion with my mother-in-law about the Holy Trinity. It wouldn't occur to me. The only thing I know about Scientology is that there is an element of self-improvement, in that way that *Thirty Days to a More Powerful Vocabulary* had in the forties. My first contact with Tom, he was carrying a dictionary. The man is hungry for education. He's constantly striving to better himself in every way. Any question that I've ever asked Tom regarding our work has been answered with wit, humor, and candor. That's all I need to know.

Let's go back to some of your earlier friendships. How close were you with Jack Nicholson?
Jack and I were roommates, so for the time that Jack and I were together and close, we were at the same level on the Hollywood food chain, which was at the very bottom. We had similar ambitions. The good-looking girls in our acting class would not go out with us because they were going out with guys who were older who could take them to the Crescendo or the Macambo. So we shared dreams and hope for the future. In that sense I was never much closer to anyone than to Jack.

Did you ever predict that Jack's career would exceed his ambitions?
Part of my vanity is being able to see this kid of eighteen coming out of the cartoon department of Hanna-Barbera, and I saw him improvise for the first

time, and I said to him, "You're gonna be a movie star." And he said, "Yeah?" And I said, "And I'm gonna direct you."

You once said that it's hard *not* to think about Jack even when you're not writing for him. True?
Sure. After all, we were in that class for seven years. I watched him improvise twice a week. I improvised with him. I learned to write as much by watching Jack as anything else.

How does an actor influence a writer?
First of all, because Jack was so gifted. He drove home the point that what an actor says is not nearly as important as what's behind what he says, the subtext. Jack never failed to show you that what he was saying was not what made you laugh. . . . It became obvious the text was almost incidental and that what was underneath it was what really counted. And also with Jack, you could almost not write a sentence too long for him to say. His cadences were such that he could carry it on and on and talk indefinitely, and it would get funnier and better, that was his gift. Even if I'd say, "I once drilled a whore with a glass eye who would then wink you off," Jack would say the line and say, ". . . and wink you off for a dollar." He added "for a dollar." In other words, he could always extend it and make it better, which is unusual. Very few American actors have the ability to handle something that's sheer length and make it better as he went on. Part of it is that his seemingly mo-notone delivery isn't monotone at all but has wonderful nuances all the way through.

I learned to listen to other actors' cadences too. Warren's are different, Tom's are different, Billy's are different. It's just that at that time Jack was so much in my head and I was doing an awful lot of writing for him, like *Chinatown* or *The Last Detail*. I don't think Jack ever did a better performance in that time of his life than *Detail*. A lot of that seemed to spill over into *Cuckoo's Nest*.

Do you agree with Bob Evans, that *Chinatown* made Jack's career?
Chinatown added a color to Jack's career that proved to be everything that it became. Up to that point he did *Cuckoo's Nest* and *The Last Detail* and *Five Easy Pieces*. *Chinatown* was something else. He played a man, a fully function-ing human being. It allowed him to take his place in a pantheon of movie stars in a way, because of the maturity of the part. It suggested both Jack's cruelty and his warmth. In spite of all the expressed cynicism of the charac-ter, he was a man who was trying to make things better . . . and failed.

What's your relationship with Nicholson now? Are you estranged?
Yeah.

Since *The Two Jakes*?
Yeah. I can talk about Jack and about friendship, but I cannot talk about the specifics. Yes, we're estranged. Did that affect my admiration for his skill or his work or the fondness of my memories of Jack those times when we worked together? Not at all. *The Two Jakes* wasn't what caused the falling out. It was all the events that led up to it. By the time of *The Two Jakes* it was a done deal. Jack and I have been, at different times in our lives, as close as brothers. I loved him so much, I loved his art, I loved his spirit, I loved everything about him. And I know so much about him. I can't honestly sit here for any public consumption and tell you what went wrong with our relationship without adopting a posture that would suggest that what went wrong was his doing and not my doing. I find that undignified and I just can't do that.

I would say the same is true of Warren [Beatty]. I cared so much for him. Both men are such powerful influences on my life that what went wrong is much less significant than the years we were friends. With Warren I became very close on *Bonnie and Clyde*. I championed that script when fifty directors turned it down. So our closeness began on a professional level, whereas Jack and I began on a personal level. There's a line in *Tequila Sunrise*, "Who says friendship lasts forever?" I can say in general that ours is a business where all of us are tempted to confuse the personal with the professional, and a lot of mischief occurs there.

I mean, look, you are so close to someone every day of your life, and then suddenly people become famous. In the beginning none of us were. I'm talking about the actors—writers have a limited prominence, minuscule by comparison. Then suddenly you are in a position of prominence, private and public, and circumstances keep you apart, yet in your mind that's one of the closest people in the world to you. A year or two will go by, and you don't realize you haven't seen them because you're seeing them in everyday life the way the public is seeing them—on TV, in the movies, in magazines. Then every few months you run into each other and say, "Let's catch up and talk." You think you're the same people, but time has gone by and you're not, you're fooled by that. Without even knowing it. And then the personal and the professional get entirely confused.

Also, people as they get older can get conservative, tend to repeat past successes, and feel a need to hold on to the past rather than forge something different in the future. The classic example of any actor who goes through various stages in his life, being a young leading man, then comes a time when a transition is necessary. Some manage to age themselves perfectly. Jack has been very good at it. Redford struggled with it and seems to be succeeding. Warren, who's as bright as any man alive, will probably do the same thing. No doubt in those times of transition it can be difficult.

Warren used to be talked about in political circles as a potential candidate. Did you think he'd ever run for office?
Warren's skills have always been at their peak as a diplomat rather than as a politician. His is the force of personal persuasion. Get him in a room of his peers and he can dominate. Get him in a public forum and he'll tend to be self-conscious, worried about saying the wrong thing.

If you're at a party and Jack or Warren is there, do you avoid each other?
I haven't seen Jack for five or six years. I saw Warren not long ago, and we were genuinely happy to see each other. I think both of us are sorry we haven't seen each other more. There's no anger or bitterness. Those things happen, but I think what you're left with is sorrow.

Does your wanting to direct take away from your being able to write for some of the actors who might feel disappointed about that?
They might have felt that not writing for some of them because I was going my own way was depriving them of something.

Did they feel that was a betrayal on your part?
I don't know if anyone would ever own up to that, or even think they feel it, but the net effect was: yes.

Who among today's younger actors would you compare to the early Nicholson and Beatty?
Early Jack had more in common with Johnny Depp. Because Jack started with Roger Corman, he didn't start off in the pedigree plays, like *Loss of Roses*, that Warren started with, and immediately [Beatty's] first movie director was Kazan. So Warren started at the top. Jack was an outsider. Johnny was in that *21 Jump Street* thing and clearly decided he did not want to do that with his life. He's been guided by his feelings of never wanting to act unless he can express himself fully. Warren began with something to protect, because he started at the top. After he'd done a series of movies that hadn't worked as well as his earlier ones, ending with *Promise Her Anything*, then he got bold and did *Bonnie and Clyde*. His boldness was a realization that he *had* to be bold. And I encouraged him.

Have you ever wanted to work with Depp?
Depp should be one of the biggest movie stars in the world. Everyone seems to know it. I wanted Johnny to do *Ask the Dust,* and he wanted to do it but couldn't get a date.

Is that John Fante novel still a viable project?
It's still a project of mine. Johnny may be too old by the time I can get it done, but he really liked it. The difference between Tom [Cruise] and Johnny is that Johnny's a little vainer than Tom. Johnny does not want to be caught dead in something that looks like he's pleasing an audience (*laughs*). Tom doesn't mind. But he does have the same ambitions.

You're also close to two of your neighbors in the Palisades, Kurt Russell and Goldie Hawn.
Goldie and I stay in touch. And Kurt and I talk often. Kurt's like Churchill—that sounds bizarre, but Churchill never really changed. The world around him changed, and he just resolutely didn't change, so it appeared that he changed. Both Kurt and Tom are possessed of more physical courage than any two men I've ever met. Tom is more discreet than Kurt—by that I mean his choices are more careful. Tom makes choices that he thinks will work and will be challenging. With Kurt, I have teased, "You're the best actor with the worst taste that I've ever seen." And he laughs. Kurt is a ballplayer who's been obliged to become a movie star now making $10 million, $15 million a movie, having been derailed in his basic, true job.

Is there anyone whose preconception you had of him turned out to be completely different than what you thought?
I've had a long history with Bob Evans. He's an example of a guy who you can't believe isn't a flaming fucking asshole (*laughs*), and he comes to be one of the best people in the world. Evans is a perfect example. He's surprisingly insightful and even brilliant on movies, catching them at a certain point. That guy has no right to look like that, talk like that, walk like that, and be that nuanced and subtle in his take on watching a movie.

You were so enamored with Evans you cast him opposite Nicholson in *The Two Jakes.* What were you thinking?
Oh geez. . . . I cast him because if Bob could behave the way he behaved on any given day of his life without acting, he could have given one of the great performances of all time. It was my arrogance that I felt that I could get him to behave and not act. But he had acted. It's one thing to take a person who's never acted, it's another to take one who has and break his habit.

Did Evans get angry with you over this?
Oh yes. He got angry at me. But who gives a fuck? I love Bob, what can you say? He's got one of the great hearts.

Was it Evans who got Polanski to direct *Chinatown*?
The great thing about Robert Evans is that he forced Roman into material he might not have picked himself: *Rosemary's Baby* and *Chinatown*. Roman picked *What?* and *The Vampire Killers*.

You fought over the ending to *Chinatown*, and Polanski prevailed. Who was right?
Roman and I have been much misunderstood about this. We agreed that it ended darkly. The only difference was I felt it was too melodramatic to end it his way. The way I had it figured it was just about as dark, but Roman felt it needed that finale. I was wrong, and he was right. Roman is one of the most gifted filmmakers of all time. As the years have gone by I see that he taught me more than anybody. The best working relationship I ever had was with Roman. By far. He's a fucking giant.

What made Roman so good at narrative?
Guts is what makes Roman so good. A willingness to take the time with what other directors consider shoe leather and want to get through quickly. He understands that the credibility of a melodramatic story is to let the fucking guy take his time finding who he's got to find.

You worked with him on *Frantic*, which didn't turn out so well.
There were just limits to what could be done. I tried to deal with the relationship between Harrison Ford and Emmanuelle Seigner [now Roman Polanski's wife]. Both Roman and I were somewhat victimized by public attitudes about us. I think it would have been more interesting to make it a story about a man who goes to Paris to honeymoon with his wife to recapture something that had died with his medical success, then loses his wife literally, and recovers through having this affair, remembering what it was like to have loved his wife. That affair should have taken place that way, and didn't.

Any impressions of Harrison Ford?
I knew Harrison before that. He almost did *Two Jakes*. Harrison's a powerful presence. A very careful, cautious, guarded man. One who, in a way that I admire, takes care of himself better than I've been able to take care of myself. He's a good man. I asked Harrison to play the lead in *Without Limits*. We

couldn't get this fucking movie made for love or money, so at a certain point I thought of Harrison as Bowerman. He never read the script. He was in the middle of *The Devil's Own* and said he just wanted to go home. He's an actor of greater range than his choice of roles would indicate. There's a lot of things he could do that he's chosen not to do. But he does what he does better than anyone else on earth. What the fuck can you say?

Are you sorry that you've directed only three movies?
Yeah, kind of. I hope to change that. I didn't really have any choice—it would have been too disruptive to my family, to my older daughter, I would not have been able to have had the time I had. If I had had a more amicable divorce, it might have been possible, but it wasn't. I hope I live a few years longer and can be livelier and healthier and maybe get a few more movies in.

Is there any classical novel you'd like to turn into a film?
The Charterhouse of Parma. It's a great story. Stendhal's like serious Dumas. He was the most Italian and sumptuous of the French novelists. And nowhere more so than *The Charterhouse of Parma*.

How have other writers influenced you?
Like everyone else of my generation, I was profoundly influenced by J. D. Salinger. He was the first guy who used language that seemed to me to be suggestive of what I heard on the street. And also, he used refrain and kind of careful imprecision, almost coincidentally with the time that you started being able to hear less and less of the lyrics when Elvis Presley sang. It's no accident that Elvis and Jack came up at the same time. In the forties there was Dick Haynes and Sinatra and crooners like Al Martino—you were hearing every goddamn word. And then Elvis came along grunting, "You ain't nothin' but a hound dog," and suddenly what was behind it, the subtext, became more important than the lyrics. In Salinger what was behind "If you know what I mean," which was a constant phrase, or calling somebody a "phony"—the unwillingness in trying to get too specific in communicating, knowing that you'd fail, doing it indirectly with refrain, was in fact the way people talked. That affected me. People very often are loathe to say exactly what they mean even if they can articulate it, and furthermore, we tend to suspect people who are too articulate. Who are the actors who seem to us to be the ones that we believe? "Yup." John Wayne. Henry Fonda. Gary Cooper. Clint. Monosyllabic guys. We tend to believe they're more honest precisely because their feelings are almost too important to be able to put them into words.

What screenwriters influenced you?

Robert Campbell. Chuck Eastman—Adrian Joyce's brother—wrote *Honeybear, I Think I Love You,* a very influential screenplay in the fifties that never got made that affected me strongly because there was a guy who was able to use life around him and push as far as anybody writing a novel was going to push. James Agee's published screenplays affected me, particularly *Noa Noa,* about Van Gogh. One of the great scenes in screenwriting that I've ever seen, read, or imagined was between Van Gogh and Gauguin. Gauguin was a tough guy who gave up banking and left his family to pursue painting. Van Gogh was in many ways a hothouse flower, as driven as he was. There's a scene in which they're painting—as Agee describes it, first with the colors of the landscape as Van Gogh sees it, then as Gauguin sees it. Vincent is always annoying Gauguin, who has the sensibilities of a banker. A daddy-long-legs gets caught in the paint on Gauguin's canvas, and he brushes the spider away. Van Gogh goes to pieces, because it loses a leg, and he starts to clean the paint off the spider and says, "There, there, it will be all right." He's talking to the daddy-long-legs. Gauguin looks at him and says, "I want to paint your picture." It's a scene of close-ups of the two men, with Van Gogh unable to keep still knowing he's being judged by the portrait painter. Gauguin says, "Sit still, Vincent, and let me finish the goddamn thing." He finishes it, and Van Gogh asks to see it, and now the shoe is on the other foot, it's Gauguin being judged by Van Gogh. It's Gauguin who is nervous: "What do you think? What do you think?" Whatever he thought of this psychotic child, he knew that Van Gogh's gifts were prodigious and would take very seriously his comments. And Vincent says, "Well, Paul, it's very good, but you painted me as if I've already gone mad." That scene floored me, because it depends in its entirety on silences, these two guys, and a canvas which you don't really see.

What films have most influenced or affected you?

Renoir's *Grand Illusion. Rules of the Game.* Ingmar Bergman's *Winter Light* and *Smiles of a Summer Night* are two of my favorite films. *Seventh Seal.* I like *Wild Strawberries,* though I'm not as fond of it as other people are. *Dr. Zhivago,* which one recognizes as very sloppy in terms of detail, but *Zhivago* and *Lawrence of Arabia* both moved me. I've rarely had the experience of coming to some real understanding of what it's like to walk out of this house and be locked out forever, which you get in *Zhivago. Dr. Strangelove. Paths of Glory* and *2001: A Space Odyssey. Giant.* I like the strong emotional effect of movies, and I'm always grateful for that. One of the best movies ever made is *Double Indemnity,* in terms of just dazzling skills, and it ages well. It ages better than *Sunset Boulevard,* although I like that one very much too. Certainly *The Mal-*

tese Falcon. I recognize John Ford as wonderful, like Milton, but like John
Milton, I'm not drawn to read him. In recent years—there's one movie in the
last five years that's stuck with me: *One False Move*. It's in a class by itself.
When have you ever seen a movie where for 60 percent of it you have no
fucking idea who the protagonist is? That's the advantage of a movie without movie stars. And the end of that movie, when he asks the little boy to
stay with him, it's not sentimental, and the moment is over with and it's fad-
ing before you realize the full implications of it, that was his son. It was
amazing.

What did you have to do with *Marathon Man*?
I came in at the end of the movie. I suggested that Dustin make Olivier eat
the diamonds. I also wrote a love scene, thirty seconds, with Dustin and
Marthe Keller, where there's food all over, and she says, "I can't move," and
he says, "Neither can I," and she says, "Thank God." I thought, okay, that's a
good love scene. I go to see the dailies with John Schlesinger and Bob Evans,
and—Dustin always liked me for this—the next thing I know I'm on my feet
yelling at the fucking screen. I was beside myself. This is how they shot it:
She said, "I can't." He said, "Neither can I." She said, "Thank God." I said,
"What does that mean? I can't suck your dick? I can't do what?" The whole
meaning was lost—it *had* to be "I can't *move*" another muscle. I can't grind
my pelvis one more time. It couldn't just be "I can't." Because then the audience asks the question: can't what? If you force the audience to think, even
for a nanosecond, it destroys the whole purpose of the scene.

**When you did some work on Norman Mailer's *Tough Guys Don't Dance*,
did you ever speak with Mailer?**
Briefly. He came out here and asked my opinion about the screenplay. We
talked. I'm a huge admirer of his. I learned something from him. I made the
remark that all writing was about loss. And just as quick as you can imagine
he said, "All *your* writing is about loss." And I thought, okay, he's got my
number. He taught me something about myself in a fucking hurry.

What would you like to see taught to young screenwriters today?
Those screenwriters that I've admired brought other disciplines and other
lives to their writing. They've worked in other professions, they were journalists who had been exposed to all walks of life, which gave them a broad insight into the society. That bleeds into their films, which gives it vitality that
maybe screenwriters who go to cinema school and feed on old movies could
use.

What has the enormous success of *Titanic* signaled to people like you?
In the eighties we had superheroes, from Superman to Robocop to Super
Arnold and Super Sly, fatuous infantile daydreams of potency that arose
from a country that considered itself impotent. They were not sophisticated
or very much related to life, so there was a falling off there in terms of films'
willingness to communicate issues that reflected the human condition.
Maybe in the nineties we're seeing a change via a popular film like *Titanic*.
It's a real event, with life-and-death issues. It may not be on the level of a
Robert Bolt screenplay, to put it kindly, but the issues are ones that kids
have never really seen in movies before. Maybe there is an appetite for that
now. People see that 1,500 died—how do they do it? What would it be like
for me? The spectacular nature of it, and the fact that it was true, arouses in
people what such drama always does: you want to know what that experience was like without having to drown. And if you could behave well. The
people and the environment, the ship, really happened. It hit the country
with the fucking force of revelation.

THE ACTOR

ANTHONY HOPKINS

IT TOOK ANTHONY HOPKINS twenty-five years, acting in sixteen plays, forty-two television dramas, and eighteen movies, to get to the point of being cast as a jailed serial killer who, in a total screen time of just twenty-seven minutes, shook up moviegoers like few characters ever did in the history of the cinema. Those twenty-seven minutes made Hopkins the kind of star he had dreamed of being when he was a lonely, tormented boy growing up in the shadow of Richard Burton in Port Talbot, Wales. Thomas Harris's *The Silence of the Lambs* gave both Hopkins and Jodie Foster the roles of a lifetime, and both were recognized with an Academy Award. He portrayed Hannibal "the Cannibal" Lecter, the captured killer with a penchant for raw liver and fava beans, and she was Clarice Starling, the young FBI trainee catapulted into the deadly center of a hunt for a serial killer who skinned women.

For those who were surprised at the power of Hopkins's performance, one only had to look at his body of work to see it coming. A classically trained Shakespearean actor (who dislikes acting in Shakespearean plays), Hopkins appeared in eight of Shakespeare's plays in London and Los Angeles and on film. For British and American television he has convincingly portrayed Charles Dickens, Georges Jacques Danton, Lloyd George, Edmund Kean, Guy Burgess, Adolph Hitler, Mussolini, and the Hunchback of Notre Dame. His first film was *The Lion in Winter* with Peter O'Toole and Katharine Hepburn in 1967. In other movies he starred as an eerie ventriloquist in *Magic,* as the doctor to *The Elephant Man,* as Captain Bligh in the third remake of *The Bounty,* and as a rare-book dealer in *84 Charing Cross Road.* Following *The Silence of the Lambs* he appeared in the acclaimed Merchant-Ivory production of E. M. Forster's

Howard's End, as Von Helsing in Francis Coppola's *Dracula,* as the proper but suppressed English butler Mr. Stevens in *The Remains of the Day,* as C. S. Lewis in *Shadowlands,* as Nixon and Picasso in films by Oliver Stone and Merchant-Ivory, as Dr. John Harvey Kellogg in *The Road to Wellville,* as John Quincy Adams in Steven Spielberg's *Amistad,* with Brad Pitt in *Legends of the Fall* and *Meet Joe Black,* and in *The Mask of Zorro, Instinct, Titus,* and *Mission Impossible 2.*

It was his performance as the psychiatrist Dr. Dysart in the Broadway production of *Equus* that caught the eye of the novelist Thomas Harris, who wrote to Hopkins, upon learning that he had been cast as Hannibal Lecter, "My standard for how to project intelligence is and has been for twenty years your performance as Dr. Dysart. . . . What an extraordinary piece of work."

Hopkins's extraordinary work as an actor was recognized by Queen Elizabeth in 1993 when she knighted the Welshman. It was an honor that Hopkins wasn't expecting, and though he considers the goings-on of the royal family a kind of soap opera, becoming Sir Anthony Hopkins was nevertheless a humbling experience considering where he came from.

He was born on the last day of December in 1937. His father was a baker, and his mother worked with her husband. Young Tony, though attracted to the smell of bread, didn't help much around the bakery. School was a disaster for him. He had no friends and felt as if he came from another planet, the lessons were of little interest, and he often lapsed into total silence for weeks on end. When his teachers voiced their concern about him to his parents, they put him in a boarding school. But Hopkins still felt "like a Martian." He was shy around girls, didn't play sports, and didn't know what he wanted to be.

After World War II ended, he discovered the movies and became fascinated with American gangster films like *Sahara* and *High Sierra* with Humphrey Bogart, *The Last Gangster* with Edward G. Robinson, and *Scarface* with George Raft. "Those sort of movies had a big influence on my life," he recalls.

Another big influence was seeing Charlie Chaplin in *Limelight* in 1952. Chaplin's sadness reminded him of his grandfather. Hopkins, then fourteen, wrote to the great comedian, and Chaplin responded. "I knew I couldn't become him," Hopkins realized, "but he was the signal that started me, because I could understand the failure. Just slightly off course. Like Lecter—people who are somehow trapped in something themselves."

At seventeen he discovered acting, and by some miracle (and a talent for playing the piano), he won a scholarship to the Welsh College of

Music and Drama in Cardiff. After two years he was drafted into the British Army, where he served as an incompetent clerk. In 1960 he became an assistant stage manager at the Manchester Library Theatre, then joined the Nottingham Repertory Company. In 1961 he won a scholarship to study at London's Royal Academy of Dramatic Art. While there he met an American student who had studied at the Actors Studio and who introduced him to the teachings of Stella Adler, Stanislavsky, Stanley Meisner, and Lee Strasberg. Stints at two other repertory companies in Leicester and Liverpool followed, and then, in 1965, he was invited to audition for Sir Laurence Olivier, the director of the National Theatre. "I thought I was going to be discovered overnight and become a big movie star within three days of stepping onstage," he said. "None of that happened." Still, within two years Hopkins was designated as Olivier's understudy, and he was considered to be in training to one day take over the directorship. "I was told that I had the promise of becoming one of the great actors in England." But booze and a hot temper turned an opportunity into a nightmare.

While appearing in *Macbeth* and rehearsing for *The Misanthrope*, Hopkins blew up over the direction of John Dexter and quit the National Theatre. His decision was final, even though he was warned that one simply didn't behave that way, and that he would probably be destroying a promising career. Hopkins didn't care. If there was one thing he couldn't take it was someone who told him what to do, and in the world of the theater that put him at odds with every director who wanted to cast him.

His drinking became a problem ("I was drinking myself to death," he admits), and he often sank into deep depression. His first marriage lasted just four years, and when he walked out he left behind a baby daughter, with whom he had little to do as she matured. In 1973 he married again, this time to Jennifer Lynton, whom he met while filming *When Eight Bells Toll* in 1969.

After falling asleep at the wheel while driving in Arizona, Hopkins realized that he needed help and found a well-known organization for alcoholics. "I suddenly realized I was face to face with people who felt exactly like me," he said. "I thought, God, this is what I've been looking for all my life. I knew why I drank, because I simply didn't fit in as a kid, I had all those lost feelings, I wanted to become an actor, I wanted to be somebody. When I came to America, the last place I intended to come to was a self-help for alcoholics. But God had other plans."

His sobriety tempered his rage, but he has never lost his edge as an actor. Though the Oscar and his knighthood have brought Hopkins the formal recognition he once craved, I didn't know what to expect in the winter of 1994 when I went out to the Miramar Hotel in Santa Monica, where he likes to stay when he comes to Los Angeles. I'd read about his comments that he understood characters like Hannibal Lecter and Adolph Hitler because he *was* them, or at least some part of him was. I had no doubts the man had demons, and I wondered whether they would surface when we talked.

But Hopkins was preparing for his role as an even-tempered English butler, and for the religious thinker C. S. Lewis, whose faith was rocked when the woman he passionately loved died of cancer. He was affable, controlled, polite, verbally pugnacious, and, at times, outrageous.

Hopkins isn't a man who keeps his opinions to himself. He doesn't look kindly on his profession or on the prima donna behavior of his fellow actors, and he's bold enough, and confident enough, to say what he feels.

I saw him twice before he left for England to make *The Remains of the Day,* and twice more after the movie was done and he had been knighted. At one of our sessions I brought along a copy of *The Silence of the Lambs* for him to sign. He obliged by writing how much he looked forward to having dinner with me, where we could dine over a plate of raw liver, fava beans, and a bottle of Chianti. Wishing me pleasant dreams, he signed it "Hannibal Lecter." Before our last session I went out and found a copy of *The Bunker.* Since I already had the cannibal, I thought I'd like to see what he had to say as Hitler. "All orders must be obeyed without question at all," he wrote, and then he initialed it "AH."

With your knighthood, must we address you as Sir Anthony?
They say "Sir Hopkins." What do Americans think of all that?

It's duly noted. But never mind what Americans think, what did *you* think when you found out about it?
It was a big surprise. It's nice. I'm very honored, as I was with the Oscar, so it's been an incredible year. I don't know how to use it, maybe I can get special tables at restaurants.

Which is a bigger honor for an Englishman, an Oscar or being knighted?
Well I hope this won't get in the English press, but the Oscar, because I'm a movie actor. Getting the Oscar was a great moment for me. It changed my life because it knocked a lot of myself down inside of me. Not crippling self-

doubts, but doubts that I wanted to be rid of. I think praise is a very good thing to have in one's life. It's better than a kick in the ass.

When I was a little kid, I used to be picked up by my father and thrown into the air, and I always wanted to touch the ceiling. And I thought, well, I've touched the ceiling. It's like they let me out of the cage.

Will it be just as fantastic to get a second one?
One is enough. I got an Oscar, so I'm off the hook really. I've done everything I've ever wanted in my life. The knighthood is another thing.

I nearly blew it all some years ago, and I had sort of a resurrection. So many people don't survive drugs or survive the horrors that I did, and I came through it. And then *Silence of the Lambs* came out of the blue, and I was given an Oscar, and then I was given this knighthood, and now I've done this amazing film called *Remains of the Day*, which really is coming home to me, and next playing C. S. Lewis. So I'm getting these parts now, and I'm thinking, what the hell's happened? Why are these parts coming to me?

My agent says, "This is a very exciting time in your life." I say, "What are they talking about?" They are all excited, but I say it's all bullshit. I mean, agents are agents, actors are actors. There's nothing exciting about it. I love going to the studio, I love going to location and getting into the dressing rooms; all that ritual of going to makeup, putting the clothes on. If they want me to wait there for three days, I don't care. These assistants run up and say, "Sorry to keep you waiting." I say, "Just make sure my agent gets the check, that's all." I read books, I relax, I sleep. I love it. I always save my energy. I don't hang about. I stay away from other actors, I don't want to have lunch with them. And as soon as the shot's over, the day's over, I'm in the car and I'm off. I don't want anything to do with it. This friend of mine said, "It's easy for you to say that." Well, it is, it's easy flying a jumbo jet when you know how. It's the same for me: it's easy because I know what I'm doing, like a computer.

Another knighted actor, Sir Laurence Olivier, said that acting is a masochistic form of exhibitionism.
What a lot of crap. No. It's all *bullshit*. Bullshit. It's a crock of horseshit, all of it. I don't know, maybe I'm shallow; I don't have much going on in my mind. The only quote which is fairly accurate for myself, and I meant it, I think actors are all pretty rather damaged goods. I came into therapy to see if I can get through my neurosis. Acting in itself didn't fix me, and being successful at it didn't fix me. But it showed me the way.

Why did you want to be an actor?

It's all I know. I've been getting away with it for thirty years. I became an actor because I wanted to do something new that would get me out of the rut that I was in. I wanted to just make a mark somehow, I wanted to become famous, that's all I ever wanted. I'd seen Brando and Montgomery Clift in early films, and that's what I wanted to become. I wanted to become an American actor. My longing to come to America was a more powerful influence than anyone like Olivier, who was the greatest actor of his time. But looking back, I remember I wanted to become an actor because Richard Burton had made it in my hometown where we both lived, he escaped from there and made a career for himself. I didn't care what it took, I just wanted to become somebody like that. I just didn't want to be what I was. So I sort of followed in his footsteps. He was quite instrumental in my life really.

Why the need to escape? How traumatic was your childhood?
I was an idiot at school. I didn't know what time of day it was. We lived in the rural part of an industrial steel-working town. And when I first went to school, I was in a completely alien environment. I can remember the smell of stale milk, drinking straws, and wet coats and sitting there absolutely petrified. And that feeling stayed with me, the fear stayed with me all through my childhood and right through adolescence. That gnawing anxiety that I was freaky, that I wasn't really fitting in anywhere. I didn't know what was expected of me. I couldn't achieve anything, and I couldn't accomplish anything. Maybe I was dyslexic. So I wasn't popular at all. I never played with any of the other kids, didn't have any friends. I wanted to be left alone right through my school years.

Did you ever do anything to attract attention?
Just after the war I was in a little school called Bridge Street School, and every lunch I could get on the bus and go home, which was about a good three miles. But I would never get on the bus, I would run beside it, like an idiot, like the school clown. I was so ill when I got home, it's a wonder I didn't have a heart attack. I was throwing up because I was exhausted. I used to race the school bus, and naturally it would get ahead of me and I'd catch up at the bus stop, and kids would say, "Come on." I would do things in a weird way, like I wouldn't go to my own birthday parties.

What did your parents do about your fears and anxieties?
I was an only child, and my mother and father were a little worried because I just didn't seem to grasp anything. My parents sent me off to a boarding school, and I lived away from home from the age of eleven. That sense of po-

tential failure still hangs around me in the back of my mind. I still don't hang around people, I'm not gregarious with anybody.

And this stems from your being so withdrawn as a child?
Oh yes. In school I wouldn't speak to anyone for four weeks. And I was punished.

How were you punished?
They would hit me.

The teachers?
The teachers, yes. They'd slap me about the head.

Would you speak when you were called upon? Or you just wouldn't speak?
No, I wouldn't speak, I just wouldn't speak. So I was hauled before the headmaster, and he talked to my mother and father and said there's something wrong with me, I wouldn't speak for weeks.

How old were you?
Fourteen. In 1953 I was reading Trotsky's *Russian Revolution,* and I was asked if I was a Communist or a Marxist, and I didn't know what they were talking about. The book was taken away from me. Then some of the kids would call me "Bolshie, Bolshie, Bolshie." And I went completely into myself. I thought I'd defy them all, and that stayed with me the rest of my life, that I would show them all one day. That's why I became an actor.

Whose fault was your withdrawal—yours, or your classmates who teased you?
I just hated the rejection, I hated being sneered at by other kids. I get a recurring dream, that I'm outside of the group. And I don't belong, and they show me that I don't belong. And it's always going back to school, or it could be amongst a group of adults in a dream and they turn on me, humiliate me, and I wake up. It takes me a few minutes to come to terms that it was a dream, it's so vivid.

How do they humiliate you?
They call me crap; "you're nothing, you're so worthless, you're nasty, you're a vicious person." Once I get back to my senses, I take it as a good sign that I'm no longer that, because I'm very aware of what you could do through self-contempt. So my life is a remarkable revelation to myself.

As a child, did you have any religious beliefs to fall back on?
No. In school once, when I was about four, they'd been reciting the Lord's
Prayer and the Twenty-third Psalm about "Our Father who art in heaven
. . . ," and I couldn't comprehend it. Whenever I mentioned this, my father
said, "It's a load of rubbish, God." So I believed for years that it was all very
self-determined and you just suffer in this uncomfortable universe. My father's philosophy was: "You're going to fight. It's dog eat dog! You don't
trust anyone and don't give anything away."

How much of a force was your father in your life?
He was a man of colossal energy. But a lot of the energy didn't go anywhere.
He was just spinning his wheels. He was exhausting to be with. My father
said all bakers are mad because they have such a violent temperament. I remember him getting a loaf of bread because it had gone wrong and tearing
it in a rage and throwing it at a tray of cakes all over the wall in frustration
because it hadn't worked. In the Depression years people did anything to
survive and people cracked.

Did you ever work with him in the bakery?
No. He said, "You don't want to come into this business, do you?" And I said
no. And he said, "You'd be hopeless."

**With your problems at school and your lack of interest in his work,
your father must have thought it a miracle that you got through school
at all. Is it a major accomplishment to survive the English school
system?**
Yes, it is. The public school system is one of the most insufferable systems of
all. I'm glad that I was in that system because it gave me enough rocket fuel
to get out and do something different. It pushed me into huge rage and
anger for many years: to hell with everything, don't trust anyone. I look back
at it now and think it wasn't that something was wrong with me, it was
something was right with me. I may have hurt a few people along the way,
but it got me what I wanted. Just beat your own drum, that's what it was
with me. But I was beating myself up because I felt weird.

Despite the suffering, what were you good at as a boy?
I was good at impersonating teachers. I could imitate mannerisms: walks,
body movements, voices. That was my way of getting back. I really developed
it when I became an actor.

Did you ever mimic anybody who walked in while you were doing it?

Olivier once. I was doing a speech, just fooling around, and he was standing right behind me.

And what was his reaction?
He said, "Is that supposed to be me? Doesn't sound anything like me." But it was a good impersonation. When we were together making *The Innocent* in Germany recently, I did John Schlesinger, and he said, "Oh, fuck off." Schlesinger is an interesting character, he's very precise and he's quite volatile.

When I went in the Army for my military service, there was a Sergeant Brolins, and I used to be able to imitate his voice. I'd stand outside the huts and call everyone out on parade half an hour early. They'd all come out and I'd vanish. I suppose it's all a residue of my childhood. Somebody said of me once, "What is with Tony, always the jokes and laughter, fooling around, what's he covering up?" Maybe she's right, maybe I am covering up something.

Besides your talent for mimicry, didn't you also find some release through music and drawing?
Well, I was captivated by Beethoven and his music, and I wanted to become Beethoven. I can compose and improvise. When John Schlesinger heard me playing piano one day, he said, "Let me put that in the wedding scene." So we did it. I always manage to sneak a little of my own music in my films.

Do you still draw?
I used to draw when I was a kid, used to lie on the floor while all these war planes were dropping bombs. There was a woman called Bernice Evans, eighteen or nineteen, and she came to the house one day to see my mother, and she looked at my drawings and said, "They're very good, aren't they?" She said, "If you want him to have lessons . . ." and I was sent to this little school that Bernice had in town, once a week on Friday nights, and she taught me how to paint with poster paints, very bright. Then, in the summer in 1947, this man came up the stairs and in the room. He had a bright checked jacket on and very piercing eyes, and she said, "Anthony, this is Richard, he's an actor."

It was Richard Burton?
Yes. Never met him again until I went to ask for his autograph when he became a bit more famous. But he went out with Bernice.

And what about you? Did you go out much or were you sexually naive?

Just a bit dumb. I didn't know what it was about. It was something you didn't talk about. Especially a Welsh background, I was very closed off about it, didn't want complications in my life. And so I closed down. It's all rather baffling and mysterious. So I never had an easy relationship over the years, then gradually I began to really like women. But I was very shy of women for a long time, fearful. I was a bit of a recluse. I went out with a girl just briefly, and I went out with a girl at the Royal Academy. In 1961 I went out with an American girl for about six months, and that was a bit of a traumatic experience. I was just besotted with her, but she was ephemeral, elusive. One day she said, "That's it." It's all such a big deal that's made of everything, whether it's sex or acting. Now I think it's no big deal. You function, you get on with your life, and one day it's all going to be over, that's the end of that.

After public school what jobs did you hold to get on with your life?
I worked in a steel company in Wales for eight weeks, in 1955. The fitters would come in and say, "I'd like two dozen steel bolts and two pieces of piping." And I'd always get it wrong. I remember one man said, "You're not really connected, are you?" And that's what I felt most like in those years. I couldn't get anything right. My father would say the same thing. "Take this bread to the shop. No, forget it, get out." He gave up quickly. Mind you, I got out of a lot of duties and hard work. In the Army I qualified for a clerk's course, and I was in the chief clerk's office for eighteen months. I could not type, and I couldn't do anything right. And the staff sergeant was sitting there looking. He said, "I was just wondering, how the hell did I give you this job?" I was so stupid. I'm stupid.

I just couldn't make anything work. I got into a repertoire company, the Manchester Theatre, and the director had had it with me. Everything was a disaster. Finally they gave me some small parts, which I couldn't do. So I didn't start off with much promise. But I had no intention of doing work for the rest of my life, which is why I became an actor.

Did you have a feeling of belonging when you were with other actors?
No, not at all. I didn't get on at all. I still don't get the sense of belonging.

What did you learn when you studied at the Welsh College of Music and Drama?
Not very much, because I was too young for it really. I learned some speech, and the history of the theater, and makeup and all that. Then I left when I was nineteen, I went on a tour of Britain for the Arts Council. Then I did my national military service for two years.

Did you try to get out of the military draft?
They said that if you drank a bottle of vinegar it would cause a heart tremor and get you out of the Army. I was hoping I could have something wrong with me, but there was nothing. I couldn't fake it.

After the Army you enrolled in the Royal Academy of Art. Did you finally settle down by then?
I was a troubled student. I didn't like dancing and ballet, I couldn't stand all that stuff, so I used to skip those classes and go to the movies. But I worked quite hard on what I chose to work on.

Did you worry much about technique at that time?
You have to learn to speak clearly, which is the British system. I can understand why the American actors think that's for the birds.

When you joined the National Theatre, Olivier was its director. Did you become friends with him?
He was an old man, and I didn't get that close to him, but he took me under his wing. He liked me because I was a bit odd and I was pretty feisty. He liked physically strong people. He was not a very strong man, he had very bad legs and always complained about them—they weren't thick enough, they were spindly. I was always naturally kind of muscular, and he'd come up and say, "God, lucky man." He said you've got to be strong, you've got to have stamina.

Did he ever give you any kind of advice?
Yeah, he said, "Work hard. Be courageous. Do the impossible. Do the outrageous. Don't ever be calm or tame. And don't waste your time doing the movies. You're a fine actor, you ought to stay in the theater for a while. Don't sell out, keep that training going." But British actors all want to sell out now. They keep saying about Richard Burton that it was a waste. What do you mean it was a waste? He did what he wanted to do and made a lot of money, married a famous movie actress, and did some good. He certainly shook the rafters, made a bit of noise.

You made a bit of noise yourself when you quit the National Theatre in the middle of a rehearsal for *Macbeth* in 1973. Was it a self-destructive act?
No, it was the most creative thing I've ever done, because it got me out of where I was. Unfortunately, I left a lot of people in the lurch. But I just had to get the hell out of there, I would have gone under if I'd stayed.

So it was self-*constructive*?

It was. At the time I thought, oh my God, I'm a terrible, irresponsible wreck, and I've destroyed my career. It was quite a cold, calculated thing. Here I was being groomed to lead the company, and I just wasn't fit for it, not intellectually, emotionally, physically. I wasn't interested in becoming a classical actor. I was drinking too much, and I had a lot of fire and anger in me. And on top of that having this director, John Dexter, who I later worked with on *Equus* and became good friends with, but at the time I couldn't take John. So I left. I woke up at 3:00 A.M., and I had this voice going around and around in my head. And I thought . . . I'm not going to go back there. So I phoned up my agent, and I said, "I'm out, I'm not taking this insanity, being screamed at by this pig of a man. It's not important. I value my mental health, or what's left of it, more than I do the theater. I'll drive a taxi, I'll do something. I don't care." I'd painted myself into a corner. I had to make a break with myself and with the past, I just had to get all those chains off me. I put the phone down and walked across Green Park in London, and the birds were singing and the cabs were driving by and buses, and I thought, it's over, I'll never have to go back again. I have no future. And within a few weeks I was out in the desert sitting on the back of a camel with Leslie Caron doing *QB VII* for an American film company. Beginning of a whole change in my life.

To go from Shakespeare to a TV miniseries might seem like a backward step for most actors. But you don't see the worth or virtue in either the Bard or yourself, do you?

I don't like virtue, and I don't like worthiness. I don't like valor. Why keep being so nice? It's something in me, I can't stand that. My father couldn't stand all that stuff. I don't say that I'm not a phony, I'm as phony as everyone else. We're all phony. We're all charlatans, we're all flawed, we're all liars, nobody really carries the mantle totally in their lives. But there's a part of it I can't stomach. Who gives a damn about a theater that was built four hundred years ago? Who cares? Pave it. Who cares? It's dead stuff. It's like the bloody Bard. Whether this *Lear* is better than that *Lear* . . . who gives a damn? You're doing what fifteen thousand actors have done before you. How the hell do you find something new? It's a fucking nightmare.

What about the truism that every actor should do *Hamlet*?

Most actors want to do *Hamlet* when they're at their craziest. I was the same way. I think it's a death wish.

So actors should forget Shakespeare?

I suppose it's good to have done it. I've done quite a bit of it, but I don't find it enriching. I never know what the hell I'm doing. I don't like Shakespeare. I'd rather be in Malibu.

You're harsh on your profession. Are you also cynical about people in your profession?

What's so special about being an actor? Actors are nothing. Actors are of no consequence. Most actors are pretty simple-minded people who just think they're complicated. Films? Actors? What is it? I remember when I'd heard about De Niro in *Raging Bull,* and I thought, I've got to go see this film. I went to see it at a small theater in New York—and the smell of urine, and pissing, and a couple of people asleep . . . it was like that moment of truth: is this what it's all about? And when I went to England in 1978 to do *Kean,* I went for a long walk one cold, bleak, British afternoon, back to those depressing areas of my life, the Waterloo and the Old Warwick, and it was now dark, it closed down for about two years. There was vomit on the sidewalk outside, and garbage, dog shit, the paint was peeling off the doors, and the theater itself was a very narrow-looking place. I walked to the stage door, it was all boarded up. I thought it was so important. Then I wandered up to the West End, opposite the theater . . . all those actors, captured for eternity on these ridiculous posters, and I thought, it's all such a pain for nothing.

"Here lies Ozymandias. . . ."

Yes. For nothing. I occasionally go and see a play, if it's a friend of mine, and I'll go backstage afterwards, and the smell of rotting garbage outside restaurants, it's so depressing. You look at this grotty, dirty little dressing room, and there's the actor, who looks like he's just been in the ring with Mike Tyson, for fifteen lines, and you say, "Well done," though he looks like death. And he says, "Oh, I got another show tonight." I come out in the bright sunshine, and I walk and I think, I don't have to do that.

An exercise in futility?

Yes, it's an exercise in futility. And it's the same with movies. If you can't enjoy doing what you're doing, what's the point of doing it?

Did you enjoy your first movie, *The Lion in Winter?*

Yes, though I was just a young, brash, very nervous actor. I had a lot of opinions about myself, you swing between tremendous arrogance and tremendous self-contempt. So I was pretty nervous, and pretty scared and unsure of myself. But I loved standing in front of the camera, I loved working with Hepburn and O'Toole. I could feel a sense of power and a center of strength in me, and I thought I must never lose it, never let go of this sense of center that I had in myself, which I'd never felt onstage.

Did Katharine Hepburn advise you not to overact?
No, she said, "You don't need to do anything. You'll understand, just relax." Then she said, "You don't have to act. You've got a good voice, you look good, you've got a big frame, you're going to look good on film. And you don't need to push it. You've been in the theater a long time. Don't act. I'll do the acting. I'm always overacting . . . that's the way I am, but you don't need to do that." She was right.

Did you know Peter O'Toole before you did this film?
No. Never met him. He was electrifying. The most exciting and dangerous actor I've ever worked with. We had some wild times together.

How wild?
Fights.

Physical or verbal?
O'Toole and I, both smashed, ready to beat each other up. He was mad. Drank as much as I did and probably more, and he had that kind of yearning zest for life. He'd been provoking me. And we sat in the car park with our coats on, and I was going to deck him . . . and he said, "You wouldn't hit me, would you?"

How was he provoking you?
He hated the Welsh. I didn't give a damn about race, Welsh, Irish, it's all the same to me. A lot of Welsh people are anti-English. I've got no bones to grind, I told O'Toole. He said, "You're like that other Welsh bastard, Richard Burton. You're a fucking misfit, play the piano and all that stuff, and you're a stargazer." Because I like astronomy. It got up his nose for some reason. He was pretty smashed, and I'd had a few, and we were in the restaurant, and I suddenly got out of my chair and leaned across the table and said, "You bastard, come outside." I meant it, I was going to deck him. I didn't care.

Did you care about what the critics said about your performance in
Magic?
I don't know why I did that film, they should have gone to somebody else, an American actor, a New York actor like Al Pacino.

Critic Pauline Kael felt you used all the emotions of a dummy.

Who's this? Never heard of her. I'm always wary of knowledgeable people who are very critical. We have them in England. Jack Tinker, one of our foremost critics, works for one of the tabloids; it's the most irritating writing, because he creams his jeans over any Vanessa Redgrave performance. It's all bullshit, all these endless analyses of films.

When you did *The Elephant Man,* did you feel it was a worthy picture?
It was very sentimental, deeply sentimental. I struggled somewhat with that. I used to cause a bit of trouble, I used to attack directors. David Lynch was going through an odd period in his life. He was very unsure of himself, and I always went for the jugular with people like that; in those days I was too tightly wrapped up. I was very intolerant of people. I said, "I don't want to speak all these lines." And David said, "You've got to." So I cut a lot of my own lines. The funny thing is, I can look now and see somebody like James Ivory, who is like David Lynch, doesn't seem to direct you at all, but now I enjoy that. Ten years ago I would have found it intolerable.

You also found Shirley MacLaine intolerable when you worked together in *The Change of Seasons.* What was the problem?
We didn't get along too well. We didn't speak to each other. She didn't like me. She's very clever and talented, but she likes to run everything, she likes control. That's okay, but I can't be bothered with that circus. You've got one director, you don't need three. You don't need the actress telling you what to do.

You probably wouldn't enjoy acting with Barbra Streisand because she would always be directing.
No, I give them five minutes, I'm not going to put up with that. It's not that important, none of this has any consequence at all. And dubbing, editing, all that bullshit—do your job, go home. If somebody asks me, "Do you want to be involved in the development of this production?" "No, give me the script, point the way to the studio and show me the camera, and I'll do it." I have no interest in developing, in producing, in directing anything.

What interested you in appearing in a third remake of *The Bounty*? Why the fascination with the subject?
I wasn't fascinated, they gave me the part and I did it. I'd seen the film when I was a kid. I thought [Charles] Laughton was terrific.

How do you compare Clark Gable's Christian to Brando's?
Brando kept changing sides. I'm a Brando fan, but that film was a mess. I liked Gable.

That TV miniseries you did, *Hollywood Wives,* was also a mess. Why'd you do it?

Just for a laugh. I was living in England, and I wanted to sell my house in Los Angeles, and my agent phoned up and said, "Do you want to do *Holly-wood Wives?*" And I said, "Is it porno?" He said, "No." I said, "Okay. How much they paying me?" I had a good time. I never saw it.

The other miniseries you did, *The Bunker,* wasn't done for laughs. Was it difficult to get inside a mind like Adolph Hitler's?

I enjoyed doing it. When I was playing him, I thought there must be a clue. What is his personal tragedy, his grief and his great loss? And I went back and looked at movies and the Olympic games and the glorious days of the Third Reich, seeing him standing there speaking "Sieg Heil." What a dream that must have been for him and for those corrupt men around him. And for the German people, eighty million people on their feet saying, at last the savior has come. And that's what they believed. I read *Mein Kampf* closely—the genocide policy, it was there, it was self-evident. With the Russian tanks moving in and Germany collapsing and falling into rubble, he must have felt a tremendous sense of betrayal that the people had let him down.

I knew so much about Hitler, and I also knew the old man in him. He's sort of a Lear figure: the decrepit old man in the bunker and the loss of his dream; the greatest dictator in the world ruling over a million square miles of rubble and ruin. Extraordinary. I understood him. Understood his need for sweet cakes and his tea parties. I styled Hitler after my own grandfather on my father's side, who was a bit of a tyrant. Self-educated and full of all kinds of extraordinary opinions and philosophical insights. He was Victorian, had a hard life, but he was hard as nails, confused, frustrated, powerful, and a sentimental ogre. Which Hitler was as well. But my grandfather didn't kill anyone, he wasn't responsible for the death of two million people.

I was a bit scared of him when I was a child, because he was tough. My father was a little scared of him. And I can always remember when I saw him standing in the street one day when I was about twelve, thirteen years of age, and my grandmother died, and he was standing there with a shopping bag, and he looked stooped and bent. I thought, that's what I'll use for Hitler. The broken man.

That scene in the Chancellory garden, which is documented footage of Hitler, his boys in their caps and their ears sticking out. The last shot of Hitler, and he's going around greeting and thanking the young boys who were twelve, fourteen years old. A broken man, shaking and patting the little boys on their cheeks.

You've also played other frighteningly evil men, on stage in *Pravda* and on screen as Hannibal Lecter in *The Silence of the Lambs*. Why the fascination with the dark side?

I've played very bright people, and very monstrous people. In *Pravda* I played a man called Lambert LaRue who was like a male version of Margaret Thatcher. He was like *Jaws*, in the way sharks move. This man knew exactly what price people had, and he knew that everyone had a price. He was ruthless, and he had a juggernaut kind of wit. It was a wonderful catharsis for me to play it because he attacked everything. Nothing was sacred. I loved playing that part because he saw through all the bullshit. He knew that contained in each human being is the jungle. That's a pretty bleak look at life, but there's a part that is exciting. It's like Lecter sees the human jungle inside each human being, he sees the dark side. It's a nihilistic truth, and it's a Nietzschean view of the world.

Before you filmed *Silence of the Lambs*, Jonathan Demme said he was repelled by the idea of doing a film about a serial killer. Were you as well?

No, I didn't think it was an exploitation movie, it was a very well constructed thriller. I had no qualms about playing Lecter, because he's a piece of fiction, a product of the imagination. A bizarre, strange, intriguing character.

Do you like being labeled the scariest man in the movies from one part?

Is that what they call me? It'll be somebody else next week.

Demme felt that Lecter stands apart from all other characters in all other works of fiction. And that you knew exactly what to do with the part. That you got the joke. What was the joke?

Well, only Jonathan can explain that. The joke, I suppose, is that Lecter's the boogie man at the end of the dark tunnel, to which we're all drawn, the shadowy figure in all our dreams. And I knew he was very attractive, and that there would be sexual undertones to it.

You also knew something about him as a reptile or a lizard.

I devised, for playing him, a cross between a cat and a lizard, somebody who doesn't blink, who is absolutely still for hours at a time. Like a praying mantis, or a spider on the wall. When you see a tarantula on the wall, it's stationary for hours, and suddenly it goes, *tsst . . . tsst . . . tsst. . . .* That's the most terrifying moment. The movement is real terror. For Lecter, he just stares, and watches, and then he moves.

Rod Steiger said that you got Lecter from him.

That's Rod's joke. "I taught you everything you know, Tony."

Didn't you say you got Lecter from Brando?
The walk at the end is Brando. I thought, I must walk like a cat. I've got two cats, and I love watching cats stalking things. Just get this slightly female walk. When I was walking, I thought—this is Brando.

You also said you heard the voice when you read the script.
Yeah. I knew it. I knew his voice.

And it was your idea to slick back the hair?
Yes, it's just the way I saw him: sleek hair, greased back, very tight, like he's bursting to get out of his skull. I wanted it like steel. I saw him as a man very taut and very economical. I also wanted to have the prison uniform tailored so it was very tight. I knew the look I wanted. I went to Jonathan Demme one day and said, "You know, when we go into the big cage scene, I see Lecter in a kind of boiler suit. What I'd like to see is just white pants, white T-shirt, white shoes, no laces." I just wanted to get that look, because I remember when I was taken to a dentist when I was a child, the white so scared me. I thought there was something very clinical and clean about shining wash basins and the horror that's in that place of awful, pristine white. When I put the wardrobe on and did the makeup, I just went on the set and out came the voice of Lecter.

Were you concerned at all about the glorification of violence? That some sicko like a Jeffrey Dahmer would see the film and be influenced by it?
No, I didn't think it glorified violence. The cinemas are full of violent films. Like *Rambo* and *Texas Chain-Saw Massacre* and Schwarzenegger movies, they are very violent, and they are so dehumanizing. Schwarzenegger's stuff is anti-human, anti-humanity: the human being turned into a machine state, Superman. They are very entertaining, but there's something almost fascistic, something very odd about it, but they are also very camp.

Do you see *The Silence of the Lambs* as a strange kind of fairy tale?
Yes. The story's about Clarice, it's not about me—it's like some strange Gothic fairy tale that she's sent out by the king to kill the monster, there's an evil scourge in the land, and he says, "Slay the dragon, but you've got to go talk to the prime dark angel." And she goes down into the bowels of hell and meets this dark angel, who is always in the half-light. It's all very erotic. It's a romantic figure, the Angel of Death, he makes her strong, and he

opens her up. Now go and get him. It's a very primitive, archetypal fairy story in a way.

Was it a twisted sort of love relationship between you and Jodie Foster?
Yeah. Lecter is great mischief, he's the devil really, he loves seeing people under pressure. And he knows all the moves she's going to make, and he doesn't even look at her, but he knows where her shadow moved. When she turns up at the very beginning of the film, he must think, what an ironic sense, what a brave little girl she must be. It's like a giant cat with a mouse, and he says, "I'm going to play with her and see what she's really made of."

Would he ever dare taste her?
I think he just enjoys toying with her. He's destroying her and rebuilding her. He loves her in a way. He'd never hurt her.

Why are evil men so often very sexy?
Power. Evil has its own power. Power is erotic. Remember when Kissinger was secretary of State and he had all those women, all the young girls around. Politicians are very powerful, and directors are powerful. People who run industries are powerful, they are erotic symbols. Power is sex. Richard III is sex. I don't think Hitler was sexy, but people used to have orgasms when he spoke. Because they fill a need on a mass level.

Are we drawn to these people because we all have a darker side?
We all would like to be machinelike and have no emotions. I long for it all the time. Have no emotions so that I could make no mistakes and be ice-cold. I'd love to be like that. But I can't be, I'm trapped in my own personality, which is constantly getting me into areas that I don't want to be in. I really long to be somebody who is ice-cold, brutal, and tough and uncompromising. Of course, I'd probably hate myself.

Some say the film is about reaching God, that eating one's victims or skinning them is the sacrament made literal.
That's all bullshit. You know, somebody once came up to me in a restaurant and put a plate of cold liver in front of me; suddenly, out of a character I've played, I've become this kind of creature.

That creature will probably earn you more than $10 million for the sequel.
That's what they say, yeah. I asked Jonathan, "Is there any news?" And he said, "Well, Tom [Harris] is writing. He's a slow writer."

Is there any doubt in your mind about playing Lecter again?
Only if the script is good. If the writing went nowhere, no, I wouldn't do it.
Why spoil it?

You've made Lecter a signature role in your career, but excluding your-self, who might you have chosen to play it?
Jack Nicholson. When I got the part, I always wondered why they gave it to me.

Do you find it ironic that your big hit is a movie that you're in for only twenty-seven minutes?
Is that all I'm in it for? That's amazing.

Did you feel you'd been let out of the cage after that movie?
Yes, it broke all box-office records in the West End theater. I went with a friend of mine, and we sat in the car across the road, and I looked at the lines of people, and I saw my name up there, and he said, "What do you think?" I said, "The weird thing is, I don't feel anything. Nothing changes. I look in the mirror—same boring face is looking back."

Yet that boring face has transformed into the face of monsters, mad men, and tyrants. Have these roles given you insights into the darker levels of humanity?
Yes. It's interesting watching people in power. Like watching Saddam Hus-sein; his whole body movement when somebody goes to meet him. When he went to the hospital after the Iraqis were bombed in that hotel. This sol-dier—who may have been politically completely opposed to him—you see his reaction is like standing before some colossus, some monster figure, some boogie man. And you watch people with Hitler, you watch people with pow-erful people, it's the same thing. Watching the Saddam Husseins, when they're talking, they don't actually look at the people they're with. They make the other people around them invisible. Olivier had that quality, and Francis Coppola has a bit of it. Powerful people have a way of making other people feel invisible, they have the power to ignore people, like you say "Good morning" to them, and they cut you dead. It serves to destabilize the other person, that's the way they rule.

John Huston was like that.
I'm sure he was. A lot of directors are, a lot of moguls are. It's a very danger-ous area when directors start to feel their power: keeping people waiting, not answering their phone, turning up late. Gandhi said that being late is an act of violence, an act of terrorism, because you unnerve people. Going on to say

"Good morning," they walk past you. I personally want to kill them when they do that. Because I think rudeness is a real spit in the face. There's a lot of pigging and rudeness in this business, it's one of the most insufferable parts of it. So when I occasionally become a director, I go over the other way to be kind to people, because to make people feel they're anonymous, to reduce them to numbers, to unimportance, like actors who treat people from the props department with a contempt, don't thank them for giving them a prop or don't say "Good morning" to the electrician or to the sound man—it's unspeakable. I've seen it, I've watched it happen. Actors and directors are fucking horrible, it puts me in an intolerant rage.

You've said in the past it was directors like Peter Brook, Tony Richardson, and Ken Russell who have become so powerful in England that they used the actor as a puppet. Is that how you still feel?
Yeah. Got no love for them at all. Richardson was one of the worst ones. Those directors, I hate them. I don't understand why actors don't stand up for themselves when they're being treated . . . abused, by some director, and they put up with it. Why not stand up and fight against maniacs? I do fight it, I don't put up with that. I won't work. I hate directors who are interfering, passing notes. It's not worth getting out of bed in the morning if you've got monsters, I don't care how great they are. I've walked out of two films. One was with some British jerk director who was crying in rage because I dared to challenge him. Because I don't give a shit about my career. I don't like anyone bullying other people. On *Dracula* an assistant director shouted at the cameraman, and I stopped and said, "Is this a concentration camp you're running here? Don't shout in front of me, just go fuck yourself, keep out of my way." I don't want to be a hero, I don't want to be everyone's champion, but if I see it, I'll stop it, I won't put up with it. I'm glad my anger is alive and healthy, I don't want to become too docile.

Did you also feel that way about Sam Peckinpah when he sent you the film for *Straw Dogs* and you told him he had a menstruation complex?
Yeah. Sex and violence, that's all. . . .

What did you think of the film when you saw it?
Terrible.

So when you have to portray anger now, do you just think of a few directors and it comes back?
Yeah. I must say that 90 percent of film directors I've worked with have been terrific. The theater is a different story. That's the breeding ground of such fabulous bullshit. Intellectual bullshit. These directors come straight out of

Cambridge University with new innovations about Shakespeare. Hamlet
dressed up as a Nazi. It's wanking, you know.

Isn't a case often made that the director is the director, the father figure?
Oh! I can't stand it. When you think of the history of what the human
species have gone through. The knowledge that has been brought forward
about people's rights to not be controlled by other people. From national
histories, the Holocaust, brutality, war, down to the shop floor. Nobody can
have power over you. Why we still put up with this bullshit, I don't understand. If you let these sharks get at you, they'll tear your innards out, they'll
destroy you. Why bother with these people? They make life miserable for
everyone on the set. That's one area that I've decided in the last few years
that I can well do without.

**You mentioned the power of Francis Coppola. What kind of tyrant was
he when you were filming *Dracula*?**
Francis is an enormous personality, very charismatic, he's a controller, a dictator, a tyrant in his way. I say all these things with a positive feeling. *The
Godfather* was one of the greatest films made, and *Apocalypse Now,* a big,
sprawling film of epic proportions. I watched him in that documentary
about the making of that, and there he was in the swamps, up to his chest in
water, directing the helicopter. I think this isn't a man who is covered in
Gucci leather sitting in an office in Burbank. This man really does put his
money where his mouth is.

Were you pleased with the way the film turned out?
It was a big bold film, I've never seen anything like it. The only criticism I
would have is, if I were Francis, I wouldn't do so much. He threw too much
on the screen. I'd just say, "Right, we don't need all these shots." But that's
the way he works. When he makes pasta, he puts everything in it. He's an ex-
cessive person with huge appetites.

Many people were hoping it would be a scarier movie.
It wasn't scary. No. I didn't find it sexy either. I didn't find it erotic. It is
funny, though, isn't it?

Yeah. But that isn't why one goes to see a Coppola film about Dracula.
When my wife Jenny and I first saw it, I looked at her—she's very, very conservative in her taste as far as films go—and she's sitting there going, "What
the fuck is all this about?" She said afterwards, "I've never seen anything like
it." The images have still stayed with her. So it hit her, because she wouldn't
have crossed the road to a Dracula film.

Did you know how you were going to play Von Helsing before you started filming?

When I read the script, I thought, how the fuck am I going to do this part? It doesn't really have much of a clue in it. I remember doing fantastic preparations. And then we started rehearsing, and working with Coppola is an odd experience because he improvises, so you don't have a text to work on, he changes it all the time. There's a kind of chaos, because everything is thrown at you. He throws ideas as you're walking . . . and you grab at them. It's pretty chancy to work with a man like Coppola, because you are on the cusp of a disaster. The only way to work with somebody like him is just learn your lines, show up, and don't ask questions, because he seems to know what he wants to do. He gives you anything you want as long as you keep out of his ego.

Was it Winona Ryder who suggested you for the part?

Yes, she did. Coppola told me that Winona had brought the *Dracula* script to him, and she wanted me. She's amazing. Twenty-one years of age, and she's got an extraordinary brain, extremely well read and knows herself.

Is it true that you're uncomfortable around young, accomplished actresses?

I can never really relax, especially with actresses. I met Meryl Streep in London, and she'd paid me great compliments, and I didn't know what to do or say. So when I get frightened, I give them a hug and I get very physical. With Winona Ryder, I could never quite relax with her; the same thing with Jodie—Jodie and I were slightly nervous of each other.

What about young actors, like *Dracula*'s Gary Oldman?

Gary Oldman is a very exciting actor. He reminded me of me in a way. As I was some years ago. He's very obsessed, obsessive, which is good as long as it doesn't destroy him. I hope I've grown out of that obsession, because it's so uncomfortable living in an obsession like that. He's got that thing that O'-Toole had, that wonderful quality of sheer bloody madness. Gary doesn't stop. He may be a bit of a pain in the ass to some people, but at least he's there, he's functioning, he's very alive. If anything, Gary has to just calm down a bit.

Your own madness and obsessions coincided with your drinking years. How big a drinker were you?

I was a problem drinker, I drank for fifteen years, which is not long. I had done severe damage to myself, I put on weight, I'd done more damage to my emotional equipment, I was just very shaky and thought I was going mad. I felt it was hopeless, and I wanted to end it all. My life was beginning slowly to fall to pieces, I was a damn nuisance to be around.

Did you drink while acting as well?
No, but I may as well have been drinking because I was so hungover and intoxicated. You can function well while drinking. I did it quite successfully.

How long has it been since you last had a drink?
Seventeen years.

Did you ever worry that you would lose your edge if you gave up booze?
Yeah, initially. I didn't care, I just wanted to get this monkey off my back, and I did.

Is that when you found [a certain self-help organization]?
You can't print its name, you know.

Why?
You have to respect the anonymity of the tradition. You mustn't print that. I would be very angry if you print that.

All right. How did you get help?
I wound up in a self-help group, and I found there were people who were just like me, and their job is to help people who suffer just like themselves. A network is there night and day if you want it, and it saved my life. I'm so indebted to them, I try to observe the rules and traditions.

Did you decide to seek help after you drove from Los Angeles to Phoenix and didn't know that you'd done it?
I remember doing it, but I'd fallen asleep at the wheel, I was intoxicated, and I came back to Los Angeles, and I reached my wit's end. I could have killed somebody in my car.

Is that how you thought you were going to die? In a car accident without even knowing?
That was horrifying. I thought all my problems from when I was a little kid come back to this inability to fit in and live peacefully in the world. This feeling of being an outsider. And when you take drugs or booze, it makes you fit in for a while. That's why it's so attractive. Booze is just narcotics in a bottle. It's a depressant. And anything you can get to fix you is an addiction. Whether it's sex or food or work or success, if it becomes a fixation then it's

an addiction, and you become dependent upon that addiction. It can ruin your life.

Didn't Robert Morley talk to you about your problem?
Yeah. I resented it.

What about other drugs—marijuana, acid?
No, I never messed with that stuff, but I had enough tequila in me to know what an acid trip was like.

How often do you go off by yourself into the desert or the mountains?
Well, I love driving. I take off quite often. Mickey Rourke and I took a wild week in Utah, Wyoming, Montana, Idaho. I went from Boseman, Montana, to Spokane in one day and drove right down through Idaho to Boise the next day, did a four- or five-day trip.

Was your drinking part of the cause of the failure of your first marriage?
I don't want to talk about that.

At all?
Nope. It's over. It was my problem. My fault. Produced one child from that and got divorced.

We don't know much about it. . . .
I don't want you to know anything. It's over.

Can we talk about your daughter?
No. Because she's changed her name. She wants to get on with her career.

Are you friends with her?
Oh yeah. I saw her just recently, but that's over as well. You're not going to get anything out of me. I'm keeping the personal parts of my life that would be painful to my ex-wife and daughter. I accept full responsibility. It was just something that didn't work. It's over. It's been and done, it's over.

Didn't you once play a character in *The Good Father* where you had to vent your rage against your wife?
Yes. The director, Michael Neal, was a very complex man. He wanted to talk about the part and degrees of rage and anger. I said, "Listen, let's just shoot it, I know all about anger." And he said, "Yeah, but let's talk about it." And I

said, "No, look, I bring the child back, I dump him on the mother, she slams
the door in my face, and I kick the door, that's it. There's nothing about degrees of anger. I know this man inside out and backwards, he's me. I've done
all these things, I've been through a marriage, I've been through a disastrous
divorce, and I've got all that violence in me, so let's just do it." So he did.

Did you like the results?
I didn't know what the hell the film was about, but it looked quite good.
There was one day when I was showing her the kid's bed and a little room
that I've got for him. And I walked out of my first marriage, which was a disaster, and I left my child Abigail. As I did it, I just broke down, which I've
never done before. I've always kept myself in charge of my emotions, but I
just broke down. I felt ashamed and very angry with myself. It's the first time
I acknowledged that anything had any ties on me, because I've always tried
to deny emotion. It kind of shook me.

So your personal life intruded on your life of make-believe?
Yes, the hurt the children go through over divorces, with their innocence
and adult stupidity. It hurt me that I'd been irresponsible. But I wasn't fit
for marriage to bring up a family, it was a mess.

How old was your child then, when you were playing this role?
About fifteen, sixteen maybe. She has a very small part in *Remains of the Day*.
She's a good actress.

Did she ask you to get her a part?
No, I just went to the producer and said, "I'd like my daughter to do this.
What do you think?"

Did she have any problem with that?
No, she loved it.

Do you give her advice?
No, when we were on the set together, I stayed away. She changed her name
so they didn't know who she was. We were in a scene together. She's one of
the housemaids, and she's with my father as he's dying, and she wakes him
up when I come into the room. She said, "I was nervous." And I put my arm
around her and said, "You looked terrific, it was great."

Does she know your basic feelings about it all being bullshit?
No. I don't try to disillusion her about that.

You also said seeing her was like seeing yourself in drag.
We do look a little alike, but she's got all the burning questions I had in
there. She's much smarter than me. She's very determined.

**How long did it take for you to become friends? Was that a hard
process?**
We got close a few years ago, and she came and stayed with us. And because
she was doing her own numbers, playing some sort of scenes for herself, trying to impress me or being manipulating, I said, forget it. I just withdrew. I
always withdraw from people. I try not to let people absorb too much of my
energy. Once people start latching on to me and try to draw things out of
me and control me, I wave them good-bye, sometimes forever, and I won't go
back. I don't like being controlled by anyone.

**But when it comes to your own daughter, don't you have to have a rec-
onciliation about that?**
Not necessarily. I was quite prepared to go into the wilderness without her. I
was prepared not to see her again. It doesn't matter to me, you see. We have
to be tough and callous about it all, live our lives; it's a very selfish way of
looking at it, but I don't have a conscience.

Do you have contact with her mother as well?
No. After our scene together I wrote to her mother and her grandmother
and said, "She did really well at this, and I'm so pleased for her." But that's
as much.

Your second marriage has lasted for twenty years. How did you meet her?
I was up in Scotland for a film called *Eight Bells Toll,* and she was working for
the production company. I arrived at the airport worse for wear, having a few
drinks on a late plane—I'd missed the other one—and her boss said, "One of
our actors is missing, and he's probably going to turn up on the next flight.
Could you go down and meet him and give him his call sheets for tomorrow
morning? He's a bit of a nuisance; his name is Tony Hopkins." And as I got
off the plane, she was there, and as soon as she saw me she thought, "That's
him. I'm going to marry him." And she took an instant dislike to me. I was
rude like lots of actors.

Did you even notice her?
Nope. And a few weeks later I was at a party, and I asked her out. She wrote
to a friend of hers and said, "I met an actor called Anthony Hopkins, and he
was quite offensive, but I feel drawn to him in some strange way."

Are you uncomfortable with your former intensity, that you just want to wipe it away?

Yes, I am. I want to forget it. It was a stage in my life when I was very unattractive, very tiresome. It really sounds weird, but everything to do with acting, the intensity of acting, the meaning, the importance of this to me now, is incomprehensible. My whole attitude about it all has changed so drastically in the last couple of years, the whole acting business has changed. It's work, it's a job, it's something that I do quite well, and I enjoy it. It doesn't consume my brain, it doesn't eat me up anymore. It's none of my business anymore. I just show up and do what's in front of me, it's the only way I can function.

So you are a very changed man, from what you were to what you are. You're really two different people.

It's like having slipped off the edge. I feel this sort of emptiness, there's no resistance for me. I've done a few television interviews lately, and I was looking at myself. If I were not me, but watching this man, I would have thought, what an extraordinary attitude to his work. Because I feel detached from it. It's like all my ambition is gone. I'm not very comfortable talking about all this, it leaves me puzzled, as if, "What importance is any of this?" It's of no consequence at all to me.

Still, to get an insight into who you are, we have to look at who you were.

The only negative emotion that I feel is, I get scared when I get cornered by the intensity of this business, by people who say, "You've got to do this, this is an important career move." It's the only violent feeling I have. I don't give a shit about anything, and yet because I don't care about it anymore, something else has come into my life, which is a real profound enjoyment of it.

Lao-Tzu said, "How do you clear muddy water? You don't stir it, you let it settle to the bottom."

That's it, it's a feeling of settling, like I've settled. And the funny thing is that everything is coming to me.

Were you surprised by the overwhelming critical acclaim of *Howard's End*?

I wasn't. I thought it was going to be a good film. It was received well in England, and that surprised me, because the English don't like anything that we do. They knock everything, like they always have a go at Ken Branagh. Well, he's the only filmmaker we've got in England.

Is there much of a film industry in England anymore?

No film industry at all in England. I don't think people care, give a damn about it. The British public, they're television addicts. And yet the cinemas are beginning to fill up, but it's all American movies. We don't have any British movies, not much to speak of. I think the first British actor that really worked well in cinema was Albert Finney. He was a backstreet Marlon Brando. He brought a great wittiness and power to the screen. The best actor we've had. Burton had it as well. The problems with the British film industry started in the sixties, when directors made films for their friends but not for the general public. They were making films about washing lines and brass bands in North Country towns. Talking about "the industrial north." So what? Who cares?

You've expressed your admiration for Finney. Who else have you found extraordinary?

I suppose Olivier was, in his way. He represented something.

What about Mick Jagger, who acted with you in *Freejack*?

I was only with him for a few days, he's just an ordinary guy, very pleasant, easygoing.

If Jagger's ordinary, what does that make such icons as Elvis and Madonna?

Madonna and Elvis are just self-creations . . . that's their genius, they invent themselves. I don't know if they're human. I'd like to have met Orson Welles. Welles was a mess at the end of his life. It's not worth it, is it? Lonely, sheer loneliness. And Brando, though I know nothing about him except what one reads in the news.

Do you have an opinion about Brando and George C. Scott rejecting their Oscars?

It's insulting. It's so criminal. It's fucking pompous of them. Who the hell do they think they are? People in a very good industry which has been very good to them and they make a lot of money, they're very rich in a luxury business. People who get the Oscar and use it as a doorstop for the toilet door—what are they trying to prove? It's like somebody gets up to get the Oscar in evening suit, a tux, and wears tennis shoes. So big deal. You're making a gesture? You're showing us what a rebel you are? You are showing us what a conservative arsehole you are. They are assholes. I admire Scott and Brando, they are terrific, great actors. Why demean themselves, why do that, why insult people who want to see them? Why turn on them and piss in people's faces? Because that's what they're doing. They are turning around and farting in people's faces, and that's an insult.

Is the disdain you think they have for their craft or for themselves?
For themselves, and a tremendous amount of pomposity. It's beneath them, that sort of thing. That's bullshit. I just find it a bit sad, great actors that they are. Why didn't they just enjoy it? I mean, especially Brando, extraordinarily gifted, nobody can touch him. Why turn it all to shit?

Who are the actors that you most admire?
Faye Dunaway, she's one of the best American actresses. I like Pacino very much. De Niro. Michelle Pfeiffer, Jodie Foster, Johnny Depp, Winona Ryder. My favorite actors are American actors.

You're leaving out your fellow countryman and Oscar winner, Emma Thompson.
She's a really great actress. I don't know what it is about her. She's one of the most intelligent actors I've worked with because she keeps it all very simple, very direct, very clear.

Does she work at all the way you work?
We work in exactly the same way. I've done two films now with her. There's no bullshit with her. That's a compliment to myself, isn't it? We get on so well together because we seem to keep it light. You get into the character, and then you do it. I suppose it is complex, but it doesn't feel like work, because it's like driving a car. She asked James Ivory, "How should I age?" Then she came up with something brilliant. All she did, she wore brighter lipstick, had long, very high varnished nails, and smoked a cigarette. It was a hardness, and it was extraordinary—that was her contribution.

Actors like Pacino and De Niro seem to spend a lot more time than you do getting into their roles.
I know Pacino and Dustin Hoffman and De Niro work very intensely. And they produce wonderful performances. I can't do that. For example, on *Remains of the Day* I thought I'd better go and study some butlers. A friend of mine introduced me to a butler at the Palace. I expected to meet a dummy. He's a very nice young fellow, didn't speak with a kind of upper-class accent, not vain. Just an ordinary, straightforward guy. And he was one of the top butlers. So I thought, well, that's the way it is. This butler I'm playing, Stevens, is a unique butler. His problem is that he's so intent on being the perfect butler he just waves good-bye to his whole life. He's a bit of a fanatic.

He's over the top, he tries to do everything so precisely, a perfectionist. His tragedy is, he can't forgive himself, and he begins to slip as he's getting a little older. He has longings, yearnings, and he can't understand them, because he's so closed off. And that's his problem. He's a man so lacking in self-knowledge it's heartbreaking. When I read the script for *Remains of the Day*, I started looking at scenes and putting them together, because once you've learned the dance steps you're free. I don't go along with this idea that you've got to wait for the lines to come. I don't think they come to you, you've got to learn them. Maybe that's why a lot of American actors say all English actors are just facile. Maybe they've got a point, but for me I've got to learn the text. That's the most important thing, because in the text lies all the essence.

What tricks do you use to help you learn your lines?
I take sections of the script or play, and I'll write it all out in longhand. Then I tape it to the wash basin, and I learn it in parrot fashion. Say it out loud twenty times. I have little marks in different colored pencils that look like cartwheels—a four-stroke asterisk surrounded by a circle, which means "five." I put them in my notebook—they're the number of times I've gone over it. It's an obsession really. I know that if I've done it 150 times, I really know it so well, it's there in the nuance of my brain. Sometimes I learn the end of the play first.

I also do old magic tricks, like knock myself on the head three times in order to remember something. I know the text so well that I don't have to act it, and when the other actors have it you start playing tennis with it, hitting the ball back to each other. Everything starts to flow, and your body responds because what you've done is concretized thoughts.

Well, it certainly seems your life has been more like a game of racquetball, bouncing off four walls and the ceiling, than tennis.
I love the bizarre arrangement of life, the choreography of life, where you don't know what's going to happen next. And my life has been a choreography. It's been such a series of dreamlike events.

The wisdom of Sir Hopkins: life is a choreography. Expect nothing.
Ask nothing, expect nothing, and accept everything. That's it. I say to myself every day, like a meditation: "It's none of my business what people say of me or think of me. I am what I am, and I do what I do for fun, and it's all in the game. The wonderful game, the play of life upon life itself, nothing to win, nothing to lose, nothing to win, nothing to prove. No sweat, no big deal, because of myself I am nothing, and of myself I've been nothing."

Where is that from?
I made it up, it came to me at a moment of severe depression ten years ago, sitting in a hotel in Rome. I was having an ego problem because I hadn't got what I wanted. I was sitting in this garden with a notepad, trying to write a book, and I wrote that down. It became clear to me. I repeated that over to myself like a mantra, and ever since a lot of extraordinary things have happened in my life.

And you haven't been depressed since?
Well, I suffered through a sort of clinical depression about six years ago, and Jenny said, "Maybe you're always depressed. You're Welsh, you're an actor, maybe you ought to accept that's what you are." And I said, "No, I can't accept that. This is a role I'm playing." I think we play roles in our behavior, emotional games with ourselves. If we act as if we're depressed, then we'll be depressed, and if we act as if we're troubled, then we'll be troubled. I think too much thinking can wreck you. I can sit in the sun and think my way through the universe and just make myself miserable. People have too much time on their hands, too much time in order to get bored. I feel more at liberty now, I feel free of a lot of bugs. All my problems have always come from an argument with myself. And recently I stopped fighting with myself.

Did you go into a depression when your father died in 1981? Were you at peace with him? Or were there things left unsaid?
I was never very demonstrative emotionally or affectionate with my dad. I'd drummed that out of myself, I didn't trust emotions or feelings at all. I gave his hand a squeeze before he died and said, "I love you." That's the first time I'd ever said that in my life, and I sort of muttered it, and he gave my hand a squeeze, and then he died. It was funny going to hospital to see him, and I thought, well, that's the end of that. Kind of sobering thought, it does slow you down for a moment.

Did you ever kiss your dad?
When he was dead.

Do you have any fears about your own death?
I don't. I know that in the end there's a peace, a real peace, and maybe darkness and nothing. I don't have morbid thoughts about it, I'm in a state of grace, I suppose. Maybe it's Zen. My epitaph, if I ever have one, will be, "What was that all about?"

JODIE FOSTER

JODIE FOSTER GAVE ME THE CHOICE: we could talk over breakfast or in the conference room of her publicist's office. If this was to be a profile, I'd have opted for breakfast to see what I could learn by watching her eat. But an interview needs quiet, so we met on neutral grounds. She came in wearing a gray Armani suit, a cotton striped blouse, and no makeup. She knew that I had screened her film *Little Man Tate* with my seven-year-old daughter, and since it's about a seven-year-old child prodigy, Jodie was anxious to hear my daughter's reaction as well as my own. The film was something special for Jodie because she not only acted in it but nurtured its development, talked it through meetings, and proved to any doubters that she could control a set for her directorial debut.

Jodie took a seat not on the couch but on the floor, where she stirred a Styrofoam cup of coffee and then twisted and bent the plastic straw throughout our conversation. She was obviously used to talking; she's been in the business since she was three and Coppertone thought her cute enough to put in its first commercial. Ever since, she has lived her life as much in front of a camera as behind one.

When I interviewed her in the summer of 1991, Jodie Foster (whose real name is Alicia, though she's never been called that) was twenty-eight and she had appeared in twenty-eight films—a pace she deemed slow because she felt she needed time to regenerate after making a picture. After spending her childhood years doing commercials, she had gone into TV, then did her first feature, *Napoleon and Samantha,* before she was ten. At eleven she played Ellen Burstyn's daughter in Martin Scorsese's *Alice Doesn't Live Here Anymore,* and a year later, in 1976, she chilled us with her portrayal of a child hooker in Scorsese's tour de force *Taxi Driver.*

A child prodigy herself, Jodie attended the Lycée Français, a private school in Los Angeles, where she delivered her graduation speech in French. Her mother raised her and her two older sisters and brother by herself, and Jodie grew up barely knowing her father, who remarried, started another family, and remained in Los Angeles. It was her mother who made all her career decisions, though Jodie was always involved in the process. She obviously made the right ones, for Foster's career has never faltered. She even went to college—to Yale naturally—as she continued to make movies.

What people often remember when they hear the name Jodie Foster is another name she would rather not talk about: John Hinckley, the deranged psychopath who so wanted to impress her that he shot President Reagan on March 30, 1981. In an unmailed letter to Foster found in his hotel room, Hinckley wrote that he was in love with Foster and planned to kill the president in the hope that "this historical deed" would gain her "respect and love."

What it gained Jodie was security guards, who watched over her throughout her years at Yale. Never comfortable in the spotlight, this incident made her turn even more inward. She spent time whenever she could in Paris, where she maintains an apartment. She talks to the press, but she is always in control of what she says . . . and what she won't say.

She continued to make movies, appearing in *Foxes, Carny, The Hotel New Hampshire,* and *Five Corners,* among others, but it wasn't until she let it all hang out as a rape victim accused of provoking her own rape in *The Accused* (1988) that Jodie Foster entered the ranks of major serious actors. Her Oscar-winning performance brought her new respect within the industry, and she managed to follow that with another chilling and Oscar-caliber role as the FBI trainee Clarice Starling who goes head to head with one serial killer, Hannibal Lecter (Anthony Hopkins), in order to capture another in Jonathan Demme's huge hit *The Silence of the Lambs.* After starring in and directing her first feature, *Little Man Tate,* she directed *Home for the Holidays* in 1995 and *Flora Plum* in 2000 and acted in Woody Allen's *Shadows and Fog, Sommersby, Maverick, Nell,* Robert Zemeckis's *Contact,* and *Anna and the King.*

Since *Little Man Tate* is the first film you both directed and acted in, do you feel twice as much about it compared with any of your other films?
Oh, absolutely. *More* than twice!

And will you be doing twice as much publicity?
I always do what's appropriate for the film. I did so much PR for *Silence,* and I've never done as much PR for a movie as for *The Accused.* But a movie like *Little Man Tate* needs a different kind of handling. It's not a date movie, it's not an action film, or based on a Stephen King novel, and I don't want it to be sold that way. It should be done on a more grassroots level. I want to do high schools, I want to go to smaller film festivals, go to Planned Parenthood. That's more appropriate for the film. I thought about publishing a piece about it, but then I thought, why? I'm going to say it all in interviews anyway. I actually like doing interviews because you get to work out how you feel about things.

Is your move toward directing something you've always wanted to do? Or are you covering yourself for the time when you're considered "too old" for certain parts?
No, I always wanted to direct from the time I was a kid, but I didn't feel that I was mature enough. When I found this piece, it's the only movie that I really felt I understood enough.

Was it winning an Oscar that gave you the chance to direct?
This project came before the award. But it is absolutely a function of clout. I would not be able to have gotten the kind of budget that I got if I was not the actress in the movie, if I didn't cut my price and appear on the head of the marquee in a basically supporting role.

How long did it take you to direct *Little Man Tate*?
A lifetime. You can learn in five minutes what you are supposed to do technically, but it's the going beyond what you're supposed to do, it's the imagination that takes really a lifetime—knowing what movies can and don't do.

Jonathan Kaplan, who directed you in *The Accused,* called it a very personal and brave first movie to make. In what ways was it brave?
In his mind it was brave because it doesn't hit you over the head and say, "Look at me." It's about people. They are not grand, they are not princely, there are no helicopter crashes. . . .

Not even a slap!
Not even a slap, exactly. There are no night shots. There's no paint to paint over stuff, it's just pure. Even though it's a comedy, it's like a sponge seeped in sadness, there is sadness in every moment of this movie.

What are the main themes that *Little Man Tate* deals with?

What's the push of an artist who is a prodigy? The most interesting part about a prodigy is not so much that they know math or something else, it's that they are a herald to a new age. When the great prodigy comes, it means they are necessarily alone and things will change from then on. Who will the next Renaissance man be? Who is this boy going to grow up to be? He's born of these two women's sides, both of them are half of him. And he is all the things that they can never be. So it's a balance.

I do like the idea of an unconventional relationship between a child and her parent. These are three unconventional people, basically, who do not fit into society. They are misfits. It's about these people trying to find an un-conventional way in a world that keeps shoving conventional happiness down their throats. The movie is sensitive but not a sentimental movie. It's about love, but it doesn't say "what the world needs now is love sweet love." It doesn't bang it over your head and put little smiley faces on your lunch box.

It's also about intimacy, and that doesn't necessarily have to be parental. A lot of this movie is about boy meets girl, gets taken away from girl, and girl loses boy, the girl calls boy on the phone, he says, "I'm busy," the boy comes back and says, "I'm sorry." It's romance. It's about two people who are in love.

And it just so happens that the two people are a seven-year-old boy and his thirty-year-old mother. Do you think that some who see this film will compare it to your own life and interpret it as a valentine to your mother? With the psychologist character that Diane Wiest plays as rep-resenting the movie industry in your life?

In some ways that could be definitely true. Although it's not an autobio-graphical movie at all, it doesn't have anything to do with my life. I identify with all the characters. Binary opposites are something that I'm obsessed with. People are continually dancing with opposites. The world of men and women shouldn't be about women trying to be like guys and guys trying to be like girls, it should be about allowing that dynamic and that dance back and forth. It's not about trying to be the same. Tate's relationship with these two women is about balancing two sides of himself: the masculine and the feminine; the side that's ill formed, about chaos and inspiration, and the side that's about saying, "If I put the green paint with the blue paint it will make this particular color." So it's a very traditional dilemma in the forma-tion of the self and the formation of the artist. You have to have the outer self and the inner self, the public self and the private self. Everything in my life is about trying to balance two very separate identities, and in some ways that's what those two women are.

How influential were J. D. Salinger's stories on you?
Franny and Zooey is my favorite book. It changed my life when I was a kid.

Was it Salinger's ambiguities? His ability to not say as much, or even more, than he does say?
What fascinates me are layers of meaning, in terms of building characters. So much of what fascinates me about being an actress is what people don't say, the things that are implicit. That's why I was a literature major and why I stunk in history. 1917 . . . like who cares? I'm not interested in facts, I'm interested in truth, which is different.

Brando told me: "Shaw said that thinking was the greatest of human endeavors, but I would say that feeling was." What do you think?
I agree absolutely. It's the continual saga of my life anyway.

Would you say you lean more toward romance or cynicism?
I'm both. "Cynicism masks an inability to cope," said John Fowles. That's quite true. It is a protection for people who are too romantic.

Have you had any new insights into acting now that you've directed?
Yeah. There are a couple of things I realized. One is that I can be really fascistic with actors. One thing Jonathan Demme showed me was a certain freedom and openness and patience to allow an actor to find something, instead of continually telling him where it's going to be, when it's going to happen. It took me a long time during the shoot to realize that. Because I love structure, I love directors giving me as much structure as they possibly can, because if I can have twenty things on the left side of my brain, then my right side can be free to do whatever I want. But not everybody works that way. So much of it is about being able to give people freedom. As the movie progressed I learned that lesson.

I also got very specific about what I wanted and what I didn't want. If I didn't want the two-shot, I didn't shoot it, because I was worried it would be recut.

The great thing about directing is all the research you could ever possibly want as an actor you get as director. And the other thing is about being involved in the text. You know why every single line is there, and you stop asking those questions which you often ask as an actor.

Is the movie you shot the story you sold to Orion?

Scott Frank and I worked a lot together because there have been so many drafts of the script. The draft that I signed on to originally, there is no resemblance to this movie at all. It was not a movie really about two people and a child. It was a movie about a kid who went to college and wacky things in fraternities. But I got fascinated by the two women pulling him from side to side.

You have a golden rule: never make an actor feel like shit. How often have you been made to feel like shit in your career?

Not as often as other people. I was very lucky. But yes, this movie has a lot of overtones of subtle psychological abuse. How people deal with children, how people use children as props, how mothers sometimes use children against each other. Acting is the perfect, vulnerable, childlike moment where you are in the hands of somebody and where it's very easy for a director, as a father figure, or as a parent figure, to subtly work away at your psyche. That's why I work very little. I only do one film a year. I have to be really strong before I get on the set. I have to regenerate, because you get broken down when you make a movie. And if you don't spend the time and effort regenerating yourself to this very self-confident person, you can't do what's right for the character because your ego's involved. I have to be able to just totally shed my ego. I have to be strong enough and centered enough to know what the story is to be able to tell it and not get my own personal stuff involved. And you don't know who the director is until you get on that set. He could be Hitler. You're not always going to have the greatest guys.

Have you had to work with any Hitlers?

I had a bad experience with one particular movie. I thought that I could take on anyone. I never considered myself vulnerable to any kind of psychological insult. I'm not like an actor type, you could say anything to me. And I got on this set, and for some reason he insulted my soul, and it really took me a long time after that to be able to work again with confidence.

You obviously don't want to mention names, but was this when you were very young?

Old. Twenty-something.

Right, old!

The only thing you really have as an actor, the only armor you have, is confidence. And when that gets chinked away at, you can't be good. You have to be in a place where you feel so incredibly overconfident about who you are that you can allow yourself to be torn down.

Does directing satisfy your need for control more than acting?
(*Big smile*) Oh yeah. But it doesn't satisfy my need for performance. There is a side of me that needs to perform, and that side will never go away. Only acting can do that.

You got the nickname BLT (Bossy Little Thing) on *The Accused*. Did they take out the "L" when you became a director?
No, because I'm still so short. But in this one I told them to call me Boss Woman. Bossssss Woman!

Now that you've joined their ranks, who are the directors you most admire?
I'm a big fan of the French movies from the late fifties. I had a French education, I spent a lot of time there and lived there, and there is a side of me that has a French sensibility.

We'll get to that part of your life, but sticking with directors, you worked in Woody Allen's *Shadows and Fog*. Did you learn anything from him?
It was amazing how kind of okay I was about his very different, strange way of working. Nobody reads the script, nobody knows what the movie's called or what it's about. They don't tell you where you're going to be or what time period it is. Basically, it's his movie, it's in his head, and as long as you don't bug him and don't talk about the film, you'll get on great with him, because he just wants to talk about the ball game and food he ate and great jazz records that he loves. It's his party, his movie, and you have to respect that because that's how he works.

My part was small. I didn't have particularly any kind of character. It was in a brothel, and I was just another character in a brothel discussing the universe. They were long takes, and I knew I was going to have to be in one position for a take, so I found the most comfortable position reclining on someone. I couldn't take the movie seriously because I didn't know what it was about. I was just this very frivolous, know-nothing character. Usually that would bother me because I don't know how to act without telling the story, but that's how he wants to work. He wants you to just be natural. He usually says, "Say whatever you want to say, just make sure there are no pauses."

Are there any other directors whom you could so trust to work so blind?
Almost Scorsese, even though that's a much more dangerous category. But
both of those directors have a continuity to their work, and that's about the
evolution of their character. As the years go on, each film evolves their character and the things that they believe in. And their vision. Most American directors hop on a movie, they go, "Oh, *Days of Thunder,* I'll take that. *Top Gun,* I'll
take that." Whatever comes around. But when you develop projects that are
about yourself, your character, it has to have a spin on your own life. You can
say that with Truffaut, with Malle . . . they always have consistent images.

Do you feel Scorsese is our best director?
Yeah, I do.

**Now that you've become a hyphenate, are there any favorite old films
you'd like to remake?**
There's an old style of comedy in the forties that I love, all that language and
wit, I miss that. Preston Sturges stuff, language comedy. I'm tired of people
falling down stairs. Physical comedy is just not as funny.

**Success allows you a certain power in the industry, but it's still a male-
dominated world. Recently a female brain surgeon resigned her position as a tenured professor of neurosurgery at Stanford because she
didn't feel she was treated as an equal to the men. Are her problems
also yours?**
I've been incredibly lucky. I've been in a position where I haven't had to have
the kind of insults that a lot of women do in business, but there are absolutely and will always be subtle pieces of sexism every day of my life. In
some ways the greatest thing that my mom ever did for me was empower me
with this delusionary confidence. I remember sitting under a lemon tree outside my house when I was five or six, and my mom came out and she said,
"You know, you're just so lucky to be a woman now, because you can do anything you want to do, you can be a lawyer, a doctor. . . . " The message that I
realized even then was that she couldn't and that I was going to be different,
that my life was going to be very different.

**You're certainly different, but you're still a woman in what many
women believe is a sexist business. Peter Rainer in the *L.A. Times* called
women an endangered species in the movies. Do you agree?**
The vicious cycle in female films is that you perpetuate any human female
characters as props. Then you hear, "You can't have just a woman on the
marquee, nobody will care." Well, yeah, because they are not humans. You

give them these little nothing parts where they are the girlfriend-of, or the sister-of, of course they are not going to care in the movie. *Thelma and Louise*—you put two women on a marquee that actually *do* something, that have character and are human beings, then you say, "Wow, they made money. So let's do it again." It is a responsibility of women in power to change the system from within the system.

Meryl Streep has been pretty vocal about the inequities of the business. Women—with perhaps the exception of what Julia Roberts will get for her next film—don't get paid what men do. Are you struck by that?
It's not something that I go to bed at night worrying about. A movie like *Silence of the Lambs* will do more for the inequities of women on the marquee than federally funded campaigns. *Silence of the Lambs* in a weird way is a more important film than anything that has happened in a long time—for a film to make $125 million and the hero to be a woman. This movie will change the next twenty copycat films that are made after that.

Was the success of *Silence* because the hero was a woman or because of the story?
It absolutely was the story, but that's why I picked the story. The movie is frightening, but there are a lot of frightening movies out there that don't get repeat business.

And what made *Silence* different from those others?
Because they didn't have those eight-page-long dialogue scenes between Lecter and Clarise. If this movie had been done at Disney or had been "Disneyized" at any other studio, the first thing they would have taken out would have been those long dialogue scenes. As far as I'm concerned, that's the tension.

How much convincing did you have to do to get the part?
Oh, I ran after it. Every day I would call my agent and say, "You tell Orion when this thing comes through that I want to make this movie." Originally Gene Hackman was set to direct it, but he bowed out on the first draft. I think because it was a lot of work.

Your performance and Anthony Hopkins's were so striking, I wondered why the film was released so early in the year. Usually such a film would be a fall release for Academy consideration.
There were studio reasons. Thriller or horror films almost never win Oscars. They get nominated, but they almost never win. When it was released at the

beginning of the year, the market was open, all we had was *The Doors* and *Sleeping with the Enemy*. It was like a perfect niche for making money. And it was more important for *Silence* to be a commercial success than it was for a movie with great performances to be looked at for great performances. Though Tony Hopkins won't be overlooked; it's just too wonderful a performance in too flashy a part. And I don't think the movie will be overlooked.

Jonathan Demme gave you a lot of credit for helping direct the film. What were your contributions?

The only contribution I really had was my character . . . but my character *is* the movie. That's the one thing that I can bring to a movie, the story and the literature of it, and the layers of meaning. And those Lecter-Clarise scenes— that's why I live is to do stuff like that!

How challenging was the part for you?

This was exhausting. But fun. Because when you do eight-page-long scenes, it's like doing a play. That dialogue is so rich. The scene where he's trying to ask questions about her and she says, "Did you draw all this from memory?" And he says, "Memory, Agent Starling, is all I have instead of a view." "Well, maybe you'd like to put this view on our thing. . . . " "Oh, don't insult me with that questionnaire, do you really think you can dissect me with that blunt little tool?" "No, I only hope that I can understand you, I came here to learn from you, and I'm your student."

Those lines are so rich with meaning, and it doesn't matter whether the audience gets it. It's the seamlessness of that. Of working with the five different things that are all going on at the same time, in the spaces between the dialogue. "Memory of the violent world, of a world out there that I could control, is what I have instead of a view. And you are now my new view, and you are the one that I will torture. This will now be a part of my memory." It's that idea of judgment: "If you're coming here to judge me, I'll bite your face off. If you're coming here to treat me as a human being and look at the truth and not the facts and not judge the facts, then we can have an intimate relationship and I won't abuse you, because you haven't abused me." There is so much going on in that stuff.

To get into the role, how much did you learn about cannibalism, sexual psychosis, and ritual dismemberment?

I know everything that every character I play knows. But I don't want to get into the curiosity factor of violence, because that's obviously a dangerous topic. But I'm absolutely fascinated with violence in our culture.

With serial killers?
With the fact of violence as an established piece of American culture. It isn't just serial killers, it's about child abuse, subtle abuse. Those things that make the hero the hero and the villain the villain. There's a part in the book where Lecter says, "I will not be trivialized into a series of events. I exist, I'm here." There's a certain nonjudgmental quality to that. You can say, "My mother did this, my father did that," but the fact is, the character's here and I was there.

You spent time with John Douglas, an FBI specialist in serial killers. What did you learn?
I learned everything the character had to know. I don't want to go into it, especially since that part of my life is over now. There's a certain heroism to John Douglas that I loved. He loves his job, and when he discusses it, he discusses it with love and happiness. What is it that makes him happy doing what other people find very grisly? Well, it's about the fact that he's making a difference. That his lot in life is to be the one, when other people sit back in their armchair and say, "Oh no, I don't want to think about that," he is the person who is obsessed with it enough to change it.

Did you worry much about the glorification of violence before you decided to do it?
I'm not the filmmaker, I'm just the actor. And I feel very responsible for my character. But it's not the information that's bad, it's how it's used. You can take a two-by-four, and you can either hit somebody over the head or you can build a building with it.

That's the reasoning of the NRA—they support the sale of guns because it's not guns that kill people, but people who kill people. Are you for or against gun control?
I don't discuss it.

It's pretty straightforward.
Am I for or against it? Absolutely for it. Guns are not information. It's an entirely different issue.

Do you worry that some sicko will see a picture like *Silence* and get some new ideas on how to kill people?
I don't believe in censorship of anything. I believe in not going to see something. I believe in making a decision about it.

What about when it gets to child pornography? Or the resurgence of something like Nazism in Germany?
This is what I think, okay? I do believe there are moral and societal imperatives. I know that putting rape victims' names in the paper is not against the law, never has been, and never will be. But the issue is not the legality of it, the issue is not the censorship of it. It is that there are moral imperatives and moral decisions. And the legal system, which is about date and proof, is not the be-all and end-all of what's correct. *The Accused* is a perfect example of that. Everything is not black and white.

When your sense of morality is jolted, do you ever feel a need to speak out, being in the public position you're in?
The one thing that you'll see from everything that I talk about is that I'm not political. It's not part of who I am. I don't like being a spokesperson. It upsets me. And I don't feel honest about it. I can't be a spokesperson just because I'm an actor. It bothers me.

So you don't feel that you should talk about things that move you or that you feel passionately about?
Yes, I do. And I will respond to them in a responsible way. My movies, that's how I express myself. I can't be forced to be somebody I'm not.

Was it when you made *The Accused* when you first felt this?
I always said acting wasn't stimulating enough, that it wasn't intellectual enough, that it was beneath me in some way, that it was never going to be enough for me. And what I realized was that I was playing safe. And it was up to me to invest in it, with a gravity, to take that extra leap. *The Accused* was the one moment in my life where I really realized that what I wanted to be was an actor. That it was ultimately completely and totally satisfying.

Didn't you also say that about *Taxi Driver?* That it was "the first time I realized there was a craft and it's not just an imitation of yourself."
It was the first time I was asked to do anything other than play myself. I didn't hear, "Oh, just act natural, just be yourself." It was very much about creating the character. But I was twelve years old.

Is it true that you didn't really know how to judge your performance in *The Accused?*
I didn't know if it was any good. All I knew was that it was true. I just kept thinking I was making a fool of myself. It's so different than anything I've ever done. I just got so insecure on it.

While some would think the rape scene would be the hardest thing to deal with, you found the solitary dance you had to do more difficult. Why?

It was hard to do it and have it look spontaneous and unhesitating. It was very important that it be the most beautiful moment in her life. She's had this undeniable rage, and now we see her at a time where she's free and equal and unself-conscious and sensual and one of the guys. It was very important that we not be looking at her face, thinking that she's going to get it.

You've played rape victims before—in *The Hotel New Hampshire* and *Five Corners*. Did you talk to many victims before you did these roles?

You don't really have to talk to victims, they are everywhere. As soon as you say you're doing a movie about rape, boy, it's amazing how many people, how many women, have been raped.

I know you've said that you don't learn by winning Oscars but rather by disappointments. But you said that *before* you won your Oscar for *The Accused.* Does that still hold true?

I think it's very true. Disappointments are absolutely instrumental in people's lives. Those are the situations that force them to make choices, and it's not the accolades or the Oscars or the money or the rewards, it's the disappointments that force them to evaluate and center themselves, or force them over the edge. The one thing the Oscar gave me was, I realized that I had been at the "big party" of the year. And I didn't have to do anything I didn't want to do. It made me realize that all these people sitting around going, "Got to get this kind of movie, got to do that kind of movie, got to do a light movie, got to do a comedy that makes $120 million"—it's just bullshit. I don't have to do anything I don't want to do. I felt as if this was just a brief indication of saying I will be rewarded if I just do what's right. And not consistently worry about what other people are going to think or how people are going to perceive me.

How do you think people perceive you? How complicated a person are you?

I'm inordinately uncomplicated. I may be more complicated than I think, but I may be too young to know.

How isolated are you in your private life?

It's a balancing act. I have very, very few friends, but the ones I have I'm very close to.

Do you make new friends?
Very rarely. But I have great new acquaintances.

Your success came very early. You were *three* when you did your first commercial. Were you the Coppertone kid in the poster getting her suit pulled down by the dog?
No, I wasn't the poster, that came before I was born. I was on the first commercial they ever made.

Any memories of that?
Vague.

How far back does your memory go?
I remember commercials that I did or TV shows. I don't remember as much like going to school.

Can you remember a time in your childhood when you were not acting?
No.

Were you ever called by your real name, Alicia?
Always Jodie, never Alicia.

You've said that you never had the illusion of anonymity. Talk about that.
I don't mean to say that I was this big celebrity, but there was always a public side to me, even from the time I was four years old.

Has it been difficult always being in the public eye?
Yes, but I don't know anything else. It's just something that you accept, the way you accept being a diplomat's child or a Kennedy. The way you accept being black or anything that somehow sets you apart.

You have two older sisters and a brother—was there any jealousy with you doing commercials?
Not that I was aware of. My brother was an actor. He did two series that both lasted for many years. He was in *Mayberry RFD* for four years, and then he did a TV show called *Hondo*.

I understand you and your two sisters are all Scorpios—does that mean you all get along?

My sisters were a year apart, and they fought like cats and dogs. They were like Laurel and Hardy, they were so different, the two of them.

How did your mother keep your head from getting too swollen?
I don't know. She would continually say, "What do you want to be when you grow up? Acting's a good hobby, isn't it? It's a fun thing to do." She was preparing me for the possibility that it would not continue, which is the case with most child actors. Also, I don't think she saw me as having the personality of somebody who would grow up to be an actor. And she's right, I don't have an actor's personality at all. I'm not one of those people you ask to dance and I'll get up on a table and do it. I'm not the lampshade head that always has to have attention on me. It's something that in my personal life I find painful, being the center of attention. I don't like it at all. And I continually try to defuse attention to other people.

You certainly must have been the center of attention when you wound up in the jaws of a lion during the making of your first feature film, *Napoleon and Samantha,* when you were just ten.
That was an accident. There were three lions: the actual one, who was 110 years old and didn't have any teeth, only drank milk and very rarely wanted to do anything; a stand-in lion; and a stunt lion. The stand-in lion was brought in, and I worked with him. We were going down a hill, and the lion was in back of me, and I was a little kid. Got to the end of a shot, and I looked down, and he came around and picked me up, turned me sideways, and shook me. I watched everybody run away in panic. I went into shock. The trainer came and said, "Drop it." The lion dropped me, and I went falling down the hill. When I woke up, I was on a stretcher in a private plane. My mother and I had long discussions about it, and since I was going to be okay she felt it was important for me to get back and work with the lion, which I did two weeks later.

Do you have a scar?
Yeah, on both sides.

That's better than a tattoo.
Yeah.

In your youth you were compared with Shirley Temple and Tatum O'Neal. Most child actors don't last as long or make it as far as you have. Is it more talent or luck do you think?

There's talent, there's luck, but there's also very specific management. And my mom spent a lot of time trying to disassociate me from the pack. For example, *The Breakfast Club* era, not having me be involved in that group.

The Brat Pack.
Right. My mom's very astute, and she felt it was very important that I be recognized on my own. Where there would be big things like the cover of *Newsweek* or *Time* talking about child actresses, she declined for me to be involved because she said it would serve me badly. And we always discussed everything. *Taxi Driver,* we discussed the meaning of things. I really am very lucky to have had somebody who was a real person who was there to protect me and who wasn't enamored with the possibility of a flashy career. Because you do live vicariously through your children's successes, so much of it was about her really wanting me to be respected and taken seriously. Which isn't something that came in her life as easily.

Your mother has said that your strength maybe came from being raised without a father. Would you agree?
I don't know. For a lot of people that's been a disaster in their lives. I don't talk about him. It's something that doesn't exist in my life, so I choose not to talk about it.

I'll drop the subject.
No, no, that's your job to ask. And it's my job not to answer.

Have you ever reflected upon the importance of fathers?
I had a close friend, and I went and stayed with her and her parents at their shore home. I never had a father, and it's not something I sit around and go, "Well, I never had a father. . . . " It's not a big deal, I just didn't have one. But we went out on a boat with her father, who was a crab fisherman, and he said to her, "Okay, turn to the right, put the pot down, see, this is a soft crab. . . . " He was showing her something, but not teaching. And I realized why she would always love her father like that, how deep this was. They did that together, they had that. It was something that was so not a part of my life. Because what you do in a family of women is you talk about everything. You go to a movie, and you talk about it. You go to eat Chinese food, and you talk about that. It's just a very different experience.

At fourteen you told *Cosmopolitan:* "I don't know why adults are so shocked that kids know about sex. Most of us know what goes on from age ten." Did your mother tell you?

There wasn't anything kept from me. My mom was really very verbal. Mostly as a reaction from her background, which was Americana in some ways. A little white-bread puritanical, Catholic schools, convent. She was bound and determined that I would never have that kind of guilt and ignorance.

Were you brought up a Catholic?
No. I'm going to limbo. Never been baptized. I didn't know anything about religion until I went to college. My mom was pretty down on it when I was growing up. But I had a very strong set of beliefs that were passed on to me. Very strong moral code in my family. Things you don't do. For example: if you are in the Mafia, you don't rat on the guy. I got these lectures about how you don't betray your friends and you do not lie, and in business situations, just because somebody screws you over, you don't screw them, because good behavior is its own reward. I got all that stuff. But religion is not the originator of morality.

So you've never prayed to God, even as a kid?
Never. I did believe in the Easter Bunny, however.

You've said that your childhood was filled with dreams of getting out . . . .
I can't imagine I ever said that. That's what my mom's childhood was like, that's very much a part of her life. Every day of her life she thought about when she was going to leave that town in Illinois, and that is a very big part of the female heroes that I play. The girl in *Carny,* that's all she wanted to do was get out of Richmond. Or the girl in the FBI in *Silence.*

Your mother has had such a strong influence in your life. Were there ever things you wanted to do that she wouldn't let you?
Yeah. I wanted a moped in Paris when I was thirteen. It was a major bone of contention between the two of us. Every kid in France had a moped, and I wanted to scoot around Paris and obviously risk being killed. But I went out on a moped when I turned fifteen because I was not going to let that stop me. The first day I went out I had a major accident. I was riding with this guy that I really loved, he was French and he had two, and I didn't even know how to drive. So here I am looking around and ran right into him. He was cut up and bloody and his moped was ruined. I was okay.

Did you continue to see the guy?
Yeah, but we decided it was not a good idea for me to be riding a moped.

Mom was right again. Did she find out?
I don't think I ever told her. I'll tell her now.

How significant was it for you to have learned French and to have lived in France?
It's a big part of my life, it always will be. It's a real safety net for me, Paris. I still have a place there. It's like a womb, a very comforting place for me.

You've said your mother has saved you from social disgrace. Such as?
She taught me tact, diplomacy, politeness. She taught me to send thank-you notes. To say "yes, ma'am" or "no, ma'am." To never try to hurt people's feelings because it would be fun. She taught me how to be a public person in a way that was graceful.

Did she also teach you to appreciate Marlon Brando?
My mom was fascinated with Brando when I was a kid. We had Brando books all over the house. She made me go to a Brando festival down at the Vagabond Theater. I've seen every Brando movie ever made. I'm totally fascinated by him. He's a powerful human being.

Didn't you go to school with some of Brando's children?
Yeah, sure did. Miko, and one of his daughters too. Miko was a friend of mine. He was a great kid, a big goofball. Miko's mom, Movita, was a beautiful woman.

Did you ever have problems with classmates because of what you did?
I don't think there were problems, but I was different.

Who was your favorite writer when you were a kid?
Baudelaire. I really was obsessed with the darker side of things.

You got into Berkeley, Stanford, Columbia, Princeton, Harvard, and Yale. Why'd you apply to so many, and how'd you choose?
My mom was out of town, and the applications had to be done. I got so paranoid about it I sent in as many as I could get. Then I went on a trip to visit them all. Nobody gave me any guidance. I chose Yale because it was close to New York but it wasn't *in* New York. I liked that it wasn't an ivory tower; it was in a tough city, it wasn't a Barbie and Ken school. And it was a really good microcosm. Whereas Harvard was so much the crème de la crème, I just didn't feel like I fit in.

Did you make many friends at Yale?

All my friends I met on the first day. Isn't that funny? My production designer on *Tate* was my roommate in college. He was from L.A. We had a wild apartment. Junk everywhere. We had a train, flashing Christmas lights all year long. I went to Japan and brought back all these wild Japanese toys. We had a big blowup plastic pool with animals on it, only it was attached to the wall. We had a huge Twister set on the wall. So all our toys were art pieces. My bedroom was Japanese minimalist, like a futon, an orchid.

You majored in literature and wrote your thesis on the novelist Toni Morrison, who told you things and then asked you not to write about it. Why?

I interviewed her before my thesis. My professor did me a favor by basically getting me an interview with her in order for me to discuss my topic. It was never for a publication, but here I had this most incredible interview, and she said that was not part of the deal, and I agreed. Good interview, though. It was one of those four or five hours in your life, just a very big event for me.

How difficult was it having to have security guards while going to college?

I've spoken on the topic, so it's not like I ever have to talk about it again. But it is hard being a public figure. And there are times when you are more public than others. Thank God that's not always like that.

I know we're skirting around an issue you plainly don't want to discuss, but in *Vanity Fair* you said you felt at that time it was your "God-given responsibility to endure this martyrdom." What did you mean?

I don't know. The writer was talking about my psychological makeup. And I said, "I'm here for you to stick darts in me, go ahead. You can have any conclusion you want, but you're not going to get it out of my mouth."

You're tough, Jodie. In *American Film* you said, "I've done weird things when pushed to certain extremes. I've let myself be rolled over by a steamroller, then said, 'Please! Roll me over some more!'" Do you remember saying that?

It comes from work, where the production wants me to hang off a cliff at five in the morning and I'm like, "Yeah, okay! My job!" Let myself be taken advantage of in movies because I want to be one of the guys and I don't want to be the histrionic actress who won't do anything. I want to be the person who takes chances and is adventurous. I don't want to be the idiot who sits in her trailer and says, "I can't do that."

When did you stop thinking that all actors were stupid?
I don't know (*laughs*). It was a defense mechanism when I was in college. Because I didn't think I would be able to continue in the business, because I never thought I would be able to make a living at it. I had to make sure that it was something filled with dumb people.

Do you think you're more vulnerable now that you've accepted that you are able to make a living in the business?
Yes. Much softer. As I grow older I grow softer. I think *Tate* is the end result of a long battle for softness. It's the simplest movie I've ever made. The most direct and the most honest. And the softest character I've ever played.

Why do you believe that men start out liking themselves but women have to learn to like themselves?
That's always a quote that ends up haunting me, because taken out of context it sounds sexist when in fact it is a very feminist commentary about how men in our society are dubbed "human" immediately. The human experience is the male experience, and the aberrant experience is the female experience. Within the forming of the male psyche, men are given direct messages about who they are supposed to be. And women are continually given confusing and mixed messages, things that don't make sense. Like, "Yes, you should grow up and be a business person; no, you shouldn't work and have children because you won't be a fulfilled person if you don't [have children]." These messages get even more confusing as the years go on. It builds in you a way of coping with being disappointed that I don't think men are as equipped with.

In 1987 you told *Interview*: "Girls from single parent homes really want to get married. I do. I really believe in marriage." Still?
That's funny. There's a yearning for family because a single parent relationship with a child is a very, very intimate experience. And that's what you know of love—that absolute intimacy. And you won't settle for anything less.

Would you like to have children one day?
Yeah, I do. If I don't have them, I won't feel like I'm some kind of failure particularly. I just know it will be a different path. But it's definitely something I'd like to do. *[Foster gave birth to a son in June 1998.]*

What about films you'd like to have done that you turned down or didn't get?

There were a lot of films that I was turned down for that I wished I could have done. But I don't talk about movies that I didn't do because it's not fair to the actors who did them.

Your mother has said that the one thing no one ever thinks about your doing is comedy, which you're good at. Do you feel that way?

It's just so hard to find a good comedy. I could find ten good dramas for one good comedy. And I refuse to be in a bad one, so I don't do as much.

Would you still like to do a musical?

Yes.

Some years ago you said you didn't watch TV but saw every movie. Do you watch TV today?

Not much. I'm a CNN junkie. And *Nightline* I watch too.

Your mother said in *Rolling Stone* that you don't have enough sense about danger and that you'll open your door without looking to see who it is.

She shouldn't say that in print, should she?

Are her fears real?

I am too trusting, but I'm learning.

Is smoking really your only regret?

That's actually the only thing I ever did that I regret. I smoked in college until '86, then I quit for three years. I smoked the first day of shooting *Little Man Tate* and quit the last day of shooting.

Some have said you appear to have a certain anxiety about your appearance and body image: that you dress a certain tailored way, then you appear in oversized glasses or revealing dresses at the Oscars. Are you comfortable with your looks?

I love glamorous clothes, I love getting dressed up to a formal thing. I love Armani's stuff so much, it's so timeless. You can buy something, and ten years later you can still wear it. I love beautiful objects. But I also really love being comfortable. I have a style of my own, whatever that is.

What do you think of this comment about you: that you have perfected the technique of seeming transparent while being unreachable?
Well, anybody who's discussing this is a press person. My life with the press is very different than my life on the outside. It's my job. I promote movies. That's what I do.

And your relationship with the press?
I've had nothing but a great relationship with the press. And I like reading reviews of my movies because good criticism is absolutely invaluable, you have to have it to learn from.

Last question: do you believe in magic?
I have rituals and I believe in magic. I always tell my life as a series of *Twilight Zones*. My favorite one of all is the one about the black prize-fighter who's totally down and out. I always cry when I see this one. He was kind of good once, but he's not good anymore, and he lives in this boarding house with this woman and her child. The child totally adores him. He's always saying, "Joe, you're going to get that guy, you're going to pound him tonight." And the boxer says, "No, I'm not, I'm going to lose." "No, you're not going to lose, you'll never lose." "I'm unlucky kid, I'm old, I've been punched out." "You've got to believe, you've got to believe!" So he goes to the fight, and he gets really mad at his trainer, and he punches his fist into the wall and breaks every bone in his hand. Then he goes into the ring and in five seconds he goes down. On the count of five he wakes up and he's the guy on top and the other guy's down. It's fantastic! Everywhere they go afterwards it's "Joe, you were great." He starts to believe it because everybody's paying attention to him, and when he goes home the woman says, "You did great!" But the kid's just sitting there. He has tears in his eyes, and he says, "Do you believe now? Do you believe in magic?" And he says, "Well, really no, I can't, I'm too old." And the kid just says, "If you don't believe in magic it just goes away." And he wakes up. ". . . Ten." He's on the floor, he comes back . . . everyone hates him. He runs up to the kid, and he's kind of desperate. And the kid is back the way he used to be. He says, "You'll get it next time."

I don't know why I love this story. It's the whole *Franny and Zooey* thing. You must have a fat lady. And it doesn't matter whether she exists or not. But it's very important to believe that anything is possible.

THE COMEDIENNE

LILY TOMLIN

LILY TOMLIN WAS RUNNING LATE, taking time off between getting ready for her role as Miss Hathaway in the *Beverly Hillbillies* movie, preparing her five-year-old character Edith Ann for an animated primetime special à la *The Simpsons,* screening a rough cut of Robert Altman's *Short Cuts* in which she was starring with Tom Waits, and sending out boxed sets of five of her videotapes, which she sells from her garage. She was hungry and asked whether she could share a sandwich and some cookies, then remembered that the next day was Valentine's Day and asked if she could use the phone.

"It's going to sound a little bit show-offy, and I don't mean to at all," she excused herself, "but I really am self-conscious. I'm ordering flowers for a famous old movie star."

I guessed Lillian Gish, since Tomlin wrote about her in one of Roddy McDowall's photo books.

"No, Lana," she said. "I missed her birthday. And I didn't want to forget her for tomorrow. She had throat cancer, which I guess is okay to say since it was printed in the tabloids, but she's okay."

She dialed her secretary and asked her to look up Lana Turner's phone number on her Rolodex. "Call up Casa Bella, which is a florist on Santa Monica," Tomlin instructed. "I think she likes white roses, I can't remember, it says on her card. She doesn't like a huge arrangement. Or try to get her French tulips, but not too huge. Simple, simple, elegant, simple. Okay? Not too many things stuck in it. Just send it to L. Turner. Then put 'Happy Valentine's Day, We love you, Lily and Jane.'"

She hung up the phone, bit into a cookie, and apologized. "I shouldn't take this time from our interview. I'm sorry."

Nothing to be sorry about, I said. It was a perfect lead-in to talking about the influence of the movies on her life and career. And besides, this way I could tell her how I once brought flowers to Mae West, back in the early seventies.

"Oh, don't make me sick," Tomlin said. "You took flowers to Mae West? I wish I could have seen her."

Born September 1, 1939, in Detroit, Tomlin once worked as an ush-erette in the early fifties, so she saw a lot of movies. Her favorites were the "bad girl" films, which featured the tough-talking chippies who al-ways seemed to dominate the screen, like Dorothy Malone, Carole Mathews, Jennifer Jones, Jean Simmons, Ruby Gentry, Beverly Michaels, Brigitte Bardot, and Lana Turner. "I would rather be Ruby Gentry, who wrecked a whole town, than be Sandra Dee and be wrecked by a whole bunch of surfers," Tomlin once said. "I saw those bimbo-brained beau-ties in mindless beach-party movies and said, 'No, this is not for me.'"

For her it was the women in the bad B-movies. "The good women in the A-movies were either too idealized or too ditzy; worst of all, they had no dreams of their own. The bad women in movies seemed to have more daring, more guts, more strength. They definitely had more dreams."

These bad girl dreamers definitely had their effect on the teenaged Tomlin. After she saw Bardot in *And God Created Women,* she suffered what she called "Bardot damage." "I went around Detroit wearing a red shirt-dress with a black leotard underneath, the dress unbuttoned al-most to the waist. Walking the streets of Detroit barefoot as if I were in the south of France," she told her friend Jane Wagner. "I felt womanly, bohemian, abandoned!" When she saw Audrey Hepburn in *Breakfast at Tiffany's,* she suffered Hepburn damage; then Jeanne Moreau damage af-ter seeing *Jules and Jim.*

But Tomlin was also watching television, enthralled by Lucille Ball and Imogene Coca, laughing at *The Honeymooners.* When she heard Ruth Draper's monologues, she was encouraged to try some of her own. So she abandoned her dreams of medical school and, after leaving Wayne State University, set out to make people laugh. Her material came from her background—she had grown up in an apartment build-ing filled with different character types—and from them she began to build.

By the end of 1969 she was invited to join the cast of *Laugh-In,* where her AT&T operator Ernestine and her child Edith Ann seemed to hit a national nerve. From nationwide exposure Tomlin went back to doing nightclubs, and then got her first movie offer—to appear in Robert Alt-man's *Nashville.* It was a groundbreaking film, and Tomlin not only received an Oscar nomination but was voted best supporting actress by the New York Film Critics and the National Society of Film Critics. Her next film was *The Late Show* with Art Carney. And then came *Moment by Moment*, which seemed fatal to the career of John Travolta. But Tomlin went on to do *Nine to Five* with Jane Fonda and Dolly Parton, *The Incredible Shrinking Woman*, *All of Me* with Steve Martin, and *Big Business* with Bette Midler, with cameos in Woody Allen's *Shadows* and *Fog* and Robert Altman's *The Player*. She has since appeared in *Flirting with Disaster, Krippendorf's Tribe, Tea with Mussolini, Get Bruce!,* and *The Kid*.

But it wasn't her film career that made her unique. It was her one-woman shows. *Appearing Nightly* demonstrated her phenomenal ability to get into a diverse cast of characters, both male and female. *Newsweek* described the show as "a crossroads in one of the most extraordinary careers in our popular culture." Eight years later came the even more insightful *The Search for Signs of Intelligent Life in the Universe*, written by Jane Wagner, which targeted the foibles and follies of our culture with the precision and exactness of an acupuncture needle. Tomlin was awarded Tonys for both shows.

When I interviewed her in the spring of 1993, she was living in W. C. Fields's former home in the Los Feliz section of Los Angeles. We decided to meet on more neutral grounds, first at my office, and then at her publicist's. Although the setting was somewhat sterile, the company was anything but. When Lily Tomlin smiles, the room lights up. And when she laughs, well . . . you had to have been there.

So how did you become friends with Lana Turner?
I was on Jay Leno one night when he used to sub for Carson, and I was talking about Lana and my being an usherette, and I did this whole thing about when Lana pushes her hair back in *Flame and the Flesh*, when she's kind of renewed and she's going to change her ways and not ruin good men's lives anymore. It was a bad woman movie, and I was very addicted to them. They were the only movies that were of any real interest in terms of a woman's role. Everybody else, the roles women played were like suffering and kind of pathetic or manipulated, sacrificial. When I did *Nashville,* I wore that full slip because Lana had worn a full slip in *Flame and the Flesh*. Anyway, after that Leno show she wrote me, and I made friends with her. Then I got to know her when I was doing my show here in '86.

What was it like getting to know one of your teenage idols?
Well, you don't want to belabor it or inflate it so much, it's not like they levitate. In another kind of way it's like I'd rather almost never meet them. Not

that they disappoint, they don't. But it's like . . . the world is just so finite, so mortal, so simple.

You've said that you were not only affected by movies, you were molded by them. They devoured you. The moviegoing ritual was practically a religious experience.

As a teenager, movies would certainly mold your sexuality and your role-playing as a female. Like *Wicked Woman* with Beverly Michaels. You probably never saw it, because you can't get your hands on it. I remember seeing it with *The Moon Is Blue,* which was square as a box. *Wicked Woman* was this bad woman who controls the movie, she dominates everything. She's the sexual aggressor, she's doing all the lying and manipulating, having her way. You just didn't see that. There were great moments that I loved of hers. Beverly Michaels is like six feet tall and very platinum blond, and she has this very baby, young kind of face. She could look really innocent, and then her lips would snarl, and she'd speak in this New York accent to Percy Helton, who plays the little tailor down below who's always lechering after her.

Was this anything like Lauren Bacall in *To Have or Have Not?*

No, that predates *Wicked Woman,* and it's maybe a classier film, but it's not the same because Lauren Bacall still had it both ways. Beverly Michaels was like taking the Greyhound. She was truer to life. She had to work her way across the country via gentlemen with a two-day growth. I'm friends with Beverly Michaels now. She's not that old, because she wasn't that much older than I was when I was watching her. I was probably fourteen, and she was eighteen or something.

What about *Written on the Wind* with Dorothy Malone?

Oh my God in heaven! See, those were all bad girls. I was mad for them.

Did you suffer Dorothy Malone damage?

I had some Dorothy Malone damage. She was like the bad, sexy girl, and Barbara Rush was the good, sexy girl in our time.

Didn't Malone do a mambo as her father was dying?

Yeah, and kicks off her shoes—the inference is that she's a nympho. Hangs out at the roadhouse, carrying this torch for Rock Hudson, who's a really nice, solid guy. She's not a good girl. It's interesting that you mention her dance, because in *Wicked Woman* Beverly Michaels also has an old windup Victrola, and she plays a record called "Acapulco Nights" that has a similar kind of musical image.

Was Brigitte Bardot an influence at this time?

No, Bardot starts to come in the late fifties with *And God Created Woman*. That gets to be more wild. I was also affected by *Butterfield Eight*, another bad girl who likes changes. And Anna Magnani and that whole thing.

Talk about the influence of Bardot. Audrey Hepburn. Jeanne Moreau.

What can you say? You could do worse. That's quite a range, isn't it? Just like characters. I've always liked a big, wide range of type and expression.

If you could have the career of any of those three, which would you choose?

Jeanne Moreau.

Why?

Just French and she's very smart. More bohemian, and she directs too. I'd like to be Jeanne Moreau but wear Katharine Hepburn's clothes. Jeanne Moreau really hasn't made that many great movies, but I don't think she's ever cared. She wasn't that focused. You also have to isolate it to the three movies: *Jules and Jim, And God Created Woman*, and *Breakfast at Tiffany's*. I'd rather be Jeanne Moreau in *Jules and Jim*, even though she drove off at the end and killed herself.

And if you were a teenager today?

If I were a kid now at nineteen, I would probably want to be Thelma or Louise.

Which one?

It doesn't matter, Thelma and Louise are like one person.

You can't say the same about Marilyn Monroe and Doris Day. Did either of them have any influence on you?

I was more influenced by Doris Day because she was more of an icon in that era for me. We just loved Doris. She's an incredibly gifted performer. She used to play some of those comedy scenes, and it was unbelievable, the stuff she'd be asked to do, the physical activity around her room.

When Monroe died in '62 she was thirty-eight, I must have been about twenty-two. I was living on Fifth Street in New York. They announced her death on a Sunday. I remember who I was in the house with. I remember Jimmy Dean's death too. I was in a car in Detroit on a double date and was going, "Oh no!! OH NO!! Oh my God, no!" It was like role-playing or something.

Was Dean more important to you than Montgomery Clift or Brando?
Oh yes, absolutely. It took me a few years to get on to Clift, he was too subtle, you didn't get it. Jimmy Dean was in my age range, and he was behaving
in my age range.

**Let me throw some names at you of actresses beyond your age range
who may or may not have inspired you. Carole Lombard?**
She was a wonderful comedienne. But I always had that terrible image in my
mind from when she crashed and they say to Clark Gable, "You don't want
to go up there."

Ginger Rogers?
She made Fred Astaire sexy. She was so engaging on the screen, so witty in
her performances. I've met her very superficially backstage a couple of times,
and I think she's probably quite traditional in her views.

Rosalind Russell, Joan Crawford, Bette Davis?
I love all of these women because they were really larger than life during
those early years. You like buy into the Crawford image and the Davis image
and the old camp movies that they made that people just really get off on. I
met Bette Davis once. Talked to her more than once on the telephone. I
would send her flowers because we had some mutual friends. I also came to
know Lillian Gish and Helen Hayes and people of that whole generation.

Was Bette Davis intimidating?
My God, yes! I was at this dinner party with about ten people, all writers or
performers, and Davis came by. She was still in very good shape, and boy,
she was full of vinegar. You couldn't say a word at the table without her
challenging you on it. Totally outspoken, just as brash as she could be.
That's why I like to be Ernestine—we all would like to be like that.

**When you were growing up, did you dress to look like the star of the
moment?**
Well, yeah, you adopt fashion, absolutely.

How important were breasts for you as a kid?
Oh God, profoundly! I grew up in the fifties, and Kim Novak would be the
body image to aspire to. Very full-figured, full bust, full round hips. I used to
pad my hips because I thought you were supposed to have round shapely
hips from the front because skirts were made that way. Straight skirts had a
little extra material on the sides.

When I was a kid, people would say to me I looked like Loretta Young. I didn't like to have my hair pigtailed. My mother would braid my hair, and I wanted to have movie star hair. So I learned how to pin-curl my hair. I had a two-piece bathing suit, and I used to lie on top of my mother's dresser in the bedroom, with a horizontal mirror, and I'd pin-curl my hair wearing this two-piece bathing suit and admire myself. Then I'd walk around the neighborhood in this bathing suit with my hair real fluffy. I thought this was a movie star look.

Who did you think you resembled when you had pigtails?
Natalie Wood. We both had those cute little-girl faces, little noses, and when she had pigtails, we both had parts in the middle of our hair. I thought I *was* Natalie Wood. Then I thought my mother was Norma Shearer. *The Women* came out in 1939, and I saw it twenty years later with my mother. I saw Norma Shearer with that little girl, it wasn't Natalie Wood, but if it had only been Natalie Wood it would have been perfect, see? Then I could have fantasized my mother and I being in a movie together.

Did you read many of the movie magazines when you were young?
Sure. I remember all the stuff when you'd read movie magazines like *Modern Screen* about when Doris Day gets in the shower she always runs her fingers over a bar of soap so when she gets out her fingernails are real white. These things were important. So was *Seventeen* magazine, teaching you how to behave and how to talk to boys. And I was hip to *Confidential* and *True Confessions* when I was about six. We didn't have the most evolved library in our home. My family was blue-collar.

Meaning they weren't encouraging you to be anything you wanted to be, like a lawyer or a doctor?
The general feeling in my family would be, as long as the girl doesn't get pregnant and the boy doesn't wind up in the joint, you've done pretty good.

Were you always aware that there was a double standard in your house?
I was always conscious of the whole sexual double standard from a very early time, even in junior high school. I was always conscious that my mother had much less freedom than my father. I could be sympathetic about my father too, because he was uneducated, a factory worker, but no matter where my father was at, he still had more autonomy and freedom than my mother did. I really resented that.

Did your mother?

She's basically very upbeat, very satisfied, content. She really does get a lot of satisfaction out of her life. My mother would rather have the approval of the concierge than her creator. I took that line from a short story. I'm not as positive as my mother, not as upbeat. I'm much more moody. She said, "You don't have to have a lot of stuff to be happy." As I got older I began to see how witty my mother was. I don't think I'm that quick-witted. When I was younger, I was much more a parent to my mother. And my father.

Your father was a gambler, wasn't he?
He played cards, but mostly the track. I used to book my father's bets at the track, because I couldn't bear for him to lose the money. He'd lose so much money. He probably made $100 a week, and he'd bet that on a horse. So when I went with him, I'd wait until I felt like I knew he was going to lose, and then I'd hold the money. That way I'd be able to take a couple hundred bucks home to my mother.

He died young, at fifty-seven. How did that affect you?
It was meaningful. It's hard to lose your parents. I've never even gone to his grave. I can get very sentimental about my father because he died so young and I feel like he failed in some way. I look at pictures of him as a kid and his roughneck brothers. My dad is the one that looks kind of lost. His brother Lud and my dad were like twins. Then there was their older brother Elbert, who's dead now. He was just as mean as he could possibly be, beat up his wife, an awful guy. He could drink a fifth of whiskey without batting an eye. My dad drank like that too but couldn't drink, so ruined his life, his health, because he just didn't have the constitution for it.

My best story about Elbert is after he had divorced his wife and was living in some old rooming house, Daddy would get real sentimental at Christmas, and he'd say, "I'm going to go out and find Elbert and bring him back to be with the family." Of course, nobody wanted Elbert to come around because he was just as surly and awful as he could be. Mean-tempered, mean-mouthed. So Daddy had on a white shirt, and he comes back in about an hour and there's blood. Daddy had found him in a bar and sat down beside him and said, "Goddamnit, you're my brother, Elbert, and I want you to come home and spend Christmas with us." And Elbert punched him in the nose.

Did your parents ever embarrass you?
Things of modesty were embarrassing to me. Like if we'd go to the beach, and then my mother would make me change my bathing suit. People treat children like they have no sense of dignity. Even if I was seven or eight, I def-

initely wanted privacy. Or if my mother would talk about me in the third person in front of company, that was embarrassing to me. It wouldn't be horribly negative, maybe she'd say, "Oh, she's so thin." And I might be a little nine-year-old sitting there like real skinny, and she'd fuss with my hair, and I'd just be livid that my mother would do that to me in front of someone. Because I was very adult. I used to read marriage manuals, and when I'd go visit somebody, I'd go right to their bookshelves and look for their sexy books. This was when I was under ten.

See, very early I went through a realization that my parents had been children. I'd look at my mother's baby picture, and suddenly I thought that my mother was just like me. So I knew she didn't know anything. Then I thought my teachers were kids too, and I knew they didn't know anything. Then I began to understand that *everybody* had been a child, and I knew that I couldn't rely on them 100 percent.

Did you feel you could rely on anyone? Or did adults become material for your future characterizations?
I've talked about this, so I don't want to be repetitious, but it's hard not to when things are so fundamental to what happened to you. We lived in this old apartment house in Detroit, and there were so many different kinds of people in the building. And I was fearless. I can remember coming home at 10:00 P.M., eight years old, running, jumping. I'd have to jump over certain fences and swing on certain poles. And I'd hear my mother screaming for me, crazy, "Mary Jean!" because here I was, a little tiny kid, and she'd been out looking for me for three hours with the neighborhood kids. She'd see me, and she'd reach up and get a switch off the tree and whoop those leaves off. But I would never let her switch my legs. I'd run, dance, say, "Don't switch me, Mama, don't switch me!" I'd avoid her, exhaust her.

Didn't you also discover orgasms sliding down those clothes poles?
Oh geez. It was actually worse than that! I would actually hump the clothes poles. And I would tell all the women in the building who were hanging their clothes out, "Look at this great game I discovered." I would demonstrate it for them. Then somebody told my mother, and she said, "Don't do that outside." So I took my activities indoors.

Is that around the time you felt sure you had leprosy?
Oh Jesus! I used to read all these home medical books, and I read that leprosy had an incubation period of eleven years, so that at any moment you could have leprosy and not know it. It just amazed me that you could have a disease brewing for so long and not know it.

Kind of pertinent now.
Right, because of AIDS. Really scary.

How scary was it when you and a girlfriend set fire to a garage?
I was about ten when I did this. We had this old row of wooden garages, held maybe six spaces. We had an empty lot next door, and that's where we used to go to burn trash. My friend and I tossed kitchen matches through a knothole, and moments later the garage was burning down. But I wasn't plagued by guilt because I convinced myself that even though we did throw those matches in, somehow the garage caught fire in another way.

This didn't lead you, then, toward being a hood, joining a female gang, wearing black leather?
Well, in the tenth grade we formed the Scarlet Angels, but it was neither a gang nor a sorority. We were like fake hoods. It was acting out a role. Every hangout had a different style. The music and art kids hung out at Tom Thumb's; they were Ivy League and wore crewneck sweaters and desert boots. My girlfriends and I hung out at Ma's and Chris's, which was like the hoody place. The kids drank there, we were more rowdy. The guys had DAs and leather jackets and big motorcycles parked outside, but they were going to high school. And I'd have on some big old tanker jacket with a straight skirt, ballet shoes. I used to do the whole thing about hitchhiking from Detroit to Chicago in December in ballet shoes. Which was true. Henry Ford's widow is one of the girls I hitchhiked to Chicago with.

You were also a cheerleader. What did that teach you about life?
How easy it is to shock people.

Which is why they kicked you out?
No, I got suspended from time to time for shocking people on the field. Today it would be nothing. Like doing a cartwheel and having your underwear showing. Or doing some vulgar pose. Just being sexual on the playing field. Instead of going, "Rah, rah, sis, boom, bah," I was doing, "Bom de bom ba." Very soulful.

Did you ever get caught stealing bathing suits?
No. We did that because it became a challenge. Could we get every bathing suit in every color and every manufacturer? Could we get every Rose Marie Reed, every Jantzen, in every color and in two sizes? Because there were two of us and one was bigger than the other. We would brazenly take half a dozen at a time. We literally had two or three big old suitcases full of

bathing suits. We used to keep them under the bed at my girlfriend's house. We took them to the beach, and we'd change every five or ten minutes. It was totally insane. Then it all ended badly.

How?

There was . . . I don't know if I should say who she was because she's out there and that makes me a little nervous . . . maybe we can make her Asian, that's really far off. But that sounds racist. Make her a Siamese twin. Or better, two twin sisters that I hung out with. Anyway, she was really wild, and we went to the beach one day, and of course, we couldn't help but attract attention, changing bathing suits all the time. She picked up these two old boys from Georgia, and we went over to their house after we left the beach. Stayed a couple of hours, and then I said I had to go home. But she stayed. Then she called me that night and said she was going to Georgia with these two guys. When she didn't come home after a few days, they got me into the counselor's office and started grilling me about where she was, and I told, because I didn't think she should go to Georgia. These people were trashy. So I blew the whistle on her, and she never forgave me. They put her in juvenile hall. Here she was, a fifteen-year-old girl, and she turns to me in the elevator in juvenile hall and says, "I'll never forgive you for this. You're going to pay for this one day."

Did you ever get caught for shoplifting?

Yes, once. I was already grown and was doing a show in Detroit. I wasn't famous. I was in this store, and I had this impulse, I wanted to get caught, to see what it was like. I had big sunglasses, and I found out later that anybody who comes in the store that looks unusual, they start watching them. It was winter time. I saw a couple of people in the store that had very light coats, and I later put this in a sketch we did in one of my specials. I took a skirt that was very bulky, just put it in my purse. It was hanging out of my purse, and I saw the woman watching me. Unless you leave the department they can't nab you. So I'd go around and walk around one rack, then double back, watching her. She was tailing me. Then I went for the escalator, and she takes me by the elbow, and she says, "Come with me, just walk slowly, no one's going to embarrass you, just come with me." What they think you are is part of a ring. I found out all this from talking to them. So they want to know who your friends are, and they want to come to your house and see if you have a lot of their merchandise. So I had a nice chat with them.

Did they go to your house?

Noooo. I confused them. Oh, I hate to have all this written about me.

Let's talk about your early years, when you were beginning to audition for parts. Is it true that you went to read for *Lovers and Other Strangers* in 1965 and Charles Grodin made you cry?
Chuck was going to direct it for the stage. I auditioned for the part where the girl sits there stoically while her fiancé comes in and says, "We're not getting married . . . I don't love you." He's got the last-minute jitters, and she finally says, "Did you pick up your tux?" That's all she says. Well, who knows what I was doing, because there's nothing harder when you don't know what you're doing than to listen to a monologue for five minutes. Anyway, Chuck came over after I finished. He brought a chair over real quietly, and he sat down. I'm facing him, and he said, "Have you ever acted before?" And of course, I hadn't, hardly. I'd only done monologues. It was so pitying that when I got outside I went in a phone booth and I just burst into tears.

And within five years you were refusing to pose for a picture with John Wayne. How did you get from tears to that?
When I was first on *Laugh-In,* John Wayne came in. The war was still on, everybody was real political, and I was very rigid politically and felt that every act was a political act. There was going to be a big cast photo taken, and I said, "I cannot be photographed with John Wayne" (*laughs*). Today I'd like to have that picture. The same kind of thing happened when Martha Mitchell came on, and I did an Ernestine with her on a split screen. I didn't want to do that either, which I feel bad about now. In retrospect, when you think about what she went through with her husband and the Nixon administration . . . this one I really regretted, because in her book she said how hurt she was because she got that I wouldn't be photographed with her. It's really infantile in a way. Because in truth, if I were worth my mettle, I'd have engaged her.

Is there anybody now who you wouldn't be photographed with?
Probably not. I wouldn't want to be photographed in some kind of exploitive way, but to say you don't want to be in proximity to another human being because they are just so horrific and horrible, that's maybe naive.

How about Chad Everett?
(*Laughs*) You mean when I walked out on Dick Cavett in '72? They made so much out of it that it became a cause célèbre in the feminist underground. What happened was Chad Everett and I got into a little altercation. I was going to play Carnegie Hall the next night, and my Edith Ann album was just coming out, and the Ernestine album had won a Grammy, and I was certainly identified as a feminist in those days, and I dare say probably still am.

I had been going on a lot of shows that week—Mike Douglas, David Frost, *The Tonight Show*—where I'd been patronized and condescended to and dismissed. Like on Frost, Chet Huntley was on, and Lord Harlick or somebody, and they'd have a deep discussion about the environment, and then every now and then Frost would turn back to me and say, "Let's have a little of that Edith Ann." Stuff like that. I'd sort of boiled over a few times, so by the time I got onto Cavett I'm presenting my album and plugging my Carnegie Hall appearance, and then I say, "This is the first comedy album produced by a woman that's won a Grammy." And he said, "Well, why not, women are getting funnier every day." In those days the women in the audience would go "ooohhhhh" and make reactions. So then Chad comes out, and he was very big on *Medical Center* or whatever it was, and Dick started talking about Chad's ranch and his animals, and Chad said something like he had three horses, two dogs, and a wife. I was not on camera, but I probably looked out at the audience and made a little expression. Then Chad said, "I'm just kidding, my wife is the most valuable animal I own." So I said, "You own!? I've gotta go." And I got up and walked backstage. I probably would have gone back out and played around about it, but the people backstage, the producers or the coordinators, grabbed me, they were so angry, and they were shaking me. Then I got angry and went to my dressing room. Well, the best part was Chad got tears in his eyes, and then he tried to insult me a little bit, then he took out *Pageant* magazine, where he had written a poem to his wife, and he had the audacity to read this poem while W. H. Auden, another of Cavett's guests, was in the green room. And Auden was sitting there like an old beat-up pillow with stains all down his front, and he said, "Who *are* these disgusting people?" It was just outrageously funny, and afterwards it turned into a big deal. And for a long time after that kids would come and say, "My mother says she's never going to see you again because you walked off on Chad."

Did you also try to walk out on *Laugh-In* because you felt you were too hip for that show?
Yeah, I did. That's supposed to be a little self-deprecating, though maybe it doesn't read that way. I felt like my characters were being used to do material that I didn't like. Cheapening material. I didn't want Ernestine to be used with content that I didn't identify with. Or especially I didn't want her to be used for content that I thought was lame or just banal.

You've said your career all happened backwards. Meaning?
By that I meant that I got very famous on a middle-American, broad-based television show, *Laugh-In,* and had an immensely high PDQ because of

Ernestine and Edith Ann. *Then* I started playing Mr. Kelly's and any place where I could get booked and do my act, and of course, I didn't do anything like what I did on *Laugh-In,* so I used to play to basically silence. Maybe I would do two minutes of Ernestine—it never dawned on me that people would like Ernestine, because that's the only thing they identified me with, and then be confused by what else I might do. Now, conversely, people don't like it if I *don't* do something new.

How ambitious or competitive were you then as compared to today?
Now? Less ambitious, less competitive. And almost resent the time I spent being that way.

Which way?
Competitive with myself.

And not with anyone else?
Oh sure. Most actors are so kind of out there anyway emotionally. It's like identifying your salability or your PDQ with your literal, personal self, which is a grave mistake. The first time I did a special, after *Laugh-In,* I got a huge rating, because Ernestine and Edith Ann were so popular. I got an overall share of 45 or 48. In those days you could still get that kind of share. Now, unless you bleach your skin, I guess you can't do that anymore. But because we got such a big rating, they asked me to do another special, and for that one we won two Emmys, but we didn't get such a high rating. We got like a 29, which wasn't good enough in those days. I remember being devastated, thinking that I really didn't have any career or any audience, I just totally equated that rating with who I was. I didn't want to talk to anybody. I was ashamed, I thought it was all over, that I had totally misjudged everything.

And how long did it take you to recover from such a blow?
Yeah, I know, it's stupid. But slowly I began to back into a different audience, playing clubs and doing concerts. I began to be perceived of as a hipper comedian, if you'll pardon my lingo.

When you performed in clubs, were you inspired by Joan Rivers?
I go back with Joan to the Downstairs, when she was already famous. I was in the review Upstairs. I used to come down the back stairs when I wasn't on and watch her through a crack in the door. I'd be literally laughing so hard I had to stifle myself not to be a real distraction.

When Joan had her talk show, she said you're a very tough interview.

She really said that? I never thought she thought that. The last time I went on her show she brought my mother and brother out from Tennessee. I fool around with her because I really like Joan. So what I did on that show was I wore my brassiere outside of my clothing. And she didn't notice at first. Then someone from her staff noticed, so when we came back from a break she had one on over her blouse. I was supposed to be the president of Madonna's fan club. Well, my mother has really big breasts, and if I'd have known she was there, I would have had my mother come out like that, it would have been hilarious.

Robin Williams described being interviewed as a dance, "like two lepers doing a tango." How do you feel about it?
I use the phrase "broken-field stride," just trying to avoid the mines.

Richard Pryor said you were his favorite female comedian.
Yeah, I heard about that. I was so stunned. When I saw Richard working, I just loved it so much, I felt I saw into the heart of him. Nobody else was doing it. I was so gratified to be moved on that level, the way he would perform those little moments. It's not just the material, it's the whole marriage of the sensibility and someone's own humanity.

Does it bother you when someone prefaces his praise with the word "female"?
Nah, nothing matters. It's just society. We're just making it up as we go along.

When you were performing in clubs, did it ever get weird?
No. When I first performed and I played colleges, you present yourself a different way. You're cheekier, you're mouthy. And a young audience wants you to go further and further and further. I once stayed on the stage all night at the Boarding House in '75. Did everything. Having as many people as you could get out of the audience onto the stage, piled up, rolling around, doing drugs, videotaping it, taping everybody in the audience. Just anything.

Was this before or after you met and began working with Jane Wagner?
I was on *Laugh-In*. She did *JT*, this thing about a kid in Harlem, for children's programming, and it was so well received that they broadcast it at night in prime time. I was fixing to do my Edith album, and I wanted it to be different. What Jane had done was very poetic, plus naturalistic, plus styled at the same time. It was complex, like an essence, compressed. Every line almost is an observation, and yet it's naturalistic as dialogue. What I always sought in

a monologue. So I wrote her and asked if she would work on the Edith album.

You've said you'll spend the rest of your life explaining that Jane is the writer and you don't write. Has it been hard for her?
Yes, I think so.

You also said you have the same sensibilities, she's just smarter.
Yes, more verbal.

Is Jane the smartest woman you know?
She's very smart and poetic and expansive and sensitive and at the same time very analytical. Everybody who knows her knows she's pretty smart.

After working with Jane, can you go back to working on your own?
I can't. I'm not good enough.

Does she feel frustrated by your success with her words?
Only when people say *The Search* was written by us. Because it's so natural to me they can't believe that somehow I don't have a hand in it. And I don't.

You mean it wasn't much of a collaboration?
No more so than any script is a collaboration between an actor and a director and a writer. Believe me, in terms of proportion, my contribution was minuscule. You might come up with a line, but any actor in any vehicle comes up with a line here and there. When we did *The Search,* I was totally invested in the content and in the shaping of the play. It was a total love affair. It's like playing a piece of music. I'd be just as high as I could be, knowing if I did it incredibly wonderfully, the audience would just be enraptured. It's a beautiful, exhilarating experience when you're doing something that you think is wonderful and you feel people are receiving it. It's psychotherapeutic too.

Were all the characters hers?
Verbally, yes. Trudy came from the first show, *Appearing Nightly.*

Trudy the Bag Lady says she'd much rather be exploited than ignored. That true of you too?
No, I don't want anybody to pay attention to me. I don't want to be exploited or ignored. I can't take it all seriously. The only thing I could take seriously is maybe getting a nice new bag of mulch and taking the time to go out and dig in the yard.

How seriously did you take the time Katharine Hepburn, Barbra Streisand, and Meryl Streep all came to see you on the same night?
You read about that? In fact, Streisand said she got sick and left during the first act (*laughs*). I never spoke to her about it.

Does it affect your performance knowing they're out there?
Oh God yes. If I'd known they were there, I would have had dry mouth. I wouldn't be able to speak. I would have been too scared, petrified.

You mean you don't yet feel a part of the Industry?
I don't see myself that way, yet I know I am. I'm well known enough and liked enough and respected . . . it's part of my family, but it's sort of like I don't go home every year to the reunion.

How much of an aphrodisiac is fame?
Power is the ultimate aphrodisiac. Fame is too, sure. Probably more for men. I don't think men are turned on too much by famous women. I guess they are when they like to show them off or be identified with them, until they find out what it really means.

Trudy predicted that the seventies and eighties would go down as the "stealth decades": they snuck up on us, did untold damage, and we never knew what hit us. Is that Jane or you writing?
That's Jane writing. It's a great remark. I don't say things like that, I'm not that smart.

How often do you and Jane disagree?
Quite a bit. Because I'm doing a live performance, I might have six drafts of a monologue in my head at one time, and I can move sections around. But rather than rewrite, Jane will just write a new monologue. She hates to rewrite.

Most writers say there is no writing, only rewriting.
Yeah, I know. I try to tell her that.

Is Jane working on another show for you or is she writing music now?
She's working on a show for me, but she's also working on a pilot for somebody, and we have to stay involved with Edith Ann, which we're animating right now for two ABC specials in the fall.

So if Jane writes a musical, will you take singing lessons?

No. I should have been a singer, dammit! Because you get all those royalties.

Well, maybe you'll get rich off your videos. Are you really selling a boxed set out of your garage?
It's true. There're five videos, and when you buy the entire collection, you get a lock of my hair in a crystal inspired plastic pendant. But you can only get this through direct mail, it's very underground. There are even fan bonuses at the end of each tape. I thought the hard-core fans will sit through the credits, see, and then they'll be rewarded for it.

What kind of mailing do you do?
I have huge fan lists collected over the years. Maybe half a million names. Then we mostly get political groups and stuff. Part of the fun of doing this is the lock of hair and making a brochure to send out. It's like a performance. Jane calls it a performance hairpiece.

When Pat Collins had her Hip Hypnotist act, she mentioned that you were a client. Is hypnosis a useful tool?
Yes. I believe in hypnosis. I'm a very good subject. I wish I practiced more mind stuff, just like athletes visualizing themselves performing. I can do self-hypnosis.

Do you also consult with astrologers, palmists, tea leave readers?
I have this one woman in Sacramento I call because she's so much fun. And I call the Psychic Connection on TV.

What else do you watch on TV?
I liked *Kojak,* some good old potboilers, some political things, some metaphysical stuff, and Amy Fisher.

Bette Midler once said that she always wished her chest was smaller, her hair thicker, her eyes bluer, her IQ higher, her shoe size smaller. Have you had any such wishes about yourself?
Her shoe size smaller? She wears about a six!

What would you change about yourself today?
Well, I never had those wishes before, but in the last five years, because so many people get plastic surgery now, it's like an adventure. I've seen people, and they've so completely changed, even their legs, it's shocking. I've thought maybe I've just been a sissy, or maybe I've been too pure on this point. There was a time when I'd see Margaret Rutherford—there's some-

thing so sublime about her, that jaw and everything—and I'd think, if only I could have different legs and arms that you could screw on and have a different body type. So there were times when I'd say, "Oh I wish I could do that." To make that kind of transformation. But before I'd just be horrified at the idea that you would have to change yourself so radically. Now it's like some kind of flung-out fantasy, like saying, I'd like to fly to Paris for lunch. "I'd like to have my armpits suctioned." Or, "Gee, I wonder how I'd look with a different nose."

Wait till Bette reads this, she'll have plenty to tease you about.
Bette who? Oh, don't print that! (*laughs*) I just saw Bette the other day. She's not that social. I'm not either. I don't have a big circle of friends, they take too much time. They become like family, they become absolutely tyrannical in their demands.

So who among the known are you friends with?
I'm quite friendly with Eileen Brennan and Melanie Mayron. People that I've known over a longer period of time.

Bette Midler said she made you laugh a lot on the set of *Big Business*. How did she make you laugh?
Bette's funniest when she doesn't even know she's funny. And she's outrageous and real innocent. She's just . . . Bette.

Did you really attend twin conventions before you were even offered *Big Business*?
Years before, because I always wanted to do a twins movie. So I went to a twin convention. There are some really strange, rarified twins. Like if they have a green bar of soap and a white bar, they have to have two halves, one can't have a green soap while the other has white. Or if one has to have an operation, the other, whether he or she has the affliction, has to have the same scar. There's just something compulsive, they can't bear to be different.

So your interest was more along the lines of a freak movie?
Kind of freaky, yeah.

So what made you want to do *Big Business*?
I did it because I wanted to work with Bette, and I wanted to have a movie. When I'm sitting out there at the Motion Picture Home, I want to see the cassettes lined up there and say, "Well, here, let's watch this movie I made with that Bette Midler."

Is that also why you did *Nine to Five*, because of Dolly Parton and Jane Fonda?
I turned that down initially. I was doing *Shrinking Woman* at the time. It's much harder for me to do something that's been created outside like that, it's not the way I would do it, or I would want to use other examples to demonstrate the character, you know? That's ten or twelve years ago, I'm quite different now. But at that time I just hated some of the jokes. Like when Jane's husband comes over and he says something about S&M, and later she says, "If I wanted to do M&Ms . . ." The audience just howled, but I hated some of those jokes. They're sort of lame. I can't imagine why anybody thinks they're funny. When I turned it down, I was kind of heartsick because I wanted to do it because of Jane and Dolly.

So who convinced you to do it?
Jane [Wagner]. She said, "You're going to regret this. After Jane Fonda developed that part for you and then you turn around and throw that in her face? When you see whoever that other woman is who gets to be with Jane and Dolly, you're going to be so sorry that you didn't do it." And she was right. But after I shot the first couple of days, I called [producer] Bruce Gilbert and Jane Fonda over the weekend, and I begged them to let me out. I thought I was just awful. I did the Snow White stuff. Of course, they thought I was real good. I said, "Please, just let me out. I'll help you get anybody you want. I just don't want to fail the movie." Then I went to see the dailies, and I was real good. So then I was glad they didn't replace me.

You actually were a replacement for Louise Fletcher in *Nashville*, weren't you?
I didn't know for a couple of years that Louise was supposed to do the part I did. But the whole thing about the deaf was inspired by Louise. I found out later that Altman had fallen out with her and her husband. They had just done *Thieves Like Us*. How I got *Nashville* was, I had bought a book written by Cynthia Buchanan in 1971 called *Maiden*. Altman and I had the same agent, Sam Cohen, and Sam put us together. I was privileged and lucky to get into an Altman movie, especially one where I didn't have a lot of screen time and I could be brought into his fold. Then I got *The Late Show* together with Robert Benton and Art Carney. I didn't want to do it because I wasn't sure about the part. I'm glad I did it now, but at the time I resisted doing it.

And then came *Moment by Moment* with John Travolta, a film that dropped like a lead weight.

Moment by Moment was a terrible shock. None of us expected to be massacred for it. John Travolta was so hot, I'm sure it was devastating to him. Jane and I didn't escape either, by any means. I'd seen a sneak of *Saturday Night Fever,* and I loved John. And he came backstage after seeing *Appearing Nightly.* He owed [Robert] Stigwood another movie, so he told Stigwood he wanted to do it with me and Jane. We thought it would be a good movie, and there are some goofy things I do in it that I like. I had a great time with John. I felt warmly affectionate toward him. Everybody said we were just awful and I was awful and we didn't have any chemistry at all, so what can I tell you? I spent much more time with Travolta, playing around, being pals, rolling on the sand, than I did with Steve Martin during *All of Me.* Steve has a lot of propriety. I felt almost maternal towards Steve. I liked *All of Me,* though I didn't particularly like myself as this spinster character in it.

What do you like of yourself in films and videos?
I love *The Search* and my Vegas special. I like my cameo in *The Player.*

Elliott Gould saw a rough cut of Altman's *Short Cuts* and said it goes beyond *Nashville*, it's not just a slice of life but the whole pie. He thinks it's the best film Altman's done.
That's what everybody's been saying. I think so too. It's pretty much an ensemble piece, just a bunch of different couples.

You're paired with Tom Waits, aren't you?
Yes, I loved that immensely. He plays a limo driver, and we're both kind of binge drinkers. I'm a waitress, and we live in this trailer park. What Tom would do is every night he would call me after we'd be shooting and talk to me for an hour like he was Earl the limo driver, just like he was my husband. We kind of played it like teenagers that never quite grew up.

Are you more satisfied with this than with anything else you've done for the screen?
No, I'm not. I like it. I think Tom is great. I do think I could be better if I have one more close-up in my last dinner scene. See what happens is, he's so wonderful that it's hard not to stay on him. I totally understand the impulse, but I was playing the scene very differently than how they cut it for me. They make me look like I go right over to him, and there's much more resignation.

Will Altman listen to your suggestions?
He might. He might say, "Well, I'll go look at it." Luckily, I have the dailies on tape so I'll say, "Look at scene such-and-such." See, I'd like to round out

my performance. It's not *The Search* for me. It's not something that's personal or that I feel I really am communicating to you. It's wonderful, it's nice to be in a movie, there's nothing wrong with that. I'm enough of a careerist to know what it means. I'm not naive about it.

Altman's been known for his temper. Have you ever seen him angry?
No. I missed him punching Leonard Goldberg or somebody in the face during *Nashville*. They'd come down to ask him to cut six minutes out of *California Split,* and he punched this guy, and they fell into the swimming pool.

You had a small part as a prostitute in Woody Allen's *Shadows and Fog.* How differently does Woody direct compared with Altman?
Oh God, I hate not to be too smart. They're very different as individuals. I don't know Woody at all. But Altman is totally available. Altman is like this big, *menschy* patriarch. He's like if you had a father who could fall down and get drunk every night but still you somehow respect him? His humanity just moves you, it doesn't matter. Even if he's not like traditionally a good father.

Jodie Foster, who also played a prostitute in *Shadows and Fog,* said she never knew what Woody expected of her.
She didn't like it very much. I'm used to improvising. I guess I might not like it as much if I were doing a much bigger part. I'd be more concerned. But in doing that small part, I didn't mind. It wasn't a bad movie. I intuited what it might have been, but there were so many different acting styles going on.

What about dubbing? Allen doesn't do it. Does Altman?
Altman may not be very big on dubbing either. Starting with *McCabe and Mrs. Miller* and all the soundwork that he did, then in *Nashville,* all of us were always wearing body mikes. He'd just find a way to use it. I've never dubbed for Altman. He lets stuff happen. Woody does too, except the next thing you know you'll be getting a phone call saying, "Come back." On *Shadows and Fog,* when we came back, all Woody ever did was change his own lines. I don't ever remember mine being changed.

Was Woody going through his troubles with Mia Farrow at the time?
Well, if he was, I didn't know it. I came back from New York and was saying things like, "They're really nice people, a nice couple, really cute. And their children are really cute." But I'm kind of goofy that way, I don't get what's going on anyway. Woody and Mia walked to the set each day holding hands, they seemed very devoted to the kids. Mia's dressing room was like a nursery,

very much for the children. And I'd watch Woody play with his boy, he was always hugging him, picking him up, and the little boy's almost as big as Woody. Woody's really very slight.

Speaking of slight, what motivated you to do *The Incredible Shrinking Woman?*

Universal had come to me and Jane to develop this movie. It was when we were doing *Appearing Nightly.* Jane was very turned on to the idea because she loves science stuff like that. And John Landis was going to direct it originally. But then when *Moment* came out we lost some control of it. It's a cute movie, but I don't think it's what it could have been.

What about *The Beverly Hillbillies?* **Did you ever watch the television series?**

Never. But since then I've begun to watch it religiously. It's on cable two or three times a day. It's sort of charming. There's a huge audience. I'm sure that's why they're making it. Twenty- and thirty-year-olds are still addicted to it. I'm always glad that something comes along that's fun to do and I can do it. I'm looking forward to playing Miss Hathaway. People say, "Oh, Miss Hathaway . . . you're just perfect!" And I think, it's a wise woman who knows herself (*laughs*).

You'll also be appearing in *And the Band Played On* **for HBO, won't you?**

Yes. I play Dr. Selma Dritz. She was the head of communicable diseases in San Francisco at the time. I don't know what's been happening with it—at first ABC had it, then NBC, but they both dropped it. It wasn't until Richard Gere committed to it that it was able to go forward on HBO. I only got in it because Whoopi got sick. I stepped in at the last minute. I was glad, I wanted to be in it.

Do you think it will make a difference?

I think so. I'll tell you why. Because it shows very clearly the cover-up and people's lack of integrity and the idea that people could isolate and dismiss a group of people, because we're going to pay a terrible price for it.

How many friends have you lost to AIDS?

Maybe thirty. Maybe ten good friends.

You said in *The Advocate* **that you didn't think Hollywood did a good job representing lesbians and gays. You felt it was either titillation or comic relief.**

Yeah, I probably said that. Occasionally, when I do see something, I'll see some exploitative scene where two women are in an apartment, like *48 Hours*. Definitely there'll be some gay scene that's meant to be ridiculing or derisive in some way. Anything to keep the puerile interest up.

Were you offered a role in *Even Cow Girls Get the Blues*?
I turned it down. I don't know why, I wanted to work with Gus [Van Sant]. I would like to have been in it, it's an offbeat part. But I didn't love the book as much as everybody carried on in the seventies.

How difficult is it finding good material?
It's extremely hard. For me it's almost impossible, because I'm not even going to be competing for the roles that Streep and Sally Field are. It doesn't occur to anyone, that's just not the game for me.

Demi Moore has said that "there are too many good actresses to fill the few great roles for women, so you have to go out there and fight." How cutthroat does it get?
Not for me. I'm not even in the same ring with the Demi Moores. Either I wasn't smart enough to know that you could fight for a role or I never was cast in that leading-lady club.

Meryl Streep is of the opinion that there is no substitute for beauty in the movies. Do you agree?
You get an extra leg up if you're beautiful *and* you're good. Just being beautiful isn't enough to keep going. It's not so much beauty as it is youth. I look at myself when I was twenty, and I was really quite beautiful. I didn't know.

Is Emma Thompson the next Meryl Streep?
Possibly. Though I don't like to say that because what's wrong with the old Meryl Streep? But yeah, Emma's pretty extraordinary. She told somebody I know how much she liked me. I always sort of envy those English people and their kind of career, which is much more a community of actors who do a lot of different things. They're trained more in the whole craft, it's not only your art, it's your occupation.

Merchant-Ivory seems to know how to work with an ensemble, renting out huge villas where all the actors and crew live.
We did that in *Nashville*, only we had to live in motels. But I like that. I always felt I would be good if I joined the armed services. I don't mind regi-

mentation. I like to work in the theater because I love to go there every night. And I have more autonomy.

So you definitely prefer the stage to films?
Right. It's more verbal, and I much prefer words. I love words, I like the language, and I like the ideas. Even though as a person I'm much more visual. I can't create words, but boy, I love them.

Woody Allen does whatever he feels is funny, without any regard to subject matter. Do you feel that way, or are there things you'd never do?
They wanted me to do a *Tales of the Crypt,* and I could not kill someone. I was required to stab somebody repeatedly. I was like the librarian who turns out to be nutty, kind of a homicidal Miss Hathaway. I can't do any of that.

Are there any films you've seen which you wish you could have done?
Once I see the person in it, it's hard for me to imagine myself doing it. I would have liked to have a part in *Thelma and Louise* because it was landmark. I don't like to just get a part that a whole bunch of people could get. I'd much rather do something personal.

How about Clarice in *The Silence of the Lambs*?
Nah, because I don't like all that imagery. I liked *The Grifters,* but I wouldn't like to have to kill that boy in the end.

What's more important to you, your life or your work?
My work was, without realizing it. But not anymore.

Do you consider yourself a role model?
No, but I am. Anybody who is public is to some degree to somebody.

How do you think people perceive you?
I think people perceive me as talented, funny, maybe down-to-earth, or more accessible; on stage and off stage basically not different. Beyond that I couldn't say.

Complicated?
I don't think they think I'm complicated.

Do you know anybody who doesn't like you?
God yes. Lucy [Ball] didn't like me. In *People* magazine she said, "And Lily Tomlin, I don't get her." And Red Skelton said something bad about me

once in the press. I didn't care overly about Red, but I did care about Lucy. I got to meet Lucy a year before she died. Bette and I had dinner with her. I was a little scared, but she was just great.

You also met Groucho Marx before he died. Didn't he tell you that he was funnier than you because he didn't need a telephone?
Yeah, that's what he said. I said, "You are, that's for sure." I wasn't about to argue with him.

But did you write about it in your journal?
At some point. I don't keep it religiously.

Do you put other writers' names on your journal?
I have (*laughs*). Buy a leather book and put Hunter Thompson's name on it.

Ever plan to publish your journals?
No, God forbid. I'm illiterate. I live in fear that my personal correspondence will be published one day.

Are you familiar with the writings of Camille Paglia, who seems to have pissed off a lot of feminists?
Yes, some of her stuff is maybe valid, but she's so displeasing personally that it's hard to get past her. She's like an exhibitionist to me—just wants to be famous and be out there. But a lot of people do. Certainly not everything she says is wrong, it's just so theatricalized and overdone.

She believes that most men and women can never understand one another.
I dare say I fear that's true.

She also thinks that the way we urinate and the way we have sex ultimately forms the way we see the world.
I don't have any idea if that's correct or not. Do you know what that means? It's just clever, that's all.

One last quote from her: "The masculine male homosexual is the ultimate symbol of human freedom."
There's a lot of validity to that statement. I've often felt this myself, because first of all they have the masculine role to play. All the sex in the world is accessible to them. They don't have the responsibility of marriage or fatherhood. But it's like, if you really start analyzing it, it's surface. Gay men are

just like heterosexual men in the sense that beauty, youth, is absolutely paramount in a relationship. An older male homosexual has as much difficulty as an old heterosexual female in being abandoned, dismissed, discounted. Not so profound.

Is this: why is it easier to have your uterus lowered and made into a penis than to get a prescription for Valium?
That's from something I said. I probably invented an operation. In this culture, in this world, they will cut your penis off, but if you go to a doctor and ask him to cut your finger off, they won't do that. But he will cut your penis off.

Last question: if you found something valuable on the street, would you pocket it or report it?
I found a hundred-dollar bill once on the lawn at the Fairmount Hotel in San Francisco. It was at night, and I was walking my dog. The bill was on the grass. I just took it. Put it in my pocket.

THE ACTION ADVENTURE HERO

JEAN-CLAUDE VAN DAMME

TWO PRIVATE JETS and two black identical limos were parked side by side on the airport tarmac in Burbank. A tall muscular man with a ponytail, wearing a red and black leather jacket, got out of one. A shorter man, also muscular, wearing a colorful silk print shirt, his brown, almost golden hair slicked back off his forehead, got out of the other. Both men were Hollywood action superstars. They'd tossed jibes at each other on talk shows over the years, but they weren't confrontational on this hot afternoon. Steven Seagal was flying to Montana, and Jean-Claude Van Damme was on his way to San Diego to make an appearance at a comic book convention. They said nothing to each other as they got into their jets and flew their separate ways.

Van Damme, thirty-three, was with his fourth wife, Darcy LaPier, and his seven-year-old son Kristofer, from a previous marriage. Kristofer was dressed in a long-sleeved white shirt buttoned to the neck, and black pinstriped pants. The shirt was not military tight, and his father unbuttoned his son's pants to get the shirt tucked perfectly. "Remember what we said," Darcy reminded the boy. "When he does that to you, you get to do that back to him when *his* shirt is untucked."

"It is now," Kris said.

"This is a different kind of shirt," Van Damme protested.

Throughout the twenty-minute flight Van Damme doted on his son, touching his face, telling those flying with him what a good boy he was. And when Kris tossed his cookies on the plane's carpet, Van Damme apologized and cleaned up the mess.

In the waiting limo Van Damme was upset that the driver didn't leave the air conditioning on. "I'm Belgian, I need cold," he said. "I once drove a limo. Picked up a big magazine publisher from the airport. He wanted to go to Malibu and asked if I could get him there in twenty minutes. I said sure and floored it, went through all the lights, speeding, got there, opened the door. He said, 'You drove too fast.' No tip."

At the convention center, two thousand fans had been sitting in an auditorium waiting for their hero. These were people who had seen all his films, followed his career, and admired the way he moves. They were there to ask him questions, and when he entered the hall, they gave him a standing ovation. It was clear that there was a lot of adoration in the room, and when someone asked him how he felt about the cheers, he answered, "To be honest? I feel great."

"Take your shirt off!" a woman yelled to encouraging applause.

Van Damme smiled. His wife tried to, but she wasn't comfortable listening to strange women shouting to see her husband half-naked. It was something she had to adjust to, because the adulation wasn't going to stop anytime soon. Van Damme is the youngest of the martial arts–bodybuilder superstars—twenty-one years younger than Chuck Norris, nine years younger than Seagal, and fourteen years younger than the man he's most often compared to: Arnold.

He had the young audience and he knew it. He was extremely confident as he answered questions about a certain motorcycle stunt in *Hard Target*, how he learned to do a split balanced on two chairs, how he can kick six or seven feet in the air ("Do it!" they shouted). He gave the politically correct answer "Bruce Lee" when asked what martial artist he most admired. A woman stood and said she really liked *Nowhere to Run* because "us women want to see love stories." Other women shouted their agreement, but just as many boys booed. They preferred the straight action films like *Bloodsport, Cyborg,* and *Universal Soldier,* where Van Damme gets hit with wrenches and bullets, sliced with broken glass and knives, and thrown over balconies. He borrowed his wife's camera and told the audience to stand and wave their arms, he wanted to take their picture. They did as he asked and he happily snapped away.

After a half-hour of this he waved good-bye and was escorted into another room for a mini-press conference to promote his two latest films: *Timecop* and *Street Fighter.* A reporter noticed the bump on his forehead and asked whether he had an accident. "No," Van Damme said, "it's a cyst. My wife says now that I'm a big movie star I should cut it out. What do you think? Should I?" The reporter didn't know what advice to give and shrugged. Then Van Damme and his party went into the convention hall, where he created a minor furor when people recognized him. ("I touched him," one young man said after reaching out to the passing star.)

He was taken to the Marvel Comics exhibit where the famed Stan Lee, creator of Spiderman, Dare Devil, and so many other famous characters, was signing comics. Lee was thrilled that Jean-Claude came to see him. Later Van Damme said that he would try to see Stan Lee again, to see whether the cartoonist would give him Dare Devil for no up-front money but for points in a future film. When a friend said that Van Damme would never get a Stan Lee character for no money, Van Damme challenged him: "So someone else pays for it and nothing happens. If I do it, it will become a sensation, and he will be very happy to have the points."

The man wasn't always this sure of himself. He was born Jean-Claude Van Varenberg in Berchem-Sainte Agathe, just outside of Brussels, Belgium. A skinny, knock-kneed kid, he didn't care much for school, talked with a lisp, and got into trouble for mimicking his teachers. His father, who owned a lingerie shop, then a newspaper and convenience store, and then a flower shop, had him study ballet and put him in a karate class when he was eleven, where the boy suddenly became focused. Training hard every day (he could do a full split at eleven), he was participating in bodybuilding and kickboxing competitions by his mid-teens. He won the bodybuilding crown of Mr. Belgium, and also the European middleweight black-belt karate championship. He married at eighteen, opened a gym in Brussels, and became a personal trainer to his customers. But he wanted more.

Like the Hergé cartoon character Tintin, whom he admired, Jean-Claude was anxious to travel and have adventures. His ambition was to be a movie star in America. On a visit to Paris he was walking along the Champs Élysées when a photographer spotted him and offered him a job modeling clothes for Jean-Paul Gautier. Another time, in Brussels, he was "discovered" again and offered a job playing a soldier and fighting Rutger Hauer in a movie. Encouraged by his ability to be picked out of a crowd, he left his wife to follow his dream. He went to a film festival in Italy, got the business cards of a number of Hong Kong producers, then went to Hong Kong on a modeling job. He tried to break into the martial arts film industry there but had no luck, so he went to Los Angeles when he was twenty, with very little money and no English.

For the next six years he struggled—unsuccessfully placing his picture and résumé on the windshields of movie producers' cars, working as a bodyguard, bouncer, aerobics instructor, taxi and limo driver, pizza delivery man, and carpet layer. Someone suggested he change his name, and he did, from Van Varenberg to Van Damme. He married a second time, but it didn't work out because she wanted him to go full-time into her father's carpet business.

He appeared briefly as a gay biker in a film called *Morocco Forever*, and Chuck Norris hired him as an extra in *MIA*. In 1986 he landed a role as a Russian bad guy in *No Retreat, No Surrender*. But his big break didn't happen until he ran into Cannon Pictures' Menahem Golan outside a restaurant. Figuring he had nothing to lose, he called out Golan's name and shot his leg straight out and over the producer's head. Golan was sufficiently impressed and offered to make him a star. The vehicle was *Bloodsport*, a pure Thai kickboxing movie, and Van Damme felt the long wait was over.

But the movies created new frustrations. Cannon didn't release *Bloodsport* for nineteen months. In the meantime, Van Damme (who was now promoting himself as "Van Dammage," "The Muscles from Brussels," and "Wham, Bam, Thank You, Van Damme") signed contracts with independent film companies to do other low-budget films. By the time *Bloodsport* came out and became a cult success, Van Damme was tied to low-paying companies for the next five years, years in which he made action films that all made money: *Cyborg, Death Warrant, Kickboxer, Lionheart, Double Impact*. When he was finally released from his contractual obligations, he made *Universal Soldier* for Carolco, *Hard Target* with the Chinese action director John Woo, and *Nowhere to Run* with Patricia Arquette. All three earned between $31 million and $36 million domestically, and Universal became confident that, with a big budget and publicity campaign, Van Damme in *Timecop* was ready to break the $50 million barrier. Matsushita was thinking even bigger: it paid Van Damme $6 million (twice what he got for *Timecop*) to star as Colonel Guile, the computer action hero of *Street Fighter*. He has also completed *Sudden Death*, directed by Peter Hyams (who directed *Timecop*), and after my interview with him in the winter of 1995, he directed himself in *The Quest*, about a street fighter who journeys to Tibet to fight in a martial arts competition in the early part of this century, and appeared in *Maximum Risk, Double Team, Knock Off, Legionnaire, Inferno, Universal Soldier: The Return, Abominable, Desert Heat*, and *Replicant*.

His movies seem to have something for everyone—blacks are often good guys, women are treated decently, family honor and values are upheld. Van Damme fights for his brother's honor (*Lionheart, Kickboxer*) or his parents' (*Double Impact*). He's the baby-faced good guy with the short hair, well groomed, who doesn't look like he can take you out with a foot in your face. He's not as massive as Arnold, or as tall and distant as Seagal, or as mean as Lundgren, or as cartoony as Hulk Hogan. And yet, as he readily acknowledges, "I'm one of the biggest action stars in America. The others are all past forty, close to fifty, I'm twelve, fifteen years behind them. I'm the youngest. Just wait and see where I am in ten years."

Although he hasn't lacked for work, Van Damme has been hit with a few lawsuits. One, from an actor who got poked in the eye with a weapon during a *Cyborg* fight scene, was awarded close to half a million dollars in damages. Another was filed by a woman who claimed the actor forced her to have oral sex with him and then participate in a ménage à quatre.

After marrying his third wife, a bodybuilder named Gladys Portugues, and having two children, Kristofer and a daughter, Bianca, his raging hormones led him to take up with Darcy, who was married to the Hawaiian Tropic suntan-oil mogul Ron Rice. Their torrid love led to the breakup of both marriages and has caused Van Damme his greatest anguish: being separated from his children, who live with their mother in Belgium. (*In 1996 Van Damme checked into a thirty-day substance abuse program in Los Angeles but left after one week. In the fall of 1997 Darcy accused him of spousal abuse and mood swings, which she blamed on his addiction to cocaine and sleeping pills. They divorced, and Van Damme remarried Gladys. In September 1999 he was arrested in West Hollywood at 3:45 A.M. on suspicion of drunken driving. The suspicion was removed on July 10, 2000, when he pleaded no contest to misdemeanor counts of drunk-driving and driving without a license in his possession. A judge sentenced him to three years' probation, fined him $1,200, and ordered him to attend a ninety-day anti-drunk driving program.*)*

My first day with Van Damme we flew in a private jet; the second meeting was at his home in Chatsworth in the San Fernando Valley. It was one of the hottest days of the year, more than 110 degrees, and Van Damme was on an inflated raft soaking up the sun in his swimming pool. He invited me to join him, and I did. "Do people think you have a tough job?" he asked. "You don't think this is tough?" I answered, trying to balance my tape recorder on my chest so it wouldn't fall in the water. "I like to talk best over dinner," he told me, "with a nice wine." I was just happy to talk over land, with some solid footing beneath our feet.

After two hours in the broiling sun we went inside, where he showed me his elaborate ivory boat sculptures from China in his living room, along with framed giant insects from Malaysia—dung and rhinoceros beetles, a grasshopper twice the size of my hand, butterflies that hadn't lost their colors.

When I met with him in Pittsburgh, where he was getting ready to make *Sudden Death,* I had no idea that our talks would begin two hours before midnight and continue until nearly dawn, but that's when Van Damme felt most comfortable, and so we smoked Cuban cigars, drank fine red wines, and spoke about things the Belgian actor has rarely talked of in such depth. His moods changed each evening: the first night he showed me his muscles. "Look at how much better shape I'm in than when we saw each other last week," he said. The second night he was more subdued; the third, contemplative. At one point he shouted at me, "I'm only thirty-three, too young for such an in-depth interview, I'm a baby, I have so much to learn." But when I challenged his prowess as a martial artist, he went from baby to professional, asking me to stand so he could demonstrate how, in two lightning-swift kicks to my shoulder, he could easily disarm someone like Steven Seagal, who comes from another discipline, aikido, which is all arms and finesse. Van Damme only tapped my arm, but I still felt it the next day. Make no mistake about him: he's the real thing.

In San Diego you complained about the heat and lack of air conditioning. But on the hottest day of the year you floated in your swimming pool at high noon without protecting your skin. Aren't you concerned about the sun?
No, I never use those creams. I don't need it.

You really think you're Superman?
It's the genes. My mother never used creams. I sit in the sun, I get red, then I get dark.

The red part means you burn, like the rest of us. Not too smart these days, Jean-Claude.
I do not worry, it doesn't harm me.

With the way your career has taken off, it doesn't seem like anything can harm you.
You know how many people have approached me to do a movie about my life and how I made it in America? I've got so much in my head about all the stuff I've done, people will cry, they will laugh, they will go nuts about it!

That's why I'm here, to get into your head.
I've got news for you—I'm nothing special. You are talking to a guy who was not raised on the street, who didn't do drugs or crazy stuff, who comes from a simple country with simple people. I'm not deep, not super smart, not stu-

pid, just a normal guy. I've got two dogs, a house, I like to train, I love life. That's Van Damme.

The "Muscles from Brussels" is a lot more complex than that. You don't wind up with two major releases within three months by being simple. The expectations for *Street Fighter* are very high—it's supposed to be your domestic breakthrough film.
I would love the movie to be successful because the guy who did it, Mr. Sugimoto of Matshushita, put two big studios—Columbia and Universal—together for the first time since *Towering Inferno*. He put up his own money from his company, and I received a good salary, double what I got for *Timecop*. So I was crazy not to do it. And he's going to put like $20 million in promotion and advertising. He's like a big kid, a very generous man, and if it's a hit for him, he will invest more money in the business.

He's already invested more money in remaking the video game to your image. Have you seen it?
They've had six hundred people working on this one video game for the last two years, and when I asked what it was about, they said, "Top secret." I know it's unusual, and that they're using my face as Colonel Guile. So now the kids can play with Van Damme, jump, dance, kick, get punched. I'm part of a phenomenon.

And how are you in the film?
I'm funny, like over the top.

Did you feel that way about *Timecop*?
In *Timecop* I did everything—break arms, kick, jump, do a split, do karate, aikido, street-fight, knife-fight, I even fought with tools. Plus it was an intelligent movie.

Unlike the two previous to it: *Hard Target* and *Nowhere to Run*.
Hard Target was a bad script, but we had some great action scenes, and John Woo made me look like a samurai with greasy hair. The script for *Nowhere to Run* was also not that good. The writer told me, he's going to fix everything, I was in his house, he shook my hand, he promised me, but he didn't fix it.

Did you always know you were destined to be a movie star?
Absolutely. I was crazy about movies since I was born. I wanted to go to America to become a movie star. My father was against me going to the U.S. "Crazy," he said. "You'll never make it, so many kids like you, and they speak the language." Everybody tells me it's impossible, but when you have some-

thing in your head, you have to do it. It's like that song from *Man of La Man-cha*, dream the impossible dream. You can tell me many times, don't do it, don't do it, but I will not be happy until I try. And to be honest with you, if I didn't succeed, I'd still be trying. Because if you want to make it badly, you can make it. I really believe so.

But weren't you making it already with the gym you owned when you were still a teenager?
I was making a fortune with the gym, $7,000 a week, more than my father ever made. I was nineteen. I called it California Gym, it was the biggest in Belgium. I bought the machines from a Flemish importer. I was taking care of people individually, watching everybody, training them differently because some people have long muscles, others short, and nobody has the same metabolism. I'm good for that stuff. But I gave it all up—the business, my family, even though I love my parents, my first marriage—to come here. And when I came here, it was difficult—I didn't speak English, I had no work permit, but I was happy. And full of ambition.

You make it sound easy.
It was not easy, nothing happened for a long time. I learned the hard way. But you have two ways to go to Rome: you can take the freeway, or you can take the road.

Before you came to America, didn't you try your luck in Hong Kong?
Yes, for a modeling job. And I had all these business cards from Hong Kong producers, but nothing happened. I saw Jackie Chan once. I waited for him. When he came out, I said, "Hey, I love your picture, it's great." He said, "See you, man." And I'm back on the street. Then I came to America and nothing. Few people responded to me.

Did you feel like you didn't belong here?
No, I felt right, that L.A. is my place, like it's part of me, like I was here before.

Did you continue to train while you looked for film work?
I was very methodic. I was training four times a week, working at least ten hours a day, then going to casting, talking to people, always pushing, pushing, pushing.

Was any of the work you did interesting?
No. I was driving limousines. I did massage. Delivered pizza. Cleaned carpet. I was a bouncer.

Did anything ever get weird?
When I drove limousines, I took two girls from Texas, around fortyish. They asked me, "Driver, do you have something to chew on?" I said, "Yes, bubble gum." "No, we want something to chew on, something in our mouth." They were trying to take me. Their husbands sent them to Beverly Hills to have plastic surgery, and they want something to "chew on."

In other words, they wanted to chew on you?
Something like that.

And you didn't want to have oral sex with these women?
They were ugly.

Did you run into such problems when you gave massages?
My first one. This guy took off his robe, and he was naked. I said, "Do you have a towel?" "Oh, you don't need it." I start to massage his back, and he opened his legs, and I said, "Buddy, that's it, I'm leaving." He stood up, it was half hard. I have nothing against homosexuals, I got lots of friends that are gay, but that was it for massage.

As a bouncer, did you ever have to throw anyone out?
Never. It was in Newport Beach, Chuck Norris's wife's restaurant, so I drove three hours every day back and forth.

And when did you eventually work for Chuck?
I went to see him when he was with a friend and said I could train him. But he wasn't sure, so he had me spar with his friend and he sat and watched. I jumped in the air, started kicking, that guy didn't expect that. Then I trained Chuck for months, for free.

Why didn't he pay you?
Ask him. I will never ask for something. After I train him every day, he took me for dinner sometimes, and I also became an extra for him in *MIA*.

During this time you were also sticking your picture on car wind-shields, hoping a producer might call. Did you ever hear from anyone?
Nobody. I even went to the parking lots of the big studios like MGM and Fox, and also to the independent studios, which were more approachable. I always looked at the big cars, they were the producers. I put pictures of my-self and my phone number. Thousands of pictures. Sometimes I followed

some cars to see the house. People think I'm nuts, but it wasn't to harm anybody.

It sounds pretty desperate. How despondent did you get?
Before I left for America, I was on vacation in the south of France and had my dog Tara with me. She was a black chow chow, I really loved that dog. I was walking with her when I saw a man walking a big male dog, very healthy-looking, and I thought he was the perfect guy to take my dog because I couldn't take her with me to America. So I gave my dog to him, and a year later I came back to see her, but when I got there I thought maybe it wasn't a good idea that she see me, it would make her sad again when I left, so I bought sunglasses and I put on a hat so the dog wouldn't recognize me. I treated her like a girlfriend, like the love of my life. When I saw my dog walking, she had holes with no hair, and I said to myself, "You are such an idiot, you give that dog away to follow your dream, and they're treating you like shit in America, you're doing two-bucks-an-hour jobs, and here is the dog who is loving you like nobody else and you left her." I wanted to go and touch her, smell her, but if I did then she would be happy for one day and then become even more broken. Like you go back to a woman you once loved but now respect as your best friend, if you go back she thinks it's love, a woman will not understand. So I stayed away for three days, looking at my dog every day and night, like a detective. Crying behind my glasses. I left and returned a year and a half later, and she was gone. Gone. And the same happened to my parrot, a gray female I had, she loved me, she'd come on my hand, stay on my shoulder. I gave her to an old lady, and the bird died. She never called me. I will never give an animal away again. I thought, that's why God gave me such a hard time making it, to punish me. He loves the animals, they die, now you're going to suffer before you see the light.

Your suffering stopped when you finally got Cannon producer Menahem Golan to put you in a movie. How apocryphal is the story of how you caught his attention?
I tried to meet him for five, six years. Then I was coming into a restaurant, and he was coming out. I said, "Menahem, it's me, Jean-Claude Van Damme. Remember all the pictures I sent you?" He was busy doing business. So I said, "I can do great action films." And I kicked above his head, like a six-foot-two kick. I impressed him. He gave me his card and said, "Call me tomorrow."

He didn't think you were crazy? You could have kicked him in the head.

No, the guy is from Israel, he came with twenty bucks to this country, he liked that stuff. The next day I called him, he wasn't available. So I drove to his office on San Vicente. Now imagine me, I was driving taxi, cleaning carpet, delivering pizza, here I am in the penthouse of Cannon, the biggest independent company at that time. They had signed Stallone for $10 million for *Over the Top,* and I was on the sofa outside waiting for Menahem, who was on the phone shouting some deal. I thought, he likes to yell, he's a salesman. I was there 1:00 P.M., 2:00 P.M., 3:00 P.M., 4:00 P.M., 5:00 P.M., 6:00 P.M. Sitting there all day as people came in and out. He was buying, selling, building his company. Finally he came out, tucking his shirt into his pants, and I go inside. This time I think, Jean-Claude, you're here for six years, everything is shit, this is your only chance to have a small part in a movie. Don't panic, don't sweat your hand when you shake his, be strong. I felt all Belgium was behind me. Because many times people there cross my father, they say to him, "Hey, we heard your son is a punching boy in America. How's the punching boy?" My father was in shame. I gave up my gym and everything, imagine my father. So I know about how Menahem came to America with twenty dollars, so I say to him, "I came to this country with forty dollars, and I have nothing, and I hope one day I can be somebody. I'm here for six years, nothing is going well in my life, so let's cut the bullshit. I know I've got something very special. I'm very inexpensive, and I'm very good. You can make so much money with me, you can make me a star." I was almost in tears, he saw my eyes were real. I said, "Look at my body," and I started to take off my shirt. "See the muscles I have." Then I took two chairs and did a split balanced between them. "See, I am flexible. I can do kicks, everything. I'm a young Chuck Norris. Maybe one day a Stallone. So what do you say?"

He said, "My friend, you want to be a star? I'll make you a star. You got a green card?" I say yes, which is a big fucking lie. "Do you have a lawyer?" "I will tomorrow." "An agent?" "Tomorrow." "Then you're going to make a movie. You're going to be the lead in *Bloodsport.*"

My legs are like cotton balls, I can't believe it. When I leave, I'm jumping all over like an idiot. I shake hands with everybody. Then the lawyer I hired almost blew the deal. Cannon was offering me $25,000 with an option for two more films at $50,000 and $75,000. My lawyer tried to get me more money, he said they were bluffing. I almost killed him. I said I'd been trying for six years, sleeping on the street, being taken advantage of, make the fucking deal now! But then *Bloodsport* was delayed and delayed and delayed, but four months later I was on a plane to Hong Kong. Thank God it was set in Hong Kong.

Could you have done it without a green card in the States?
No. It was a good script, but they kept changing it, so all the story ended up in the garbage, and they kept losing sight of the movie. I had to recut the film myself.

How did Golan let you do that?
Because he saw the movie. He hated it. He said, "Van Damme, it's a very bad movie." I go, "Menahem, I beg you, I saw it too, let me recut it." And I cut the movie every night with the guy who cut *The Towering Inferno*. The producer didn't know I was recutting it, I was such a politician, I didn't say nothing to him, I reported to Menahem every week. Then they put the film on the shelf, so he never saw the new version. It was not released for a year and a half. Then he sold it in France and all those countries, they released it, and I flew everywhere to promote it. I paid my own ticket to Malaysia, where it was the biggest box office. Two weeks later I flew to France, did a karate kick for a magazine, did a split on the Champs Élysées. Big success. Because of the fighting scenes. Now you go to Asia, to Hong Kong, Japan, Korea, *Bloodsport* is unrentable in the stores, it's always gone. It's a cult.

And Golan didn't even know what he had?
After he saw the box office, he knew. He called me into his office and said, "Van Damme, the iron is hot. We'll do two more movies." By then I had waited so many months, I had other things I wanted to do, and also I had signed some contracts with small companies, so I said, "You said you don't need me no more." He said, "My friend, I made you a star, I'm going to sue your ass off." But he didn't pay me a penny more. Instead of giving me $100,000 for the second movie, he gave me $50,000. Big mistake. I did *Death Warrant* and *Cyborg* for him, and that was it. But I love Menahem because he gave me my first chance.

After the success of *Bloodsport* you really weren't free to work for any of the major studios, were you?
No. So many studios called me for projects, but I wasn't available for like five years. I had signed these other contracts before *Bloodsport* came out. With Cannon it was one film, two options. With another company one film, two options. A third company also one film, two options. That's nine low-budget films, below $5 million for each one. That's why I made all those movies like *Kickboxer* and *Double Impact*. One of the best scripts I ever read was called *Dusted*, but the producer fucked it up big time, it became *Death Warrant*. With this you cannot make it in Hollywood. It was like a factory, three movies a year, no cast, first-time directors. I didn't do good as an actor.

But you know what? They all made money. I became a star with those movies.

You've said in the past that they were "silly" movies.
They were not silly, for what they were it was . . . okay. I'm proud of them, and I'm not proud. You know what I'm saying?

Yes and no.
I just wish that before those movies opened people should know that they were made for low, low money, so forgive this actor if sometimes he has to scream for two minutes and he has no explosions and no bullets, no special effects.

Perhaps that's why they seem so authentic, like in *Kickboxer* where you kick down a bamboo tree.
I kicked the tree for real.

That must have hurt.
When the camera was rolling, it felt good. It was my second time in the movies, I was hungry.

You must have been pretty hungry to sign up to play the alien in *Predator*, especially when you discovered you were too small to fit the costume they had made.
I did only two scenes and had to quit because it was impossible to work in it. I wanted to do good stunts in the suit, but it was too heavy, my head was in the neck, my feet were in a cast, I was in deep shit.

But you got to meet Arnold Schwarzenegger.
Yeah. The first thing he said to me was, "I like your belt. Where did you buy it?" I go (*effecting an effeminate accent*), "I bought it on Santa Monica Boulevard." He turned around and left. Two years later I saw him on the set of *Red Heat*, and without knowing it I was sitting in his chair. He came back from his scene and looked at me, and I said, "I like your belt, where did you buy that belt?" He left nice. He's a smart man because he remembered his line about the belt.

What impresses you about Arnold?
He makes sense when he talks. He doesn't talk with complicated words, he's very direct. You look in his eyes, they are good. He will never try to hurt you or take advantage of you. He's too busy and too rich, he has his own focus,

his own mission. He's not looking at how your arms are so big and the way you dress, he's too above all that. I like him a lot.

Are you comfortable being compared with him?
Arnold is smart, and I think I am smart too. We both came from Europe—he came with weight lifting, I came with karate—and maybe that's why people compare us, but you cannot compare Arnold and Van Damme.

What about as actors? Arnold has proven himself to many critics, but there's still that question asked about you: can he act? Does that annoy you?
Yeah, it annoys me. People look at me with attitude if I tell them yes, I can act. There are two different types of acting: body acting and face acting. Brando dying in *The Godfather,* Stallone punching the meat in *Rocky*—if you can act emotionally, you can act visually, physically. You don't learn acting, it's all mood, it's all from inside, from your heart. Why do people come to see me? Because I cannot act? I think deeply I can act, but I know I'll become better. I'm not there yet. Imagine if I can do action, drama, romance, what's going to be next? How far can I go? It's all a question of wanting. But if I say that one day I'd like to be perceived like a Pacino, a De Niro, a Hopkins, they're going to say I'm a nut case.

Do you foresee a time when you will make films without exhibiting your martial arts skills?
Absolutely. But it's difficult to leave the image behind. It's difficult for Stallone to leave Rocky, he was so good, that and Rambo are like he's got a stamp on his forehead. But when he made *FIST* he was a good union guy. When you become a thing, it's difficult because you're a piece in a puzzle.

Didn't you once say that Stallone seemed confused and that he didn't know what he was doing?
Sly was stretching himself for a couple of years after he became so successful. He was the biggest star in the world, how can he beat that? It's confusing. To beat that ceiling, what do you have to do? He needs a director who can understand him. In real life he's a very funny guy, and when he's fifty-five he can do a great comedy.

Another action star you're often compared with is Steven Seagal, who apparently bad-mouthed you once on Arsenio Hall's show. What do you think of him?

I like him a lot. The first movie I saw of his, *Above the Law,* I knew he was going to be a big star. Seagal has a very quiet, strong presence, and he was very smart about something: he did action movies with a suit on. People like that.

Why did he bad-mouth you?
I don't know, he doesn't know me. When I was promoting *Timecop,* every reporter asked me about Seagal. I've only met him twice in my life. Why does he hate me?

Maybe he thinks there isn't room enough for the two of you?
We're two tough guys . . . if he loses weight, we will have enough room.

Would you like to do a movie with him?
The combination between Steven and Van Damme can be a hot movie, it's like putting Arnold and Sly together in a comedy. If Seagal and Van Damme joined forces, it could be great because people want to see Van Damme against Seagal. It's like seeing Holyfield and Tyson. But it will never happen.

Because one of you has to lose?
Exactly. And I hate to lose.

Which means, for this to happen, Seagal would have to lose to you?
No, we both have to win.

Seagal has called the people in your business pukes, scumbags, and money grubbers. Do you see it that way?
My answer to Steven Seagal: quit. Go back to Japan and work for the CIA.

Do you think Seagal ever really worked for the CIA?
Honest to God? I think if a guy worked for the CIA he will not be authorized by the CIA to go on a TV show and tell people he was a CIA expert. I don't think so.

And Seagal supposedly doesn't think you're a world champion karate expert.
When I was practicing karate, I became the best. I had the best legs in the world, and still do today. I can do things with my legs you wouldn't believe. I can jump 360 degrees. I was writing my name in chalk with my toes on the board at school. When Seagal says I'm full of shit on TV, people don't pay attention. Because I trained.

Let's talk about your training. How old were you when your father put you in a karate class? And why karate?

I was eleven, the youngest in the class. In America you have all these sports, in Belgium we had to choose from: wrestling, boxing, bodybuilding, tennis, karate. The others were too expensive, membership fees every month, equipment. With karate it was $100 a year with everything included. So I was stuck in karate. My father said to me, "It was my best investment in life. I gave $100 for my son to play karate, and he became a movie star because of that. Now he's bringing back millions. I never thought that $100 was going to make me so much money."

Who was your instructor, and did he have any special methods of teaching?

Claude Goetz. Great man. He lived outside of Brussels, and I used to run from my house to the freeway, a mile and a half, then I ran on the side of the freeway for ten miles to him, because I was training to become a champion. When I got there, he would dress me in a special thick outfit to finish my run. It was the stuff you made carpet from, heavy tissue, to protect you from dogs. And he would say, "Now, run some more." So I would run, and then I'd hear barking, his German shepherd would be after me—so strong, he was able to stop the wheel of a bike with his teeth. I used this in *Kickboxer*. The dog would catch me and hold me by my arm. Claude would say, "Stay on your feet." And that dog turned me around and threw me on the ground. Then Claude would shout, "Stop," and the dog stopped. Claude would tell me, "What you need Jean-Claude is resistance. Endurance is nice, but resistance gives you the final speed." Like when Sugar Ray Leonard fought Marvin Hagler—remember the last round? *Bang, bang, bang, bang*—Hagler was confused. That's resistance, that's the real stuff. Then Claude would take two bamboo sticks and go at me with them. Every time I opened my guard, *poke!* I had to go between the sticks to be able to touch him with my legs without being touched by the sticks. Claude trained me good.

How fast were you when you fought?

I was so fast, man. Sometimes I would hit a guy, and the judge would go, "Nothing." He didn't see. And the guy would be bleeding.

When you started competing, did you lose many fights?

Of course I lost some fights. Not many. When I was eighteen, I lost to Angelo Spitarro, who was twenty-eight, in the final. I'd been fighting for three days, twelve fights, winning, winning, winning, going home to sleep, back the next day, winning. I lost the last fight because I was so young, so nice to people. I'm more mean now. If a guy touches me, I will give him three times more. When I was young and a guy touched me, I go, "Hey." Now I get pissed. When you get older, you become more vicious, like an old wolf. I'm dangerous. I'm not to play with. I will not lose any more fights.

Did you ever get hurt when you competed?
I broke my jaw once. What happened: when you do karate, if you put one knee on the floor, the judge stops the fight. I had my knee on the floor, and the guy I was fighting came at me with full speed. *Bam!* Shot my head like a football! I stood back on my feet, fighting not to go down, but I lost control, and I hate to lose control. The fight was canceled. That guy later on became world champion, and I fought him for the championship. I broke his jaw in seventeen seconds. I did that famous kick and *boom!* he slept.

***Inside Edition* apparently has claimed that there's no record you ever won a championship. Do you have any belts to prove it?**
No belt. I received a free pair of plastic gloves, and the next day I saw my name in the newspaper. But it doesn't mean shit to me. Tell *Inside Edition* to go and look in the archives in Belgium under the name Van Varenberg, not Van Damme. They have the fight on film. Look at *Bloodsport,* you think a guy can do that and be a fake?

When you fought the guy who had broken your jaw, did revenge factor into your win?
If you fight a guy in the ring and you want revenge, you lose the fight. When you train hard, five hours a day, you cannot be angry anymore, you don't have any spirit in your body to be angry. You have to fight respecting your opponent, then you just make points. When you start to become crazy and you're pissed, you make a lot of mistakes, you open your guard, you go too close, you do not obey the rules of distance and pressure. That's how you get knocked out.

How about fear before a fight?
Always. The guy who tells you he's not scared is full of shit. Because that's what God gave you to survive: fear. If not, you'll become a kamikaze.

Are your legs considered lethal weapons?
I fought a lot in the ring, but if I fight for real, I will kill. I swear to God, I will kill. I cannot fight, my kicks will kill. Also, if I'm hitting somebody now, I'll be sued for millions.

Have you ever lost it with someone outside the ring?
Once. I was seventeen, driving my little Citroen at 3:00 A.M., and this bus driver from Morocco cut me off and almost killed me. I stopped in front of
him, stood below where he was sitting, and called him a nut case. He said,
"Fuck you." I was so pissed I kicked straight up with my leg and touched
him in his face. It was the first time I lost control. He was knocked out, and I
went into the bus and said to the passengers, "Guys, I'm sorry, you'll have to
walk." I was in the right, he was crazy. He woke up I don't know when,
maybe a half-hour later, and he went to the cops. Some people had taken my
car license, and the next morning they came to my house and said to my father, "Your son kicked a bus driver in the face and broke his jaw in five
places." My father didn't want me to have a police record, so he paid them
$75,000 at the time for me to be clean. He was so pissed. "I'm teaching you
karate to control yourself, you're an idiot, you're crazy."

Were you crazy?
Maybe. When I was fifteen, sixteen, I was jumping from the roof to the
ground. I thought I was Spiderman, Dare Devil. I once hurt my back badly.

Did you know anything about steroids then?
I knew everything about it, and I knew the consequences. I've seen people
taking it like candy, by mouth, by injection. You'll have fast results, and then
you'll pay with your tendon, your prostate, your kidney, liver.

Did you ever take any?
Never. When I was nineteen, I weighed 99 kilo [217 pounds], pure muscle. I
was a beast. Enough for me. Right now I am 78 kilo [171 pounds]. I know
what to eat, how to train.

**What about the old taboo about not having sex before a fight—is that a
myth?**
People who train are very sexual, you clean your body from the inside, you
regenerate all your cells. But making love before a fight? I will never do it. It
would be like doing something wrong. I release mentally.

Why would it be wrong?
When some people make love, they do just one fuck. When you really make
love you spend hours, you spend all night with a woman, you give a lot;
you're sweating. You want her to feel good, so you spend five, six rounds,
and the next day you have to go twelve rounds. That's seventeen rounds.

Are you saying you reach orgasm five or six times each time you make love?

I'm not saying I'm coming five or six times, it's just a metaphor.

The martial arts are often considered a metaphor for spiritual values. Seagal practices aikido, you've studied Thai kickboxing. Which is more spiritual, and which is more dangerous?

In aikido you do something with your hands, you have to grab somebody and roll them down. You don't grab a guy with kickboxing, it's bullshit. In a real street fight you don't grab people. Kickboxing, you hit first, the guy will not grab you.

What about sumo wrestling?

Dangerous! Because they are big, it's a wall coming at you, and then they throw you away. But you know why sport is beautiful? You can put a Chinese, a black, a white together to do any type of sport—basketball, volleyball, football, karate, boxing, Ping-Pong, tennis—they will compete against each other as friends, then they'll go to the sauna, take a shower, they'll see colors, sex, everything together. That's the best religion you can have. I train with guys of all colors, sweating, sparring—sport is the best bible on earth.

And when you reach the height of your sport, when you become a champion, what next?

When you meet all the challenges and become the best, leave and do something else, otherwise you become a habit, you lose the challenge, you lose being hungry. And then you lose everything. If you become the world champion as a boxer, leave the ring. Don't stay on top when you're on top.

So when Mike Tyson gets out of prison—does he come back or should he find another profession?

He has to come back—for himself, not for me, not for Don King. He has to come back and win for himself, to be the champion again and to clean himself. Then he can walk on his feet again.

Can a kickboxing champion take a boxer like Tyson?

You cannot compare. If you take the best champion in Muay Thai kickboxing, what he will do with Tyson is go for his legs with powerful low kicks. He can break your knee. Kickboxing allows elbow, knee, foot. A boxer knows from the waist up, not the legs. If Tyson comes at me, I kick him, *boom!* he's out. If I'm backed into a corner against the rope, who's going to win? Tyson?

Maybe. But a kickboxer can give him an elbow, *bam!* twelve stitches. When Tyson fights, he thinks about his next fight. When a Thai guy fights, there is no tomorrow. Elbow in the face, knee in the head. The boxer cannot use his knees, his elbows, his head.

So you wouldn't be afraid to go up against Tyson?
Now we're talking like two kids in school. Your father's a boxer, mine's a karate guy. Who's going to win? Forty-year-old businessmen love to talk about who would win between me and Seagal and Tyson. Men love competition. They want to be that guy in the ring.

So who'd win between you and Iron Mike?
I've trained for twenty years, I can give him shit with my legs, you feel the power. I can triple kick, like a mosquito. Why I hate to fight is because I hate to lose. If I go with my thumb in the eyes of somebody, I will take his eyes away. So if a guy insults me or makes fun of me, I turn my back and leave. It's good to know karate and kickboxing, but a guy who never trained in his life can come at you with a knife. Who is stronger than who?

With all the martial arts films that have come out, are there any you feel are exceptional?
Enter the Dragon. That Kurosawa movie where the girl comes to the village and the guy cleans the village of all the bandits, *Seven Samurai*. And also *The Shaolin Temple* with Jet Li. He's the treasure of Asia.

What about something like *The Karate Kid?*
It was good for kids, but I hated it.

***Enter the Dragon* was one of Bruce Lee's most popular films. Was he a role model for you?**
Bruce was fantastic, very special. The camera loved him. He was one of the first actors who came with a body on the screen. Before, there was Steve Reeves. But don't forget, before Bruce Lee was a karate guy he was *sur la planche*—on the wood. That means theater. When he was thirteen, he was acting. If you look at some of his movies, when he fights in slow motion, frame by frame, it's not too technical. But it looks great on camera.

You're saying that he exaggerated certain moves for the camera. Do you do that too?
The same. But I have my own style. I don't imitate anybody.

Who are some of the authentic tough guys on the screen?
Sean Connery's real tough. I heard stories from people. I met him once. Strong. The guy you see on the screen is the guy you see in life. I met Charles Bronson once too, he's a very powerful guy, a man's man. I love *Hard Times*. De Niro, Steve McQueen. Mickey Rourke. He was as gifted as Pacino to me, and he lost it. Maybe he can come back.

Are these some of your personal favorite actors?
Some. I love Jimmy Dean, Brando, Christopher Walken, Pacino, Anthony Hopkins, Paul Newman, Montgomery Clift, Kirk Douglas, Stallone. And French actors like Alain Delon, Fernandel, Belmondo—my favorite, to me he is a god.

What about Jack Nicholson?
He's an animal. I love animals. He eats life with big fangs.

Robin Williams?
Genius. Comedy, he's the top. So gifted.

Steve Martin?
No, I don't like him. He does nothing for me. I like Tom Hanks, John Candy, Jim Belushi.

Mel Gibson?
Very commercial, from action to drama. *Hamlet* was a good movie. You know who's great too? Johnny Depp—he's always lust. And Sean Penn—I saw a film with him and De Niro as priests, he ate De Niro alive.

Warren Beatty?
Bugsy, fantastic. That's a man with class. He knows how to make movies.

Michael Keaton?
Doesn't do it for me.

Chevy Chase?
Doesn't do it for me.

Andy Garcia?
Doesn't do it for me.

Charlie Sheen?
Doesn't do it for me.

Christian Slater?
Love him.

Keanu Reeves?
Doesn't do it for me. In *Speed,* I just didn't buy that he was that tough. If you see that guy coming at you to fight with you, are you scared? No.

What are the films that captured your imagination as a kid?
I loved American films. *Ben Hur, Spartacus, The Wild Bunch.* Later, *Star Wars.*

How often did you go to the movies as a boy?
I would go with my father on Sunday. I was expecting to see a movie once a week, but it happened once a month because he was always busy.

Was this when he was a florist?
Yes, and before that he owned a lingerie store. And then my mother did that when he started a "library," which in Europe means you're selling cigarettes, newspapers, bubble gum, like a Seven-Eleven. It was hard, he was counting on every penny. I remember once my mother took us for pasta when he was working late, and she'd say, "Don't tell your father we ate spaghetti." But I remember that smell, with mashed carrots, onion, some meat. I was ashamed to ask for a toy more than once a week because all the money they were making they were investing in something else to become more successful. And I was always helping them. I was a happy kid. You give me a piece of wood and a shoe, I would make a boat.

Did you have a room of your own as a boy?
Are you kidding? We had a very small house in downtown Brussels. My father, mother, my sister and I, we shared the same room.

That must have been awkward for your parents when they wanted to make love.
You know what? I never thought about it.

Did you get an allowance?
No, he gave me food and lodging and love. You don't give money to a kid of sixteen in Europe. I cannot see kids who have their own bank accounts at the age of sixteen. What is this? It's a joke. I gave my father everything.

Earlier you said he paid $75,000 to keep you from having a police record. How could he pay that much if you were so poor?

That was later, when he opened his flower shop and it was successful, that's when he made what for him was big money. He had all the Jewish clientele of Belgium. He was doing everything for those guys—marriages, receptions. One of his clients was Onassis. And when I was living there, I was selling flowers at night for him. My father was so good to me, I wish lots of people could have my parents. I remember when I had to have my appendix out. I was scared, but I was also very sad for my father because he was so in a panic for me. I saw his face, his eyes. He said, "If I could be in your place I would do it." I saw so much love that I started to cry. I said, "Dad, you are a wonderful father." He slept in the hospital by me, on the floor.

Other than the time you broke that bus driver's jaw, did you ever do anything else that upset him?
When I shot my BB gun into our neighbor's laundry. I was shooting at clothes pins, and sometimes I missed and it went into the laundry, and she came to my father, who yelled at me like crazy. Then I once killed a pigeon, shot it in the neck, it was a female, and my father told me she was probably looking for food for her newborn and they're all going to die because of me. Oh, I felt bad.

Did you get into fights much as a kid?
I was not a fighter, but I was making fun of people. I was always running, scheming. I never liked to fight, I liked to compete.

Did you ever steal anything?
Of course, every kid stole. A guy tells you he didn't steal, he's a liar.

What about school, did you like it?
School was prison. The system was bad, and I was bored. The teachers were making $25,000 a year, they didn't know about life, they weren't there to be your friend.

That's not their job.
That's bullshit. You want to teach a kid something, first be his friend. In America they are good, gentle, open to discussion. In Belgium, at 7:00, 8:00, 9:00 A.M., it's still dark. And the teachers were always on my fucking case because I was fooling around too much in class. I had a lisp, I talked too fast, and people said I wasn't normal. Then they changed my writing from left to right, I was a lefty and became a righty. And Belgium has two languages, French and Flemish, so we were learning in both, but I never learned Flemish, I hated it. I was worst in mathematics and history. You know why? It was the past, I was into the future.

What were you good at?
Gymnastics. Anatomy, the body. Zoology, animals, the best. And music. One day I described Beethoven's "Moonlight Sonata" on paper, with the lake, the frogs, mosquitoes, the big moon, it was very romantic, the teacher, she was crying. She loved me.

If you could change the school system, what would you do?
School should start later. When kids wake up at 6:00 or 7:00 A.M. to go to school, they don't have time to feed their body. Kids need to sleep to be healthy, bones are growing. A kid needs about ten hours of sleep a day. So many kids going to school are pale and white, they are catching colds. Kids should wake at 9:00 A.M. They should study in the morning for three hours, then do some sports. They can learn while having fun. Kids have to enjoy life because later it will be a bitch, it will be wife, marriage, problems, taxes.

And here I thought you were enjoying your life as an adult.
I love it, but I'm the exception of a movie star. Most people on the street are unhappy. All those jobs, like parking attendant, waiter, I feel sorry for them. They all want to be like me. Life is a bitch sometimes.

It can be a nightmare for some. Did you ever have any nightmares?
Sometimes, when I was young. About UFOs coming to my room. I love space stuff, but I was scared of it. And one day I had this disgusting dream. I was in my bed and the phone rang. I went downstairs, and there was this guy there who took the phone cord and wrapped it around my throat. My father was asking, "Who is it?" And I'm dying, I can't even say anything. I woke up and found myself between two pillows, suffocating.

When you weren't having nightmares, what were you reading as a kid?
Cartoons. More than any movies or *The Wizard of Oz*. You know Tintin? I would open the book, I was in the story. *Tintin and the Cigars of the Pharaoh,* I was in Egypt. He was courageous, he was not afraid to go anyplace in the world. He followed a path in life, he followed an enigma, a mystery, he did everything by himself. When I came to America with nothing, I was like Tintin. For me, it was "Tintin Becomes a Movie Star."

Tintin, though, is always alone, never with a woman. That would be hard for a man like you, who's already on his fourth marriage.

I'm young, what do I know about life? I've got so much to learn. Maybe that's why I was married so many times, because it was too early to get married. I made mistakes.

Perhaps you didn't try hard enough to keep a marriage together.
Trying is easy, faking, it's not easy. So I didn't fake. Love comes and goes. Love is a strange phenomenon.

When did you first think you were in love?
I was fifteen—she was a blond girl, cute. I was in love with a kiss. You know your first kiss? It was so new, like a breath of fresh air. Not even with the tongue, just the contact of the male and the female. It was soft, breakable, crystal . . . special.

Did she feel that way as well?
I don't think so. She never called me back. But at that time I was not too good-looking. I was a strange-looking kid, white-blond hair, big thick glasses. And I was shy, so shy.

When did you have your first girlfriend?
I met some girls at school, first love, second love, third love, but they would complain after, they were sad and brokenhearted. But there was one girl who came to live with me in my house with my parents. She was fifteen. I was in love with her for two years, and we never did sex. My dad told me, "Don't touch her, you're going to make her pregnant." She was an angel.

Did you ever pay for sex?
When I was seventeen, I went to Paris with a bunch of friends, and we went to a prostitute. She was nice, dark, flashy. When it was my turn, my heart beat like in *The Mask*. She sat down on the bed, crossed her legs, and asked, "Have the money?" I said, "Sure." I give her the money and say, "Can we talk?" I ask her, "You happy here?" She looked at me like I'm a priest. She said, "You want to talk or you want to do it?" I didn't feel like making love, so I said, "Keep the money," and I left.

Was it because you couldn't get it up?
I tried, it didn't work. If you go with a prostitute and you have to pay money to make love, can you have a hard-on?

Most men do.
I think not. Anyway, that was my impression of Paris, of hot Paris.

Has it been easier to attract women since you've become famous?
Before I became a star, it was easier for me. Because I'm a good-looking kid.
When I was unknown, I had all the girls I wanted in the world. Since I'm
known, they are scared of me.

**Four of them apparently weren't. How old were you when you first
married?**
Eighteen. She was twenty-seven, mature. She was a girl from Venezuela, very
beautiful. We stayed together for a couple of years, then she left. Or I left
her.

Why?
Many reasons. The gym, film business, me training every day, running
around, traveling, pushing hard. When a woman loves you a lot, she likes to
be your companion, but it's hard for a woman to stay next to you when you
travel. I said, I'm going to go in the film business, if I don't make it, what's
going to be her life? Maybe I'm going to be a loser. A bum. If I go into the
business and she follows me for years and nothing happens, then what? I said
to her, "I'm no good for you. I am not what I'm supposed to be. And I will
never sleep until I do my dream." So I left her to live like a Gypsy in America.

And what happened with wife number two?
The second wife, Cindy, she wanted me to be with her in her father's business. Her father told me he had wanted to become a movie star and it never
worked and I should be smart, let him buy me a nice car, house, give me a
salary, work for him in his carpet factory. I said I cannot do it, so she left me
because she supported her father.

**Your third wife, Gladys, gave you two children. She was a bodybuilder
who at first ignored your advances, correct?**
She's a fantastic woman, great woman. If I was a woman, she's better than
me. I followed her to Cancun, Mexico, but she resisted me. But when I want
something, I want it.

**A lot of men fantasize having sex with a bodybuilder, doing things in
interesting positions. Did it ever get kinky for you?**
Gladys was not too sexual. It was like sister and brother with us.

And along came number four, Darcy.
Darcy was something you cannot fight. Our chemistry, the first date . . . I
tried to fight, I tried to find every excuse to have a fight, for a year and a half

I tried to have a reason to come back to my family. Because it was too much to lose, the kids and all that stuff. And she tried too. We fought. Passionate. Unbelievable. She flew to Hong Kong when I was there. She called me from her big suite upstairs. I came, there was music and champagne, like *Bugsy*.

She was married to a wealthy man who owned Hawaiian Tropic suntan lotion. How difficult did that become?
He's a nice guy, very down-to-earth, smart man. I like him a lot. I invited him to my house for a drink. I felt bad because I'm the one who did something bad to his marriage.

Was he angry with you for stealing his wife?
He's too smart for me to know. He does not show his feelings, too much of a businessman. She knows, I don't know.

Why the need to marry instead of simply live together?
Women, they want marriage. And I like marriage too. It's building a relationship and a future together. Love is love. Marriage is a deal. Will that make the love stronger? It will make the woman happy: she thinks, he's my territory now, he's mine, my piece of luck. Maybe they feel more secure that way. But that will not elevate or diminish love.

What are the qualities that attract you to a woman?
Intelligence, charm, class, beauty, sense of humor.

And if you're having an affair, should you tell the woman you live with or keep it a secret?
I don't have an affair.

If.
If I have an affair, should I tell the woman I'm with I'm having an affair? Naturally, I'm laughing. If you want to lose the wife who loves you, just tell her you are having an affair. If you want to keep the marriage, at least to try, you tell her something happened. "I was drugged," "She put something in my tea," "I see nothing and I wake up here." Whatever. Let me ask you: if you come home and you hear your wife screaming and you walk into the bedroom and see her making love to a guy, what will you do?

It could lead to violence.
I would not get violent. I will be pissed like crazy, but I would go, "Guys, sorry to disturb you, take your time, enjoy, and when you finish, I'll come

back for my baggage, okay?" Because if I get violent, it's one more reason for her to fuck around. You want to be the champ, you act like a champ.

You're telling us, if you walked in on your wife and she was screwing another guy in your bed . . .
No, not in my bed. When a guy touch my bed, it's no longer my bed. If he touch my toothbrush, it's not my toothbrush.

And if he's touching your wife . . .
It's finished. No going back. The guy fuck you once, he fuck you twice. Same with a woman.

All right, reverse it. It's you fucking around and your wife who walks in.
You're talking fiction, right?

Fiction or fact. You have been married four times.
I never, ever fucked around in my house. I would never do that.

Are you splitting hairs here? In your house it's taboo, but outside it's okay?
You're talking about if, if, if. I'm giving you if. So when you go "if," I go "if."

So you're saying that if you walk in on your wife with another man, that marriage is over. If your wife walks in on you with another woman, is the marriage also over, or does she try to work it out?
She will leave me.

And has that been the reason for any of your wives to have ended the marriage?
No. A woman never left me because I fucked around. It's always something else, which I've already explained. Because there's nothing worse than lying. And when you love a woman and she thinks you fuck around and she's accusing you because she's heard some stories, there's just nothing worse to spend your life with someone who doesn't trust you.

What about fantasy? Jimmy Carter said he lusted in his heart. Anything wrong with that?
Many women fantasize about a guy making love to them. Married women, they are not hurting their husbands when they do that, they are not screwing around. There's nothing wrong to think about somebody else. (*It's 3:00 A.M. when Darcy comes out of the bedroom to join us. Van Damme is happy to see her.*)

Look at those eyes. If she was an actress, she would kill the screen. You put Darcy next to Kim Basinger, she's as beautiful, if not better. The woman I love, I adore her.

Is that what you want, Darcy, to be an actress? (*"No," she says.***)**
Yes, yes, she loves movies. She's a simple girl who loves beautiful movies. I would absolutely cast her.

You sound like a pretty stubborn man, Jean-Claude.
Darcy, am I stubborn? (*"When you want something," she says, "yes. You can't change his mind about nothing. He's the most stubborn man I've ever known."*)

Is that a compliment, Jean-Claude?
Yes, because it means that I believe what I know.

Do you get along with most people?
I can sit down with everybody in life, they'll have a good time with me. When I'm in good shape. When I'm upset, even with my best friend I'll have a fight. I can scream very loud, then I go for a walk. (*Darcy says good-night. Van Damme lights a Cuban cigar and is reminded of a dream he had.*)

Two times I wake up in the middle of the night, and then I wake up Darcy next to me and start to explain my dream, which is *The Quest*. First, she's pissed, but then the story is so good she starts to like it. She has to love me to put up with my bullshit.

You've predicted *The Quest* will be the *Ben-Hur* of martial arts movies. What's it about?
It's about a tough kid who's had to survive on the street and ends up being a fighter who gets invited to a martial arts tournament in Tibet in 1912. The first ninety minutes will be his story of how he gets there. It will be so fucking good—lots of heart, betrayals, deceptions, passion.

You're estimating it will cost $35 million to make, and you plan on shooting it in China. Have you raised the money yet?
I sold $25 million the first day of Cannes without any story, just the concept. I stole Cannes. It was the Cannes for *Last Action Hero, Jurassic Park*, so I planned it to be there one day before Arnold, and I bought all the small billboards at the Carlton. Arnold was having a big floater in the water, so I came up with an air balloon and got my friend, who is the mayor of Cannes, to let me do the balloon for a day, and everybody came to my part of the beach— Peter Guber, Mark Hampton, Tom Pollack. The cops came in the afternoon

and made me remove the balloon, but it was okay, by then I sold the movie
to all the buyers.

**The producer hat obviously fits you, but what about directing, which
you're also planning to do?**
I'm scared to direct, because I'm impatient. Some people in Hollywood told
me not to do it, and not to tell people that I think I can direct, because directing will take two years, with pre-production, shooting, post-, cutting. In
two years, they say, you're missing acting in three movies, missing fifteen,
twenty million dollars. As a director you are going to make half a million, or
a hundred thousand dollars. You don't have to be smart to act, so what am I
doing now, I'm killing my career.

Legitimate concerns. Why *are* you going to direct?
Because I'm in love with it. And I want to prove myself and to people that
the karate schmuck with the Belgian accent, who's dumb, who's full of muscle, who's a brute, a beast, can sometimes be the beauty. Like the cartoon.
Because people have that image—a guy who goes into the ring and breaks his
nose, that means he's got no taste. For Christ's sake, Alexander the Great,
one of the biggest warriors in the world, was gay. It happens. Napoleon was
a dictator, but he did Paris fantastic. When you act, you have to be in shape
physically; directing, you have to be a leader.

Who are the directors you admire?
Oliver Stone is really special. I love also Adrian Lyne, Alan Parker, James
Cameron, Brian De Palma, John Milius, Sergio Leone.

Did you talk with any of them about directing *The Quest*?
I talked with Stone. He's talking to me because he's got some respect, he
likes me because I came from Belgium with nothing and became somebody.
I explained to him the story, my opening scene, and he said, "Why do you
need me? You have all the shots in your head." (*Van Damme did direct* The
Quest, *which disappeared quickly.*)

**In each of your films you always get pretty beaten up before you emerge
victorious. Which is something that doesn't happen much with Seagal.
Is that part of your formula?**
It's good to see a guy who gets some beating. Because all the world champi-
ons take punches in the ring. Besides, it's just fun stuff, it's not dangerous.
In a real fight a guy takes a glass, breaks it, and goes for your face. That's
what I call a fight.

Didn't you once meet Muhammad Ali?
I met Ali nine years ago, he invited me to his house. He did some magic tricks for me. He was slow, I felt sorry for him. I was having tears in my eyes when I saw him. What a great champ.

What did you talk about?
Religion.

You don't believe much in organized religion, do you?
I believe in God. I talk to God every day. It helps me a lot. It's a big difference between religion and believing in something.

Didn't you once say that religion is only to make money?
Yes. Am I right or wrong? When you go to a church or a mosque or a temple, it's so much luxury, so much money spent just to pray. That money can be used to help people. Religion can be dangerous, look at all the fanatics. It's because of religion we have so much war. But my father told me, don't talk about religion or politics in America and you'll be okay.

Why not politics?
Because politics, it's insane. In America one mistake is unforgiven. For example, when Clinton delayed his plane for a haircut. What's the big deal? You gave your vote to him, set him up for the next four years, then you change your mind about him. What are we talking about? If in his past life he fucked around, okay, but if he can make great deals for this country as president, if he can talk about the homeless, help the medical [situation], are people going to take some guy who's like a monk, whose dick never moved but he's the worst president on earth, over the guy they elected? You need a strong person to be a leader, even if that leader sometimes makes mistakes. And no matter what you read in the paper, you don't know if it's the truth. Why am I going to follow politics and stories on TV when behind closed doors they're saying something else? But who am I? I'm thirty-three, I don't know half of what I am saying. I never follow any political stuff, I'm making movies.

Do you think it helps you in your films that you have a baby face?
It helps. Look at Tom Hanks, Tom Cruise, Harrison Ford. Baby faces. Look at Arnold, even if he's smart, strong, mature, he's got that baby look. Look at Jimmy Dean, Montgomery Clift. They're vulnerable, all of them.

Yet you've said that you prefer to look older.

Because people like me more when I'm older, they have more respect. When you're thirty-three and you look twenty-eight on the screen trying to kick ass with a big bandit, I look like a kid. To me, Arnold, Sly, and Seagal have better faces . . . you believe them.

Who would you consider to be exceptionally handsome men?
Men who are handsome? Phew. . . . Fabio (*laughs*). There are different types of handsome guys. You have the rough look and the soft look. Nicholson can be very handsome—rough, savage look. Pacino's handsome, Mel Gibson, Dean, Belmondo.

What about beautiful women?
Kim Basinger and Michelle Pfeiffer.

Kim Basinger has said that she's rarely had a good experience making a film.
She should be happy where she is, she's making movies, she can fly to all the countries in the world, she's beautiful and has a beautiful husband. Her worst experience, it's still the best.

She's claimed to have seen treachery, absolute treachery.
It's part of the business. In Hollywood you have phony people, you have to be strong and deal with it. At the end of the day she's making big money and she has a nice house. If you tell Kim Basinger tomorrow you're going to work in a coffee shop at 6:00 A.M. and serve people pancakes until 5:00 P.M., she's going to see a lot of difference.

Still, you've said yourself that you've met a lot of deceitful people in your business.
Yes, but I still love it, because I love movies.

Are there any actresses you'd like to work with?
Are you kidding? Roseanne. She's very funny. I would love to do a film with her. She is fantastic, and a good actress. So clever. And in a sense she is beautiful. Look at her face, her eyes. She's lovable. Imagine a guy like Van Damme who dates a woman like Roseanne in a movie—pure love, it can be so special. When I was young, I was crazy about Doris Day.

Roseanne's a surprising choice. Anyone else?
Madonna can be hot. You saw *Truth or Dare*? She's got something, pal. She's got tons of charisma. Imagine a movie: Madonna and Van Damme!

You've picked two women who haven't exactly sizzled at the box office.
I'll make them look good on film, don't worry about it.

How about someone like Winona Ryder?
She's very frail, very paste. I like women who look like they've been through a lot.

Like Debra Winger?
Great. And Madeline Stowe. Ellen Barkin. Barbra Streisand. She's a woman with a brain, talent, attractive. Goldie Hawn is beautiful and very, very, very sexy. She's with Kurt Russell, right? I took his movie away.

Which one?
This one, *Sudden Death,* a title I don't like. They told me he wanted to make the movie so badly. I didn't take it away, I just came a little faster. Sometimes it's good to come fast.

***Entertainment Weekly* called you egomaniacal, erratic, homophobic, and sexist. How do you plead?**
What's homophobic?

Anti-gay.
What's erratic?

All over, one day hot, the next day cold. Irregular.
I am high and low, that's true. Sexist?

To be chauvinistic, not to treat women as equals.
Wrong. What else?

Egomaniacal.
They are only right in one thing: erratic.

Well, what do you think are your weaknesses?
I love food. And I'm impatient.

That's it? What is the image you have of yourself?
I'm very happy with myself. I'm straightforward. I'm honest with people. I've got real balls. If I need to save a friend, I will go head first. So I'm more of a hero in real life than in the movies. Because in movies I let people do this

and that to me as an action star. In real life I'm very, very strong. If I have to defeat somebody to win, I'll do it.

You mean you're not a big enough hero on the screen? Isn't it enough for young women to scream for you to take off your shirt?
I'm glad they are thinking about me and that they love the guy on the screen, but if they meet the real Van Damme, they will go even more crazy. Because in real life I'm a romantic, I love classical music, I love beautiful things.

Like those Cuban cigars you're smoking?
Why does a cigar relax you so much? I love to smoke cigars—when you light up, you have to do it with small puffs, small suction, like when you make love to a woman. You can't do it like an animal. I would never smoke in public because I have an image; if kids see me with a cigar, then they think, "Hey, Van Damme is smoking, it's cool."

Speaking of kids, how strict a father do you think you are?
I believe a father has to be strict. You are preparing them for the jungle. It's a miracle to have a kid. People take it for granted. When you have that miracle, you've got to cherish and take care, you have to prepare them for life to be a winner. You have to talk to your children, spend time with them, because a father will give more advice to them than a teacher, because he loves them. But you also have to be very careful with your kids, you can fuck them up badly. One word from a father or a mother can give them sequels for the rest of their lives. When I go shopping, sometimes I see kids who treat their parents with no respect. They are telling their mother what to do, they throw stuff on the floor. My son do that to me, he's in deep trouble.

Have you ever laid a hand on your son?
Yes, once.

On his behind?
In his face. I told him something, he didn't do it, and he kept on. I was so pissed. He insulted me. Today my son respects me like crazy.

Why do you insist that he tuck in his shirt all the time? He's just a boy.
Because I don't like it.

But children today are wearing baggy clothes, they keep their pants low around the waist, their underwear shows.

That's not a style, you look like a bum. And they are all fat and have flat feet. Go to the mall, all those kids are knock-kneed, they don't do any sport, they play computer games day and night.

And they talk back to their parents and don't always do their homework.
That's America for you. That's not America for me.

But your kids are being raised in Belgium.
Yes, and they go to public school.

Do you feel guilty that you are separated from them?
Absolutely. It's a huge problem. Every day I think about it. I call my son almost every day. When I'm working out on the bicycle, I listen to music on a Walkman because I can't think right, my son and daughter are in my head every day.

Would you want your children to act in movies?
To be honest, not too much. Because I know what I came through, I've seen so much bad stuff. They will do it differently because they will have money. I don't want my son to go give a massage and the guy opens his legs. I don't want my son to see that. I saw that.

You also don't want to see a slice of melon go half-eaten.
That's because when I came to America I was unable to buy a Dannon yogurt. Taco Bell was my Sunday, I enjoyed that Taco Bell from the beginning to the end. Even if I've got millions, billions, trillions of dollars, my children are going to finish their melon. Because I paid for it, I worked for it.

And if they protest that they are not hungry?
Then I send them to bed. I will yell. Are you my child or what? You talk to me like that, you're my blood. Are you crazy? I will put that melon in the fridge, and the next day, when they wake up, there's the melon. They will eat nothing else until they finish that melon. We have this saying in Europe: who stole an egg will steal a cow. If you answer me for a melon, what will you do later when you have a car? If your father's telling you something, it's your duty as his child to listen to him. You have to respect stuff in life. That melon's life. It's a fruit.

You're one tough daddy.
It's my duty.

Are you as tough with your friends?

I love friendship. When I have a friend, I'm giving everything. I've got the
biggest heart on earth. Ask my friends.

**Your childhood friend Michael Quissy may not agree. He claimed that
you never paid him his $22,000 salary for appearing in *Lionheart*.**

Lie. I pay more than that. He made a fortune with me. I gave money to his
mother. I flew him first-class from Europe to America. He stayed in my
house, we shared food. I gave him a car. Put him in *Kickboxer, Lionheart,* two
movies back to back. Then he met a woman. He never dated too many
women in his life, and she told him, Jean-Claude is taking advantage of you.
He said to me, "I'm going to go on my own because you're bad for me."
Maybe this woman doesn't want us to be together. He left me, and now I
think he's in shame, back in Belgium doing groceries. Go ask him: Who
brought you to America? Who gave you food? Who paid your first dollar
bill? Who put you in the movies? Why are you back in Belgium? Because you
fucked up. But all of my friends, they all come back to me, they cry to me
and say they're sorry.

**Truman Capote said that when he became famous he lost 80 percent of
his friends. Is that what's happened with you?**

Ninety-nine percent of my friends. I return to my country, I go to visit a
friend, but I have to make some phone calls. He says, "Who do you think
you are?" I say, "No, no, I'm not snubbing you, I've got to make these calls or
I'll lose something." "Go to hell." It's sad. Small mind. Those guys, when you
leave the country and you come back, they don't understand your change.
They don't know about the dog I lost, the bird that died. They don't know
about me sleeping in the car. But what goes around comes around. If you do
something bad to somebody, you will pay. I always pay, trust me.

**Speaking of paying, an appeals court upheld a $487,000 award to Jack-
son Pinckney, who you apparently injured during the filming of *Cyborg*
in 1988. You stuck a rubber knife in his eye?**

Here's the story. Pinckney was a big, heavy guy working in a gym, he was a
bodybuilder, a soldier. He didn't know how to fight. There was a fight between him and I, it was raining, muddy, difficult to see at night. He was supposed to attack me, and I was supposed to kick him. He came too close to
me, and the knife touched his eye. It was hard plastic, not rubber. I felt sorry.
I drove to his Army base, I invited him to dinner. He was wearing a patch.
With surgery he'll have his vision back to normal. It was not my fault. I said,
"You should call Cannon and make sure you have insurance." "No, it's fine,"
he said. Four years later, a lawsuit. Why? I became a hot shot. He has a

lawyer, I have a lawyer, it was a great show, like a circus. I was on TV. They said, "Jean-Claude likes to hurt people to increase his popularity and his career." And he won half a million dollars.

What did it teach you about our jury system?
It scared the shit out of me. Imagine when a guy has to be sentenced to death and he has twelve people who will decide and they have no power of their own in life, only this day they have power, and if you have one leader among those twelve people who can talk well, that leader can decide your life.

There was another lawsuit, this one in December of 1993, by a woman named Tara LaBlanc who claimed you molested her in New Orleans the year before and forced her to have oral sex, and that you were involved in a foursome with her and her boyfriend and with Darcy. Set the record straight. Did that ever happen?
First of all, if Darcy saw me look at a woman, she would go nuts. I was in all the papers, it came into Belgium and France, my parents read about it. Imagine me divorcing Gladys and with Darcy and then she claims this? She was dating my trainer, she once came in my trailer to shake my hand.

And you never had sex with her?
Absolutely not. It's absurd. But what am I supposed to do? What's the next step for me? I even paid some detective to see what's going on there, but it's a long story, and I prefer to keep it off the record. My lawyer tells me to do nothing. "Today it's in the papers, tomorrow it will be gone."

Another bit of trouble occurred during the filming of *Universal Soldier* when you were arrested for speeding in Arizona. How fast were you going?
Eighty. It was at midnight, nobody was on the road. The cop put the handcuffs on me, and at the jail he took them away, but he said, "Don't kick my face, my partner has a gun, he will shoot." I told him, "I'm doing movies. It's in the movies I do that."

Wasn't there also a lawsuit you filed to get out of doing a sequel to *Lionheart*?
I filed a lawsuit because they rented a car for me on the first movie and they never paid the car.

Wasn't that because you used the phone a lot and the bill came to $64,000?
I had the car for three months. I left it with my assistant for a month, and he used the phone to call Europe. But what does $50,000 have to do with

the $295,000 profit the producer made, plus the 10 percent he has on *Sudden Death?* The guy's rich. I'm happy for him. But he should have paid the car.

That about covers some of the controversies about you—except for the one involving your *Universal Soldier* costar, Dolph Lundgren, who you apparently got into a pushing match with during a screening of *The Player*.
That was on purpose. Our movie wasn't ready, and they were going to show it at Cannes, so we had to do something to create some controversy. I came up with pushing each other on the red carpet, where we'd have all the cameras on us. He agreed, and it worked. He pushed me, I pushed him back, the bodyguards jumped in and stopped us. Then I walked on the carpet, and he stayed there like he was pissed. It was exciting, people wanted to see us fight in the movie. That movie made $100 million over the world. We used the media for that. It was my biggest movie up to *Timecop* and *Street Fighter*.

If the numbers aren't what you're expecting, you'll have to find somebody else to push.
Yeah, I'll push you, it'll be in all the papers.

"You push me, I'll push you." How's that for an epitaph?
Better: "Do what you believe is right in life, and if you don't succeed, at least you tried."

Where will that wind up? What country do you want to be buried in?
I don't want to be buried in the ground, rotting, with all those worms. What I would love is to have my body dropped where you have those big icebergs and the water is so cold and pure, to be eaten by a polar bear or a seal or an otter.

Well, you've got a long way to go before you become food for polar bears.
I'm a baby. I'm still a French piece of bread. I didn't come here as sourdough. I'm the new guy in town.

Have you always been as confident as you come across?
I'm very hard on myself always. I'm very insecure. But I believe in my dream, and I was pushing every day to make it happen. So when I hear people complaining about jobs or not having work, asking for money, it's a bunch of bullshit. When you see handicapped kids from the Make-A-Wish Foundation with no legs, paralyzed, and they come to see me with a big smile on

their face, then you know everything is possible. People don't understand in this country, they should kiss the ground in America. Go to Hong Kong and try to find some homeless. Very few. They want to make money, they clean shoes, they clean tires, they clean floors. Nobody has limitations in life except people who are born stupid or handicapped. If you saw me when I was young, I came a long way, I was not born this way. I became. I changed. I came to America without the language, without the permit, and I became a movie star. People call me lucky, they say I was in the right place at the right time. You have to make it happen, pal. You have to push hard, because it pays off. May not be as a movie star, maybe as a costar, or as a bad guy, who cares? If you want to make it badly, you can make it. When you know who you are in life, you can go so high. I really believe so.

THE STAR

HARRISON FORD

HARRISON FORD MAY JUST BE THE BIGGEST, most bankable star in the world. Seven of the two dozen highest-grossing films have had his name at the top of the marquee, and two of his characters—Han Solo and Indiana Jones—have been three-picture franchises. Born in Chicago on July 13, 1942, Ford began acting while at Ripon College in Wisconsin. He appeared in a few TV shows and some low-budget movies in the mid to late sixties, then turned to carpentry to earn a living. He had small parts in George Lucas's *American Graffiti* and Francis Coppola's *The Conversation* before Lucas cast him as the hotshot pirate pilot Han Solo in *Star Wars*. He followed that with *Heroes, Force 10 from Navarone, Hanover Street, The Frisco Kid,* and *More American Graffiti.* Then came part two of the *Star Wars* trilogy, *The Empire Strikes Back.* Steven Spielberg next cast him in the first Indiana Jones adventure film, *Raiders of the Lost Ark,* followed by *Indiana Jones and the Temple of Doom* and *Indiana Jones and the Last Crusade.* Between these he made the futuristic *Blade Runner,* the third installment of *Star Wars* (*Return of the Jedi*), *Witness, The Mosquito Coast, Frantic,* and *Working Girl.* In the 1990s he starred in *Presumed Innocent, Regarding Henry, Patriot Games, The Fugitive, Clear and Present Danger, Sabrina, The Devil's Own, Air Force One, Six Days and Seven Nights,* and *Random Hearts. What Lies Beneath* was released in 2000.

There are those in the Hollywood community who say that Harrison Ford is a bland actor, a cardboard cutout whose best performance was either in *Witness* or *The Mosquito Coast,* and that once he entered the realm of the megabuck superstar he put acting aside and has just been going through whatever motions it takes to keep his salary at the very top of what these rare performers make. There have been reports that he sings songs about himself to the tune of "I'm the $20 Million Man." But if that is the private behavior and attitude of Harrison Ford, it's definitely not the side he presents when he meets the press. That attitude was certainly not in evidence when he came to this reporter's home for lunch and a two-and-a-half-hour conversation. When he's talking to the public, it's in a whisper. He's low-key, deliberate, contemplative, and not very playful. He considers interviews a part of his job—what he must do after a movie is in the can and ready to be released. He does his job perfunctorily and then gets back into his shiny black Mercedes convertible and drives off into the distance, making his way toward the airfield where he left his airplane, which he can pilot himself back to the home he shares in Wyoming with his wife, the screenwriter Melissa Mathison (*ET, The Black Stallion, Kundun*), and their two children. (He also has two children from a previous marriage.)

On this excursion into the public eye in the summer of 1997, he was promoting *Air Force One,* a film in which he plays the president and his wife and child are being held hostage by terrorists aboard the presidential plane, requiring him to turn into Bruce Willis to save the day. But Ford was talking just before the release of *The Devil's Own,* and his costar, Brad Pitt, had openly bad-mouthed the film in *Newsweek.* Pitt's remarks to the media could not be ignored, even though one didn't expect Harrison Ford to further stir the pot. He's just not that kind of guy.

Comedian Fred Allen once said that Hollywood is a place where people from Iowa mistake each other for stars. Ever get that feeling?
Yeah (*laughs*). I never set out to be mistaken for a star, and I'm almost from Iowa, being from Illinois. All I wanted to do was make a living in an interesting way. When I left college, I knew that most of my friends were going to work the rest of their lives in offices wearing suits, working with the same people, doing the same job over and over again. I wanted something different. I didn't know very much what it meant to be an actor at that time. I didn't know anybody who was an actor. I didn't calculate the odds against success. I just thought, this is what I'll do, and set out to do it.

How many times did you hear someone tell you that you'd never make it as an actor?
Once. It was very stimulating. I played a bellboy in my first film, and I was called into the office of the guy who was head of what they called the new talent program at Columbia. He said, "I just saw the dailies, and I've got to tell you, give it up, you're never going to make it." Then he told me the Tony

Curtis story. He said the first time Tony Curtis ever was in a film he delivered a bag of groceries. He took one look at the guy, and he knew that was a movie star. And I leaned across the desk and said, "I thought that you were supposed to think that *that* was a grocery delivery boy." He said, "Get out of here!"

That guy's probably working behind a counter somewhere, and you're pulling in $20 million a picture and playing the president. Did it ever occur to you that at a certain age you were old enough to be the president?
It occurred to me, when I played the president at fifty-four for *Air Force One*, that I was probably a little old for the president.

Did you ever visit the Oval Office or stay overnight at the White House?
No. I've never been there.

What do you think of what's going on with Clinton—the fund-raising, the Paula Jones affair, Whitewater?
I have nothing to say.

How come?
Because of the framework of the question, for one thing. The framework is all focused on negatives.

But aren't the negatives what concern most of us when you're dealing with the president of the United States? As the leader of the most powerful nation in the world, isn't it a concern if we start doubting his moral and ethical fiber?
We always have a different standard when we examine the behavior of others rather than ourselves. I don't feel that I have any particular license to publicly judge Clinton or any other public official. I haven't made a personal study of the issue. I haven't fully investigated both sides of the question, and therefore I have no public response.

Have you ever campaigned for or supported a politician?
Not at the national level. I think they're well enough supported.

Did you get a chance to meet Clinton, to study him?
I had no intention of studying any particular president for this role, which is not a serious investigation of the presidency and the nature of that job. Instead, it's an action adventure set on Air Force One. The time I spend being,

strictly speaking, presidential is limited to the first ten minutes of the movie, and then the shit hits the fan and it's too late to be very presidential about it.

Are you the hero in the end?
I'm a hero in the beginning. You'll just have to pay your money and find out. Yeah, of course I am. Or he is. He does save the day.

What was it like working with Gary Oldman, who plays a bad guy?
A ball. It's high-key acting from both of us.

Do actors like Oldman and Tommy Lee Jones raise the level of your own performance?
I don't know if you can say in absolute terms that it raised the level, as though some greater quality exists, but it's fun to work with an actor to whom it comes easily. Who's able to be spontaneous and take advantage of what's going on.

Do you like to improvise?
I rarely improvise. I'd rather discuss the idea and get collaborative agreement on it before I do it. Pure improvisation doesn't often work. But I do often think about what I'm doing and will change the way I do it from one take to another.

Are there things you've seen in past characters that you'd like to do differently now?
I'm not satisfied, but I can't imagine actively thinking about changing anything. I don't have that kind of abstract head.

How was Wolfgang Petersen to work with?
He's very quick on his feet, very well prepared, very clear about what his ambitions are and is able to articulate them. Collaborative. Good-humored.

Did things go more smoothly on that than on *The Devil's Own?*
It was a piece of cake. We all called it *Air Force Fun*. It was a very smooth, clear path.

Is that usually the case with your films?
It normally is. Every once in a while there's a bump in the road and things don't go as smoothly.

Have you ever bad-mouthed one of your movies?
No.

What was your reaction when you heard that Brad Pitt called *The Devil's Own* an "irresponsible bit of filmmaking" in *Newsweek*?
First of all, I recognized the thoughts. They could have been my own. There was a point when everybody thought we should bag this stuff if it's not going to work. But we kept pushing, and then it started to work. So I couldn't argue with what he said. And I've made mistakes in terms of talking to people who didn't respect a confidence, although I don't imply that that was the case. I think it was simply a matter of forgetting that the person he was talking to was being paid to write this shit down. I wasn't terribly upset by it.

The movie received more bad press than most—was there a lot of conflict?
I think the whole adventure didn't work the way we'd anticipated it. Starting late gave everyone an opportunity to look at it and say, "What's going on here?" But the film turned out good. Brad's work was good. I was happy with my work.

Was it one you're glad was over?
Oh sure, I'm glad when they're all over, the ones that are fun and the ones that aren't. It's just hard work, that's all.

Brad Pitt's achieved major stardom at an early age. You've managed to remain a huge star over a much longer span. Do you think Pitt will come as far as you over the years?
He's already come as far . . . and further. He enjoys greater popularity than I ever did in any finite arrangement of time. I was never that popular. Never have been. I've been around for a long time, but I have never been *that* singularly popular as he is. There are a number of very interesting guys of that generation coming up who are real good actors.

How did you and Pitt get along?
We actually got along just fine. Stories of our personal animosity were totally untrue. I never had a moment's discomfort with him.

Was it a great leap in character for you—playing a cop in *Devil's Own* and the president in *Air Force One*?
In *Devil's Own* I played a New York City uniformed police sergeant. Are they great leaps in parts? They're very different to each other, and the films are very different in terms of genre. But the job is always the same. And the cop and the president both share the same head, they're all soup out of the same pot, which is my head. I have to imagine myself being a New York City policeman, which I can, easily. And I have to imagine myself being a president,

which is a little less easy because I could not imagine an ambition to be the president.

Did you spend time riding around with New York cops?
Yeah. I probably went out with them ten times. I usually picked the four-to-twelve shift, which was the most active shift. They let me hang with them and do what they did. There were some moments of elevated adrenaline, but I never really felt scared. It's a very tough job. Impossible job. I felt bad for them, and bad for the people they were dealing with on the streets.

Did you see the L.A. bank robbery shootout on TV? The two robbers were killed on live TV, and it was like scenes we'd seen a thousand times before. Only this time it was real.
That's the horrible thing, that movies inure us to the violence. I remember the SLA shootout in Los Angeles. I went to Noguchi's coroner's briefing. My best friend, Barry Farrell, brought me. It was very weird to watch it.

Which of your films most disturbed you?
Presumed Innocent disturbed me, although I was perfectly rational about it throughout the process. The circumstances of the character, his intense trials, which are not that much different to the circumstances of Dr. Kimball in *The Fugitive*. I found it very disturbing. It may be as much about the way we worked on that film as the character situation. We worked very intensely and got close to the bone.

Have you ever had a worse haircut than the one in *Presumed Innocent*?
I thought it was a very good way of describing character. It was my idea. Because this was about a guy who had the one affair of his life with this very beautiful woman in his office. I wanted to give an expression of this character that made it clear that this was not another notch in his belt, that he was a person without personal vanity, which is one of the things you need to be a cocksman, isn't it?—a degree of vanity. I didn't want this guy to be like that. I wanted this to be one very wrenching circumstance in his life. And when it turns to shit, as it does, he's devastated by it.

In that seduction scene with Greta Scacchi, what made you more uncomfortable, the crew watching or making it on the desk?
Neither. It was altogether a pleasure. To me a scene that involves making love is like any other scene, except you get to kiss a pretty girl. It's always acting. I can remember about that scene that Alan Pakula let us stage it ourselves and describe the boundaries of where we were going with it. He was es-

pecially sensitive to Greta and her personal feelings about privacy. I remember the details of that scene very well, not because it was a scene of lovemaking but because it was a scene that was extremely technical.

What interested you about *The Fugitive*, besides its franchise potential?
Let's make it clear that I wasn't interested in the franchise aspects. These days you can make a story about a dog being run over by a car and they'll say it has sequel potential because there's such a drift of real ambition out there. What attracted me was a variety of circumstances that this project seemed to fit. I wanted to work in the spring, because I wanted to work twice that year and then not work at all the next year so I could stay home with my family and see my kid through first grade and enjoy being in Wyoming for one whole year. I knew I wanted to do another active kind of picture while I still have the capacity. And it was an interesting project. The character was one of those not so well described as to be unique, but his circumstances were unique and compelling. So the elements were there to be able to say yes.

The Fugitive was about a man wrongly accused. Have you ever been wrongly accused of anything?
Never. I was *always* correctly accused. I have almost always been caught for things I did wrong, like shooting out a couple of plate-glass windows with a slingshot.

Did you see the re-release of *Blade Runner*?
No, I didn't, but it had to be better because it was free of the godawful bloody voice-over, which I was compelled to perform, if you can call that performing. There were four or five different versions of that voice-over that I was forced to record, every one of them under duress. The final version, Ridley Scott was off the picture, and the completion bond company, which ensured the completion of the film, had come on to the picture, and they were the ones who insisted on the voice-over. The last time I went to record it I found an old-style Hollywood screenwriter wearing a powder-blue hobby suit with the little belt that hooked in front sitting over his little portable typewriter in the recording studio tapping away. I said, "Hi." And he said, "Leave me alone, leave me alone." About half an hour later he reappeared with this sheaf of papers. I said, "Who's our director?" He said, "Me." I recorded exactly what he had written without protest, without context, without discussion. I just wanted to read it cold, become familiar with the material, read it again and again, and then get on to the next piece. I did each one of the speeches five or six times, and they seem to have chosen the first take of every one of them. Much to my embarrassment and chagrin, they released

this shit. I was both offended as a performer by my own lack of zeal in getting this right, and I was offended it was added to the film to start with because one of the original agreements between myself and the filmmakers was
that I would do this film if the voice-overs were removed. Because when I
first got the script, it had a voice-over in it. I said, "Look, I'm playing a detective, and I don't do any detecting. Let's put the information that's in these
voice-overs into scenes, so that we don't have to tell people about it, we can
show." Well, we did that, and yet when it was all over it was considered so
convoluted that the voice-over was necessary to straighten it out.

**When producer Robert Evans was casting for his lead in *The Saint*, he
said he was interested in finding a younger Harrison Ford type. Val
Kilmer got the part. How does that make you feel, that you've become a
"type"?**
It's come to that. What's interesting to me is it's the same Robert Evans who
was around when I was a young Harrison Ford type! But I hope there's not a
"type."

Did you ever want to look like anyone else?
Anybody else. Anybody with a straighter, thinner nose, a better chin.

**The story of your chin scar has been told. Do you have any other scars
that are hidden?**
Oh, just the one inside.

**Are there any artists or other actors whom you wouldn't mind being
compared with?**
The notion of artist seems to fly in the face of comparison. What makes you
an artist is developing what's singular and particular about yourself and giving it expression. I'd be happy to be compared with anybody who was generally understood to be good.

Have any actors experienced any anxiety working with you?
Sometimes I'm aware that somebody I'm working with is nervous, and I'll
try to make things easier for them if possible.

Do you ever get nervous?
Not really anymore. Not for acting. There's one thing that makes me nervous in life, and when I act it, it makes me nervous, and that's public speaking. Though it might seem to have some similarity to what I do, it's completely different.

Of actresses you haven't worked with, are there any you'd like to?
I'm a guy who doesn't have a favorite color or a favorite ice cream flavor or a
favorite movie. I tend to not nominate favorites.

Come on, *everybody* has a favorite ice cream.
If you can call vanilla a favorite ice cream. . . . The reason I like it is because
it doesn't include all of those other complications. It is ice . . . cream. I have
common man's taste. Although I've had more than common man's experience, so it's probably widened my palate.

**You spoke earlier of taking on *The Fugitive* so that you could take a year
off. That didn't happen, though, did it?**
Never happened. I have a hard time comprehending time except in those
blocks that are used to make movies.

Is it difficult to plan free time?
It is, because we feed opportunistically, and if something comes along that is
a virtue and has a time scale attached to it, you tend to want to take advantage of it.

Which in your case happens more and more.
What happened is that the schedule was upset by *Devil's Own* not starting as it
had been planned to start. We got pushed back four or five months, and then
it took longer than we had anticipated, and that pushed it much much closer
to *Air Force One*. I would have had nearly nine months off instead of three.

**I guess with the kind of success you've had you can't complain. Ever
marvel how many successful movies you've been in?**
Yeah.

**Have any surprised you, where you thought the film wasn't going any-
where and it caught on?**
There are a number of things that I've done where I was very surprised by
the degree of success. *Star Wars* for one. There had been no success of that
order in films ever before. So that was surprising.

**Did you get *Star Wars* because you were at the right time at the right
place: working as a carpenter outside Francis Coppola's office when
George Lucas came by?**
It was *inside* Coppola's office, installing an elaborate portico entrance that
they had built in a mill. The carpenter who was to install it ran away, and

Dean Tavouris, Coppola's art director, connived me into doing the job. I said I would only do it at night because I wasn't comfortable walking around Francis's office as a carpenter, since I had worked for him as an actor in *The Conversation* and I wanted him to think of me as an actor. So one night I worked all night, and I wanted to finish up to a certain stage before I left, and I was still there working when George Lucas walked in with Richard Dreyfuss for an interview for a film called *Star Wars*. George had said that he wasn't going to see anybody who he had earlier worked with in *American Graffiti* for this particular movie. So my agent had made no effort to get me an interview. The luck of it is that I was there. I'm not sure it had a great deal to do with the eventual outcome because it was months and months before I was asked to come in and help George read other actors for the other parts. There was no indication that I was in consideration for this part, it was just, "Do me a favor, pal."

Did you know that Al Pacino turned down the Han Solo role?
Really? I think a lot of people were up for it, but frankly I don't think anybody was offered the part. My understanding was that George had two different groups of three ensemble casting that he had narrowed it down to. The only one I know who George had seriously entertained playing Han Solo was Chris Walken.

How aware were you of the mythological elements in *Star Wars*?
I thought we were on to something when we were making it, not because of the unique aspects of it, but because of the aspects of it that were so familiar. Because I could feel the fit between the sage old warrior, the beautiful princess, the callow youth, and the guy that I played. I knew what I was meant to do, and I knew it from fairy tales, from just knowing what these human units meant, and what the expected relationship was between them. I thought, this is good fun here, as well as some sort of strong primordial themes being engaged.

Did it change you?
Going to work changed me. I spent fifteen years trying to make acting my sole profession and being able to say, "Now I'm an actor because I'm employable as an actor at any opportunity because of this great good luck. Now how shall I strategically attempt to make this continue? What should I choose?"

What were your big decisions then, after *Star Wars*? Did you get a new manager, agent, lawyer?
I didn't change anything. I'd been married for thirteen, fourteen years.

Did you expect the re-release of the *Star Wars* trilogy to do the kind of business it did?

It's pretty amazing, and that's about as much as I think about it. It's just amazing that a twenty-year-old movie can be released this way. I'm delighted that it's still of interest.

Do you make any more money?

No. There probably will be some small amount of money, but I was not in a position to negotiate for a back end when I did *Star Wars*. I was paid $1,000 a week and $1,000 a week for expenses.

Has Lucas sent you any presents since the re-release?

We talk every once in a while. He did give Alec Guinness, Mark Hamill, Carrie Fisher, and myself a small percentage of the net, which did net me some amount of money. He didn't have to do that. He did the same thing on *American Graffiti*, I got a tenth of a point on that. It made a little bit of a difference.

The success of the re-release of the trilogy will most likely trigger re-releases of other films, which may make it tougher on current films to find theaters.

I don't think a lot of them are going to work. There's less chance of *Star Wars* seeming dated because the story has an appeal to each new generation on the basis of its Joseph Campbell-esque-type themes.

Have you ever worked as well with a director as you did with Spielberg on *Raiders of the Lost Ark?*

To that point I had not worked with anybody where we had as much fun working together. It was "toys for boys" big time. I'm not sure that that experience is any longer available to me, because it was sort of a special circumstance. The character was a special prize, the kind of film was a special joy. It was a great time.

It seems remarkable to think of how you managed to appear in two action-packed trilogies.

It seems remarkable to me as well. To have those experiences and not to have been the first choice in any of them seems even more remarkable. Remember that Tom Selleck was the first choice for Indiana Jones.

The box office wasn't there for *Sabrina* as it's been for most of your other films. Were you satisfied with *Sabrina*?

I don't expect them all to do the same. I don't know how you could expect a film like *Sabrina* to do the same as *Clear and Present Danger*. It's not a common taste. I always wanted to do a movie with Sidney Pollack. I was pleased with the experience.

It was reported that you and Pollack tried to drive away from your fans after seeing *The English Patient*, but they followed you for miles until you stopped and signed autographs. Did that happen?
They were driving dangerously, so I decided if I signed autographs they wouldn't do that.

Do you understand such behavior, being on the other side of it?
No. I don't understand it.

Is it ever scary?
It's not been scary . . . yet.

Have you ever worried about stalkers? Do you have your own security?
No. Even less so now that I would appear in a magazine saying no. I have from time to time, when I know that I'm going to be in public and somebody's going to feel responsible for my security, suggested that it be done by professionals rather than a PA with a radio in her hand. I have had a number of people over the years who have not appeared to be totally in possession of all of their marbles, but I've never had any real, substantial trouble.

What was it like when you went to Harvard to receive the Hasty Pudding Man of the Year Award?
Silly. It was okay. I was flattered to be singled out, chosen. I guess I dodged it a couple of years in a row and then having been asked once more I decided to do it. It's not the kind of thing I usually do.

Would you do it again?
No.

Did you really don a wig of rubber snakes and put on a red-feathered, tasseled bra?
That's correctly reported. I knew they had something in store for me.

Were you paraded around Harvard Square?
No, that's the Woman of the Year who's led through the streets. Susan Sarandon did it the year that I did it. I just had to appear on stage briefly dressed up in that rubber wig and sit and watch the Hasty Pudding show. Then I was led backstage for a press conference, the basis on which I can say

I would never do this again. It was a very uncomfortable press conference for me.

How long did it last?
Too long. More than ten minutes and less than half an hour.

Do you agree to do publicity for all of your films?
I don't agree to do anything. I've never had a policy about these things. I understand it to be a part of my job. One does so many of these things in pursuit of what I do that I don't think of them at all, except that it's important to bring attention to the film at the time when it's out there. You do these things to try and protect the investment that people have made in you and the film.

Yet you seem to limit your interviews to short periods of time.
I've never sat down for more than two hours in a row. The reason I won't do a long-form interview is because it's just too personal. Don't need it. I'm not John Huston or Truman Capote, I'm just a simple guy who doesn't have that much to say and is not that interested in hearing it back. I've often said that what I do for a living is the most interesting thing about me. Also, as you can see, I have very little interest in The Subject. I haven't thought about The Subject. And I don't think about The Subject. I do what I do. Certainly I reflect on my life, but I don't feel I owe it to anybody to share my reflections on myself. And I don't feel that I have either the right or the responsibility to speak about a lot of issues that I don't know enough about.

Is it also about trying to preserve your mystique?
There's no mystique. And because there's no mystique there's no mystery.

How lasting do you think fame is? Do stars fade after a generation or two, or because of today's superior technology do you think people will still be watching some of your performances fifty years from now or marvel at Michael Jordan's abilities caught on tape?
He might even be selling vacuum cleaners.

Like Fred Astaire. What do you think of that?
I didn't see the commercial, but I suppose it's regrettable. The whole question of artists' rights is rather complicated.

Ever think that one day some film editor might be asked to switch your face as Indiana Jones with . . .

Somebody more popular, more contemporary. I'll be long gone and will have
spent the money.

Bet a lot of people don't know that you've done commercials in Japan.
I don't do it anymore. It was contractually understood that they were only
for Japan. They were relatively fun to do. I did them for Honda motor car,
Kirin beer, and a cellular phone company. The rules were that they were not
quite an endorsement. And they were very lucrative.

Do people think of you more as a movie star than an actor?
Yeah. It's too fine a point to belabor, but what I do is act.

Does that hurt you in some roles, like *The Mosquito Coast*?
Yeah. I loved that book, the language.

**You spoke of always having fun on your films. What about in the begin-
ning of your career?**
Well, I always have a good time. Nearly always. It's fun for me to do what I
do. Back in the earlier days, when I had not such great responsibility in any
one film, the demands of production and screenwriting didn't fall so heavily
on me, on my back. Not that I take the responsibility for screenwriting, but
while that process is going on, if things aren't ready and you're working, it
becomes complicated.

Do you view any movies as art?
I think you can make a case for film writing being, under some circumstances, an artistic endeavor.

You live with a screenwriter. Has it given you insight into that process?
I have the utmost respect for those activities where people discipline themselves to that extent and work so much alone at the point of genesis. And
when they begin to work with others, it generally becomes something else.
It's very tough work.

How rare is it to see a first draft of a script really work?
Very rare. Very. Things change when you begin making something. When
you don't have this part in your hand and you substitute another part and
you just have to assemble the thing as you go along every day.

When a script isn't good you call it "talk-story."
That's one of the things a script can do to ensure its failure, is to talk about
what might have been dramatized. And to continually be talking about what

you're doing. People appropriate emotional information more easily than that. They get bored if you don't supply them with something.

How many good scripts do you read?
I've read any number of scripts which are good in and of themselves, which doesn't mean that they are perfect for the job at hand. There's no limit for better.

Is it harder to make a good movie than to write a good book?
Yeah.

Are there any books you'd like to see made into movies?
A lot of good books cannot be done. They're too complicated, and they live too much in the mind. Movies require objective manifestations of behavior and activity. A lot of very good books are mental.

Have there been good movies made from good books?
Not in the same terms. I think you can make a really good movie based on a really good book, but it won't be the same as the really good book.

Are there any novels you've liked recently?
I haven't read a novel in at least a year. I read practical nonfiction or scripts. My wife's a voracious reader.

Did your involvement with the Dalai Lama happen because your wife wrote the script *Kundun*, which Scorsese is directing?
Yes, that was totally based on her. It's quite simple. I regret the situation of Tibet and see it as a failure to preserve simple human rights to the people of Tibet. I think he's a remarkable person who I've come to respect and admire.

Is there a saintly aura around him?
I think he is a religious person. He is a substantial scholar, and I think he's the real deal.

Were you put on a list to keep you out of China because of your speaking out at a Senate subcommittee on behalf of the Tibetan people?
Apparently. I'm sure I did a number of things to annoy the Chinese. I was nervous about public speaking, but it was a small panel. They sought our input. The ambition at the time was to prevent the Chinese from gaining most-favored-nation status without redressing some of the problems that they've created in Tibet.

One Christmas you helped feed four thousand homeless at the L.A. Mission. How does that affect you?

Being there didn't affect me one way or another, but the problem is something I think about and something I try to do some small part in alleviating through projects other than the L.A. Mission.

What insights did you take away after spending time at the CIA head-quarters at Langley for *Patriot Games*?

I didn't have a strong emotional reaction to what we saw. I never had a very simplistic idea about what the intelligence community does or doesn't do. I knew that sometimes they do right and sometimes they do wrong. What I was interested in doing was giving a moral context to the character that was not insincere.

You've said you don't quite understand happiness. With all you've got, what's to understand?

I don't understand it as an ambition. I understand it as a by-product. As a pure ambition, it's not really worthy. My work is still an awful lot of fun for me. I love going to work, when it's coming easy or when it's going hard, I still love the job. I love the problem solving.

What about the physical toll some of your movies must take on you?

I tore an ACL [anterior cruciate ligament] in my knee during *The Fugitive*. I tore a rotator cuff in my shoulder on the last film, so I'm waiting for that to heal. They're frequently accidents, not the result of trying to do something outrageous. On *The Fugitive* I tore my ACL because I was running towards the camera. When we rehearsed it, there had been a hole next to the camera I could run through; when we shot it, somebody set a century stand in that hole, and I put all my weight on my right leg to cut left to avoid it and tore it. That's not an extraordinary thing to do, to run toward the camera. I hurt my shoulder over the years a number of times—you have a side you favor when you have to hit the ground, and I generally land on my right shoulder.

I've given up winter skiing when I have a picture in the spring because I don't have an ACL in my left knee. That was run over by the flying wing in one of the *Indiana Jones* movies. And I blew it out skiing one time. A friend of mine who's a surgeon said, "I've got good news and bad news." I said, I'll have the bad news first. He said, "You completely tore your ACL." I said, what's the good news? "You did it five years ago." It took me months to remember where it happened, and finally I remembered it was on that *Indiana Jones* movie in the middle of Tunisia where there was nothing to be done about it, so I just went on. And it never got fixed. But I can still do a lot of cross-country skiing with my knee.

You've said that you have a degree of irritation with people who are undisciplined. In what ways?
People who don't do what they say they're going to do. Don't work hard at what they're doing. Give up easily. Don't prepare themselves.

Do you have a temper?
It's way under control. I haven't lost my temper in months. I rarely lose my temper. I used to yell, but I got over that.

Did either of your parents yell?
Not really.

Was it tough growing up with the name Harrison?
I was Harry until I went away to college and had the opportunity to reinvent myself. To at least that degree.

When you were a kid in Chicago, did you used to sit by the window and wave at people going to work and returning home?
People would walk down the street on the way to work and come back down the same path. Since I'd always sit by the window looking out, I'd see the same people. We didn't have television, we didn't have a dog, so outside was where all the interesting stuff was happening. I could never know what was going to happen outside.

Did anything ever happen outside that surprised you?
Pretty banal.

Were you also bullied by boys in Morton Grove, outside of Chicago, who would push you down a hill?
Yeah, I was bullied. Pushed down a hill quite frequently. It continued because I didn't fight back, but I never could see the profit in fighting back. There was no one person to directly confront. And I was getting a lot of sympathy and attention from the girls.

Who do you know better, your mother or your father?
My mother, I suppose. A nice lady, still is. They live in Laguna.

Your mother's Jewish, your father's Catholic: what holidays do you observe?
All holidays. There's an advantage there. We were not raised with any particular religious tradition. Although in those days it was thought the wise and liberal thing to do to expose your kid to all manner of forms of religious ex-

pression, so it was one weekend at the B'hai Temple and the next at the Protestant church. I don't think it went on for more than six weekends. What interested me was the sway this idea held over people: the idea of a controlling, omniscient God was something I found real interesting. I didn't subscribe to that particular theory myself, but I was interested in the power of the church and religion and how it's used. I have the same disposition now towards religion as I did then. The variety and forms of religious expression still interest me. I'm probably more understanding of it now, less willing to define myself as an atheist or agnostic. Less interested in characterization of every kind.

Variety of another kind was also a part of your consciousness because of your grandfather, who was in vaudeville. What kind of act did he have?
He was a black-faced comedian. I never saw him, he was twenty-five when he died. I only know a little bit about vaudeville. It was a rough life, and my father is very unwilling to talk about it. He had a rough time when he was growing up. My grandfather was an alcoholic. When he died, he left my father a virtual orphan. His mother was unable to care for them, so he and his brother were raised by nuns in an orphanage.

You're a grandfather yourself now. What's that like?
Great, I've got one grandson, four years old. He's terrific. And what's great is to see my kids with him. Not just his parents but also my grandson has a six-year old aunt and a ten-year-old uncle.

You were a voracious reader between ten and twelve—what books did you most enjoy?
Biography and history.

And why did you stop reading voraciously after that?
Because I began to have assigned reading.

Of the biographies you read, whose life had the most meaning for you?
Wow. That's a serious question that takes a good rummaging through the inventory. (*Long pause.*) Abraham Lincoln.

Because?
Because to a small boy reading biographies, and possibly because I lived in Illinois and was able to see some of the reality of his life, I was very touched by what he did, by the difficulty of his presidency, of his life, and the quality of the man who overcame those circumstances to do so much for this country.

Joyce Carol Oates has said that there are pleasures in reading so intense that they shade into pain. What books have caused you pain when read?
Oh gee. You ask questions, and I'd love to give you serious answers, but at the moment my mind is drawing a blank. I can read Richard Ford and get that kind of experience. I just read Somerset Maugham's *Cakes and Ale,* there's some of that in that as well.

Richard Dreyfuss went to the Galápagos Islands for a PBS documentary. Goldie Hawn went to be with the elephants in India for *National Geographic* TV. Is there any place you might go if offered?
I get asked, but I don't want to go on an assignment. There would be nothing that could entice me, because I have the opportunity and wherewithal to do it on my own. I really want to go to southern Africa, but I won't go there to do a conservation story. I'll go on my own.

So there's no issue or concern that you might publicly support or highlight?
I do it all the time, and I always regret it. I just came back from Brazil, where I was in board meetings with a group that I work with called Conservation International. At their urging once again, I said I would be interviewed by Brazilian television, and once again I saw a series of old movie clips interspersed with very short and unexplored comments about conservation. I didn't feel that it was appropriate for me to take the time on that occasion. I never make myself available to the press unless I've got something to sell—that's why I'm here now, I have a movie coming out. I don't believe that complex issues should be decided on the basis of what celebrity is endorsing it. Yes, you can help bring attention to issues, but the quality of the argument often suffers. In the cases of Richard and Goldie, they're helping expose people to these elements, I don't know that they're making an argument.

I think that they're having a good time.
I like to have adventures without the movie camera with me.

Do you have many?
Yeah, we do have lots of them. We travel.

Can you compare and contrast Wyoming and New York?
Wyoming is good, New York is bad. We do have an apartment in New York, and I love going there for a couple of weeks at a time. My kids love it, the museums and the things in the city that you simply don't find anyplace else. It's great for them to get the experience of being able to go to both.

Have you ever been near death in real life?
I've had a couple of car wrecks, that's about it.

Have you ever been robbed?
I've had houses robbed, but I never had anybody stick a gun in my gut and ask me for my wallet. Never used to have a lock on our door when we lived up here on Woodrow Wilson [in the Hollywood Hills]. One day a lady came screaming in who I recognized as a person whose name I didn't know but who lived across the street. She was hysterical. I was unable to get any information about what her problem was until either her boyfriend or her husband burst in the door behind her. And in a moment of nonthinking I threw him out of the house, never recognizing until I got him outside and got some distance between us that he had a knife in his hand. But I was on him so quick, screaming so loud, that I undid him. It's a moment I think of.

Had you seen his knife do you think you would have reacted the same way?
No. I would have tried to reason with him.

Norman Mailer has said that there isn't a man alive who doesn't have a profound animosity toward women. Marlon Brando agrees with him. Think they're right?
They must not be very happy guys. I don't feel that at all. I feel a real kinship with women. I'm comfortable with them. I like women.

What do you know in your midfifties that you didn't in your midforties?
I wouldn't know how to name it. I find these turns of mind very hard to wrap myself around. The questions that call for absolutes, even simple absolutes. My mind doesn't work that way.

Let's see how well you do with offbeat questions.
I rarely give offbeat answers, but go ahead.

What are the three worst celebrity-oriented magazines?
Peephole. Vanity Fair. Us . . . as opposed to *Them.*

What are the five most important things in life?
Kids. A good bed. Good shoes. Practical clothing. And time for yourself.

If you could repeat one alcohol or drug experience you've had, what comes to mind?

(*Laughs*) I guess I wouldn't have gone to Hogs & Heifers that afternoon. Just went out one afternoon with a couple of guys, had a few beers, and lingered too long. Guess I had too much fun. A lot of untrue stuff ended up in the tabloids. I'm usually pretty good, I don't drink too much, and when I do I usually stay out of trouble and out of sight.

Should marijuana be legalized?
Probably.

What's the saddest thing that's ever happened to you?
I suppose that would be the time around the events of the dissolution of my first marriage. No further details.

What's the single most valuable thing you've ever learned?
Not to give up.

When did you learn that?
Over the fifteen-year period of time it's taken me to begin to have a career in this business.

If you could have survived any historic disaster?
Can't think of a reference for it. Just to be happy to be alive? Or to have had the experience?

If you survived, you would have had the experience.
But would one treasure that experience? It's either the Donner Party or the *Titanic*—to have lived through the *Titanic* is one thing, to have lived through the Donner Party, it ain't over yet. I'll say *Titanic* to give you an answer to your question.

What one news story or event would you like to have reported?
Ellsberg. The Pentagon Papers. Big story.

What one event in history would you like to have personally witnessed?
The Gettysburg Address.

Is that also a period of history in which you would have liked to have lived?
No. That was a terrible time in America. I don't think I would have liked to have lived through the Civil War. I think I would have liked to have lived around the turn of this century, when things were really changing. Things are still changing very rapidly, but that would have been a very interesting time.

What about if you had to have fought in any war in history?
World War II.

If you could have been a jury member in any court case, what trial would you choose?
The court-martial of Lieutenant Calley.

For those who don't remember, William Calley was tried for wiping out a village of mostly women and children in My Lai during the Vietnam War. How did you react to that at the time? Was it something you could understand at all—a young soldier freaked out who just started firing at innocent people?
I couldn't comprehend it. I could never imagine it happening to me. What I could imagine was being a member of his command and seeing it happen and not being strong enough to stop it.

Do you know anybody who has Vietnam horror stories?
Yes. I don't remember them, though I remember books, like *Casualties of War*, in which it was all distilled. That was one of the most compelling books I've ever read.

How did you beat the draft during that time?
I was a conscientious objector.

Were you actually classified as that?
No, I never got it. I confused them so badly that they never took action on my petition. My conscientious objection was based on no history of religious affiliation, which made it difficult at that time. I went back to my philosophy training from college. I remembered Paul Tillich's phrase, which was, if you have trouble with the word "God," take whatever is central or most meaningful to your life and call that God. And I always had trouble with the word or notion of God in a stand-up form. So I developed that thesis and took the biblical injunction to love thy neighbor as thyself as the central and most meaningful thing in my life. Combined it all and typed for days. I sent it off and never heard a word. Never got called in. It lingered for about two and a half years, and then my first wife became pregnant and I got an exemption based on that. The lawyer that I had retained to pursue my case, one J. B. Teats, told me that I owed him $5,000 as a result of my wife becoming pregnant. He showed me the piece of paper I'd signed, the simple form of a retainer, which stipulated that any more desirable draft status that was achieved during this period of time would be deemed to be the result of his

interference. And he was not amused by the conjecture of the child's paternity. So for about two years he dunned me for that $5,000. I finally paid him.

We've strayed from the offbeat. If you could reverse one sports call . . .
Don't know anything about sports. I don't have the sports gene in me. I just never cared about it. There's a couple of things I like to play but not competitively. I play tennis for the exercise but never socially. I always play with a pro so I can work intensely for an hour or two and not be distracted by anything else.

If you could have invented anything from history, what would you pick?
Airplane.

If you could uninvent one thing?
Gunpowder.

If you could be the editor of any magazine, which one would it be?
Flying.

How long have you been flying?
About two years. It's something I always wanted to do and never had a block of time to do it in. I got my license last September.

How is your vision?
I wear glasses when I fly.

How was it when you first soloed?
Great. I had a few bad landings at first because I was flying a Cessna 206, which is a bit more of a handful than people normally fly during training. One bad landing I don't think I'll ever forget. I'm pretty well aware of my limitations. *[Ford's six-passenger Beechcraft Bonanza sustained minor damage when he ran into wind shear and was forced to land in Lincoln, Nebraska in June, 2000.]*

How far have you flown?
I've flown across the country four or five times. Always with somebody.

Think crossing the ocean would be different for you?
It would be different for my wife. Right now I'm flying single-engined planes. I think I'll wait until I'm flying a twin to cross the ocean. It's a hop, skip, and jump to do that if you go through Nova Scotia and Greenland.

Do you have a landing strip on your property in Wyoming?
No, I gave that up as an option when I put a conservation easement on the property. It would be nice to have a little strip, but it's not too bad to have to drive fifteen minutes to the airport.

What's your most treasured possession outside of your children?
I don't really possess my children. I guess that would be my new airplane. Seats six, single engine. But if I get my motorcycle next week, it might be a toss-up.

Do you collect anything?
Apparently I collect airplanes. And motorcycles.

How about when you were a kid?
No, I never was a big collector. Stamps, for a while.

Do you have paintings in your house? Do you buy art?
Yes. Until the walls are filled. I'm not a collector collector. I continue to look, and every once in a while I'll buy something.

If you could own any one painting, which would it be?
I'm not really good at favorites, at isolating something down to one option. At least I can't do it with any confidence. I can do it as a kind of parlor game.

So what painting would you want over your fireplace?
I'm pretty happy with what's there now.

What is there now?
A Vuillard. French Impressionist.

How about if you could live inside of one painting?
There are paintings that intrigue me about the world they describe, but I wouldn't necessarily want to live there. I don't think I'd like to live in Hopper's world, but I'm intrigued by that. By his understanding of space and light and human emotions.

Hopper might be a painter whose work you'd want to own but not live in, like, say George Seurat's *La Grand Jatte*, which was turned into the play *Sunday in the Park with George*: a bright afternoon in a Parisian park with people strolling or sitting by a lake.
I'm not terribly fond of that picture, and I'm not terribly fond of that world.

And you wouldn't want to speak French?
Not have to.

Musical instrument, if you could play one, which would you choose?
The piano. I played for a little bit when I was a kid. Also the cello I'd like to play, it's an instrument that I really love the sound of.

Is there any piece of music you would like to have composed?
No. I would like to have been Hoagy Carmichael. I like the freedom of his mind. "The Baltimore Oriole." You know the words to that song?

Hum a few bars.
I won't put you through that. But these were intensely original descriptions of lovelike moments couched in really bizarre word pictures. I'm not too good at this.

You're doing fine. If you were to be successful with another profession . . . ?
Architecture.

When you were a carpenter, what kind of furniture did you build?
I made tables, not in a contemporary design. I mostly did more traditional stuff. I did quite a few architectural homes that were designed by notable architects, and the people had additions they wanted to design and build in the manner of the existing house.

Did you work on the design end as well?
I did in most of those cases. I designed my own residences, but I don't get much time building anymore. It takes me a while to get back the tool skill to the level that I want it to be at. I haven't had a month in a row to sit down and devote to woodworking, although I still keep a shop in Wyoming that I get into occasionally. I was never an artist, I was always a craftsman. I'm a practical person, so I do practical things.

Do you get in trouble when you don't do practical things?
Like what?

You tell me.
I don't know. Almost everything I think I do is practical on some level or another.

Why don't screen doors ever work?

Probably because the weight of the top and bottom rail is not sufficient to bear the strain put on it by the pneumatic door closing. Best to go with a solid bottom half, the dogs and kids won't kick it in to start with, and you'll have more meat on that middle rail.

If you had to choose the single biggest mistake you've made, what would it be?

Did I somehow get into the long-form interview that I've been running away from all my life? (*laughs*). I don't object, but because we've run into a couple of your questions so far, I'll tell you very quickly when I don't have an answer so we can get on with this. I'll sit here and ruminate with you, but we won't get much work done. So I'll give you the fast answer without being censored if it comes. If it doesn't come, I'll tell you I just don't have one. The last one was Single Biggest Mistake. Now I have to run through my life and try and find where I made my *biggest* mistake. (*Thinks.*) Don't know.

You probably know but don't want to say.

No. Don't know. I've made a series of small mistakes. Big mistakes? I don't know what that means. Do I have regrets? I would be led to know the mistake by a regret that I carried around with me. I have no regrets. There are lots of opportunities, and I'm sure I made a lot of mistakes, but I leave them behind me. I could give you something general like I regret that I wasn't as good a father to my older sons when they were growing up. There you go. Happy?

If you could have directed any film?

I don't want to direct films.

What about TV—if you could have produced any show?

Edward R. Murrow.

Do you watch your films when they come on TV?

No. Maybe for a few seconds, that's all.

Assuming there is a God and you could ask God one question, what would it be?

Is there anything we can do, or is it all in Your hands?

Maybe plumbing is in God's hands. Why does the hot water in my upstairs bathtub turn cold after a few minutes when it doesn't happen in the downstairs tub?

I don't know, man, might be your karma.

But it also happens when my wife goes to take a bath.
You might be your wife's karma.

If you could have any writer in history write your biography, who would you choose?
I don't want anybody writing my biography.

Assume somebody might. If you could choose the writer . . .
(*Thinks a long time.*)

How many writers have you mentally crossed out already?
None. I haven't crossed anybody out, I just haven't settled on anybody.

There's a pretty wide range to choose from—you could go with a master of the internal like Dostoevski to one of the external like James Michener.
If it's between Dostoevski and Michener, then let me think of something practical, that won't hurt as much and would entertain people. Elmore Leonard.

If Leonard wasn't available, think you might write your own memoirs?
No. Maybe after I'm dead.

That would be a neat trick.
It would be a lot easier to do it after I was dead.

If you could choose the way you could die, what would you choose?
An instantaneous brain aneurysm. Drop like a rock.

What people would you choose to be the pallbearers at your funeral?
I don't know, they'd probably have to put me on wheels.

SHARON STONE

I WAS SUPPOSED TO MEET SHARON STONE for lunch at the Delancey Street Restaurant in San Francisco's Embarcadero at noon, but my plane from Los Angeles was delayed, and I had to call her publicist to let her know. I managed to get there before our rescheduled one o'clock meeting, but Stone was even later. Seeing that the room was crowded, I asked a waiter whether there was another, private room we could use. He was cooperative, and I was able to set up my tape recorders, take out my notes, and get cushions for the wooden chairs before the waiter returned to tell me that Stone had arrived and didn't want to talk in such seclusion. He led me into the main dining room where the woman who became an overnight star when she crossed her legs in *Basic Instinct* and revealed that she was not wearing panties was standing at a table where her husband, *San Francisco Examiner* executive editor Phil Bronstein, was dining with a friend.

I shook her hand, introduced myself to her husband, and suggested that we go to the private room, which was all set up for our interview and lunch. "I don't want to go there," Stone said. "I want to eat here." She pointed to a corner table that had been reserved for us. I didn't want to make a scene, but I knew if we went to that table I'd have no chance at any kind of intimacy with her. There were just too many people, too much noise. It would be an impossible interview to transcribe.

I leaned toward this famous woman I didn't know and whispered in her ear, "Trust me." Then I turned and walked toward the other room, hoping that she would follow. She did, though not without first circling her finger around her ear to her husband, indicating that I was probably crazy. But I knew what I had to do, and though she pouted for the first

half-hour of our conversation, she eventually warmed up once she realized that I was there to take her seriously for however long it took. It
also didn't hurt that she was in a restaurant that had been started by a
friend she respects, Dr. Mimi Halper Silbert, who happened to come in
before our conversation got under way. Silbert is the bubbly president
of the Delancey Street Foundation, a self-help residential education
center for former substance abusers and ex-convicts. The two women
chattered like schoolgirls exchanging gossip in a restroom.

"Did you see what was in the *Chronicle* today?" Stone asked. "They
said that my husband and I were necking in a restaurant on the first
night of Passover. They took it from the *Post*, which said we were
'canoodeling.' I said to Phil, 'Is that like not a legal Jewish thing to do?'
He said, 'Not unless you're pork.'"

Then Stone told her about going to Pennsylvania to visit her parents
with her new husband.

"My parents sent me a fax to see if Phil ate ham, before we came
home. His parents are more like they would be my parents, and my parents would be Phil's parents. His mom's an actress, his father was a ballet dancer, they're very artistic and eccentric and wild. My parents are
more solid and like Phil. I think Phil died and went to heaven when we
got up there. My parents live in what used to be my dad's hunting cabin,
but they expanded it into a big house in the woods.

"I don't know how Phil consumed the amount of food that my
mother made. Phil was on his seventh serving of potatoes, and I said,
'That's probably enough.' And my father took me aside and said, 'If Phil
wants potatoes, you have to let him have potatoes. That's my marital
advice.' They gave us their room, which was already unbelievable. And
my mom left an Easter basket outside the room. We went antique shopping. My father has mellowed so much in his retirement, he's like a different guy."

Sharon Stone has changed a lot in 1999. Besides remarrying, she also
made San Francisco her home base and is nearly finished remodeling a
ninety-year-old Victorian house outside the city. She has completed her
three-year commitment as the spokesperson for AMFAR, the AIDS organization previously represented by Elizabeth Taylor, and she has
taken on other causes that are dear to her, including raising awareness
about breast cancer and raising money for numerous social causes. She
has appeared in films like *Last Dance, The Mighty, Gloria,* and *Sphere,*
which haven't had the box office of her breakthrough film, *Basic Instinct*
(which Camille Paglia considered one of the great performances by a
woman in screen history), or won her any Oscar nominations like the

one she received for her performance in Martin Scorsese's *Casino.* Nevertheless, she believes that she's been growing as an actress. *The Muse,* a comedy written and directed by Albert Brooks, is an example of that growth, which continued in *Picking up the Pieces,* a black comedy (with Woody Allen) about a jealous butcher who kills and chops up his cheating wife, only to have her severed hand turn up performing miracles.

The Muse is a small Albert Brooks comedy. Quite a switch from the thrillers and hard-edge characters that have rattled the box office in the past.

It was the most fun. To the point where you want to say it was the funnest! Fun to the point of silliness. But absolutely focused and professional and thoughtful. Albert is a tremendous leader. He has the maturity, the preparedness. If someone came to work not knowing their lines, he could do everything to make their performance happen. He's an extraordinarily gifted man. And the movie was shot so beautifully. It's a sweet, charming movie. Albert's most accessible picture.

You are the muse?

I'm a muse for Hollywood people who believes she's the daughter of Zeus and is there to inspire people on their scripts. It's very often unapparent what she's doing. Like with Albert, part of what I do is ignore him a lot. The Albert Brooks character is very selfish, very self-centered, neurotic, ungenerous. In a lot of ways, what she does is not give to him, to make him learn to be generous. She creates situations where he has to help. He has to learn to surrender.

What other directors get to play themselves?

Marty Scorsese and Jim Cameron and Rob Reiner. I wrote Marty a note that said, "I just saw the movie. You're the funniest scene in the movie, I however *am* the movie. Kiss my ass." He's funny! He comes in, and he wants to see me—I'm by then living in Albert Brooks's guest house. She's a character who comes in and lives in a hotel, a guest house, a room, a house, and she just consumes their lives. I just wish I understood about comedy, what I get now that I did it. I would like to go back and do the movie again. Anyway, Marty is the one director that Albert doesn't let the muse see, which is interesting and funny. I think it's because of *Casino,* and also because Marty is like the biggest, he wants to have the power of not letting Marty get to me. Marty comes in and starts throwing a fit: he needs better parking, and there aren't any magazines, and he says he wants to remake *Raging Bull* only this time with a thin guy. He talks a thousand miles an hour and never stops speaking for the entire scene, and he's great. And Jim Cameron was fun. As bold and brilliant an individual as he is, he was the shyest of all of them, which was dear. Of course, Rob was just nice and fun and extroverted.

Will Brooks get behind the promotion of the film?

I called Albert, trying to tell him how he can sell the film, because when I'm done acting I turn into the Avon lady, I take it around. I have a blue-collar ethic—they give me a lot of money, and that's part of my deal. But it was like I was speaking Swahili to Albert. I think it was offensive to him. His dream is to make the movie and then see how the world naturally responds to it. This was shocking to me, because in all my years in this business I've never heard that attitude! I was as stunned as if he hit me in the head with a board.

You often say after finishing a film that it's the best work you've done. And then the movie quietly disappears and you're left with that quote.

I think I ruin everything that I do. On *The Muse* I'm not objective. I don't know if I'm good in it or not. I see when I look at it, I understand how I can be better. This is my first full-blown comedy. In my dramatic work I really do feel like I get better with every part. Even though *Gloria* was a mess, I did some of the best work I've ever done. I look at it now, and I see where I'm growing. In *The Muse* it was a growth for me to just do it. But I'm not the finest comedienne of all times. My comedy work is not on par with my dramatic work. I have a lot to learn. I learned so much from making the movie that now I'd like to do another comedy right away because I have so much more I'd like to apply. The process is very fresh for me. I'm a student. When you have a terrific teacher, which Albert is, it's pretty fabulous. Do I think it's the best work I've done? No. But do I think it's funny? Yes. I watch the movie, and I feel like I'm hurtling through space and I don't know what's happening. I don't know if I'm good or bad or funny or awful.

What comic actresses do you admire?

Carole Lombard is more my style. Or Eve Arden. I don't have that thing that Meg Ryan has, that ability for cuteness. I'm not like that.

Who would you be comfortable doing a romantic comedy with?

Robin Williams. Or Bob De Niro. He's extremely funny in general, and he gets everything in terms of acting, more than anybody.

What about Al Pacino, who always professes to want to do comedies?

I don't think he and I mesh. Given the right roles, the specific set of circumstances, any two people could work together.

You acted with Dustin Hoffman in *Sphere*. Was it at all disappointing to be in that kind of film with him?

No. My part in that movie was peculiar, complicated, and a little strange. I enjoyed it. Dustin's not an action movie fan. I am. I love to do physical parts. I love when I have to throw knives or do karate or jump out of an airplane. And I learn to do it. Tear ass on my horse across the desert, whatever it is, I like physical challenges in my work. It's like doing *Three Musketeers* movies if you were in that period of filmmaking. I don't have that sort of value judgment about filmmaking.

Is the action movie declining?

Yeah, it's changing.

How did you feel about the critical and public reception of some of your recent films: *The Mighty, Gloria, Sphere*?

I got some spectacular reviews on both *The Mighty* and *Gloria,* from the reviewers who mean anything to me. I was particularly grateful when I got good reviews in *Gloria* because I thought the picture was a mess. That they didn't make a lot of money is a little bit sad, but then Harvey [Weinstein] didn't really release *The Mighty,* it was released in two hundred theaters. It's a lovely movie, the boys did a terrific job. *Sphere,* like any other movie that came out for the year after *Titanic,* just got lost in its wake, every movie got wiped out by that movie.

***Sphere* was important to you for reasons other than your career: you met Phil Bronstein while filming in San Francisco, and that led not only to marriage but also to relocating to San Francisco. Is it true you didn't initially like Bronstein?**

Yes, I didn't like him at first.

What turned you around?

I met him, then I had lunch with him and a couple of other people. That night he went away hiking. He drove to a pay phone each day and called me. When we talked, he talked to me about some books, then he sent me the books. Then he sent me some flowers. But principally it was because he called me each day from a pay phone, that he had to drive a long way to get to, and he had to stand when he talked. So I got to know him, because it required a certain effort that was old-fashioned.

How do you know he was at a pay phone and wasn't calling from a cellular phone?

Because you could just hear it. People would be in line, or drive up and be in the parking lot waiting.

And you discovered about him . . . ?
That he was funny and bright and interesting.

Whose decision was it to marry?
His.

Did he have to talk you into it?
It was not the kind of thing I could be talked into, but it was certainly he who wanted to get married. I had no interest in getting married anymore. But of course, I had no idea what marriage could be, because my last marriage was so not that.

Were you wary? In the past you've drawn up cohabitation agreements. Did you with Phil?
It's not in good taste to talk about that.

So the answer's yes?
The answer's whatever agreements we came to need to be between us.

When did you fall in love with him?
I would say I've fallen in love with him in much bigger degree since I've been married to him.

Joan Crawford believed that an actress should not marry.
You have to imagine how different things were then: they were studio players, their lives were run by the studio. Very often their marriage choices were chosen by the studio, so that may have been a very intelligent position for someone like Joan Crawford to take, the I-don't-want-to-be-married position. So that she didn't have to play the studio game.

How much luck is involved in a good marriage?
Some, but I'll tell you, it's about whether or not you've got the commitment and the courage to do it. My parents have been married forty-nine years. They have a relationship, not an arrangement. They hang out, joke, laugh, and overtly, every day, love each other. Very few people do that.

Think married sex improves over the years?

Oh, married, loving sex? I don't care how much you might be in love with someone, like an illness, there is nothing like married, loving sex. There is no way to tell somebody who hasn't had that experience what that does to your whole life, to the way you look at the world.

For someone who has been married more than once, does what you say hold true for marriage in general?
Oh good heavens, no. Oh God, no. I wouldn't say we had married, loving sex in my first marriage.

Did you love him?
Yes, but . . . we didn't have that kind of commitment to the relationship. It's almost like there's you, there's them, and there's the relationship. And you have to work to the relationship and sometimes the choices you make aren't specifically for each other.

Is there more temptation out there for someone like yourself?
Oh, that's never been my thing. I have a monogamous gene.

Are you happier in San Francisco than in Los Angeles?
Yes. The intellectual root, the drive of this town, is much more diverse. In L.A. I can't even say it's about movies because so many people in the movie business don't know very much about movies. It's now become kind of a corporate adventure—it's become about some kind of peculiar power struggle, with movies as the bartering beads. It's nice to be in an environment where people talk and care about other things.

I really like L.A. and have a big house down there. I love to go there, and I love the weather. And my very good friends live there. But San Francisco is a very loving environment. I've worked all over the world, and this is the most loving town I've ever been in. The most accepting. People are kind to each other here, they're generous. There's dignity in being generous and decent. I wouldn't say that that is the top of the value system in a lot of other towns.

Are you hassled at all here?
People here have a different kind of integrity which allows them to experience me as a human being and not as an object that may grant their sensationalistic desire of the moment. I never, never, never have people hound me for autographs or chase me for pictures or be mean to me because I don't want to kiss their baby. Unless it's a tourist.

Do you feel that way about New York as well?
No, I get chased constantly in New York. I've worked out a very successful
deal with the paparazzi in New York, which is, when they chase me, I will
stop and do pictures if they go away. So I have to do pictures and have that
barrage every time I go outside. But you know, I just don't feel like that every
time I want to go for a walk, or if I'm in the middle of baking and I need
some butter. I'm able to have a life that is much more normal, and therefore
I'm able to have a sensibility and a sanity that is much more wholesome,
which is very important to me.

If you had stayed in L.A., would it have driven you insane?
I certainly think that it was not going to be possible for me to successfully
date or to find a relationship or get married in that town. That was not going to happen. But I do have a spectacular group of girlfriends, and guy
friends, in L.A. That's the pleasure of my house in L.A., which is so big it's
silly. But I had to get behind gates. There weren't any charming houses with
some land that qualified in the safe department. There was one, and I went
on a bidding war with Carrie Fisher, and finally I said, okay, you take it. It
was beautiful, it was Edith Head's house. It wasn't a showboat house, and
the house I bought was. And I have since made it my own. We call it The
Bunker. It's a place where nine to twelve of my girlfriends can come together
and watch a movie and have a big buffet, family-style meal.

How often are you in L.A.?
Quite a bit, every month for five days. I've taken my company, Chaos Pro-
ductions, to Arnold Milshon at New Regency, and he's godfathering my
company now.

With all you've got on your plate, how often do you see your husband?
Constantly. He's on television in the morning—they do a little spot in the
news that talks about what's in the paper. His last group meeting of the day
is at five. So even if he comes home after that, it's not before six-thirty. When
I met him, he worked seven days a week, like a movie schedule, all year long.
He hadn't taken a vacation in five years. Since then things have changed a lot.
(*A waiter comes in. Stone orders a big bowl of matzo ball soup.*) This woman who
runs Delancey Street [Dr. Mimi Silbert] is a spectacular individual and one of
my husband's best friends. Most of the people here are ex-cons and drug and
alcohol abusers. Serious criminals. It's extraordinary what she does. Because
our penal system is so fucked up. When I did *Last Dance,* I watched tons of
tapes of interviews of serial killers, and I could see by the misshapenness of
their heads that 80 percent of them had fetal alcohol syndrome.

How much time do you spend on causes you believe in?
Oh God, so much. In the last ten years I've always had offices, but the truth is, I don't go to them. I like to work at home. So now my office is in my apartment. It's a terrific way to work if you can. In our new house, which we're remodeling, we've taken one of the bedrooms and are making it into my office. We've opened the attic up and made that Phil's office.

Have you met a lot of new people through your husband?
Yes. People I would never have gotten to meet. People who think and talk about other things, who do really good things in the world. It seems like all my husband's friends do something special.

What new friends have you made on your own?
I'm able to make girlfriends up here. I met a girl from my neighborhood in a restaurant, and my God, it's so great—I now just stop by her house and she makes me a cup of tea and we shoot the breeze. I'm a big fan of [the artist Jean-Michel] Basquiat, and I met this girl from a small town in Pennsylvania who came out here and opened this art gallery. We've become really good friends, and I'm hosting a show for her, a tribute to [Robert] Rauschenberg. We're giving the proceeds of the opening to my church that's building a family center. They said they were going to name the floor after me.

You seem pretty involved with this church. What denomination is it?
I think it's probably called Methodist, but it's completely nondenomina-tional. I'd been trying to find a church to go to in L.A., but they would al-ways sell me out for the PR, and there would end up being these fucking *Globe* reporters in the parking lot and chasing me around in the church. It should be illegal for the press to follow you into church. But when I was up here making *Sphere,* I started going to this church, and it's been terrific. There are no crosses because they don't worship the concept of suffering, guilt, and punishment—which I'm so not into. It's about joy. Love. Making the loving choice, being your best, being true. And they have the best choir. You dance for the first forty-five minutes. Thousands of people go, it's standing room only. Black, white, Chinese, Jewish, Buddhist, Christian—it's an incredible environment.

I've always been very interested in religion. My parents were Protestants. When I was ten, I decided I wanted to go to Baptist church, so I went sepa-rate from them. And I went to Baptist school. Their idea of Baptist was the preacher held your head under the water, and I didn't want to do that. I studied a myriad of religious philosophies, even Scientology. Ultimately I've come to the conclusion that I'm a Taoist Buddhist who believes in God.

When you decide to get involved in a cause, do you get advice from a lot of people?

No. I usually don't talk to anybody. I make my decisions from my gut. When I surrendered to being an artist, I became sure that my heart and my instinct were smarter than my mind, so I try to listen to that. A lot of the things that I agree to do I'm advised not to do. People disagree with my choices more than agree with them. Cindy [Stone's publicist] was very supportive when I wanted to do AMFAR, but we knew going in that wasn't going to be easy or popular. When I took it, it wasn't popular. Now we're doing great. The last big thing, where we honored Clive Davis, Tom Hanks, and Barbara Walters—and Whitney Houston, Barry Manilow, and Puff Daddy performed—that was like, wow! When I started I was auctioning the salt-and-pepper shakers off the table, we had nothing, there was no perpetual motion happening.

Your three-year goal was to raise $76 million. Have you come close?

I don't know. I suspect they came up with a figure they hoped for. I don't work like that. I do the best I can. I never ask overall what we made. I did an auction in Dallas, and we made $750,000, which was good. We had an auction for Francis Coppola—he's providing an acknowledged citizenship for homeless people in the northeast community by giving them post office boxes and voice mail, so that these people can get jobs. He had maybe $12,000 worth of retail, and we made twenty-six grand. I asked at the end, how'm I doing? Because I do a lot of auctions. One for the ballet last year, one for my church. This auctioneer thing is sort of out of control—I get offers every day to do an auction for charity. I have to narrow it down.

How do you prepare to run an auction?

I get cover sheets, and I study what the material is, so I have in my mind a humorous field of reference on the items, or some historical reference. AMFAR is the least prepared—they never give me anything in advance. I'm always flying by the seat of my pants trying to make it happen, which adds a certain energy. When I speak for them, I make some notes. I have a different way of public speaking. I used to write something and read it, but that's boring. Then I was on a Friars Club dais for Barbara Walters. I read my stupid thing, and then I watched Sid Caesar, Carol Channing, Henry Kissinger, Diane Sawyer—an extraordinary group of people who knew how to do public speaking. I was most educated and informed by Kissinger. He had notes and had a particular way where he really spoke to the people who were there. He had subject matter, reference points, but you could see that he was really listening to the room and seeing what was happening, taking that energy and rolling it into himself and making it a powerful presentation. It was very good. So then I decided to try it like that. Sometimes I'm at the event before something happens that informs me what I'm supposed to talk about. I have a faith that I know something will happen, but sometimes I'm walking to the mike before it does.

You got some unwanted attention when you said that eliminating coffee cured you of cancer. For the record: you never had cancer, did you?
I had lumps in my entire lymph system: in my neck, under my arms, in my groin. It made the doctor turn white. I took antibiotics, and they didn't go away. They freeze-dried my blood and sent it to a lab in Boston, and the diagnosis was positive. Then it was gray . . . it just went on and on. I had this terrific doctor who said to me, "You don't have cancer. I think you're allergic to caffeine." He told me every single thing to take out of my diet—and ten days later it was all gone! I have no use for caffeine ever since.

My gynecologist gave me this book, *Eating for Your Blood Type*. My blood type is A+, of course. It tells you what you should eat and what you're predisposed to physically in terms of exercise. I'm so like not jumping and running. It also tells you what illnesses you're predisposed to and what you're not predisposed to by your blood type.

So what are you looking out for?
Breast cancer. My friend and I both got voted Woman of the Year up here for our breast cancer awareness stuff. We're writing a poem for our acceptance speech. She's a well-known published poet, and I'm a goofball. So her part is deep, and mine is like: Boobs, tits, cantaloupes, watermelons, ta-tas, "Come in, Radio Free Europe," . . . that's my part.

Who's got the most beautiful breasts you've ever seen?
(*Pulls out her top, looks down at her own, laughs.*) I'm very happy with my own. You have to be happy with what you have. When I was young, I always hated my hips and thighs, and I thought I had a giant ass. Now that I'm older I think, Oh, I have a woman's body, and isn't that nice. Yeah, I can't look great in pencil skirts, but you come to appreciate yourself, it's part of maturing, accepting you.

You've also said that you finally have grown into your face.
And my voice. I've had this froggy voice since I was twelve. And I was always sporty, which is really peculiar on a teenager. It started to work for me professionally when things started to take off, where I could play characters who had a knowingness and a kind of edginess that didn't make sense when I was younger.

You've described growing up as an intense, weird kid who made everybody uncomfortable.

Sometimes when we're uncomfortable we have an inflated sense of how we affect others. I suspect I had much less effect on others than I imagined at the time that I said that.

In what ways did your father drive you toward perfection?

He felt that I was so special that not to use that specialness to its fullest would be wrong. The mistake in that is the judgment of what special is. Now he's more accepting of what special is for all his children. He admires and appreciates all of his children equally now, but when he was younger he thought he had a responsibility to push me to my greatest possibilities.

When did he become proud of you?

I don't know, though I know that he is. If he picked my life, he wouldn't have chosen for me to be an actor. I wouldn't pick it for my kid either, but for much different reasons.

Were there any actresses you were particularly attracted to as a child?

I was a little in love with Rita Hayworth. And with Ava Gardner.

Part of your biography stresses your high IQ in high school. Did you once win a high school essay contest?

I didn't win a contest. When I was in school, they were having an experimental educational program. I started school in the second grade when I was five—I could do the work, but I couldn't socialize, I was completely overwhelmed. The children were twice my size. So they put me back in first grade for the rest of the year, which gave me the horrible feeling of, now I'm failing. Now I was with these babies who were learning their ABCs, which was worse. Then I went to this Mensa program in the fourth, fifth, and sixth grades where we had special classes for part of the day. Then in high school they sent four of us to college, so I went to college and high school at the same time. In college I studied writing. So that's what was happening—I was chosen to do this college writing program.

Have any publishers expressed interest in the short stories you write?

I just performed them, which was very cool. I have a friend in L.A. who has a musical group, and we performed in a bar a couple of times. He wrote music to go with my words. It was very interesting.

You let *Esquire* quote one of your stories: "Style is what you do with your mistakes: Barbra Streisand's nose; Clark Gable's ears; Danny De Vito's size; and Cher."
Bruce Vilanch was there when I read that story, and he thought that was hilarious.

Ever hear from Streisand or Cher about that?
No. I know Barbra, because her kind-of stepson, Christopher Peters, I dated for a long time. I had dinners at her house.

Do you like her?
(*Long pause*) She has lived so long with such huge fame, and she has chosen with that fame not to live in the rest of the world—I can't relate to that.

Do you see that happening with your costar in *The Quick and the Dead*, Leonardo DiCaprio, whom you've dubbed a genius?
I knew the second I saw that kid, he's just the one. If he survives fame, he'll be the finest actor ever. If he survives it.

Do you think he will?
I don't know.

You told *Movieline* that none of the other kids have his depth and breadth of understanding, and wisdom and character. Five years later, do you still feel that?
Yeah. And I love Kate Winslet too—they were very well matched. She's remarkable. But anyone like him? No. No. Leonardo's like Mozart, there's not a lot of that. People don't know it really yet, because of the kind of movies he's done, and because he looks like a kid—but like the eight ball says: "It will be revealed." It will be revealed with Leonardo. If he makes it. It's such a hideous thing, what's happened to him. I can't think of anything worse.

What do you mean?
For him to be so famous. It's just awful.

At what age is someone mature enough to handle fame?
I was thirty-two when I got famous, and I was barely holding on. And because I come from such solid family, and because I have the same friends I've had for twenty-five years, there was so much that was already a constant in

my life, I had so much life already. I had tremendous support. And I also had a life to look at.

Fame is an ugly thing. I was watching Marilyn Manson interviewed on TV the other day. He was saying that Jesus was the first celebrity and set a certain standard for what celebrity is. He's very interesting—he's a lot smarter than your average sensationalistic rock lunatic. And sensible.

You've said that your will is what made you famous—not your talent or charm or superficial qualities. How willful are you?
I don't think it's my will that's kept me famous. I think that I learned my craft and love my job and respect that I work for the public. That's probably kept me famous.

How would you describe yourself?
I wouldn't, I'm so sick of me.

***Entertainment Weekly* described you as having the humble beginnings and exquisite fashion sense of Joan Crawford; the bald, playful sexuality of Marilyn Monroe; the man troubles of Lana Turner; and the take-no-prisoners glamour of Elizabeth Taylor.**
Well, I haven't killed any of my boyfriends yet. I've been asked to play Lana Turner too.

In *Elle*, you're described as a sex symbol: "Steely, ambitious, unforgiving." Is that you?
What that writer did was step into a fantasy day with me, and write about his fantasy. But I don't think anybody can be described in a quick series of adjectives of any kind and have it be at all accurate.

How ambitious are you?
More than ambitious I would say that I'm unsatisfied. I'm one of those people who always wants to do a little better, achieve a little more. Is that ambition? Maybe.

Is it hard to be a sex symbol?
(*Taking airs*) Well, for me it just came naturally. Everybody has their thing. It's figuring out what's your thing. I certainly never thought that was going to be my thing. But it's funny to me that it is. And that it happened to me later in my life, it has a certain kind of joy and humor to it. If I was twenty-two instead of thirty-two, it wouldn't have been that funny, it would have been a nightmare, and I'd probably be dead. But it's pretty fun as a grownup.

What did you think of Gwyneth Paltrow's parody of you on *Saturday Night Live*?
She's very young, and in that rarefied air that's a little thin, it's like she's not quite getting enough oxygen. She's being guided by people in some situations who have bigger plans than her. I don't know yet what I think of her. I would like to think that she just doesn't know, that she's just young. I would like to think that she will eventually spend her fame valuably.

The women in the generation before me cut the path for women like me to walk freely in the world. The women in this next generation don't really know what that cost. They don't totally get it. So they don't respect it. It's a lot easier for me to be an individual, to be self-employed, to make my own decisions as an actor, than it has ever been in any generation before me, and those women before me worked very hard to make choices and to change the way the game was played. Part of the way you do that is that you handle yourself when it comes to you. These kids that are coming up don't have an awareness of that, they don't understand why it's so easy now. When fame comes upon people who are really young, they don't know that they're being eaten by it, they think they're being fed by it. That's what intrigues me about Angelina Jolie, because I think she gets it. She has that tattoo on her stomach that's so intense—it's in Latin and says "That which feeds you eats you." Can you imagine what you must know at that age to have done that to yourself? But probably since the Oscars that young lady [Paltrow] has a better understanding of what it is than ever before. I wish her a lot of luck and stability, because she's got a lot of talent.

Is this your warm way of saying you didn't really appreciate her parody?
I didn't appreciate it. And I particularly didn't appreciate her being malicious about my husband.

Which was?
She said something nasty about him. (*When introducing him, Paltrow-as-Stone added, "Isn't he creepy?"*) I just don't think she gets it. I don't want to believe she has any malicious intent, I want to imagine that she's just that naive.

The tabloids have you splitting with your husband—how do they find these things out?
You know what happened? Someone we knew was doing that, making up those stories.

Have you had it out with that person?

Some of my friends have, but I haven't. Well, it blew up on itself without me doing anything, and I eventually did discuss with this person how I felt. I said: "My sadness is not because I've lost trust with you about my privacy, it's because I've lost trust with you about my heart. Because you've somehow forgotten that this hooks to me and is about me inside. Where's that part of you gone to lunch?" I have a philosophy about this particular thing, which is, I either love someone or I don't. If they do this, and if I know that they're doing it, it doesn't make me not love them. What I generally choose to do is observe them, I watch the process, and I try to figure out what it is in them, what's happened to them. It's become more interesting to me than offensive. I obviously adjust the degree of closeness that I entrust with that person. But it's my friends that seem to decide whether or not they're going to kick him out. I don't know how to explain this. I don't have that kind of hateful feelings about that stuff anymore. I don't know why I understand it, but I do. And I forgive it, because it's a completely other thing that drives people to do that. It's something about the way they feel about themselves. It's very little to do with me. This is what I try to tell my other friends, who get hurt and angry about it. What you have to learn when you get so famous is that just because it has your name on it, it doesn't mean it has *anything* at all to do with *you*. So what I'm trying to do as this person's friend is see what it is with him, what's his pain that's making him do that? Any of my good friends will fuck up and do something peculiar as a result of my fame. You have to understand, if you're famous, that it's going to fuck people up, that nobody's going to handle it great 100 percent of the time, not even your best, best friend. They're going to do something that they shouldn't do.

Has your husband's profession given you new insight into journalism?
His impression of the media and their reaction to celebrities has changed more than my experience has changed. Because he's never been on the other side of it before. Last time in New York he walked down the street and people started screaming, "It's Sharon Stone's husband!" He said it was the most horrifying, hideous experience. Because he's so not that. He's not that kind of guy. Nobody bugs me when I'm with him.

What should news journalists be doing that they're not?
Being accurate. It's much less important if someone is accurate when they discuss my life than when they discuss Kosovo, but it's not separate. Because it's an ethical standard. When people make up stories about me, it hurts me. I understand it comes with the territory, but it hurts my family, and that I don't understand. Or when they discuss my family or Phil in ways that are

inappropriate, because they are not public figures—so I don't think they should be up for that kind of speculation. It's not right.

But it's also inevitable.
But the laws have to change. The laws about what's a stalker and what's appropriate and how close people can come to you on the street. I just cannot have people throwing my mother on the ground. That happened once in a bad way, where she got hurt. It was when I first got famous, and we went to a movie in Century City. We started to get rushed by some paparazzi, and she said, "You run for the car, and I'll be between you and them at the bottom of the escalator." I rushed because they will push me right up against a wall, and I really do get hurt. It's not a joke. So I'm running, trying to get to the car, and I turn around, and they pushed her onto the escalator and then started jumping over her. She was getting smashed into the escalator stairs and getting hurt. It was horrifying. I had to turn back and get her, because if I didn't it wouldn't stop. People do things like get in her car. Or they hit your car, keep rear-ending you because the California law says you have to stop.

So, is the media the enemy?
I have so many friends who are journalists. I end up making friends with people who come to interview me, or I do their shows, because they're the people you can talk to. But your publicist will always tell you that you can never be friends with a journalist, because ultimately and eventually you will get hurt. It's drilled into your head.

I had a journalist really fuck me and my friends in a big way, a guy who clearly had his own cross to bear, of being the son of a celebrity. He wrote nothing but lies. He took everything that everybody said out of context, and he wrote things that I said that I never said. I got phone calls from people you wouldn't believe. My best friend was crying, people were just broken by this. He was so insistent that I wasn't who I was. He just kept insisting that I had to be really unhappy. He would come to me and say, "I just had lunch with four psychiatrists who say you *have* to be unhappy." He was mad. Insane. He couldn't believe that I could play a character in *Basic Instinct* and not have to be like that. He was like a man possessed. Poor thing.

Journalists often come in with a preconceived idea of who you are, what the story is, and you're there to fill in the blanks. So I always come in a little bit like, "Here we go again." It's boring.

Does the same hold true with photographers? You've appeared on so many magazine covers. Did any photographer ever trick you into a pose you didn't like?

The one Annie Leibowitz shot for *Vanity Fair [for the April 1993 issue—Stone is without makeup and bare-chested, covering her breasts with her hands]*. I just hate that because I felt so betrayed by her. I did that whole shoot and worked really hard with her for several days, because she was very insecure about shooting me and felt that everything had been done and she didn't know what to do. I was very excited to be photographed by her because she's so talented. We were in the middle of *Sliver*, and I was tired and not feeling well. When we finished, we were in the dressing room, and I had taken my hair down and taken all my makeup off and she said, "I just want to take a picture of your back, would that be okay?" I said, "Sure, but I'm wiped out." So she took the picture of my back, and then I turned like this *(with hands over breasts)* to leave, and she took my picture and put it on the cover. That was a cheap shot. That picture is mean-spirited. I didn't like it, and I didn't like what she did.

What magazine cover meant the most to you?
When I was on the cover of *Rolling Stone*, I thought that was just the coolest thing. This was in the very beginning of everything.

You were also on the cover of *Playboy* twice.
When they called me to be on the cover a second time, I said I'd only do it if they did the Q&A with me. I read that interview recently—I was such a baby and so clueless.

What magazines do you take seriously?
Time. (She asks the waiter for hot chocolate and potato bread toast.)
I'm in the phase where I'm eating like a child.

You're not pregnant, are you?
No, but I'd be delighted to be at any time.

Have you looked into why you haven't gotten pregnant?
There is no reason. Yes, I've looked into it.

What about adopting?
Oh yes! Oh God yes! However many children we make, we will also adopt children. I know a terrific adoption agency. *[In the spring of 2000, Stone and her husband adopted a baby boy.]*

Diane Keaton adopted.
I think she is so swell. Her physical comedy is so pure. I really love pure talent.

Let's talk about that—who are the talents you feel are pure?
Judy Davis just sends me. Judith Dench. I've seen *Mrs. Brown* so many times
that we don't call it *Mrs. Brown,* we call it *The Movie. Impromptu* with Judy
Davis was like this for me, where she plays George Sand—something in her
performance is so inspiring to me, I've watched it a thousand times. I'm in
the process of maybe doing a movie with Billy Connolly—he's just swell. Pure
talent? Lynn Redgrave. I was genuinely happy when she got the Golden
Globe instead of me. Meryl Streep—what a talent. I voted for her for Best Actress for *One True Thing*—because of this one scene where Renee Zellweger
starts yelling about her dad, Bill Hurt, and Meryl Streep is on the floor, dying of cancer, trying to sort out the family album, trying to get all this stuff
organized before she dies. And the daughter comes in with this rage, and she
has this speech about how when you first get married what you think you
will put up with and what you think you won't and then it becomes your
family and then it's what it is. Meryl's technique has always been better than
anybody's technique. Sometimes I am more moved by someone who has a
more raw kind of talent. I was particularly moved by her work in *Sophie's
Choice* and *French Lieutenant's Woman,* but sometimes I would rather see Anjelica Huston crawling across the floor with the guy with the bag of oranges
because you don't know what's going to happen, and that sends me. But this
work she did was so informed and revealing and generous, that she took off
the mask and put such a private piece of her personal information in her
work, which is riveting. Just an amazing little moment. She is a really big talent. Geoffrey Rush is like that, he's like the god of acting. Robin Williams. It
astounds me that people don't understand the depth of his dramatic talent
and range. I told *Movieline* when they asked me which actor I wanted to work
with, Robin, and they wrote because he was so funny. Nothing to do with
him being funny—his ability, his tenderness is infinite. There's something in
him that has an enigmatic comprehension of the soul in his work. The humor allows people to be with it without being terrified or ripped in two, because it's so profound. He's amazingly gifted.

Any memories of working with Robert Mitchum?
I loved him. He was sweet with me. He did this one thing one time that was
terrific. When we were doing *War and Remembrance,* it was my birthday, and
we shot one of those ungodly twenty-two-hour days. He had them make me
a spectacular birthday cake, and he, Hart Bochner, and Barry Bostwick were
going to take care of me all day—that was my birthday present. So they
rubbed my feet, my shoulders, brought me tea, and spoiled me all day. It was
wonderful. I remember sitting on the set one day, and he was sitting forty
feet away on a folding chair, and he kept leaning over and staring my way,

and I asked, "What the fuck are you doing?" And he said, "I'm looking up
your dress!"

Were you wearing underwear?
Well, yeah. He's the kind of guy if he pinched your butt, it was a compliment, it wasn't insulting, it was flattering and funny. We met once at the
Biltmore in Santa Barbara to have tea—I had tea, he had four hundred
drinks—and then we were going to meet some friends of his. I didn't want to
ride with him because he just really hammered the booze, so I followed him.
We just went from one person's house to the next, half these people were
having cocktail parties, it must have been the way people lived up there, and
we had the best time. He was just a lot of fun. Told great stories.

**What about Steven Seagal? You always refrain from commenting about
Seagal and *Above the Law*. What did he do to you?**
I just think he's an individual who isn't worth the ink it would take to write
about him.

So you don't believe he's a reincarnation of a Tibetan holy man?
I don't believe that the Dalai Lama believes that.

Do you have an opinion of Marlon Brando?
I think Brando's very interested in people's discomfort. It's like a study for
him. I don't know him, but a friend of mine was the butt of his practical
jokes.

What about Jerry Lewis?
He seemed really angry. But he was fantastic in *The King of Comedy*.

Dolly Parton?
I love her. How about her mouth like a sailor? She's really special, I like her a
lot. Talk about pure genius. And Marty [Scorsese]—pure genius.

Jim Carrey?
I had a mini-breakdown watching *The Truman Show*. I started to panic at a
certain point and had a hard time being with the comedic aspect of it. I
think Jim Carrey is a fucking genius. His performance at the Oscars this year
was outstanding. He really gets it in a big way, and he seems to be doing better. Fame hit him. . . .

Along with $20 million per picture.

That's another thing that isn't so good. Not just the fame, but the money changes everyone around you. For me, I wanted everybody to be in it with me, I wanted them to have it too, but then you have people turn into sycophants. You create a bad gravy train, and you just fuck yourself.

On the other hand, gravy trains can lead to interesting dinners.
I had a very good dinner with [director] Harold and Susie Becker, Jimmy Woods, Jack Nicholson, Marty [Scorsese], Candice Bergen, Faye [Dunaway], and Garry Shandling. That was a very good group. Candy Bergen is a scream, she is truly, truly funny. Shy.

Are there any actors you feel close with?
The ones I like to hang out with are Faye [Dunaway] and Shirley MacLaine.

Dunaway seems incredibly fragile and vulnerable.
Faye's great, really intelligent. She seems like a lioness because of the way she behaves with her fragility, the way she aggresses with her entire being when she feels fragile or scared. She's extraordinarily talented and beautiful. People get an impression of her that is so different from the truth of her. In truth, she's so dear, but she acts out in a way that really misleads people about who she is. But you're absolutely right.

And do you share MacLaine's concept of an afterlife?
Yeah. If you're not trapped in the idea that this is all there is, the concept of death is kind of exciting and terrific. My husband is not very keen on this. I think it's most important that people know that you love them and that you're current in your relationships, so that if it is today, you're on top of it.

Do you live each day as if it could be the last?
Not in some kind of desperate, accelerated sense of it. I like to stay in and not go out of the house for days on end sometimes. I was thinking about that the other day. Well, what if that was it? Great. I'm very content with my life.

Have you ever been in awe of anyone?
Yeah, a lot. I'm in awe of Mimi [Silbert]. Of Janon Cecil Williams, he's the pastor of my church, and his wife. They do the most amazing things. They've got 40 programs, they feed the homeless 365 days a year, they've got buildings to put homeless families back together, rape counseling programs, hooker rehabilitation programs. (*Stone's husband enters: "We're leaving. Sorry to interrupt." She gets up, they hug.*)

Is Bette Davis your favorite actress?
No, although Marty and Bob [De Niro] said that I would be the next Bette
Davis if I don't do plastic surgery.

Would you consider doing plastic surgery?
Yeah. My husband thinks it's awful. But I think when your face doesn't go
with your body that it looks really dumb. Like Goldie Hawn said in *The First
Wives Club,* if you want to freshen up a little bit, that's okay. As Joan Rivers
would say, you repaint your car. But that thing where you have a mask that
stops at your jawline and you have this baggy old body underneath, that
looks so stupid, I wouldn't do that to myself.

What are you in need of now?
I have really good genes about aging. I'm lucky to be forty-one and I see
women thirty-one that I look younger than. For a while I thought they were
the exceptions, but the older I get the more I realize there's an exception
about the way that I'm aging. It's two things: one, that I have really lucky
genes; and two, when I was fourteen, my mother gave me moisturizer and
said, put it on every time you wash your face, at least twice a day. That probably has been enormously helpful to the aging process.

**Mae West's aging secrets were cocoa butter on her breasts and a daily
enema.**
Eeyew. I've been asked to play her. I liked her. I think if you have a wholesome life and you're not a drug addict or an alcoholic and you don't do
things to excess that are bad or even supposedly good for your body—it's
good to have a drink now and then, good to have a steak or smoke a cigarette once in a while.

What about marijuana?
Terrific! It should be legalized. It's much better for you than alcohol. It's terrific medicine and has been enormously helpful for so many people. Marilyn
Manson said the people who abuse drugs make it bad for all the rest of us
who just want to use them. Marijuana's a terrific thing.

Cocaine?
No, cocaine is an evil, horrible, awful thing.

Mescaline or peyote?
I personally am too fragile to take hallucinogenics. I would lose my
mind.

Have you ever?
I had someone put LSD in my drink when I was nineteen, and I had a very
long trip. I did it with so many people who were tripping that as soon as it
came on I knew I was tripping and I called my roommate, who sent a cab for
me and helped me through it.

I always thought if I got incurably sick I would drop acid.
If I got incurably sick, I would take heroin before I'd take acid, because those
opiates can be very soothing. But I wouldn't want to take heroin because I
have no interest in being addicted. I am addicted to winning, and that's
enough to wrestle with every day.

**So James Woods was right when he said you don't have to steal every
scene, you have to *win* every scene?**
Uh-hmm. Especially with him, because Jimmy is voracious as an actor. People acquiesce to him. If you acquiesce to an actor of that intelligence and
magnitude, you disrespect them. So when I get in a scene with Jimmy, it's
like getting in the ring. I'm not going to play that game, I'm going to step up
and really play. When we first worked together, he was very outraged by that
behavior. Now he really enjoys it, and our relationship is very good as a result. I love working with him, because he doesn't back down from me either.
Gene Hackman wouldn't give me an inch [in *The Quick and the Dead*], and I
was so proud that he wouldn't, that he respected me enough to do that was
a big deal to me. To be pandered to or have someone give me the scene is a
horror to me, because what's that? There's no passion in that, no risk in
that. And there's certainly no unknown thing that will occur from that behavior. I love working with people like Jimmy and Gene and De Niro, Sly,
Arnold. I love these guys who are going to get in there and really go for it,
whether it's an action movie or a drama. In fact, I'd love to do a romantic
comedy with Arnold because he's a wonderful comedian. The thrill is to play
in whatever the venue or genre is and have the person be really willing to
come out and play. That is where it's at. So yeah, I play to win. Though I
think I would be different now, because I understand as a grownup woman
winning in a different way. I'd like to play movies where I win as a couple,
not as an individual. I've often played characters who are isolated or individ-
uated or just insane, so I'm at a point in my life where I would want to play
doubles, which I never got to do very much.

Why won't David Letterman play with you?
Because he's afraid he could lose, and I don't think he could stand that for
a second. I have fun on every other show. I particularly like Dennis Miller,

it's like a tennis match with him. Jay Leno is the most professional, to-gether, terrific showman. He does his own warm-up; when you cut to com-mercial, he'll say, "We were talking about this, and if you say this, you'll get a laugh." He will literally lean over and give you a joke. Because he plays for his show. I respect that. Letterman is so smart and funny that I wish he would play, but not enough that I would want to do it anymore. I went three times.

Paul Verhoeven, who directed *Basic Instinct,* thought you could capture the evil and the charm of the character because those elements were present in you. "She can be so goddamn mean," he said. "She really knows what buttons to push to get to you. She's manipulative. She's very hard to know."
He also said wonderful things. You'd have to understand him to know what a compliment that all is. I think that, essentially, because he's not available to love me all his life, appropriately, he's made a choice to hate me. But it's the same thing.

Whatever happened to the sequel to that film?
They wrote a pretty good script, and I've been harassed to do a sequel. It should have been four years after the first.

Well, the third *Godfather* was what, seventeen years after the second?
Well, there's this nostalgia about gangsters and that period and a story that's ongoing. *Basic Instinct* was a thriller. What happened is that things that were happening in society and in the movie came together in this moment; I don't think that we are as a society like we were then. Things have so dra-matically changed since then. I don't think it's timely. Also, I had like a World Series–winning home run with that. I don't think there's any reason to take that away from my life, I'm happy with the win. [Stone changed her mind when she was offered $15 million to do the sequel, which will be re-leased next year.]

What ever happened to two other projects: *Manhattan Ghost Story* and a remake of *Bell, Book, and Candle*?
Manhattan Ghost Story I've been crazy about for ten years. Then they wanted Julia Roberts and somebody else, then it went to another studio . . . if they ever got it together and offered it to me, I would be delighted to do that movie. I have a real strong connection to the material. I have no interest in a remake of *Bell, Book, and Candle*.

You said about Hollywood that you can only fuck your way to the middle. For those at the bottom, isn't that called progress?
(*Laughs*) I suspect it is.

How seductive was Robert Evans in convincing you to do *Sliver*?
He's not seductive at all. In fact, I don't even know him. I did *Sliver* because Joe Ezsterhas wrote it, and because we had the same agent and my agent talked me into it. It had nothing to do with Bob Evans. Partway through the show Bob Evans asked me to come over to his office because he wanted me to have a better relationship with Billy Baldwin. I didn't get it with Billy Baldwin. Here's Bob Evans telling me that I should seduce Billy Baldwin, referencing this by telling me how he once seduced Ava Gardner. The whole time he's telling me this he had one of those milk carton boxes of malted milk balls, which are going all over the floor and banging into the walls, and I'm thinking, it's just miraculous that he's not in a padded cell. He's cuckoo for Cocoa Puffs. Is he alive or did he die?

Still producing movies.
He got married for five minutes, right?

Maybe the secret to longer marriages is what you do together. Do you and your husband work out together?
Oh God no. He goes where they bang things and play that horrible music. I can't get into that at all.

How do you keep in shape?
I do this thing called Pilates, which I love. Nick Nolte's trainer is the one who taught me in the beginning. It's wonderful, you work out laying down, which for me is like fabulous. I'd rather bathe than shower just so I can lay down. I'm pretty thin now.

Stallone said that exercise to you is three pieces of Dentyne.
Because he's such a health nut. I was like a marshmallow on toothpicks standing next to him. He's sweet. And funny! We have really a nice relationship.

Do you have any special diet?
I think I'm becoming a vegetarian again. I see that lately. Like I was making dinner last night and made my husband a pasta sauce with chicken and ugh, you know?

Are you a good cook?
I am a really good cook. But we have a really little kitchen right now with an ick electric stove, so it's hard to cook in there.

Tell me about the time you got hit by lightning.
I was seventeen. I was holding an iron, filling it with water, and our well got hit by lightning, and it came through the faucet. It lifted me like a giant had picked me up and thrown me. I hit the refrigerator and slid down. My mother was there, and she slapped me to straighten me out and then took me to the hospital. I had an EKG. There was so much electricity in my body after that.

My dad was putting a concrete floor in our garage and was troweling it off to finish it, and there was an electric pole with a light on it which got hit by lightning, and it hit him, burned him.

How many near-death experiences have you had?
A number of them.

What's the closest to death you've ever come?
(*Long pause*) There was the lightning thing. Then a horseback riding accident. I had a serious car accident after *Total Recall*, where a woman was driving the wrong way up Sunset Boulevard. I had meningitis when I was twenty-two—that was really unbelievable. I woke up and couldn't move from the waist down. Couldn't move. I was put in a quarantine hospital. I lost twelve pounds in the first four days. I'm probably on my sixth life by now. The time I contemplated death the most was when I had a stalker who threatened my life. That's a serious thing.

What kind of stalking was it: letters, phone calls, appearances?
One time it was letters that were postmarked increasingly closer and closer until they were hand-delivered. Then someone spoke to the person, but there are no laws about that sort of thing. Then I got another letter saying he knew it was me come to him in another form and he was coming to take me away where no one could find us. That's more frightening than death. A death threat, yeah, okay, you die. The other thing? No. That's a bad thing.

What happened to him?
I finally caused such a fucking scene! During the bad part of it is when O.J. killed Nicole. Because of that and the impact that it had on the world, I was able to get the police to wake up a little more. Fortunately, he was not an American citizen, so Interpol was incredibly cooperative, and he was deported.

What area of the world was he from?

Europe. And if he leaves his country, we get notified. Then I had a couple of other people who called—two guys who in their country were ex-military guys who wanted to start a Hollywood security system. Their concept was that they would scare a celebrity and then save that celebrity, and by that reference they would be able to start a company. Can you imagine that? We were able to track them through the international police because they would call and talk to my manager for a long time.

Have you ever sued anyone?

I've sued once and won. But there are others that I think about. If I was going to sue, there's a doctor I would put out of business. To sue someone is often a bad idea because it hurts you so much. I also think that these things that people do that are so wrong, it's a part of their learning process and their destiny. *Karma's* such a pop word, but there is a responsibility and a reaction to everything that you do. I don't think it requires my attention for that person to have a reaction to their bad behavior.

What was the suit you won?

I had a lawsuit with Harry Winston. He had given me this necklace to wear, to be my signature piece and therefore be representative to Harry Winston. I wore it on sixty-two television shows and interviews. A year later I had my assistant call so we could get some kind of paper so we could properly insure it [it was valued at $400,000], and we got a return call from a detective that I would be arrested if I didn't return it. It was like, huh? You know, when they lend you jewelry, someone brings it over, and if it's valuable, a security person goes with you, and then they pick it up that night or the next morning. They don't leave them laying around your house for a year. That's the only reason I sued. If they would have called and said, "We screwed up, we can't do it," or, "The person who did it didn't have the authority to do it," we could have had a conversation. But they had a policeman leave a message that they were going to arrest me. I said, no, we're not going to do that. That's a different story. That's like saying I'm a criminal. That's when you have to sue, because the person is giving you permanent damage to your reputation.

But didn't it hurt your reputation?

Well, the details are that they settled. I had them give the check directly to AMFAR. I didn't want anything from them, other than for them to get into reality. It turned out that they were selling part of their company or going public or something and you can't do that if you had outstanding. . . .

Who's the doctor you would like to sue?
He's a doctor who was very negligent with me. *Very* negligent. I don't want
to get into it, or I would sue. When people are unethical, it doesn't require
me to explain that to the destiny of their lives. That's who they are. That's a
character choice. We all make mistakes, and the measure of who you are as
an adult is what you do about the mistakes you make.

What major mistakes have you made?
I told off a former agent in front of his colleagues when I shouldn't have. It
was inappropriate behavior on my part, immature and unprofessional.

Did you apologize to him?
Oh yes, more than one time. Because I think the person is very special,
which was why I was so hurt and disappointed by his behavior.

Were you once strip-searched by Japanese customs officials?
I was strip-searched in New York coming back from Japan, body-searched in
Japan. We had a couple of undeclared things. The person I was with was carrying more than the amount of money he was supposed to carry—he was
Italian. I had a Cartier watch that was undeclared, and I kept the box because I was so excited that I had the watch and I didn't think about it. I was
twenty. Also, I had on a black Israeli paratrooper's jumpsuit and a black hat
that I had bought in a used clothing store in Paris, so I looked like a nut. We
just fit that profile.

Was it humiliating?
Frightening. It's not like I trust the legal system so much that I imagine that
I have to have something on me to end up having it on me. And I didn't re-
ally understand what was going on.

Among movie people you've met, who has most impressed you?
I was really impressed with John Huston. More than any other person I ever
met in the movie business. He was so loving to me. And very, very sexy. He
had a powerful charisma. I just met him on one occasion, before I was famous, and he signed his book to me. He wrote: "To Sharon, with high expectations for her future." I can't tell you—it was such an encouragement, it
was like out of control. When things were really bad, I'd look at it and
think, for whatever reason and whatever moment, he gave me that encouragement.

Who else signed their books to you?

Lauren Bacall. She's a handful. I had gone to see her in *His Girl Friday* in L.A. I bought the seats beside me so that nobody would talk to me, and I went by myself. Because I just thought she was *it*. Then I stood outside her dressing room door alone in the dark to get her to sign my book, and man, she didn't come out forever! She wasn't exactly warm when she signed my book and got in her car. But later I had the opportunity to meet her. In fact, she spoke for AMFAR and has been very helpful. When she didn't get the Oscar for *The Mirror Has Two Faces,* I lost it. We were making *Sphere,* and I watched it in my trailer, and I just cried hysterically. But I think she's tough, that she alienates people. But I have more fun when I run into her at events than almost anybody else. She's hilarious, and the stuff she says is true. I just think she's great.

Have you ever wanted to write a book?
People keep asking me to do one, but I just can't imagine doing it.

Are you a big reader?
I like to read, I read all the time. I like Evelyn Waugh. I love Camus. I love philosophy. I love Kierkegaard—*Fear and Trembling* is one of my favorite books. I read that book when I first got so famous, I was really looking for something and found it with that book.

How'd you find it?
I like to go late at night to Book Soup [in Los Angeles], and I said to one of the people there, "I'm having an existential crisis, I don't know how to better explain what's happening to me, and I need something to read because I'm really struggling." He recommended it to me.

When did you read García-Márquez's *One Hundred Years of Solitude?*
When it came out. I gave it to a lot of people who didn't really get it. I like Borges. Did you read the one about the existence of God? I just love that. Octavio Paz touched something in me, and I exchanged some faxes with him—we tried to meet before he died, but he was too sick. *The Tree Within* is the most incredibly beautiful thing. To read him you need silence and time, his paragraphs explode.

Any American writers move you in that way?
Of course I love Tennessee Williams and Hemingway's short stories. Truman Capote. When I was young, I liked Cheever. I think I'm more of a broad than a lady. I appreciate Fitzgerald, but it's not my thing. I'm not a Jane Austen gal. She doesn't stir me.

I'd think that a broad would like Elmore Leonard.
I do. And I also like Jim Thompson. Jim Harrison. I loved *Dalva*. And *A Woman Lit by Fireflies*. Mark Twain. I liked his book about Joan of Arc. I thought Saul Bellow's *More Die of Heartache* concept was kind of wonderful. I read all those Updike books and thought they were interesting at the time.

If Jodie Foster somehow decided she didn't want to play Clarice Starling again in *Hannibal*, Thomas Harris's sequel to *The Silence of the Lambs*, how fast would you jump to get that part?
Before they'd finish the sentence I would do it. Anthony Hopkins is a prince among men, aside from being a terrific actor. Just to be near him is such a joy. He's so kind. When I first went to the Oscars after *Basic Instinct*, which was a huge big deal for me, I walked past him, and this was just after he played that part, and he was so kind to me. I love when talented people are also good people.

In *Elle*, you said: "I love to be around people who, whatever they do, they're the best at it."
And that they love what they do.

Let's play "Best and Worst." What's your favorite quote?
Katharine Hepburn's quote on aging, which is: "Aging is like watching a car crash in slow motion." That's hilarious. I also like that quote from *Buckaroo Banzai*, which is, "Wherever you go, there you are."
    There's this Buddhist quote, where they didn't believe in life and death. This guy's son died, and he was crying. And his friend said, "If death is an illusion, then why are you crying?" He said, "Because the illusion of losing your son is the hardest illusion of all." That's so beautiful.

Favorite speech?
One that Teddy Roosevelt gave that I really liked. The one: "It's not the critic that counts."

Best shotgun?
Winchester always made really good guns. I had a Baretta pump that was pretty amazing. Before I gave them to the police.

After what happened in Littleton, Colorado, when two Columbine high school students opened fire on their fellow students?
Right.

You issued a press release saying: "One of the greatest things my father taught me was respect for my country and gratitude for the rights that we as Americans hold dear. My mother taught me the dignity of following my heart. Our world has changed and our children are in danger. I choose to surrender my right to bear arms in exchange for the peace of mind of doing the right thing." Did you get much attention from this?

I wasn't looking for publicity—I gave the press release to the police because it was a public action. I didn't want to impose my point of view on others, as much as I wanted to encourage others who share my point of view to do it as well.

And did anyone you know willingly give up their guns?

No. But someone should organize a day in every town to give up their guns. Make it July 5: Be Independent of Your Guns Day!

Were any of your guns valuable?

Some were. Mr. Glock visited me and gave me a bunch of guns, and made me engraved handmade guns. They were collectors' items: silver and Wild West scrawlings on the barrel.

Why didn't you give those to a museum instead of to be destroyed by the police?

Because they had my name engraved on them.

In the past, did you ever pull a gun on anyone?

Yeah, in my L.A. house. I had a circumstance where I had a guy outside the gate and I could see him on the security camera. He was cutting a hole in the gate. I called 911, and no one came. I called 911 again ten minutes later, and still no one came. And he started to climb the gate. He was up on the gate. I called 911 a third time, I said, "This muthafucka's on the gate." They were not particularly helpful. So I decided that I didn't want him to get on the property, because if he did, then I would have to shoot him, and I didn't want to have to shoot him. So I opened the front door and hit the button that opened the gate so it would swing with him on it. As it swung open, I pumped my shotgun and said, "I'm gonna blow your ass all over the street." And I heard him land when he jumped and his footsteps running off.

Were you scared at the time?

I was more angry than scared, that I wasn't getting help. It's not the first time that someone's tried to break into the house or come over the fence, but it made me mad.

Now that you've given up your guns, you can't chase anyone hanging on your fence as easily.
I'm not sure confronting a psycho going over your fence is the smartest thing to do anyway. I'd rather lock myself in the house than have guns in my life anymore. I still carry a short Louisville slugger bat and a taser in my car. The taser is a great thing, you only use it if someone is in contact distance—it knocks them down and provides you space to get away. But I'll tell you something, when I had my guns, I would hear noises in my house and I'd be afraid. Since I gave my guns away, I've been sleeping like a baby. Having guns doesn't inspire a sense of security.

Especially when you travel. What's your most memorable travel experience?
I love Paris. I've traveled so much, I'd really have to think about that.

Favorite hotel?
The Ritz, in Paris.

Worst hotel experience?
In Victoria Falls in Africa. They had shag carpet, and they didn't have a vacuum cleaner. They had this carpet for ten years, and they came in with a bucket of ammonia water and a rag and damp-ragged the shag carpeting. But they had ticks that would live in the carpet, so when you got out of the shower you had to put your see-through stained towel on the ground, walk three steps, spin the towel, walk some more, until you got to your shoes, because if you got bitten you would get tick-bite fever. It was pretty awful. This was right after their civil war—there was no import or export, nothing to eat, undiscovered land mines, no international phone system. And yet it wasn't quaint, rustic, or charming—it was scary.

Favorite restaurant?
Hmmm. Petrosian in New York.

Best beach?
In Mauritius, off the southern tip of Africa. The most beautiful thing I've ever seen. You can literally float with the current around the edge of the island twelve feet above the ocean floor and see every grain of sand.

Most exotic place?

When I was in Africa. It was so primitive in Victoria Falls, you could walk through the rain forest by yourself, see no one, no sidewalks, no lights, sit on the edge of the cliff, where you could see zillions of feet down, and have the thunder of the falls vibrate through your body, and you'd be soaking wet in the rain forest with rainbows all around you. And if you went there in a full moon, the moon made moonbows. Beautiful.

Most incomprehensible?

Prison.

Most depressing?

Pediatric AIDS ward.

Best designer?

Banana Republic.

Hair color?

A really good natural redhead on a woman.

Ice cream?

Seduto's French vanilla bean.

Dessert?

An absolutely fresh homemade chocolate éclair.

Do you make them?

No, or I'd be Sophie Tucker.

Who has the best legs?

Cyd Charisse.

Best smile?

Children.

Face?

Ava Gardner.

Body?

My husband.

The best kiss you've ever had?
My husband.

The best movie kisser?
Robert De Niro.

De Niro's not a guy who likes this interview process.
It's anxiety. When he took the time to hang out and talk with Phil, I really realized what a huge thing it was, and what a big statement of affection for me it was, because it's so hard for him.

When did this hanging out occur?
Recently. Quincy Jones's birthday is right after mine, and we're friends, so we spend birthday time together, and Bob came over in L.A.

Best sex stimulant?
Laughter.

Sex scene?
A scene that didn't have sex in it. The scene in *Witness* where Kelly McGinnis is washing and Harrison Ford is looking at her through the screen door.

A lot of people say the scene between Donald Sutherland and Julie Christie in *Don't Look Back*.
They say that was real sex.

Scariest moment in a movie?
I was frightened when I saw that John Malkovich–Clint Eastwood movie where Malkovich plays a guy who's going to kill the president *[In the Line of Fire.]* I was so frightened at one point during that movie that I literally thought I was going to have a heart attack. Something about his performance really hit me.

Your best movie?
It's yet to come, I hope.

But of the ones you've done?
Casino was a special thing, a dream come true for me to work with them. I don't have any rational sense of judgment about it. It was everything that I wanted to do, to work with Bob [De Niro]. Everything I studied and trained for, everything I addressed as an actor, was to work with him. That was my

goal. To work with Marty was almost inconceivable to me. It's beyond belief to me even still that it's a part of my life. Best movie? I don't know. Certainly my most astonishing experience.

What's your favorite movie?
The animated *Jungle Book*. When we started *Casino,* Marty asked me that question, and I told him, and he said he had a print, which I couldn't believe, because prints like that are in a vault in Tennessee, if you want to screen it, it's a big deal, because I've tried. I said, "If I do a really good job, can I have it?" Five months later we finish the movie, which was an arduous process, it kicked my ass playing that character, and at the end I came in my trailer and the film cans were stacked on my chair.

Favorite artist?
Between Max Ernst and Egon Schiele. I have a Schiele drawing and an Ernst triptych painting that's very beautiful. I have a very interesting collection.

Is that what you mainly collect?
Paintings, yes. And photographs. I have a couple of first edition books like Cocteau's *Opium*. I have a Cocteau drawing that's pretty nice too. Of the Nymph.

Favorite TV show?
I love *Homicide*. Love it. I love *The Sopranos*. *Oz* is too much for me. I really like *Chicago Hope*.

Any comedies?
I'll watch *Golden Girls*. And *Dharma and Greg,* she's delightful. I liked *Ellen*. I'm thinking of playing a gay girl in a comedy. You know the *If These Walls Could Talk* series? That they did about abortion? They're going to do it this year about pregnancy. I'm going to do one. Ellen DeGeneres will be my partner.

Your sister's involved in charity work. What do your two brothers do?
My older brother is an actor in commercials and is getting started doing movies. He's also a writer and wrote a good script he's shopping. My younger brother's a carpenter and a construction worker, a very sweet guy and an exceptional Mr. Field & Stream—fishing, hunting, loves to be in the woods.

Is Oliver Stone also your brother?
No. If Oliver Stone was my brother, I would have straightened him up by now (*laughs*). He's a brilliant man who could be much kinder to himself than he is.

Why do you think most little girls draw pubic hair on their Barbie dolls?
Because it's organically offensive to be made into that thing that a Barbie doll is. Because there's so much admiration for Barbie they want to make it more real.

Why is masturbation a sad thing for women?
I don't think it is.

You've said in the past it was lonely and sad.
That was about my character in *Sliver* and her masturbation. But I don't think that way.

Have any actors been violent with you?
Physically violent? Yes. A lot of times because I don't back down from guys who are expecting me to back down, they sometimes push because they don't know what else to do.

You're against the death penalty, but what about exceptions for people like Jeffrey Dahmer? Or the woman who drowned her two children in a car? That Russian serial killer? Or Milosevic?
You can't make it a movable line. To kill people as an example as to why you shouldn't kill people is stupid.

Two more questions: do blondes have more fun?
I feel better about myself when I'm a little blonder. I feel more fresh and up. There is kind of a lift, because it's the most light reflective color of hair, and having that light around your face gives you a lift.

Are people envious of you?
Sure, come on. I got to be tall and blond and a movie star. That's a lot to get in life.

THE CRITIC

GENE SISKEL AND ROGER EBERT

ON FEBRUARY 24, 1999, GENE SISKEL DIED from a brain tumor at the age of fifty-three, breaking up what was arguably the most famous public couple of the last two decades (Regis and Kathy Lee, Siegfried and Roy, and Mark McGuire and Sammy Sosa notwithstanding). The most influential critics this country has yet produced, Gene Siskel and Roger Ebert brought so much passion to their individual views of the movies that they became more known than most of the actors they critiqued. In a time when the average cost of making a major studio film is over $52 million and the average cost to market that film is $25 million, the importance of a trusted critic is to help balance the barrage of hype and blarney made possible by budgets like these. It seems appropriate that this book should end with a conversation with these two entertaining, erudite, and cantankerous adversaries, who always went at each other with vigor and humor. It's how we came to know them, and how I'd like to remember them.

It was a Wednesday morning in the winter of 1991, and Roger Ebert was late. Gene Siskel was already on the phone, not wanting to lose any time while waiting for Roger to arrive at the CBS building on North McClurg Street in Chicago, where they taped their *Siskel and Ebert* syndicated movie review show. When Ebert appeared, he walked into executive producer Larry Dieckhaus's office, glanced at the trade papers on a circular table, and mumbled something about Spike Lee's movie, *Mo' better blues,* which he had recently seen. "It could lose the ending totally. Spike got careless." Then Ebert talked about one of his passions, the laser disk and how he talked Siskel out of buying a THX Lucas system. "See, I'm late, but Gene isn't even here yet, is he?" he asked Dieckhaus. "Gene's been here," Dieckhaus calmly told him. "He's in makeup now."

Roger grabbed a forbidden muffin before going into makeup and popped it in his mouth. Both he and Gene were on diets—Roger because he needed to be; Gene because he didn't want to be "the balding *and* the fat guy."

Finally ready, the two men walked into studio 1, where they sat in movie chairs and got ready to challenge each other's opinions of five current movies. Running through the scripted portion of the show— text they'd previously written about the movies under discussion—Gene read Roger's line: ". . . *Mo' better blues* this week on *Siskel and Ebert*." "See the line above that?" Roger asked. "Says *Roger.* Doesn't that mean you're not supposed to read it?"

Roger adjusted his new glasses, but from the booth the producer told him that a white line around the rims showed on camera and asked him to switch back to his old ones. "Why can't I find a good pair of glasses?" Roger complained. Gene took Roger's glasses and tried them on. "God, they're like bottles," he said.

As they had done for the two decades their show had been on the air, they were both wearing sleeveless sweaters under their sports jackets. They released some of their energies (and hostilities) by playing "Peas Porridge Hot," clapping their hands and making contact with each other just before they were ready to roll.

On camera, Roger began previewing Walt Disney's *The Jungle Book* but floundered over Rudyard Kipling's first name. He did another take, this time blowing "Kipling." In the booth one of the crew members said, "This is what Gene usually does." Roger tried again, but this time his voice cracked and he asked for some hot water. "He *never* does this," his director said. Later, when Gene read and stumbled, Roger was quick to say, off-camera, "Where do you think I caught it?"

After both men faintly praised *The Jungle Book,* Roger said, "I guess I'd recommend it for what it is . . . rather than what it isn't." Off-camera, Gene remarked, "We'll leave that for Bertrand Russell to interpret."

As Roger began to give a thumbs-up review of a film called *The Unbelievable Truth,* his female producer in the booth said to their director, "Now I understand why Roger liked it—it reminded him of David Lynch. Talk about a major waste of time. Talk about amateurish acting."

So even this country's two most powerful movie critics could be contradicted by their own people. In America people have two jobs: their own and criticizing movies.

In less than an hour the show was recorded and they wouldn't have to face off for another week. But they would see each other. As their show gained in popularity, Siskel and Ebert became what some called the Laurel and Hardy of movie reviewers. They were invited to speak at various functions, and they were frequent guests on TV talk shows like David Letterman, Oprah Winfrey, and *The Tonight Show*. On this particular day they were scheduled to appear before a group of sixty media-wise high school juniors at Northwestern University.

When they arrived, they were told that these students weren't "journalists" but hoped to work in television. Roger immediately jumped on that. "If you want to go into TV," he said, "begin with print. Or you'll become the laughingstock of whatever small station you'll wind up in."

Siskel supported what Roger said. "Everything I want, I get by writing. I wrote a one-sentence job application. I wrote my marriage proposal."

Roger's advice to them was to write a letter to some editor every day of the week and to read newspapers and national publications. Gene said that he was never a letters-to-the-editor kind of person when he was young, but he strongly believed they should keep a diary. "Write one paragraph a day about anything." He pointed out that though they were mostly known for being on TV, it was writing sentences that helped them *speak* sentences. "You might be thinking, 'I don't want to go into TV news, I want to go into programming . . .'"

"Oh good," Roger quipped, "then just go for the lobotomy immediately."

Roger then got personal about how he rose to the top of his profession. "Nothing like being one of the highest-paid and most successful journalists, because when you're fat and can't see, there must be something you're good at."

To which Gene commented, "Nothing like cutting to the quick."

Having heard the stories of each other's lives so often they could speak for the other, they decided to do just that. Roger would tell Gene's story, and Gene would give them Roger's. But two sentences into Gene's life, Gene began to interrupt Roger to correct his hyperbole. Roger called Gene "Robocritic" because Gene often paced and constantly pointed his finger, as if he were a lawyer trying a case. When Roger said that if Gene were a trial lawyer he'd want his colleague to defend him if he committed a crime, Gene was quick to ask him what kind of crime Roger thought he was capable of committing.

"Probably murder," Roger said. "Unfortunately, after I'd committed it, you wouldn't be around to defend me."

When Gene began Roger's story, he talked about how extremely smart Roger was as a boy and how very secure he was in his view of the world. "As an only child, what he said was paid attention to." Roger added that he was the editor of his high school newspaper and president of his senior class. When Gene expressed some surprise at the thought that Roger might actually have been *popular* as a fat kid, Roger said, "I wasn't that fat when I was in high school. I was on the swimming team." It was an opening too wide for Gene to ignore. "Well, we know you could float," he said. The appreciative audience laughed. Siskel beamed.

Gene told the students that Roger was more interested in himself than Gene was in himself. "I'm more interested in the other person."

Roger differentiated their ways of thinking. "Gene's a vertical thinker, I'm a horizontal thinker. Gene narrows in, I'm more expansive." That's why it worked between them, Roger thought. But Gene wasn't so sure it was that clear-cut. To him their show succeeded because they rarely regarded the audience. "We regard each other as the audience. When our show is working right, the audience is eavesdropping on us."

"Gene and I are not part of each other's chemistry," Roger added. "We come whole. Complete. As if the other is superfluous. Our idea is to blow the other sonofabitch out of the water." He added that the other "copycat" review shows on TV didn't have what they did to make it work. *Sneak Previews* "tried to cast for chemistry, but they didn't get it." "They hung in there for a while," Gene said, "but they didn't have the goods."

Roger was asked to make the distinction between a critic and a reviewer. "A critic tells you what he thinks," Roger answered. "A reviewer tells you what you think."

Roger took exception to being linked in the public's mind with Siskel, but Gene said it didn't bother him. After a couple of hours telling stories, giving advice, and running each other down, Roger called for an audience vote: "Who likes me more than Gene?" A few hands went up. "Who likes Gene more?" A few other hands went up. "A lot of you didn't vote," Roger said. "I really want you to like me."

"Who do you think you know better?" Gene then asked. This time the vote was more for Siskel, which surprised him.

But what came out in this calling for votes was how truly competitive these two guys were. They had been competitive all their professional lives, each trying to outscoop the other for their respective Chicago papers, the *Sun-Times* (Ebert) and the *Tribune* (Siskel). They were two grown men, highly intelligent, at times quick-witted. Ebert had even received the Pulitzer Prize in 1975 for his film criticism, yet they could squawk and bicker over the pettiest matters. To them, however, nothing was petty, it *all* mattered. They were obsessed: with the movies, with themselves, with how they were perceived by others, with who was better, smarter, funnier. And they were forever reviewing their own performances.

When the meeting with the students concluded, Gene told them, "I'll never have a forum like our show in my life. It's fabulous." And he positively glowed when one of the students came up to him afterward and asked, "How can you stand working with Roger? He's so opinionated."

Not only was that the very reason Gene could stand working with Roger, but it was the reason their work was so watchable. Although Gene would often try to explain himself, Roger felt there was nothing to explain. Coming across as sure and all-knowing, he exhibited an arrogance that could annoy some and was pure enjoyment for others. And when the two disagreed—which wasn't as often as most people thought—it made for good television.

Roger Ebert, the shorter, fatter one, was born in 1942 in Urbana, Illinois. Gene Siskel, the taller, balding one, was born in 1946 in Chicago. Ebert was a precocious only child. Siskel had two older siblings, and after they were orphaned before he turned ten, they all went to live with their aunt, uncle, and three cousins. Ebert filled his imagination with books. Siskel filled his with numbers: he could multiply at four years of age and was doubling numbers up to one million soon after. By fifteen, Ebert had become a sports writer for a local newspaper and published a science-fiction fanzine called *Stymie*. Siskel attended a military academy his last two and a half years of high school and was so judgmental that he was constantly grading his own signature.

Ebert went to the University of Illinois, where he edited an alternative paper and then the college newspaper. He cofounded the Collegiate Press Service, which later evolved into the Liberation News Service, and joined the Campus Film Society, where he began his serious involvement with film. Siskel attended Yale, majoring in philosophy and planning to become a trial lawyer. His mentor was the novelist John Hersey, who advised him to never do anything for money, to have more than one career, and to hope for serenity rather than happiness in life.

Ebert went to graduate school at the University of Capetown in South Africa for a year and at the University of Chicago, but he never passed French or wrote his doctoral thesis on Dwight Macdonald, Edmund Wilson, and Paul Goodman. Siskel got a public affairs fellowship from the CORO Foundation and went to California to work on the state senate campaign of Dave Roberti, then joined the Army Reserve, where he got into journalism. In 1966, at twenty-four, Ebert became a general reporter at the *Chicago Sun-Times*. Siskel was twenty-three in 1969 when he joined the *Chicago Tribune* as a neighborhood news reporter. After becoming movie critics for their respective papers, Siskel also began reviewing movies for CBS's WBBM-TV, and Ebert for ABC's WLS-TV. Ebert also taught a film class at the University of Chicago extension division.

In 1975 the two were paired for the first time as battling film critics for public television's *Opening Soon at a Theater Near You*. That evolved into *Sneak Previews*. They went into commercial syndication in 1982 with Tribune Broadcasting and were called *At the Movies*. Three years later they moved to Buena Vista Television and became *Siskel and Ebert in the Movies*, then just *Siskel and Ebert*. It is estimated that they were seen in more than eight million homes weekly, and their thumbs were considered worth more than their combined body weights in gold if they went up rather than down for the movie under review.

Both critics' newspaper reviews were syndicated nationally (Ebert claimed to appear in over two hundred papers, Siskel in over seventy), and Ebert had his annual *Movie Home Companion* as well as a collection of movie-related essays (*A Kiss Is Still a Kiss*) and a journal of the Cannes Film Festival, *Two Weeks in the Midday Sun*.

Ebert is married and has homes in Chicago and in Michigan. Siskel was married with two daughters and lived in Chicago. When I first met with them in Los Angeles, they each warned me about the other. Ebert said that Siskel would never sit still, that he'd pace, make phone calls, point his finger at me every time he made a point, take forever to make that point, and be totally unable to tell a joke without blowing the punch line. Siskel said that Ebert would never ask me anything about myself, and that he would answer every question as if he were an absolute authority, even though the majority of his stories would be embellished. Sure enough, both men proved right. When you work as professional antagonists for so many years, you obviously pick up on the behavior of the other. Siskel never did sit still—he paced around the room as he pointed his finger and used two sentences where one would have done. As for jokes, he tried one and, yes, blew the punch line. Ebert did indeed speak with a sureness of his own convictions and never asked me about myself, though in Chicago he got points for bringing down a copy of my Huston book for me to sign.

In Chicago we talked individually and together in conference rooms, at restaurants, and at their homes. They were America's two most popular film critics, and among other things, I wanted to see whether they really did hate each other as much as they liked to make it appear on their show.

Do you think a lot of people who watch you think, these guys have got to be an act, they have to be each other's best friends?
EBERT: Anyone who would look at our show and would think that should get a brain transplant. You can't look at our show and think that.

Do you really dislike each other?
EBERT: Sometimes we do really dislike each other.
SISKEL: Sometimes we don't.
EBERT: And it differs from show to show, and sometimes during the show. On most shows we like each other. Sometimes during a show something will be said that will make some of the hairs on the back of the neck curl. And anybody can see when that happens and when it doesn't happen. It's not manufactured.
SISKEL: When people ask me, "What *is* your relationship like?" the best answer I can give is, it's what you see. If you see a little bit of dislike, there's probably a lot going on.
EBERT: In other words, it's probably *more* intense.

But in a sense, are you two like actors playing a part where you know you have to play the role of antagonist at times?
SISKEL: I'll tell you honestly that *nothing* like that is conscious.
EBERT: My nature is to be antagonistic at times, especially with Gene, who brings out the antagonistic in me.

Do you guys hang out at all when you're not doing the show?
EBERT: We have more or less decided that for the good of the show it's better for us to be apart except when we're doing the show. I don't *ever* discuss movies with Gene except on our show.
SISKEL: There's a very practical reason. I was told this at my newspaper a long time ago—"Write it, don't talk it." If we were to talk it out, it wouldn't be as good as it is on the air.

What's so hard about being a movie critic? Isn't it true that everyone has two jobs: their own and criticizing movies?

SISKEL: It's also said about sports writers. We're talking about popular culture, and people feel free enough to comment on it.

EBERT: Everyone who goes to see a movie certainly has an opinion about the movie. It's interesting: I would never think to question our music critic's review. But he wouldn't hesitate to come in and say, "I think you were wrong about the new Woody Allen picture." That's one of the intriguing things about movies is that they are a popular art form, so everybody feels equally competent to talk about them. And why not, as long as you're talking about your own reaction—which is all a critic really does.

Is what you do really work?

EBERT: Yeah. People may envy the job, but they don't realize you go to 400 movies a year and review 250 of them.

SISKEL: I think the job is cultural reporting, social commentary, art criticism. It's consumer information, consumer advocacy. We perform all of those functions. I want films to be better if I'm a moviegoer, and I think critics *really* want that and have the forum to help make them slightly better.

What qualities should a great critic have?

SISKEL: In criticism there is a certain rigor implied: having principles, holding to them, measuring what you're saying, trying to be accurate.

EBERT: A critic should be honest in expressing his own feelings, have a good background in his subject matter, have passion and love for the movies, be able to write clearly and entertainingly, and have a great deal of stamina.

How do you stack up to such criteria?

SISKEL: As a critic I think I try very hard to say exactly what I think. And in a medium in which we are well known for the binary thumbs-up and thumbs-down, I try to be able to give the mixed review. But most pictures fall into that middle ground, so I really wrestle over which way my thumb is going to turn. And how many stars I give, I care a lot about that. It's not flip.

EBERT: Gene's strongest point is, first of all, he's an extremely good, highly competent and skilled journalist. I actually respect Gene. He's always on the phone, and he usually knows things, like who's in town, when can I get to them, how can I do this without Roger finding out.

You praise his reporting. What about Gene as a critic?

EBERT: As a critic, to my way of thinking, he's lacking in enthusiasm. He's just a little bit too standoffish and cold about the movies, though he will give you a pretty good idea of what's in a movie. He's the critic from Missouri: you have to show him. He thinks the movie is going to be shit, and if it is, that just confirms his suspicions.

I go to the movies anticipating a good time. Gene goes fearing a bad time. And that is an insight into our basic personalities. My glass is half-full, his glass is half-empty. Gene is always trying to anticipate what will go wrong. I generally assume that things will go right. These are two fundamentally different personalities at work here, and they reflect themselves in our reviewing. Siskel: I've heard Roger say that before, and I don't believe it's true. I want movies to be good. I'd have to be a masochist to want them to be bad. But if you were to stop me any day and say, "Gene, do you expect to see a good movie or a bad movie today?" I would tell you I'm expecting to see a bad movie. The reason is because most of the movies I see are bad. I'm being practical in telling you that most of the things that people create aren't all that interesting, and that's too bad. What keeps me going is that I have a real strong desire to see something great. And when I see it, it lasts for a long time.

So what you're saying is, your pessimistic outlook isn't a weakness. What weaknesses do you think you have?
Siskel: Well, my scholarship in silent film is awful. I haven't seen them. Federico Fellini told me, "I've done nothing that Von Sternberg didn't do before. We directing now haven't made any major improvement since the silent era." That means that if I'm going to be a measurer and stand in judgment, then I have to have complete information. So I'm aware of the films I haven't seen, and that is a failing.

Since you're on record as seeing films you like many more times than once, why do that when you could be spending that time seeing movies you haven't seen?
Siskel: Well, I don't have a real good answer for that.

Okay, Roger, it's your turn.
Ebert: If you ask me for my weakness, I would say that if you look at the star ratings that I give to movies, I'm usually about a half a star too high. Gene will tell you that my greatest weakness is I get overenthusiastic. I'm a cheerleader. One of his favorite lines about me is that I bring my audience with me everywhere I go. Nobody laughs at my jokes more than I do.

Gene, on the other hand, doesn't tell jokes. I've only heard him try to tell a joke twice in fifteen years, and he blew the punch line both times. Gene is not a raconteur. After fifteen years on television, he still doesn't know how to talk economically. He rambles. Sometimes he gets very impatient, and then his language gets more and more terse and shorthand. At one point he was impatient with a Teleprompter operator who was showing him a piece of copy when he wanted to see another piece of copy. He kept saying, "Other, other." And the prompter operator then gave him a different piece of copy that was still not the right piece of copy. Gene came up with the classic line, "*Other* other." And everybody just broke down with laughter because that was so typical.

One of the big differences between Gene and myself is in the area of competence. Gene prides himself on being incompetent when it comes to anything technical. He actually becomes retrograde. No human being alive has had more trouble with computers than Gene Siskel.

Is it as bad as he says?
SISKEL: It's bad. Yes, I have never successfully programmed my VCR.
EBERT: He's never successfully installed his telephone answering machine either.
SISKEL: That's correct. And I still write with the same first little computer that I learned on. In addition to not having a natural facility for it, I think I also have a disinterest in it.
EBERT: What frustrates me is that Gene could make life so much easier for himself, and save himself so much trouble, if he would get himself a Macintosh computer. But he doesn't want to make the effort to save himself the effort.

What if you gave him that as a present?
EBERT: I'm not going to give him no Macintosh as a present!
SISKEL: Beautifully elegant sentence there.
EBERT: I think there's a streak of masochism in it. If you look at Gene real carefully, you'll find that he almost always finds a way to make things harder for himself while saying that it makes it easier. My instinct is generally, this is the plan, we've made it, let's stick to it. His instinct is, let's see how we can change it in such a way that we can steal from Peter to pay Paul, with both Peter and Paul being hours of sleep. The story of Gene's life, if you work with him over a period of fifteen years, is just a constant trail of computers that lost his file, malfunctioning machines, malfunctioning alarm clocks, late flights, delays, misunderstandings, bad communication, can't do what he said he'd do for you now because he's still behind on doing something else for somebody else. Everybody who works for him and with him is familiar with the telephone calls from everybody else he works with. Channel 2 is

always calling the *Tribune,* the *Tribune* is always calling *Siskel and Ebert, Siskel and Ebert* is always calling channel 2. Gene's wife, Marlene, who is a saint, deals with this by refusing to get involved with it.

SISKEL: For some reason, Roger has a need to prove to himself, and maybe to the rest of the world, that he is better than me not only as a film critic but as a human being in every single facet of his life imaginable. He's like a dog with a bone, and I'm the bone. If I were perchance to be better than Roger in some facet of life, it's simply because it's meaningless or trivial to Roger. And if he probably put his mind to it, he'd be better than me in that. If the person that he just described sounds like a total incompetent boob who would be lucky if he or she were ever employed by anyone, the contrary facts are that I've been employed by the *Chicago Tribune* for twenty-one years, by WBBM-TV, which he refers to as channel 2, for sixteen years, and have just been hired for a new job with *The CBS Morning News.* I've received offers from other people of significant stature recently. And do the show with Roger for fifteen years. I'm sure everybody has their method, but I think I'm a pretty good worker.

EBERT: We once did a press tour for the *Siskel and Ebert* show where we had eleven flights. An itinerary laboriously worked out, where we would go to many different cities. By the time we finished that trip, Gene had changed every flight. We had to change from Eastern to American to get from Dallas to Miami because Eastern wasn't a safe airline. Then we had to change from Delta to Eastern to get from Miami to New York because then we could get to New York earlier. I said, "How did Eastern suddenly get to be safe again?" He said, "Well, these airplanes hardly ever crash." "Well, then why did we have to change the other flight?" "Well, because everything being equal. . . . " I mean, he always has an answer.

SISKEL: Well, I would hope that if I did something I would have an answer, so I put a positive spin on that. I'll bet there weren't eleven flights. And I'll bet I didn't change all of the ones, no matter what the number was. Based on my history of Roger and numbers, I'd guess the number may be closer to seven, and the number that I changed probably was four.

All right, Gene, what are Roger's strengths and weaknesses?
SISKEL: I'm aware of the films that he has seen. He will do some shot-by-shot analysis of pictures; he does a course. I envy that because that helps him be a good critic. Roger is very good on story construction. He can break the story down with the genre. His other strength is that he's a beautiful writer. He writes first draft, and it's readable, printable. You have to rework my copy; I'm not a natural that way.

A weakness of his is sometimes he goes with the first draft too easily. His thinking is a little glib, a little sloppy. He isn't tight enough, rigorous enough on the pictures.

EBERT: I produce twice as much work as he does. He thinks of me as lazy because I make it easy for myself. He thinks of himself as a workaholic, but most of his workaholism consists of spinning his wheels. I review every major movie that opens for the *Sun-Times,* and I have a piece in every Sunday. He does little one-paragraph mini-reviews for the *Tribune,* and he has a piece in about once a month. Who works harder? I have a book that comes out. I've written four books. I've got a serial that I'm writing. I teach a film class at the University of Chicago. And yet he thinks that he works harder than I do. He gets very little done, but it takes him hours and hours to do it because he always puts it off. Somehow he thinks it means you're working harder if you arrange to work all night long. The question is not how hard you work but how much you produce, and I'm much more productive than he is. In terms of print for our newspapers, I write about five times as many words a year as he does.

SISKEL: Roger's a furious worker. He's an elegant worker. But compulsive. I do not view myself as a workaholic but as basically lazy. I don't have the greatest work habits. I'm not a natural, like him; I'm more of a plugger. I have a set of responsibilities that Roger doesn't have, and that's my family. It's the sustaining pleasure of my life. And if that means that I can't work as much as he, I'll take that deal anytime.

Who's smarter?

SISKEL: I think I'm a little bit more intellectually rigorous, and a little bit more circumspect. I'm not glib, as he can be. Which is why maybe I'm the better critic. I don't think I'm any smarter than him about movies. About one's self? I would say yes, and I don't say that with bravado or particular pleasure. About life? Probably not appreciably. And I suspect that Roger will say that he is smarter about each and every one of those things.

EBERT: People ask which one is the intellectual and which one is the populist. My answer is I've got him surrounded. I am *both* more intellectual than he is *and* more populist than he is. He is Mr. Middle of the Road. I teach. I go to film festivals. I'm on panels. I contribute to film magazines. He just grinds away with his little one-paragraphs at the *Tribune* talking about how sloppy I am.

SISKEL: Roger, lighten up. You've got a great mind—lean back, enjoy it. I'm no threat to you, big guy. You know, if it were true that I was as incompetent, malfunctioning, as pedestrian as you're claiming I am, I should be basically shot.

Before this turns into a duel, let's focus for a while on the movies. Why should we care about the movies?

SISKEL: For all kinds of reasons. They have the potential to be one of the most visceral art forms. And the most democratic, not having a pretense around them that they push people away. I think that everybody can easily get lost in them. Even if you go with your mate, you can have a private experience with a film. I feel like that I'm really covering the national dream beat. Also, they can tell us something about what's going on in the world. What we're thinking about and what we're afraid of. And the people who are the real artists are making their frames of film worthy of hanging in a gallery. I asked Martin Scorsese what would be a single image in his work that described a lot of what he felt. He pulled out *Raging Bull*, and the image that he came up with was in the title sequence right at the beginning. It is in the ring—it's misty and smoky, and De Niro is shadow-boxing, facing away from us—he felt that that was emblematic of the battle that people face in the bedroom, in the kitchen, in the workplace, in life. That image is as rich as a painting. We ought to revere film images that much.

EBERT: They're the only art form that really records the way people look, move, and speak in what approaches lifelike accuracy. Imagine what it would be like if we had movies from the Elizabethan period. Wouldn't you like to see a British war film from the Crimean War? Or an adventure set in India during the Raj? Five hundred years from now the fact that these movies exist is going to be so incredibly interesting to people.

SISKEL: Also, everyone that I talk to in all fields—music, TV, writing—they all want to make it in the movies. Writers get all gooey when their work is going to be made into a movie. They get silly. That's the big game. I learned that from Paul McCartney when I was the first to tell him that *Give My Regards to Broad Street* was an awful picture. He asked me, "What did you think?" Meeting Paul McCartney was very exciting for me, but I said, "Well, you never lied to us. I can't lie to you. I thought it was terrible, everything about it." He was shocked. He got very angry. He almost threw a glass of orange juice in my face. I said, "Look what you've done. So you made a bad movie." He said, "You don't understand. Inside of Paul McCartney there's a little boy that's me." I said, "Is it true that the movies are the biggest thing, even for you?" I mean, here's a guy who was in a great movie early on, and a pretty good one after that. He said, "Yeah."

Why are we all so starstruck?

EBERT: Robert Mitchum was being hounded by autograph hunters, and he said to his wife, "Why do they think I'm such a big deal?" And she answered, "Because they're smaller than your nostril." And that's it. We have this very,

very lifelike, voyeuristic, escapist experience involving these larger-than-life beautiful people who have been made up, photographed, costumed, scripted, and directed to look as attractive and interesting as possible. So of course they carry some of that aura around with them in everyday life.

Why do you think that stars always want to be liked?

EBERT: Think about it for a second. The impulse of the actor probably takes place at an early age, when they are taken to a performance and they notice that most of the people sit in a dark room and look at an illuminated stage upon which some of the people walk around and talk. Most people at that point immediately put themselves into the audience; some people say, gee, I want to be up there on the stage. What you are saying when you put yourself on the stage is: I am of worth and interest. I am interesting and intelligent and attractive enough that people should pay money to sit in the dark and look at me while I walk around here with the lights on me. Now, since that kind of egotism is fairly fragile, actors of course are insecure because they keep wondering if people will stop buying tickets. It's an industry legend that until the last year of his life Henry Fonda was afraid that he would never work again—that's how insecure he was.

What stars made you feel larger-than-life by just being with them?

SISKEL: On my thirtieth birthday, in 1976, Cary Grant invited me to join him in Palm Springs. He didn't know it was my birthday. I had done an interview with him for the paper over two days. And it was fabulous. *Fabulous.* That was probably as much fun as I've ever had on an interview. We talked about LSD and all the stuff. When it's really good like that, then you believe you're in the movie with them. He had a favorite Mexican restaurant, and he had a little too many margaritas, and we came back, and he put his arm around me. You feel debonair. You feel witty. Or you hear the piano and Cole Porter is playing. It's too much. John Wayne is the other one who had that effect on me. It has to do in part with what he represented, which was a *big* movie star when I was a little boy. When I interview actors who become stars when I'm an adult, it's not quite the same thing. It's a lot of fun to be in the presence of Jack Nicholson. He's bright and a great mind, but he would be sort of like an older brother compared to Wayne, who's sort of a father figure. I went with him to a café in Dallas, where he caused such a stir—the waitress crossed herself before serving him! He *was* big.

EBERT: John Wayne was the first big star I ever interviewed. It was in Fort Benning, Georgia, on the set of *The Green Berets.* Wayne came walking toward me in full battle gear in the hot, blazing Georgia sun, stuck out his hand,

and said, "John Wayne"—the two most superfluous words in the English language at that point. I visited his house in Newport Beach once, and he demonstrated all the rifles. He had a big rifle collection. "This is the carbine I used in *Stagecoach*. This is the piece of shit the Army's giving our boys to use in Vietnam. This is the rifle the commies are using to kill our boys; it's a much better rifle." He was a very funny guy, a master of the put-on. There was a British journalist there who was trying to get the angle that John Wayne was this right-wing Republican who was in favor of the Vietnam War. So he said, "What do you think about Nixon's conduct of the war?" Wayne looked at him and said, "I think that Nixon has conducted the war with honor, and there's only one thing better than honor: inner."

Robert Mitchum has also always seemed bigger-than-life to me. One thing I've noticed in being with him in situations—such as once in Pennsylvania where we got lost driving to a movie location (Mitchum was smoking pot the whole time), we went back and forth across the river several times, seeking help and guidance and aid from people like snowplow operators—is that everybody knows Mitch. I was in an elevator with him, coming down from his office in L.A. once. There was a woman in the elevator. She got in and saw who it was, and she couldn't look at him again. She just stared at his tie. When we got to the ground floor, as the door was opening, Mitchum said to her, "Thunderstruck, or just like the tie?"

Mitchum can be a very difficult interview. What is it about him that makes him worth the effort?
EBERT: An interview with Mitchum doesn't involve you asking him questions and him giving you an answer. It's about sharing some time with him while whatever happens, happens. He's the last guy alive who still deserves comparison with people like Bogart and Gable and Cagney. He's the last of the black-and-white film noir stars. He carries a weariness with him, a cynicism, a presence. There seems to be more to him; there seems to be a mystery to him. That's what you always got out of film noir, was the feeling that there was some question that these people wanted answered, but you didn't know what it was.

Who's been the easiest to talk with?
EBERT: Woody Allen is one of the easiest for me because he's so smart. Another one would be Mel Brooks, who is always on. If you talk to Mel Brooks for thirty minutes, you have thirty-five minutes of material. As far as conversation and good humor, the best in the business is Michael Caine. He is a true raconteur. He is *lots* of fun to be around. In terms of positive vibes in the room and good feeling, Dolly Parton actually has the aura that you

would associate with a faith healer. If you're in a room with her, you come out feeling better. I don't know how she does it, but I just walked out, and it was like I'd been strapped to an ozone machine. Oddly enough, on the plane flying back from Dallas with Gene, who had also interviewed her, he said the same thing.

SISKEL: Yeah, she's a delightful person. Another interview that I liked was Meryl Streep. I asked her on camera in a live television situation if she could teach me something about acting. I said, I'll say a line and you critique me. So I said, "I love you, Meryl," and she said, "All wrong." I said, why? She said, "Because when you said 'I love you' to me, you were thinking about how you were saying 'I love you.' You were presenting it to me. In a real acting situation, and in real life, if you're saying 'I love you' to someone, you're not thinking about how you're saying 'I love you.' In that moment you're thinking about one thing: do *they* love *you?* That's where the center of your energy should be. It should have been on me, and searching me to see if *I* love *you,* and not thinking about, as you were, how you were saying 'I love you.'" That little paradigm case is a great instruction about the nature of acting. I've told that to other actors, and they've said, you're not going to get better advice than that. That it is obviously seeking the truth of the moment.

EBERT: What she was giving Gene was essentially this Sandy Meisner technique, which is to say that the subject of every scene is the other person rather than yourself. The Method would center you in yourself; Meisner centered you on the other person. One of Gene's real strengths as an interviewer is telling people what he thinks. It's just amazing. When he had Tom Cruise on channel 2 in Chicago, he told Tom Cruise all about how he, Gene Siskel, felt the first time he met John Wayne. See, this is what the viewers want. I congratulated him. I said, "Gene, that was a fabulous interview Tom Cruise had with you, in which he was able to get you to talk about your relationship with John Wayne."

Speaking of Cruise—is he the biggest star today?

SISKEL: Right now Tom Cruise is just about as hot as anybody in the movie business. I saw it at the Oscars. With fifteen minutes to go, every big star was in, and no one moved because one star hadn't arrived. Everybody—the fans, the press, everyone—was waiting for one person. Everyone wanted to see Tom Cruise. It was fascinating to me. Their quiet was palpable. When I did that interview for TV, there were 150 people standing around watching him. It was crazy. I haven't seen anything like it in a long, long time.

EBERT: Tom Cruise is the biggest star in America today, but do we have to necessarily inflate him into the greatest actor in the history of motion pictures in order to get him onto the cover of a magazine? A lot of the hyperbole that you read in magazines is really addressed not at the reader but at the editor, to convince the editor that it deserves the kind of coverage you're giving it. I am utterly bored by celebrity interviews. Most celebrities are totally devoid of interest. Who wants to read a sixty-inch interview with Tom Cruise? I don't—and I write them! Life is too short to want to know about Bruce Willis. Have you read Shakespeare yet? Dickens? The bane of the celebrity interview is the Dreaded Hotel Room Interview. Sit in a hotel room for fifty minutes and talk to somebody. *Nothing is happening!* I love it when something happens.

One thing that is sad is the manipulation of the celebrity carrot to the press by press agents, where they offer you a celebrity under certain conditions. It has led to a situation where perfectly nice guys who can talk very easily to the press get hooked up with press agents who create so much ill will for them that in the end you wind up really having to make an effort not to resent it. I wonder sometimes why people hire bad press agents.

On the subject of Cruise and the younger generation of actors in their twenties, do you feel differently talking to stars who are twenty years younger than you?
EBERT: Oh yeah. The real movie stars are the ones that were movie stars before you were eighteen. The thing is who calls you "Mister" and who you call "Mister." Whenever I spoke to Mr. Wayne, or Mr. Mitchum, or Mr. Douglas, or Mr. Newman, or Mr. Scott, I was properly respectful. But when you're talking to guys like Tom, and Tom, and Tom (*laughs*)—the three Toms.

Do you call anybody "Mister" today?
EBERT: As a courtesy, until you're introduced or invited to call somebody by their first name, you do call them "Mister." I would say "Mr. Brando."
SISKEL: In writing letters requesting interviews, I usually use both names.
EBERT: Like "Dear Marlon Brando:"?
SISKEL: Yeah. I did that to Tom Cruise. "Dear Tom Cruise."
EBERT: I think the easiest way to solve it is, once again, just go back to good manners and say, "Dear Mr. Cruise." Obviously my manners are the best of anyone at this table. One peculiar thing for any American to do is to sound at all at ease in dealing with English titles. I once interviewed Alec Guinness. I can't call him "Mr. Guinness," and I can't call him "Alec." The correct form is "Sir Alec." Then, of course, Americans get all tangled up. "Good morning, Sir." It sounds like you're the waiter. And you don't say, "Good morning, Sir," to a Sir unless you *are* his servant.
SISKEL: With all respect to the British Empire, I would probably call him "Mr. Guinness."

EBERT: That's silly. You wouldn't go to Gerard Depardieu and call him "Mr. Depardieu." You'd call him "Monsieur Depardieu," wouldn't you?
SISKEL: No.
EBERT: How about "Signor Mastroianni"?
SISKEL: No, I probably wouldn't.
EBERT: "Mr. Mastroianni"?
SISKEL: It's no big deal.
EBERT: Would you go so far as to say "Pope Paul," or would it be "Mr. Paul"?
SISKEL: Jeez, this is boring.
EBERT: Who got boring on it instead of making a little anecdote out of it? I told a neat little story, and then you started droning away with your useless addendums and footnotes, which is always the case.

So, guys, besides each other, who's got the biggest ego in the movie business?
SISKEL: I'm sure it's like a sixty-way tie for first place. If you are used to being waited on hand and foot, and making as much money in one film as rich people make in their entire lifetime—not the average working man, but *rich* people—and if you are turned by the press into an instant expert on everything, and if your feet never touch the ground, or you never take the bus, and if you never went to college—and so many of them did not—although I suppose it could be argued that it's tougher making it in the acting profession than it is making it through college—well. . . .

Besides the pampering, can you name names?
SISKEL: It takes a lot of balls to make *Cannonball Run 2*—to have an audience that loves you for making the first one and then do a sequel where you know you're going to make money off of your fans and give them a race which is the height of the movie and is mostly animated, it was venal. It didn't care enough to do what anyone would want Burt Reynolds to do if they were going to see the picture. That takes a real big ego. My next candidate for a big ego would be George Segal. He's done good work, but I guess he couldn't handle the stardom.
EBERT: When you say, "Who has the biggest ego?" there's an implicit criticism. You're actually asking, who's the biggest asshole? I would say that the biggest ego of anyone I've spoken to in the movies belonged to Ingmar Bergman, but I would want that to be heard as praise. He has a very highly developed sense of self, of who he is, what he thinks, and what he cares about. He's one of the most impressive people I've ever met. We sat in a little cloistered cell almost, in his studio that he uses in Stockholm. It's the place that he goes to think. It had an army cot, a table, a chair, and an apple in it.

And a box of a special kind of Danish chocolate that he liked. This was a man who had really thought about things, really has something to say and knows how to say it. I was very impressed. Woody Allen has an extremely well-developed and healthy ego. This does not mean he's conceited; it doesn't mean he's insufferable. It just means that he takes himself seriously, and he should.

In terms of just dynamic energy and infectious enthusiasm, very few people are the match of Martin Scorsese. I gave him his first print review. It was his first film, his student film, *Who's That Knocking at My Door?* I said, "In ten years he'll be the American Fellini." Well, of course, that was wrong because there's nothing similar between Scorsese and Fellini. But he called me up, and he said, "Geez, do you think it's gonna take that long?"

Roger, have you ever talked to Woody Allen about his apparent obsession with Bergman?
EBERT: We've talked about it. It's not so much that Bergman had an influence on Allen as that Allen's own obsessions are similar to Bergman's obsessions. The most startling thing Allen ever told me was that not a day goes past when he doesn't seriously consider the possibility of suicide. I've always felt with Bergman that, for him, life is an option that is exercised daily.

Woody's as smart and as perceptive as anybody I've ever met. He once sent us a letter when he made *Zelig*—and I have a copy of this letter. Gene thinks I stole it from him, and he's right. "Dear Boys: As you know, in the past I have often suggested that you pick the scenes that you want to use on your show. But with *Zelig* I have decided after a lot of thought to have the policy that there are not going to be any television clips released for this movie. The movie is so hard to explain that I feel any television clip at all will be misleading. However, I recommend that you take any clips that you want from *Mommy Dearest* and identify them as being from *Zelig*, as this can only help me at the box office. Sincerely yours, Woody Allen."

Robert Duvall said that when an actor wants to learn about acting he goes to an acting teacher, not a critic. "Critics can't teach actors anything because they don't know anything about acting. So how can they judge films?"
EBERT: He's changed the subject in the middle of the sentence. I don't recommend that an actor learn about acting by going to a critic. I recommend that a potential moviegoer read about the movies by going to a critic. I don't think the people who make movies should read the criticisms. I'm not writing for the people in the movie; I'm writing for the people who might go to the movie. My job is not to be an actor, a director, a writer, an editor, a com-

poser, or a set decorator. My job is to be an ideal member of the audience. I might know more about being a member of the audience than Robert Duvall does.

SISKEL: I ripped Goldie Hawn real hard for *Bird on a Wire.* Saying, "She's forty-four years old, why is she playing dingbats?" Here's a woman who has executive-produced some of her own projects and is presumably a smart businesswoman. Why doesn't she honor herself, and women, and forty-four-year-olds? In a weird way, when I'm knocking her for acting infantile at age forty-four, I'm her best friend. I'm telling her something that few people will tell her. I'm paid to do that. She can think I'm awful, and she turned away from me at a party that we were both at, but I'm her best friend . . . because I love movies and because in some way I love what she *can* do. So don't reject the critic. The critic has something to say to you.

EBERT: I don't think that Gene really believes that. He believes it, but if he stopped to think about it, he's not writing for Goldie Hawn, he's writing for his readers. And he's speaking for his viewers.

SISKEL: You're right, I don't have her best interests at heart, but I have her public's interest at heart.

John Simon says, "Without criticism, the artist receives no serious answer." Does an artist need a serious answer?
EBERT: Some do, some don't. I still believe that the critic primarily writes for other people interested in the same art form. The proof of that is that much of the great criticism has been written about people who are already dead. Samuel Johnson was certainly not hoping to help Shakespeare when he did his edition of Shakespeare's plays. But what he was trying to do was bring Shakespeare's plays to his contemporaries and to reinterpret him. That's what a critic can do.

SISKEL: I think that it can be healthy.

Simon, though, often takes offense at what an actor looks like. He's been known to criticize Streisand because of her nose. Is that healthy criticism?
SISKEL: I'm one of his few defenders. I'm more favorably inclined intellectually toward that attitude than disinclined. Here's why. These actors use their bodies. They'll always tell you that's their instrument. Okay. If that instrument is distracting to you, I think you do have an obligation to report it.

But Barbra Streisand can't do anything about her nose.
SISKEL: We all know that they can do anything they want these days. You can cut down a nose.

You'd recommend an actress permanently alter her face so certain critics might like her better?

SISKEL: I believe that somebody can be physically cast wrong, yes. Will you subscribe to that? That's really the nut of what he's saying, and that's what I subscribe to: that somebody can be physically wrong for a part.

EBERT: His contention is that if we are being asked to pay money to look at someone, we have the right to say why we don't want to look at them. A certain amount of tact is necessary in cases like this. I don't think I would mention Streisand's nose in print any more than I would mention it to her in person. I generally feel that what makes people interesting is the spirit that shines through.

While we're talking about the physical, Gene, six years ago you told *Playboy* that Nastassja Kinski was the actress you'd most like to see naked. Roger refused to answer that question.

SISKEL: That's right. I couldn't believe that he would not answer that. He was not answering honestly, I know that.

EBERT: I was not being dishonest. Somewhere in Hollywood or France there's a woman who I might like to see with her clothes off. But why should I violate her privacy by mentioning her name in the pages of *Playboy*? She didn't ask for that kind of singling out, and it would be rude of me to do that. For me to say that I want to see actress X with her clothes off is a version of a dirty phone call. I might as well call her up and say, "I'd like to see you naked." When you say that you would like to see Nastassja Kinski nude, the fact that you would say that, what does it tell us about you? Doesn't it indicate a certain lack of civility or taste?

SISKEL: It depends. I have seen her nude in movies, and it was pleasing. If it was an issue for her, then she should have remained clothed.

EBERT: This is ironic because you are a movie critic, so you are supposed to be an expert viewer of the film. In making that statement, what you have done is you have completely forgotten that you were looking at a fiction film. All you were talking about is that you saw a particular woman take her clothes off, and she must have wanted to do it. So you're assuming that she, as Nastassja Kinski, wanted to take her clothes off so that you could look at her. Therefore, what you're doing is you're cutting through all the layers of fiction and all the layers of motivation, and you are essentially being a voyeur—which reinforces my point. It's bad manners to say things like that. If you could say that she played a character in the movie called *Exposed* who had a scene that you found quite erotic, then that would be a compliment to her as a professional actress. But for you to even forget to mention that at all is essentially showing your hand. This is sort of like the justification of the rapist: well, she seemed to enjoy herself. You're taking it totally out of context.

SISKEL: Actors use their voice, they use their bodies—they use all kinds of things.

EBERT: Certainly they do. There's nothing wrong with saying that somebody's sexy or attractive or sensuous. But when you start naming lists of people that you'd like to see naked, haven't you crossed some kind of a boundary in terms of behavior or taste?

SISKEL: I don't know that I was making such a list.

EBERT: Well, you were essentially asked for the number-one person on your list: who would you most like to see take off her clothes? And you eagerly volunteered the name of Nastassja Kinski.

SISKEL: And I enjoyed it. I don't think it's a big deal.

EBERT: You made it a big deal by saying that I was dishonest.

SISKEL: It could have been sloppy thinking.

EBERT: Okay, so I'll ask you this question: when you answered that question, was it good manners or bad manners for you to mention her?

SISKEL: Ah, I think I have pretty good manners generally.

EBERT: How would you like to read in the paper that somebody you never met would like to see a member of your family naked?

SISKEL: How about let's getting it real direct. Let's say someone said they wanted to see my wife naked, and I read that.

EBERT: How would you feel about it?

SISKEL: It wouldn't bother me.

EBERT: That's interesting. There was a time when nobody would have understood a remark like that and it would have been grounds for a duel. No gentleman would ever say publicly or privately that he wanted to see a lady naked, whatever he might have thought.

SISKEL: And you know what? I don't know that I'd want to return to that time. At some level, I suppose, I would feel a compliment toward her. I wouldn't be offended by it.

EBERT: That's *extremely* bad behavior. There's just been a general lowering of manners in our time. Can you imagine forty years ago any public figure being quoted on who they would like to see naked? Today it's just considered to be part of the fodder of celebrity journalism. Can you imagine anyone asking H. L. Mencken who he would like to see naked? Or George Bernard Shaw? Or H. G. Wells?

Is it bad behavior to look at a naked actress in the pages of a magazine?

EBERT: I think that one of the most ludicrous magazine features in America is *Playboy*'s "History of Sex in Cinema," which lovingly details, year after year, every last nipple and buttock that was seen for even the briefest flash on the screen. And has all these ludicrous montages of color pictures of somebody with a little pubic hair showing. It's partialism taken to a sick degree. It's obsession with part of the body as opposed to the whole person.

Now you're taking on the *Playboy* philosophy?
EBERT: I know what the *Playboy* philosophy is about. I don't think it's what Christie Hefner believes in. Let's say that actor X does allow part of his genitals to be glimpsed as he jumps out of bed. I'm not interested in seeing a freeze-frame of that moment in some kind of a fuzzy photograph in *Playboy* magazine.

Do you object to the centerfold as well?
EBERT: The erotic content of a photograph is different from the registering and coverage of every single glimpse in motion pictures. A *Playboy* centerfold might indeed be a celebration of the beauty of the human body. And since the Playmates at the time that they appear have no identity other than their exterior form, it can be seen almost in an abstract way. When I look at *Playboy*, I look at the centerfold first. So does everybody, I'm sure. It's like looking at a traffic accident: you can't help yourself. In the middle pages of this magazine a young woman has voluntarily posed for nude photographs. Women who pick up a copy of *Playboy* also look at the centerfold first. Not because it's erotic but because they're curious.

And couldn't one be curious about seeing an actor or actress without any clothes on in a love scene in a movie?
EBERT: The moment that an actor takes off his or her clothes, the movie changes from a fiction film into a documentary.
SISKEL: I remember something Spielberg told me about sex scenes. He feels that it's almost impossible to do a sex scene without the audience having the reaction, "Oh, that's what they look like."
EBERT: I am not arguing against nudity in the movies. All I'm saying is that acting has traditionally consisted of putting on costumes, not taking them off. Actors have traditionally been in the business of pretending to be somebody else other than themselves. Well, the moment that the actor completely unclothes, the actor abandons character and becomes self to some degree.

Unless you're that good of an actor. *The Emperor's New Clothes*. Or a foreign actor who is not also a celebrity.
SISKEL: This gets into some very practical matters. The reason that that doesn't happen to us, a Western audience, in [the Japanese film] *In the Realm*

of the Senses, which I loved, is because I don't know those people. As opposed to having a celebrity disrobe—"Oh, that's what they look like." So you notice the discoloration on Richard Gere's back or shoulder blade. He has a splotch of some kind. That's where it does become a little documentary. I guess I don't see [naming who I'd like to see naked] as a big deal. I certainly didn't intend it as a dehumanizing remark, robbing someone of their dignity. I just thought that it was another way for me to answer the question of who turns you on in the movies. For a long time both Roger and I have said that we thought Kinski to be extremely erotic.

As a matter of fact, wasn't she one of the rare times you agreed about something physical: that you both had a weakness for the sensual lower lip?
EBERT: The lower lip. Gene is a big fan of lower lips, and I am too. Rosanna Arquette has a wonderful lower lip.
SISKEL: Okay. With that remark, have you robbed her of her lip-ness?
EBERT: No, I haven't. I have not.

Is it all right, then, to discuss other parts of the anatomy besides full lower lips?
EBERT: Yes, Gene, why not make it specific? Describe to us your ideal of the perfect female body. Do you like big breasts? Little breasts? See, this is interesting. You won't answer that because you would find it embarrassing to answer that question.
SISKEL: No, you're telling me why I won't answer. I don't particularly think in terms of film that that has any real. . . .
EBERT: You're evading it.
SISKEL: No, I'm not evading it.
EBERT: You're getting very antsy now.
SISKEL: No, you're enjoying that I'm thinking that the subject is really not relevant to an interview about film. That's all.
EBERT: You have volunteered the name of somebody else. What is your taste? Instead of mentioning a name, why won't you describe your own taste in women, in the perfect female body?
SISKEL: You could argue very easily that if I answered the first question, which I answered with Kinski, then the answer to your question would fall right out of there.
EBERT: Oh, you like women who look like Nastassja Kinski.
SISKEL: Ipso facto.
EBERT: Nobody else, right?

SISKEL: Wait a second. You wanted to know what I like in the looks of a woman, and I'm telling you Nastassja Kinski comes about as close to perfection for me as anybody I have seen in the movies. If you know what her body looks like, you know the answer. That's my answer.

EBERT: See, he's very embarrassed by this.

SISKEL: I'm not embarrassed by it! I'm giving you an answer.

EBERT: You won't use words. What is it about her that you like?

SISKEL: It's obvious.

EBERT: What's obvious?

SISKEL: Every part of her body. You name the part, you've got the answer. I'm giving you a complete answer. How about you?

EBERT: I, by definition, won't answer that question.

SISKEL: Well, I have.

EBERT: Okay, good.

SISKEL: Now, on the question of taste, I've heard you scream out at screenings, "The movie gets four stars: three stars for her being in it, four stars if she removes clothing."

EBERT: I think that actually the first person to yell out such a thing at a screening was you.

SISKEL: No.

EBERT: See, you would never remember that.

SISKEL: No, you do that. That's your thing.

EBERT: Oh see, isn't that amazing. That is just a bald-faced mistruth. He does it constantly.

SISKEL: No, I don't.

EBERT: Yes, you do. He doesn't remember doing it, though, because he has selective amnesia. You can ask anybody on our staff if we don't both do that on occasion. I don't deny that I have occasionally said things like that at screenings because I don't deny that I have libidinous feelings. That I feel "lust in my heart," to quote another famous *Playboy* interview. I don't understand why Gene denies that he's ever said it at a screening.

SISKEL: I have not done what I said that you did. That is, specifically say, "Three stars for her being in the picture, and if she will remove clothing, four stars."

EBERT: Well, you're probably not funny enough to have thought of saying something like that. For years you have said *similar* things.

SISKEL: I might have said, "I'm in love." That's about as far as I go. But you've called out and said, "The most beautiful woman in the movies!" Do you know who you said that about?

EBERT: Yes, I do.

SISKEL: Do you want to reveal that?

EBERT: I don't know. Why don't you reveal it for us?

SISKEL: Daphne Zuniga.

EBERT: Daphne Zuniga. She is. People don't realize it because she's been photographed badly in many movies. There's a movie that was made that nobody ever saw called *Modern Girls*. Now, when I was saying that she was the
most beautiful woman in the movies, Mr. Siskel was agreeing with me.

SISKEL: I do not agree with that.

EBERT: But you felt that she was gorgeous.

SISKEL: Absolutely not. Roger, I want to tell you something. One of the
things that you do is that if you hold a strong position, you find it very, very
hard for someone to hold a counterposition. I am telling you that not then,
and not now, do I rank Daphne Zuniga as one of the most beautiful women
in the movies. I know that you feel that way, and I don't hold it against you,
I just don't share that.

EBERT: I have also gone on record—now, this is a sore point between us—as
having great admiration for Katherine Harrold. And once when we were doing our show and we were reviewing a horror film that she starred in, in
which I thought she was very effective, Gene accused me of having this feeling and said, "Instead of reviewing her movie, why don't you ask her to dinner?" Later I received a letter in the mail from Katherine Harrold saying that
she had seen the show and was very flattered, and the next time I was in New
York we should have dinner together. I asked Gene if he had sent me this letter as a joke, and he said yes. It was only two years later that I found out he
had *not* sent me the letter (*both laugh*).

SISKEL: You believed me.

EBERT: Oh yes, of course I did.

SISKEL: I was very clever, I guess.

EBERT: It turns out that Katherine Harrold thinks I was extremely rude because I never answered her letter. Because Siskel told me that it was from
him.

Would you have gone out with her?

SISKEL: Of course he would have!

EBERT: Sure.

**Well, this certainly has been an entertaining insight into the minds of
what *Spy* magazine considers the two most powerful movie critics in
America. Do you accept that?**

EBERT: According to a scale which is completely contrived. It can only really
be appreciated as a joke.

SISKEL: I think it's pretty obvious that we have the most power right now. Our names carry a greater endorsement than other names. But the way that they went about arriving at it I don't think made a lot of sense. The fact is that we have the largest audience of people who are interested in the movies watching us for our opinions right now.

So how come *Spy* magazine says Gene's the most important critic and Roger's second?

EBERT: Well, first, that was all tongue-in-cheek, their entire criteria for judgment was completely silly and goofy—which everyone will agree to. In other words, the article is completely meaningless as a real value to anyone's influence. Secondly, what they're measuring is not necessarily flattering. They're really giving you your power not on the basis of your circulation or your influence, but on the basis of how much your opinions have corresponded to the box-office performance of movies. Gene gave *Batman* a favorable review, and I didn't like it. Therefore, he got millions of dollars of extra points in the *Spy* category system. But if you really look at it, he can't count the *Tribune* at all. He's not their critic, Dave Kehr is. I have two hundred papers, he has—what? Sixty-five? I don't know. I just took the *L.A. Daily News* away from him two weeks ago. He's got *The CBS Morning News,* but he doesn't review movies for them. Where does he review? Only on our show and for channel 2, the third-rated news in Chicago. Channel 7 is the number-one rated news in Chicago. Nevertheless, Gene wanted to win. I don't care really, except I do care, because he always manages to manipulate these guys. He gets some writer from *Spy* magazine and talks to this guy until the guy will do anything to make him stop talking. Gene's telephone conversations are famous for being endless. Anybody who's engaged in negotiations with him finally tells him things like, "I'll do anything you want if you'll just stop calling me." It must be said that Gene lobbied furiously to win, and that I would have placed first if it hadn't been for Gene's telephone calls to that publication.

SISKEL: Now I think I've figured out what the trigger may have been for Roger's wild overstatement of everything about me. The thing that's been bothering him was that *Spy* magazine thing.

EBERT: What Gene can't figure out is that, despite all of his efforts, I always seem to wind up on top. I'm smarter, funnier, I'm a better writer, I'm a better talker, I'm better on television. It's just astonishing. For all of his efforts. Now, I'm sure that Gene would be happy to tell you that he's smarter, that he's a better critic, that he's better on television.

Gene, how much power do you feel you wield?

SISKEL: I must say, because of the *Spy* magazine and people are now bringing it up to me, I'm a little bit more aware of it than I have been in the past. I live in Chicago, I work in Chicago. I don't travel that much, so I'm not in the media centers of the country where I would hear more about my power. So I haven't been all that aware of it. I guess that we can sell some considerable amount of tickets, and possibly prevent as many people from going. I got a lot of reinforcement for my power out at the Oscars this past year. When I go out to L.A., I get treated pretty well by these people, and that's why I should get home real quick. I don't need any more power, and I don't need any more money. I don't need any more fame. And I know who's really big, and I'm not.

You two have been parodied in the media and in movies like *Hollywood Shuffle, Summer School, Will Vinton's Claymation Festival, Back to the Beach, Amazon Women on the Moon*. What do you think of these parodies?
EBERT: Well, the most amazing parody, the one that had Gene and myself picking our jaws up off the floor, was Danny Thomas and Bob Hope doing us on *The Bob Hope Special*. I mean, when you grow up with Bob Hope, it's like if we were to look up at Mount Rushmore and there were two more guys up there, and it was Siskel and Ebert. Bob Hope and Danny Thomas! It was just . . .
SISKEL: . . . shocking.
EBERT: It was stupendous! It was amazing. So that was a high point. Another personal landmark for both of us was being satirized in *Mad* magazine, because we grew up with it. You know you've arrived when *Mad* magazine does a parody of you.
SISKEL: I don't like crossword puzzles in the paper. I always thought, what do you end up with?
EBERT: With it all filled in! It's empty, and now it's full. It's like what God did with the universe (*laughs*).
SISKEL: I know it's the process of testing yourself. Anyway, whereas I used to completely flip over crossword puzzles, I will now fairly regularly scan to see if I'm either a clue or an answer. And we are regularly clues and answers.
EBERT: And it's usually me. You know why? I'm the answer because "Ebert" has two *e*'s. It's a fabulous name for a crossword puzzle.

How much of a landmark was it when you first appeared on *The Tonight Show* with Johnny Carson?
EBERT: Johnny Carson comes under the rule of People Who Were Stars When You Were Eighteen. I would have to be on the Carson show a great many times before I would get over the shock of being interviewed on the Carson show by Johnny Carson.

SISKEL: When we're behind the curtain for one of these things, particularly with the Carson show, which was again a big thing because when you were a kid you watched it, we will often say we should be watching the show, or "here's where you get punished." When I saw him walk through the door—it was a jaw drop for me.

EBERT: Before I saw Johnny, I saw Ed McMahon and Doc Severinsen, and my knees were already jelly. Then the band started to play: *dah-dat dah-dah-dah*. I was thinking, *get me outta here!* We were so frightened. There's even a picture of us holding on to each other. I was saying, "Gene, we're a couple of midwestern boys who belong back in the Midwest." There was no way that we belonged on the Johnny Carson show. We were way out of our depth.

Did you call him Johnny or Mr. Carson?

SISKEL: I didn't call him anything.

EBERT: I didn't call him Johnny.

SISKEL: I did all of the hick things in connection with that show. I took a picture sitting in Johnny's chair after the show was over. I took a picture with my daughter sitting in Johnny's chair and my wife and I as the guests. I took home one of Carson's cue cards of one of his jokes.

Since everything between you is so overly analyzed, how are you feeling right now about each other?

EBERT: It's just maddening sometimes to work with him. And I think that he probably is kind of tired of working with me on occasion too.

SISKEL: I've felt estranged from Roger in the last month or two. On our sliding scale of getting along or not getting along, I feel we've been drifting apart a little bit.

Like it or not, you two are linked like Siamese twins. What are your gut feelings about being known as "Siskbert"?

EBERT: I do everything that I can to do things that I do by myself. I'm very proud of the things that I do as Roger Ebert. I really, really, *really* resent references that seem to link us together as two halves of one opinion. And I am at pains to suggest that the *Siskel and Ebert* program is something that I do once a week with Gene, and I come to the show as a complete entity and interact with him for half an hour. But the two of us are not in any way, shape, or form a critical team. The other thing that pisses me off is that a lot of people seem to think I'm Siskel, and Siskel claims that *nobody* ever thinks that he's Ebert. I think he's lying; I think he does it to push my buttons. I think he must occasionally be called Ebert by somebody. People call me Siskel at least half of the time. It's the deal with the devil: "The good news is, I'm going to make you famous. The bad news is, nobody will know who you are." At least with Martin and Lewis you always knew which one was Martin and which one was Lewis.

SISKEL: It doesn't bother me if somebody calls me Ebert. What's fascinating to me is that that would mean something to him. That a perfect stranger didn't know his name? Or got confused? These are not issues to be annoyed over. I feel I'm secure in my own identity as a critic and don't try to reach a middle position with Roger at any time. At the same time I recognize that the power that I've been given to act independently and have a resonance, and to be sought out for opinion, is due not entirely, and not even halfly, if you will, to the fact that we work together.

Do you think that I would be sitting here talking to you if you were not together?

SISKEL: No, you wouldn't be. I think I have a real good fix on what the situation is. And there are instances where we do come together on an issue, where we do have very similar attitudes, such as violence directed at women, colorization, the A-rating, stereotyping in the movies, the televisionization of movies. . . .

EBERT: Letter-boxing . . .

SISKEL: To do those shows, obviously, we have to reach an understanding. We have to say, yes, that's an issue for both of us. It doesn't in any way diminish me if people view me as part of a program. It's *enhanced* me. And every week I separate myself out from him; I have no problem with that.

EBERT: One of the things that gets me is we're usually quoted as "Two Thumbs Up!" I liked it better before we had the thumbs. Then at least you were allowed to have an opinion, like, "I enjoyed this movie," or, "A hilarious film." It's almost as if the two of us are little jack-in-the-boxes, and all we can say is, "Two Thumbs Up!" "Two Thumbs Up!—Siskel and Ebert."

Do you pay much attention to your names quoted in ads?

EBERT: I don't care about whether I'm quoted in ads. I don't read the ads to see if I'm quoted or not.

SISKEL: I don't have to ever see my name in an ad again. It's embarrassing. When I saw the size of type that they used in *Die Hard 2,* I thought (*gulp*).

How often do you feel ambivalent about giving a film a thumbs up or down?

EBERT: We have plenty of reviews that are somewhere around the middle. You just have to kind of jump one way or the other because of this idiotic business of only being able to vote thumbs up or thumbs down. I'd like to give a sideways thumb occasionally.

What are your opinions about some of the other TV reviewers, like Gene Shalit, Joel Siegel, Leonard Maltin?

SISKEL: Gene Shalit is well known for having a punning vocabulary; Joel Siegel engages in a lot of alliteration. As a writer, I just think that those things are kind of false. I prefer the more direct speech pattern and writing style. Leonard Maltin has a good sense of film history and is an asset to that program.

EBERT: I'm not interested in giving my opinions on them. Leonard Maltin is a good friend of mine, and his book is quite useful.

Who are the critics that have most influenced you?

SISKEL: I'm of the age that Pauline Kael and Andrew Sarris had a big influence on my life. Kael with her enthusiasm and attention to detail, and finding the relevant detail to illustrate the point. And Sarris for his Americanization of the auteur theory and giving these film directors their due as artists and as authors. Of the people who are working now, they're the ones who have to get the lion's share of the credit.

EBERT: I've always been a big fan of Pauline Kael's. I like Stanley Kaufman, Manny Farber. I don't read other critics for their opinions, I read them for their style and for what they see in a movie. Dwight Macdonald's film column in *Esquire* was the first contact that I had with serious first-person film criticism. He became one of my heroes, along with Edmund Wilson. I don't read Gene's reviews because I don't want to know anything about his opinion of a movie before we tape the show. We tape live on tape. Unless somebody completely screws up, the entire show is first draft. You're watching it as it happens. So I don't want to know what he's likely to say, what he's said before, what he might say again. Only very rarely has he said something that has changed, affected, or influenced my mind. I suppose over the last fifteen years we have both said something that the other guy had to concede was a good point. But in the heat of battle it doesn't usually happen that way.

Would you say that you've learned anything from each other?

EBERT: The whole idea of visual analysis of a film is something he has picked up from me. The notion of how the left and the right are different, the top and bottom, foreground and background. The notion of the strong axis. These are basic cinematic rules of thumb. The place in a composition where an object seems to be most at rest is just to the right of center on the so-called strong axis, or "golden mean," as Renaissance painters called it. You can look at any painting, and you will find that it is organized with the strength on the axis, like that door and that window on the two panes behind you. Or it's moved off the axis to create tension. What directors do is

they frequently put the person in authority in a scene on the strong axis, so
that they will even take a hero and move him off to the left if they want him
to seem more vulnerable. The left is more negative, the right is more positive. Movement to the right is more positive, movement to the left is more
negative. Diagonal movements or compositions tend to want to escape the
screen. Horizontal and vertical compositions tend to want to remain at rest.
Movement toward the camera is aggressive, movement away from the camera is recessive. The camera moving toward something is aggressive, the camera pulling away is disinvolving. Closer shots are more subjective, longer
shots are more objective—both in terms of distance and in terms of dura-
tion. Things in the foreground have dominance over things in the background. Things at the top are heavier than things at the bottom. Movement
is always dominant over things at rest, which is why the director can get you
to see something small in the back of the screen if it's moving, instead of
looking at something large in the front of the screen that isn't moving.
Many of these notions are known instinctively by people. It's not like a director sits there directing his movie with a textbook open. I first got turned on
to looking at movies in those terms by talking to a man in Chicago named
John West, who is now director of cinema in the Chicago City College system. There are books you can read, like *Understanding Movies* by Louis Gian-
netti, or *Art and Visual Perception* by Rudolph Arnheim. So I started talking
about movies in this way, and this was a new thing for Gene.

SISKEL: (*Laughs out loud*) Let the paper record "raucous laughter." You know,
it never had occurred to me until I met Roger—he said sarcastically—that visual material would ever be a way of discussing the medium of film. I know
that Roger has one of the biggest egos in the world, generated out of massive
insecurities obviously. Until tonight, I didn't realize how massive and how
insecure.

Is there anything you've learned from him?
SISKEL: Let me think (*pauses*).

I'll let the record show there was a forty-second pause.
SISKEL: Roger has a real interest in matters technical and technological. I
have to give him credit for being more on top of something like laser disks
than I was.

What do you feel you've taught Roger?
SISKEL: Roger didn't know the three-part rubric for judging acting, which
George C. Scott gave me. And that is: (1) Who dominates, the character or
the actor? (2) What choices do you make as an actor, fresh choices or famil-

iar ones? (3) While remaining in character and coming up with fresh choices, can you do all that and give the audience a joyous performance? So, I passed that on to Roger.

Did Scott tell you who he felt met his rubric?
SISKEL: He said, "Cagney was the best." And it's true. There is that joy that he had of entertaining. You can measure actors on each of those scales how well they do. Burt Reynolds is lousy on numbers one and two—he doesn't make interesting choices—but look at number three, joy of performing. His needle goes way wide.

Have studios or directors ever given you scripts to read?
EBERT: I won't read them. I have a form letter. A film critic is the last predator in the food chain. He should review the movie after it's made; he shouldn't be rewriting it before it's been sold.

Dwight Macdonald decided to stop being a film critic when he felt that "as the years go by one has already reviewed, under another title, almost every new film one sees." Have either of you gotten close to that point yet?
EBERT: There's never been a point where I've been bored with the job, but I've always felt there has to be a finite length of time that I want to make it my business to process every major commercial movie in the world every year. The fact is that eventually you do feel that you've seen a lot of films before. I have in my *Movie Home Companion* a section called "Glossary of Movie Terms." We did a show based on some of the things in there, such as The Fallacy of the Talking Killer. If you're seeing your first James Bond movie, you're not so apt to pick up on the fact that the Bond villain inevitably talks when he should be pulling the trigger. But in every single Bond movie, every single villain says, "Ah ha! Mr. Bond. I now have you under my control. You are my archenemy; I am going to kill you. But before I kill you, I'm going to show you my entire layout here, tell you all of my secret plans, invite you to dinner, and allow you to seduce my mistress, who will then give you the keys to the dungeon so that you can blow up everything." Every Bond movie would be over already if the villain had done what he was supposed to do when he was supposed to do it, which is pull the trigger.

Then there's The Fruit Cart. Sophisticated moviegoers all over the country now realize that whenever you have a chase sequence in a foreign or exotic locale, one of the cars will sooner or later inevitably topple a fruit cart. All of the melons will roll into the street, and the enraged peddler will jump out into the street and shake his fist at the retreating automobile.

SISKEL: I'm still as enthusiastic about movies as I was twenty-one years ago. The good ones will let you run through bad ones for a long time. When I saw a picture like *Do the Right Thing*, I was still going to see it a year later. That picture had about five months of active life in my head. *Die Hard 2* was another. I sat there enthralled.

You often bring up *Do the Right Thing*, Gene. What is it about that film that so captivated you?

SISKEL: I particularly was impressed with it in the year that *Driving Miss Daisy*, a film allegedly about racial issues, would be the most celebrated film of the year. It's like I wanted to say, no no no no; look over here, and you'll see a beautifully made film, and a film that's much more real. *New York* magazine ran a cover story saying, "Race Is the Issue." They were referring to the mayoral campaign of David Dinkins and Ed Koch. I believe that statement, "Race is the issue," applies to all of America at all times. Race is really the issue, and we will be judged on how we handle the racial issue in this country. This is the picture that, to me, best reflected and illuminated the racial conflict in America. Better than any other picture I've seen. So here's a picture that handles a major issue in a first-class way and is visually and stylistically first-rate, classic filmmaking. It had a rich musical score, beautiful art direction, sweeping camera movements, bold, crisp dialogue. I think he told the truth, and he told it in a poetic fashion. Like, here's what happens, here's how the hottest day of the year boils over. And right now, the temperature in America is ninety-eight in a lot of neighborhoods. It's like he just handed people a book of what can happen and of how things happen.

EBERT: I really started the *Do the Right Thing* bandwagon on our show. I saw it at the Cannes Film Festival and wrote two pieces about it before Gene ever saw it.

Well, rather than repeating what you do on your show, let's talk about the show itself. What's kept it fresh over the years?

EBERT: The fact that we have not gotten bored with doing it, and because we are still highly attuned to each other's opinions. If he disagrees with me, I take it personally, and vice versa. We are still so competitive. We know how to push each other's buttons in such a way that there is a real feeling of risk when we're taping. For both of us.

How much pleasure do you each get from seeing the other guy sweat?

EBERT: If it's real sweat, no pleasure at all. We both enjoy putting the other guy on the spot. But in situations where we're both on the spot, neither one of us enjoys it.

SISKEL: We're in a profession where a lot of people don't lay themselves out and confront competition. Journalists will crap on each other in bars, in restaurants, to their bosses, to their colleagues—but they won't face their competition in any real way. We do, and you've got to learn from that.

Had you guys known each other before you first started doing this?

SISKEL: No. We really hadn't had any extended discussion.

EBERT: We had had no meaningful conversation on any subject.

SISKEL: We just sort of glancingly observed each other. The fact is that there was only one guy who could really hurt me in my profession other than myself, and that was Roger, because he could beat me on a story. Or write a better review.

And how much tension was there?

SISKEL: There was tremendous tension.

EBERT: Oh, unbelievable.

SISKEL: We were going after the same audience every day in Chicago. It was a slugfest at every level. We were point men in a very visible column on a very visible beat. It was important if I had an interview or a scoop on a story—anything—it was terribly important. And that built up over years and years. I started in '69, and we started in the fall of '75. So for six years, day to day. And now we're going to sit down together? Wow! Again, fear. What if he blows me off the screen? What if I say something wrong? Roger is the guy that I feared the most.

Who structured the show?

EBERT: Our producer, who put us in the balcony. She devised the basic set. She told me, "Don't think of it as a camera. Just think of somebody that's watching the show, and talk to them." So I said, okay, I'm going to talk to Mr. Dudak—he was my landlord on Burling Street. Gene was always on me for that.

SISKEL: I used to say that I recently got a call from Mr. and Mrs. Dudak, and they both said they preferred me, even though Roger was speaking to them.

EBERT: Today, if I look back on tapes of the early shows, I find it startling that Gene and I agreed to work with a trained dog. And I find it even more startling that we later agreed to substitute a trained skunk. When we were on *Sneak Previews,* we had the Dog of the Week, and then when we went to *Tribune,* we couldn't use a dog anymore. We could use ourselves, we could use the balcony, we could use the screen. What was distinctive about the show, what they might sue us about, was the goddamned dog. So we got a skunk for the Skunk of the Week. And the animal trainer wanted to give us a turkey vulture for the Turkey of the Week. It would perch on Gene's head or something—I don't know. I feel that something basic and fundamental inside of me has changed in such a way that I could never again work on television with a dog or a skunk. And even at the time Gene and I used to ask each other, "Do you think Pauline Kael would appear on television with a trained animal?"

Can you critique your show?
SISKEL: I have routinely asked directors and people in television what they would do to improve our show. I've asked Warren Beatty and Steven Spielberg. Both of them said that they would spend more time on a movie. I think we should do that. I would like to see a show devoted to one film. I think we ought to do a documentary on how we come to an opinion of a film. We did it about ten years ago, and we ought to do it again. I think we could spend a little more time on detailed analysis. Let the argument go on a little longer, not make it so snappy. Let it get uncomfortable, let it get a little more like life. Not maybe as glib. I think it could be very dramatic, and also real in a way that I'd like to break through some of the forced congeniality and assuredness of television. Everybody's in control at all moments, so there's something wrong with you if you're not in control. Well, there's not something wrong with you if you're not in control.
EBERT: Maybe I should be a little harder on movies, and maybe Gene should be a little easier on them. I probably have an excess of enthusiasm, and he has a paucity of enthusiasm. Sometimes we're criticized for not dealing in high-level, in-depth film criticism. And that's true; we are not a high-level, in-depth film criticism show. This is two people talking about the movies. But we have a lot of younger viewers who watch the show, and it seems to me that what we're telling them every week for half an hour is that there are standards and that it is your job to make up your own mind about what you think about a movie. It's okay to have an opinion; it's okay to disagree with someone. There's more than one way to look at a movie. We try to alert people to clichés and repetitious stuff and recycled ideas and themes. This is good because it sinks in over a period of time.
SISKEL: Another influence is that people realize, through our show, that people who are critics love the subject that they cover, not hate it.

Do you think most people are watching you because of your opinions or because of the potential for watching two people argue with each other on television?
EBERT: We don't argue that much.
SISKEL: And we don't disagree to be disagreeable. We probably agree 70 percent of the time.

EBERT: A lot of our discussions are based upon mutual enjoyment of sharing things about a movie that we've both seen and observed. We rarely get really angry at each other. When we do get indignant, we're often both indignant at a third party, such as the people who perpetrated some piece of shit that we had to sit through this week. The notion that the show is about Gene and myself doing a Punch and Judy act is not perceptive.

I'll tell you where I think people get that idea: there's hardly any disagreement or any real conversation on television. In the early days of television there were open-ended talk shows with people like David Susskind, Irv Kupcinet, and others, where people who disagreed with each other came on the air and fought. Then for a long time that disappeared, and there was all this blandness. Now you have some confrontational stuff on TV, especially on some of the cable stations. But still basically it's very rare for anyone on a polite show to express disagreement.

How powerful a medium is TV?
EBERT: I don't think television is as influential as people think it is. It is basically watched by people who see it very passively and are not really moved to action by what they see. I know that occasionally Siskel and I have been able to influence the fortunes of movies. Usually we don't have much influence on the big movies; either they're going to succeed or fail on their own. But little movies that depend upon word of mouth, I think that our show works like word of mouth. Siskel and myself talking to each other are like you talking to a friend about a movie.

Is seeing a movie on TV still a movie?
SISKEL: No, you're seeing television when you watch a movie on TV, not a movie. The thing that is so wonderful about film and made such a big impression on me as a kid is the scale. You know all the theories: you enter the dreamlike state; the light comes from behind your head; you surrender to the image; you're pulled around like in a dream. It's just the opposite of home video, where you're, in effect, the projectionist. You run the movie, you control the light level.
EBERT: The bigger the screen, the better the sound, the better the experience.
SISKEL: The shoe-box theaters really hurt the movies. Younger audiences see movies as basically enlarged TV, so they really won't demand that the movies be that much different than TV. They won't know the difference, and it will all fall into the main slop-bucket of entertainment.

How would you change the movies if you could?
SISKEL: I would have the studios dedicate money out of their receipts so that one-half of 1 percent of the gross, or one-tenth of 1 percent of the gross,

goes toward film preservation and film education. I would put in an education and preservation tax on the movies. And toward reestablishing a writing workshop within the studio. I'd try and slow down the scriptwriting process, to come to the set on the first day of shooting with a completed script. A lot of pictures that I see are not even half-baked, they're an eighth-baked. They don't have a second act, let alone a third act. They just have an idea for a film. They get a couple of stars to sign on, and they're gone. I'd like "mo' better" programming at film societies on college campuses. I would like bigger screens and better sound. As the screen size shrinks, so does the imagination of the people who are going to fill that screen. We're demanding increasingly less from our movies because they don't look or sound like that much of a big deal. They don't dwarf us or dominate us or rush over us. They're the rowdy neighbor, they're not the mystical, magical stranger.

EBERT: The people who don't love films are frequently the people that run the studios because they have gotten to a point where the pressure is so intense and so unreal at that big-money level to perform and to produce that they want to hit one out of the ballpark every time. They don't have the attention, they don't have the space on their desk to make room for a smaller picture, an independent picture, a roll of the dice with some kid who might have something that he could offer. So they spend it on big pictures that, in many cases, they feel quite cynical about. And eventually they become cynical themselves.

SISKEL: An exception was Tom Pollack at Universal. He did take the risk on a $6 million or $7 million picture. It was *Do the Right Thing* and Spike Lee.

EBERT: He took another risk on *The Last Temptation of Christ.*

SISKEL: Yeah. So this guy is a real hero. He deserves recognition.

20th Century Fox, which put out Russ Meyer's *Beyond the Valley of the Dolls*, which you wrote, Roger, isn't very high on your worthy list, is it?
EBERT: Fox just wants to disassociate themselves from that film. I mean, any studio that would make *The Adventures of Ford Fairlane* and doesn't want to acknowledge *Beyond the Valley of the Dolls* is badly confused. *Ford Fairlane* is a failed attempt to deal with some of the same material in *Beyond the Valley of the Dolls*, which is a camp rock-and-roll horror exploitation musical. Still, it's the movie that won't die. It could be as successful as *The Rocky Horror Picture Show* if Fox got behind it and showed it at midnight here and there.

How much did you get paid for that?
EBERT: $15,000. Pretty good in 1969. I've written about five or six screenplays for Russ altogether. *Beneath the Valley of the Ultra Vixens* was the only other one produced. He's got a screenplay that he's trying to sell right now that I wrote

in 1976 called *Up the Valley of the Beyond*. Only now there's a conflict issue involved. The way I handled it was to never review any other Russ Meyer movies after *Vixens*. Then, as I became a national film critic, I got out of the screenplay business altogether. I don't believe that a film critic has any business having his screenplays on the desks at the studios.

What do you like about Russ Meyer and his films?
EBERT: We share a lot of the same sense of humor and the same imagination. They're outrageous, melodramatic cliff-hangers. He's an extremely original director. His work will last and be interesting in the next century once the issues of sex have stopped obscuring what he's really doing, because he's not really making sex films at all.
SISKEL: No, you don't eliminate the sex angle in Russ Meyer. You look directly at it. Russ's distinguishing trait that's a positive is that he puts a lot of joy in sex on the screen, and that's healthy and fun. In the seventies he got sort of a violent turn in some of those sex romps, and I didn't care for that.

Well, Gene, here's your chance: want to review Roger's movie?
SISKEL: I haven't seen *Beyond the Valley of the Dolls* in twenty years. I thought it was gratuitously violent. And it didn't make me laugh. Somebody sticks a gun in somebody's mouth, and it kind of linked sex and violence in a not particularly healthy way. I thought it was distasteful. That was my reaction to it. I gave it a very negative review. I gave it one star.
EBERT: I think it was pretty sensational. Even today it plays like gangbusters.

Well, Gene's entitled to his opinion, Roger. At least you've got your Pulitzer. What did that mean to you?
EBERT: It relieved me a great deal, because two years earlier Ron Powers, the *Sun-Times* TV critic, won the Pulitzer. So I spent twenty-four months in suicidal depression before I won it myself. They say that when you win the Pulitzer you get a real short résumé. I don't bring up my Pulitzer on the show very often because I'm sure it's constantly on Gene's mind.

Gene, are you envious?
SISKEL: Of course. I would have loved to have won one. My editors entered me a number of times, and I didn't win. At the time Roger won his, we were in such a binary competition that it hurt.

Gene, Roger has said in the past that your greatest flaw is circumspection bordering on paranoia.

SISKEL: For the first time he's hit on an interesting category. I think he *lacks* circumspection. I think that a person who is so full of himself that he doesn't see that maybe he's entertaining a party at which the guests have left, physically and intellectually, that's a flaw for him. I know I'm circumspect. My mind is of the bent where I try to get what I think is the right answer.

Bob Strauss wrote about you guys in the *L.A. Daily News*. He said that your points of reference are widely dissimilar. "Ebert's enthusiasm is piqued by the technical aspects of film and analytical criticism, while Siskel seems to look at things in more philosophical, emotionally informed terms."
SISKEL: I don't know how tight that sentence holds up under scrutiny. We tend to think philosophical is intellectual, and we tend to think that emotional isn't. So it seems to be giving me a lot of ground there.
EBERT: It is an astonishing statement because I think that almost anybody would agree that I am more emotional than Siskel. I would say that all of the terms that he uses would describe me. And that Gene is more box-office-oriented and more oriented toward the efficiency of a movie in terms of the way it accomplishes its task.
SISKEL: Look at the different answers here. I defended Roger for having emotions, and I took a compliment aimed at me and parsed the sentence. And what does Roger do? He takes it as an insult to himself. There's a real juicy one right there for you.

All right, let's not hold back. Just how low has your relationship gotten?
SISKEL: I'll tell you one of the lows of the relationship. Fortunately, it was off-camera. We were doing *Saturday Night Live* for the first time. We were both pretty scared. It was live television. The rehearsal had gone badly. We had never worked off of cue cards. We were blowing it left and right. It was just humiliating. Then it came time to cut lines. We got into a situation where Roger was counting lines and saying, "You have more lines than I do." I began belching nervously. We were hostile, and we felt we were both going to go down in flames. We did the show, and we did okay. We never worked with a cue card again when we did the show.
EBERT: The key thing you have to remember about Gene is that in situations involving fear, his defense mechanism involves anger. Before live audiences he becomes extremely rigid and abrupt. We were in a room with a typewriter, and Gene began to grow concerned that the cuts would involve a diminishing of his role. I tried to start counting words, to prove to him that this was

not the case. He went ballistic. So that by the time that we went out on the air we were both complete basket cases.

SISKEL: What about your behavior during any of this? You described my behavior, but what about your own?

EBERT: I was the one with the typewriter who had been writing the script. Gene was stalking around dictating. I just couldn't reason with him. It happened again on *The Arsenio Hall Show.* Gene was told by some functionary what we were supposed to do at the beginning. Later the executive producer gave us different instructions. When I tried to inform Gene, he said that he already knew exactly what he was supposed to do. Then, when I tried to say, no, Gene, it's been changed, he said, "Very well, do whatever you want," and he clammed up. This is what he often does. He gets very rigid in a situation like that. Then once he gets on the air, he relaxes. What happens is there's enormous tension before we go out, which leaves me uptight, and once we get on the air he's relaxed. My way to deal with this is to have no contact with him whatsoever until we go out to do such a show. I absolutely don't want to see him or talk to him, because then I won't get any of the bad vibes.

SISKEL: It's interesting how he describes things in terms of what I did, but I don't get a feeling of . . .

EBERT: In the case of *The Arsenio Hall Show,* all I tried to do, in a placating and reasonable way, was to say, Gene, they've tried to tell us to do something a little bit differently than you think. And you wouldn't listen. Then we went out there, and we blew it because you didn't know what you were supposed to be doing. I was not angry. Our producer, their producer, and me were all three unsuccessful in getting you to listen because you went rigid.

SISKEL: I don't remember that. I don't. I think Roger gets more nervous than I do on live television.

EBERT: The way that it seems to work is that Gene gets extremely nervous in the green room and expresses it in an aggressive way that affects me in such a way that by the time we go on the air, he's gotten rid of all his aggression and I've got it. So that it works best for me if we don't have any contact at all before we go out.

SISKEL: I would agree. It's better, just like on our show, for us not to be in contact with each other.

Is there an all-time low for each of you?

SISKEL: He would think it would probably be the card game on an airplane. I would say it would probably be an episode involving going to an airport with a car. He taught me a game—it was a rummy game. It involved a discard pile and meld pile. As soon as he taught me the game, I began beating him on it regularly. At one point he felt that I had discarded something when, because of the little plastic tables that they have on an airplane, I just conveniently put something down. It became such a big deal with him. He starts raising his voice: "I'm never playing with you again!" and he throws the seat up. I was in shock. The stakes we're playing were pennies. That was an all-time low because it was so trivial.

In the car on the way to the plane, Roger wants to get to the airport real early. I don't like to waste my time sitting in an airport, so I get there at what most people would think of as late. We were at the studio, and I thought we could do some more work in a staff meeting rather than go to the airport and sit there eating peanuts or having a club soda at the bar. Just as a precaution, I called the airport and found out that the plane was delayed, so that gives us fifteen more minutes. He wouldn't hear of it. When I wanted to keep the meeting going, he got very upset and was verbally abusive. And I don't personally handle getting angry or being yelled at very well. I don't like it.

EBERT: Gene has switched so many signals on me that all he has to do is suggest that something be different and I get mad. I'll give you an example. We were once on the Letterman show. Letterman said, "We'll give you a limousine, and we'll bring you from LaGuardia to Rockefeller Center. We'll tape the show, and we'll take you back to the airport." This is fine with me. Gene is immediately thinking, "Maybe I could go to this art gallery while I'm here." So he gets upstairs at the Letterman show and says, "Can you arrange another limousine?" They say yes. We go back downstairs. The original limousine is still waiting. The second limousine has not arrived. Gene gets into it and tells the driver to take him to the art gallery. I'm standing in the middle of the street trying to block the limousine and saying, "Look, I didn't change any plans. I want to go to the airport. You're the guy who changed your plans, wait for your limousine." Gene's response to that was to roll up the electric windows and tell the guy to drive off. The second limousine never arrives, and I took a taxi to the airport.

Did you confront Gene about it later?

EBERT: Oh God, I'm still talking about it now, and that was eight years ago! Oh, I talk to him. He will not respond. He just goes into the stone-face routine. Gene's response to criticism is silence and deafness. Gene has often said that when we get mad, I explode and he implodes. The madder I am, the louder I get; the madder he is, the quieter he gets.

SISKEL: (*Laughs*) Jesus Christ! My recollection is that I had a limited amount of time to get where I was going. I had been told to take that limousine, and they were ordering another limousine for Roger. There was time for him to make it to the airport. I think that's a fact that was left out. The only way I was going to get to where I was going to go was if I left right then and there. I felt under duress, because he was getting angry. When he gets angry, it can be very unpleasant. It's easier to cave in when he throws a tantrum. At that point I just didn't feel like caving in. I wasn't gleeful when I did it. I felt badly doing it. I guess that day I felt I'd had enough of being bullied. Roger's had people give in to him all his life. He's a tyrant all the time, with everybody. I'm one of the few people in this world that can stand up to him, and that must frustrate him terribly. *Terribly.* The story is interesting in that you're dealing with someone who always got his way, and with someone who grew up in a big family and didn't always get his way. I think I'm the sibling that he never had. I know that. The best definition that I've seen of our relationship is that it's a sibling rivalry and we both think we're the smarter older brother.

EBERT: The all-time low was the famous fight over a coin toss that led to just unbelievable unhappiness and verbal anger. It had to do with who was going to lead a certain special show, who would talk first. I wanted to talk second, you see, because the first guy introduces the show; it's the second guy who sets up the show. Now, the show was my idea, and I wanted to explain to people what it was about. So we flipped a coin, and Gene won the toss. So I said, "Okay, you go first." He said, "No, I get to choose. I choose to go second." I said, "That isn't fair. We were tossing over who was going to go first. You won the toss, you have to go first." Gene says, "How can I be said to have won anything if, as a result of having won, I have to do what you tell me? Obviously, as the winner I should get a choice." Well, this led to an extremely angry confrontation because, of course, eventually I had to blurt out, "I want to go second because it was my idea." And it just went on and on. If Gene had lost that coin toss, Gene would have said, "Oh, too bad; I go second." He was just being that much more manipulative than I was being. By his way of doing it, he got his choice. We didn't toss over anything. He wins, he gets his choice. He loses, he has to go second—which is what he wanted. You understand? Because Gene had made these private rules in his mind, he couldn't lose.

SISKEL: Again, the portrait of me is just absolutely horrible. I mean, I am an ogre of immense dimension. You would have to have such a low opinion of someone that you could pull off what he is accusing me of attempting to pull off. It flabbergasts my mind. Isn't it interesting that the guy who views me as Machiavellian is *truly* being Machiavellian? It's sort of traditional that the person who wins the coin toss gets to pick what they want to do. He had a buried agenda; I didn't. Again, this is the syndrome of the only child, who always got his way and always wants to get his way. I think Roger's got some big problems. As a newspaperman, I'm telling you, you've got a good story on the psychosis of Roger Ebert, and I would say, run with it. As I read it, the guy is extremely frustrated that he doesn't win all the time.

EBERT: You've talked to both of us for hours and hours: which of us do you think has a greater need to always be right?

To be diplomatic about this, I would say that perhaps Gene wants to be right more, but that you think you are right more. You don't have the need to be right.

EBERT: I have more innate confidence in the fact that I am right. I just assume I'm right, partially out of conviction and partially as a pose, because it drives him up the wall.

After all these years, Roger, do you feel that your own character starts to change to outmaneuver him?

EBERT: Yeah. I think that I was a much more trusting and sweeter guy earlier on. I always feel that Gene is thinking of the angle, so I have to think of the angle too. And I always feel like I lose. He always gets the angle on me. He gets the limousine, he wins the toss.

But you got the Pulitzer Prize.

EBERT: Yeah. That's the only consolation I have.

And he gets *Spy* magazine.

EBERT: Well, he manipulated *Spy* magazine.

Before we start that again, let's go back to your childhoods and see if we can get to the bottom of all this bickering.

EBERT: Maybe in Gene's life he had too many people tell him when to shut up. A lot of his behavior may come out of military school.

Hold on. Let's do this systematically. So, Gene, was it military school then?

SISKEL: I went to Culver Military Academy for my last two and a half years of secondary school. I was doing so-so in high school, and my parents thought that I could do better, so they sent me to private school.

When you say your parents, it was really your aunt and uncle, wasn't it?

SISKEL: My parents died when I was very young. My father died of a heart attack when I was four, and my mother died of cancer when I was nine. The three of us were taken in by my aunt and uncle, and I grew up with them since 1955. I refer to them as my mother and father, and I refer to my first cousins as brothers and sisters. It's really a story of being saved. It's always been the most beautiful act that I've ever been witness to.

You were probably too young to have many memories of your father, but do you remember being told of your mother's death?
SISKEL: I was told, apparently, while I was watching a baseball game—and I denied it. It didn't register. I thought she was still alive significantly after she was dead. I couldn't handle it obviously. I used to pray for her to get better, after she was dead.

Since this interview is mainly concentrating on the relationship between you and Roger and your relationship to the movies, let's focus on how the movies influenced your childhood.
SISKEL: I would walk eight blocks to the theater every Saturday with my friends. A big theater. A Mediterranean-themed palace with lighthouses and twinkling stars in the sky. Red velvet all over the joint. One picture that made an impression on me was *A Star Is Born* with Judy Garland. I remember the colors were richer than I had seen before. I also remember it was adult and there were problems. I remember being taken to a drive-in to see *A Streetcar Named Desire.* I remember being in the backseat and hearing people yell and scream. I grew up in a very happy home and didn't hear that. The movies, there was something potent there. It was adult. That's what movies meant to me, plus one other thing: admission was a quarter, and I was given two quarters so I could buy my refreshments. This was the first time in my life where I was really turned loose. Even though the movies were adult, I was as much of an adult as I could be at seven, eight, nine years old going to the theater. I could choose my food. I wasn't served by my parents, the selection was mine. There was a little delicatessen next door to the theater, plus the candy in the theater. You had your choices. There was exotic food. There was a sour tomato that one kid in our gang liked. I couldn't go near it. But it was exotic, and that's what the movies were.

    I saw *Peter Pan* six or seven weeks in a row there. We'd go back every week. *Song of the South.* So they were adult and magical and totally unlike TV. For instance, *Lady and the Tramp.* It was a big deal for me when I saw it in 1954. I suppose most boys think that they're the Tramp and they want to have Lady. The movie with the strongest emotional pull of my youth, and it has to do with my psychological history, was *Dumbo.* The separation of the mother was terrifying to me. And also the flying of Dumbo. It was like my whole ego was riding right on his trunk when he had to fly and believe in that mouse. I felt I had big ears and I feel most people feel they have big ears somewhere stashed in their life.

EBERT: With me, my whole life centered around the Princess Theater on Main Street in Urbana. It was nine cents, and you got a double feature, color cartoons, a newsreel, a serial, the coming attractions, the advertisements, and, twice a year, Dan Dan the Yo-Yo Man came and had a yo-yo contest. You could win a Schwinn bicycle. I wanted to be a yo-yo professional.

Your father also died when you were young, didn't he?
EBERT: He died of lung cancer in 1960 when I was a freshman in college. He had been an electrician at the University of Illinois, and my mother, who died three years ago, was a bookkeeper. Two weeks before my father died I won the Associated Press sportswriting contest for the state of Illinois. Because he knew that I won that, that award is really more important to me than winning the Pulitzer Prize.

Is Gene correct in saying you were a spoiled, pampered child?
EBERT: I had what can only be described as a very happy midwestern child- hood. I was a little overachiever. I have been a natural writer from the time I could write. I wasn't any good at sports, and I sat around the house all the time reading. I went to Boys Nation when I went to high school and was elected Secretary of State. I won the Power for Peace essay contest and got to take the train to Chicago in 1959 and shake hands with Richard Nixon. But in no time at all I became left-wing and in college joined the Students for a Democratic Society. My membership card was signed by Tom Hayden. I gave him a dollar, and he put it in the pocket of his flannel shirt.

Was it in college where you began to get seriously interested in film?
EBERT: Yes, there was a film critic at the university who seemed to know everything about the movies, and I was very impressed by him. We used to have long conversations. And there was the Campus Film Society. That's where I did all of my basic filmgoing, everything from *The Maltese Falcon* to *Ikiru*.

How different are movies today as compared to when you were both kids?
EBERT: When I went to movies as a teenager, we went to see what adults did. Now adults go to the movies to see what teenagers do. People over the age of twenty-one hardly ever make love in the movies anymore. They sit around and tell the kids they shouldn't be doing it. It's amazing. And today the best American directors are not trying to make great movies, they're trying to make successful movies. Today you couldn't get *2001* made; you couldn't get *Taxi Driver* made—it doesn't have *enough* violence, and it has the wrong kind

of violence. It's not escapist violence, it's introspective, meaningful violence. Even *Raging Bull,* it's the best film of the eighties, but you couldn't get it made today. It didn't make much money, and it never gets good ratings on TV.

There's also a decline in foreign films. What are the differences between American and foreign films?

EBERT: American films are about story; foreign films are about character. Foreign films will follow a character wherever he goes; American films will take the character wherever he is needed.

How important is the Cannes Film Festival?

EBERT: In Europe it's extremely important, because it's the launching pad for the summer movies. And it's also the most prestigious award that a film can win outside of the Academy Awards. It's broadcast live every night on every national television network in Europe.

You point out that for many stars being at Cannes is the nearest they'll ever get to scoring a winning touchdown. Why?

EBERT: For American stars. An American movie star can go through a whole career and never get applauded, except when they walk into the Oscars and three hundred people in the grandstand shout their name. Most American movie stars don't appear on a stage. Most movie stars, big as they are, never have the kind of feeling that a rock star has. What must it be like to be Mick Jagger and spend twenty years going into stadiums containing eighty thousand people who scream at you for three hours! Never before in the history of humanity has there been a stardom like that of the modern rock star. Then they get over to Cannes, and suddenly here are sixteen television networks, people shoulder to shoulder for blocks in every direction. They go inside, their movie is seen by four thousand people. It's exciting for them.

Are you two still in competition when you're over there?

EBERT: One year *Vanity Fair* gave a dinner in a little sidewalk restaurant near the port of Antibes. Of course, I was dutifully going to go see a movie first, so I got there a little bit late. Siskel was seated directly across from Princess Caroline of Monaco, and I was seated at the extreme other end of the table, behind a tree. So I couldn't even see Princess Caroline, all I could see was bark. I'm sure Gene shifted all the place cards around.

SISKEL: Let me tell you something: there were no place cards. And I wasn't seated *directly* opposite Princess Caroline, my wife was. I was seated one over.

EBERT: Every time I went over to kind of lean over Gene and try to have a little chat, he kept moving his chair around to keep me away.

SISKEL: Absolutely not.
EBERT: I thought, this was my thanks. For twelve years I've been asking him
to come over here. I said, "Gene, why don't we trade seats for a while?" Not
on your life; get back behind your tree.
SISKEL: That's classic Roger Ebert invented dialogue.

But did you want to keep him away?
SISKEL: Was I delighted that he wasn't anywhere near me? You bet. I find it
very hard to be at a party with Roger because Roger, even if he's a guest,
thinks he's the host.
EBERT: There are basically two kinds of people at any party: people sitting
around, waiting to be entertained, and people who come looking for an audience. I like the people who come looking for an audience. I have a place in
Michigan that has a long dining room table, and I was thinking of getting
all of the chairs on one side to have only a right arm, and have all of the
chairs on the other side have only a left arm, so that all the guests, as they re-
clined, would have to look at me. I decided not to go ahead with this, although I felt it would add a great deal to my legend for eccentricity.

And where would you seat Gene?
EBERT: Oh, I'd put him right at the foot. Right at the foot.

**Roger, Andrew Sarris had some advice for you. He said: "I would advise
Ebert that what is at risk in his very accomplished Laurel-and-Hardy
routines with Gene Siskel is neither his aesthetic integrity nor his emotional sincerity, but, rather, what I have perceived in private conversations as an irreverent wit being steadily eroded by too calculating a def-
erence to the banalities of a mass audience."**
EBERT: I think that that's some of the best criticism I've ever received, and I
know exactly what he's talking about. I take that to heart. He's right, that
that is a danger.

Any other dangers lurking?
SISKEL: We get rewarded, and attention is paid to what we think. That's our
job. Most people walk around and their opinion is not valued or listened to.
As a result, if other people think we have something to say that's important,
we probably do too. Therefore, you've got two very strong-headed people
who begin to think that their opinion lurches over into fact. I think Roger
loses track that it's an opinion and not fact.

What effect has being a film critic had on you over the years?

SISKEL: If you're a critic more than half your life, you judge everything all the time. Constantly. I've seen so much tumult on the screen that I read the world as more violent than it probably is. I'll be walking down the street, and I see action coming. The visual that I'm seeing will be movielike. I was in a cab, and I heard a bank robbery report on the radio. What I thought about was the shot of the robbers in their car hearing the report, which is a standard scene in every movie about bank robbery. They just always happen to be tuned to that channel.

Do you also relate your personal life to the movies?
SISKEL: The job I had in the Army Reserve very closely measured to experiences in *Full Metal Jacket.* My wife appeared on the early news show that she produced; she is not unlike the Holly Hunter character in *Broadcast News.*

Gene, you get personally involved with the movies in another way, by collecting movie memorabilia, don't you?
SISKEL: I've got the white suit that Travolta wore in *Saturday Night Fever.* I loved that picture and have seen it ten times.

What did it cost you at auction?
SISKEL: $2,000. In terms of what I was prepared to pay, it was a bargain. Now it's probably worth twenty times that. *[Siskel later sold it for over $20,000.]* Sylvester Stallone says it's the most famous suit in the world. I've never put it on, but I don't have to worry about it being destroyed, it's polyester. It will outlive even the plastic bag it's in. I'm also the proud owner of the boom box, the baseball bat, and the pizza delivery shirt from *Do the Right Thing.* And I have an early script of Scorsese's *Mean Streets.* That was an important film for me, just as the Nicholson pictures from *Five Easy Pieces* and *King of Marvin Gardens* through *The Last Detail* were. But now when you ask people who starred in those, nobody says Jack Nicholson. The dominant image of Nicholson for many people is The Joker and the Laker games. Smilin' Jack. Here was a man who, to his everlasting credit, gave us a portrayal of a modern American man that was unique. He made these pictures that really show an alienated modern guy in an exciting way. And the kids don't know it.

Gene, you've told us about some of your favorite movies. Roger, what are yours?
EBERT: *The Third Man, La Dolce Vita, Notorious, Citizen Kane, Taxi Driver,* and *Gates of Heaven,* a documentary about pet cemeteries.

And who are your three favorite actresses and actors?

SISKEL: I hate that shit. *God,* do I hate that stuff!

All right, Gene, I'll note that you refuse to play. How about you, Roger?
EBERT: Robert Mitchum, because he embodies the soul of film noir. Robert De Niro, because he takes more chances than anybody else. Jack Nicholson, because he has a gift for making the audience into accomplices. Ingrid Bergman, because of the ethereal quality of her persona. Marilyn Monroe, because there was never, ever anybody else like her; because she was able to convey carnality through innocence in a way that still remains a complete mystery. Meryl Streep, just because she tries so many different kinds of things, so she never does the same thing twice.

Five favorite directors?
EBERT: Welles, because of his flamboyant and joyous use of visuals. Scorsese, because of his energy and intensity. Bergman, because of the clarity of his images and his thought. Ozu, because of the serenity and humanity of his work. Cassavetes, because of his inspired untidiness.

Favorite scenes in movies?
EBERT: Orson Welles being discovered by the cat in the doorway, in *The Third Man.* Also in *The Third Man,* the scene where Orson Welles and Joseph Cotton ride on the giant Ferris wheel and look at the little dots on the ground below. And Welles's famous cuckoo-clock speech. Donald O'Connor going through the wall during the "Make Them Laugh" number in *Singing in the Rain.* HAL 9000 reading the lips in *2001.* The speech in *Citizen Kane* where Mr. Bernstein talks about the girl in the white dress that he saw on the Staten Island ferry many decades ago, but "there's not a month goes past when I don't think about that girl." In Ozu's *Drifting Weeds,* the scene where the traveling trooper and the mother of his child sit quietly after all of the travails they have gone through and enjoy each other's company. In *Raging Bull,* the scene where De Niro tells his brother, "Maybe you didn't even know what you were saying. Maybe you said it, and you didn't know you were saying it." In *Bonnie and Clyde,* Bonnie's mother saying farewell to her at the picnic. In *Five Easy Pieces,* the scene where Jack Nicholson tries to communicate with his father, who has had a stroke, and he can't talk to him. In *Notorious,* the scene where Cary Grant and Ingrid Bergman walk down the stairs with Claude Raines, and the Nazis are at the foot of the stairs, but, because of the dramatic logic of the situation, they can't do anything about it. The Nazis can't stop Cary Grant from leaving the building with Ingrid Bergman. The Fountain of Trevi scene in *La Dolce Vita.* The scene in *Casablanca* where Humphrey Bogart tells Paul Henreid what he needs to be told in order to believe that Ingrid Bergman really loves him.

Best love scenes in movies?

EBERT: Whenever I'm asked that question, I quote the answer that Marcello Mastroianni gave me. His answer was, "I like it when Mickey kisses Minnie, and the little-a hearts in the air between them go-a *pop!pop!pop!*"

Now give us yours.

EBERT: That's my answer too.

You can't steal someone else's answer. Come on, Roger.

EBERT: I like the scene in *Casablanca,* "Do you remember Paris?" That sequence. I love the love scene in *The Third Man,* which consists of Alida Valli knowing that Harry Lime—Orson Welles—is a bad man, but she loves him anyway because she can't help herself. I love the acknowledgment in *Say Anything,* a very underrated movie. The fact that John Cusack loves the girl in that movie because she's smart and not because she's pretty. The unreachable image of Anita Ekberg in *La Dolce Vita.* Marcello Mastroianni projects on her everything that he desires, but he just can't have her because she just isn't paying attention. One of the strangest love scenes in the movies is the one between Jodie Foster and Harvey Keitel in *Taxi Driver,* where he comforts her, holds her. And the music is playing as they dance around that horrible tenement room, and he whispers those endearments to her. There's something very disturbing about that. The love scene between Marlon Brando and the body of his dead wife in *Last Tango in Paris,* in which he has that monologue, angry at her for dying. Gene Kelly's solo dance in *Singing in the Rain.* He's so in love with this girl that he's laughing and dancing and singing.

See, when you talk about love, it doesn't necessarily mean two people in bed. It means other kinds of love. The old man in *Ikiru* who decides that since he only has two months to live, he's going to try and accomplish one good thing. And when we finally see him in the last shot of the movie, he is dead, covered with snow in the swing in a park, with the children. It's a love scene. It's the icon of his love for those kids.

All right, Gene, you can play again. What genre of film is the most review-proof?

SISKEL: It may be the comedy. It is very, very hard to argue someone out of a laugh, or into one.

EBERT: The sex film.

SISKEL: That too.

EBERT: If people think it will turn them on, they don't care what anybody says about it. In fact, most sex films are never reviewed.

Are porno films healthy or unhealthy?

SISKEL: I know that they can be degrading, but I think that they possibly can have a therapeutic value as well. I once interviewed a sex therapist who said that porno films were healthy for the basic reason of simply showing to people who have never seen the anatomy the organs, up close. Supposedly a common fear is that the vagina has teeth. And someone could say, "No, it doesn't. Look!"

Are orgasms usually portrayed from the male or female point of view in the movies?
SISKEL: I did a story on the visual grammar of sex scenes in American movies, and the orgasm is always the point of view of the woman. Richard Gere is one of the few actors who consistently has dared to be photographed orgasmic, out of control. I applaud him. I want films to open up in the bedroom. It's an area that obviously a lot of people are conflicted about.

An area you seem to be conflicted about, Roger, is the change in value systems in film schools across the country.
EBERT: I feel that the film schools are more commercially oriented than ever, that the film schools have the values of the business schools these days. Film schools used to have the values of the liberal arts schools; now film schools are more allied to the business schools in terms of their values: success, money, achievement, and power rather than vision, imagination, truth, and social change.

Your own value systems sometimes go awry when it comes to tearing each other down. For instance, Gene says that you can't wear a brown sweater on camera because you look like a mud slide.
EBERT: That's one of Gene's feeble attempts at humor. Gene also says that there's a dollar bonus for any cameraman who can *not* take a close-up of me. One of the little-known things about Gene is that from the height of an astronaut circling the earth, the only objects visible are the Great Wall of China and his forehead. He has the only receding hairline so spacious that it has applied for its own zip code.

You guys enjoy taking shots at each other, but can we cut to the bottom line?
EBERT: In the context of an interview like this, I'm almost being prompted to attack Gene, but actually I do admire him and like him a great deal more than you might think. As it is, I see more of Gene than anybody else in the world, except for my girlfriend.
SISKEL: He knows me better than anybody outside of my family, and in certain areas knows me better than anybody else in the world. Whatever else I

may think of Roger, I do think highly of him and of his mind. He can be a very good person and an exceedingly good friend, although . . .

There. See, I knew it all along.

SISKEL: . . . on our show, sometimes I feel I am trying cases every week, with Roger as Hamilton Burger and I as Perry Mason.

EBERT: He *would* choose Mason because that's probably the extent of his interest in fictional detectives. Gene has always wanted to be a trial lawyer and has really felt that he was wasted on film criticism. I would not have even *thought* of choosing Perry Mason. Now, what does that mean in terms of his rigorous thinking?

SISKEL: What it means is . . .

Enough, gentlemen. Enough.

INDEX